The Gun Digest
SPORTING RIFLE TAKE DOWN & REASSEMBLY GUIDE

2nd Edition

By J.B. Wood

DBI BOOKS
a division of Krause Publications, Inc.

STAFF

SENIOR STAFF EDITOR
Harold A. Murtz
ASSOCIATE EDITOR
Robert S.L. Anderson
PRODUCTION MANAGER
John L. Duoba
EDITORIAL/PRODUCTION ASSOCIATE
Karen Rasmussen
ASSISTANT TO THE EDITOR
Lilo Anderson
ASSISTANT TO THE PUBLISHER
Joyce Gately
ELECTRONIC PUBLISHING MANAGER
Nancy J. Mellem
ELECTRONIC PUBLISHING ASSOCIATE
Laura M. Mielzynski
GRAPHIC DESIGN
John L. Duoba
MANAGING EDITOR
Pamela J. Johnson
PUBLISHER
Charles T. Hartigan

About the Author

Guns, especially automatic pistols, have always been a part of J.B. Wood's life, and it has now been more than 40 years since he began working as a gunsmith. Fortunately, Wood has been able to combine his mechanical talents with writing about them, which he's been doing since 1962. In that time he has had more than 800 articles published in *Gun Digest, Guns Illustrated* and in most of the monthly gun magazines. In 1977-1978 he authored a two-book series for DBI Books, Inc. *Troubleshooting Your Handgun* and *Troubleshooting Your Rifle and Shotgun*. From 1979 to 1981, Wood wrote and photographed the original six-part *Firearms Assembly/Disassembly* series, a monumental task that turned out to be the best reference ever printed on the subject at hand. Currently, he is revising the series to include recently introduced guns and more guns for which detailed takedown and reassembly instructions may no longer exist.

In 1974, J.B. Wood began a regular monthly relationship with gun magazines. He was Gunsmithing Editor for *Guns & Ammo* magazine for 8 years and Contributing Editor to *Gun Digest*, is Contributing Editor to *Combat Handguns*, and is currently Gunsmithing Editor for *Shooting Times* magazine. Because he is so well briefed on firearms in general, and self-loading pistols in particular, Wood is considered an international authority, and has testified in many court cases involving firearms as an expert witness. In addition, he has done mechanical design and redesign work for a number of domestic and foreign arms makers. Currently, he is a full-time gunsmith, writer, and firearms consultant and lives in rural Kentucky.

CAUTION: In regard to the mechanical and safety aspects of the guns covered in this book, it is assumed that the guns are in factory original condition with the dimensions of all parts as made by the manufacturer. Since alteration of parts is a simple matter, the reader is advised to have any gun checked by a competent gunsmith. Both the author and publisher disclaim responsibility for any accidents.

ISBN 0-87349-201-3

Library of Congress Catalog #97-66761

CONTENTS

Index/Cross Reference

INTRODUCTION

During the years I have been a professional gunsmith and gun writer, one of the most frequently asked question by readers has been, "How do I take it apart?" When the limited space of a column answer permitted, I gave the routine takedown steps.

In many cases, I had to tell the reader that nothing had been published on his particular piece. Occasionally, I recommended that the reader try to obtain an instruction booklet from the manufacturer or importer, but this was not always the best answer. In the case of some imported guns, the direct-translation was somewhat humorous to read, or was of little help in actual disassembly and reassembly. In the case of guns no longer made, the instruction sheets are often valuable collector items and are not readily obtainable.

Obviously, something was needed in this area—a book that would cover takedown and reassembly of most of the modern guns, a number of older ones, and some of the tricky aspects of the more well-known pieces. This is the idea behind the book you have in your hands.

In the area of reassembly, many of the published instructions end with the words, "Reassemble in reverse order." In most cases, this may be the only instruction needed and nothing more will be said here. In others, though, this procedure is insufficient. In this book, reassembly directions will seldom be reduced to a single line in order to avoid an embarrassing trip to the gunsmith carrying a box full of parts. I am confident that the reassembly tips given are clear enough to permit the easy reassembly of all the guns covered. The tips do not include each and every step along the way—only the more complicated ones. You shouldn't have any trouble.

There are elements in total takedown that require, in many cases, the special tools and skills of the gunsmith. The very knowledgeable amateur may be able to detail strip certain guns to the last pin, spring and screw, but some mechanical aptitude is necessary. This book is designed for both the average gun person and the professional. While it covers routine field-stripping, it also covers complete takedown and reassembly.

For simple takedown, the tools needed will seldom be more than screwdrivers of the proper size. Complete takedown will often require several other tools, some of which are not available at the corner hardware store. For this reason, I am including a section on tools, as well as a list of sources for some specialized items.

There are a few general rules to be observed in the takedown of any gun. An occasional rap with a plastic mallet may be necessary to free a tight assembly, but for the most part, no force should be used. Never pry; always wear safety glasses as compressed springs can be dangerous. Never take a gun down outdoors, over tall grass, or indoors over a shag carpet. Read the instructions through, at least once, before you begin.

I assume a certain basic intelligence in the reader, and will not start each set of takedown directions with the repeated advice that the gun must be entirely unloaded. *Before you start the takedown of any gun, make a thorough visual check to be sure it's empty.* Check the chamber and magazine *and* be sure they are *empty*. In this area, any mistakes could be very hazardous to your health, so be certain.

An exploded drawing accompanies each gun to aid you in assembly/disassembly. Those drawings also serve to orient parts and their relationship to the firearm's actual function.

An important addition to this book is the comprehensive index and cross-reference list, linking the rifles covered here to guns of similar or identical pattern. When these are included in the count, the instructions in this 2nd edition can be used for the takedown and reassembly of over 403 rifles.

Small mechanical variations are noted on the data page for each rifle, in cases which would cause no takedown or reassembly difficulty. If the variation involves a different procedure, it is so noted in the assembly/disassembly instruction.

J.B. Wood
Raintree House
Corydon, Kentucky

A Note On Reassembly

Most of the firearms covered in this book can be reassembled by simply reversing the order of disassembly, carefully replacing the parts in the same manner they were removed. In a few instances, special instructions are required, and these are listed with each gun under "Reassembly Tips." In certain cases, reassembly photos are also provided.

If there are no special instructions or photos with a particular gun, you may assume that it can be reassembled in reverse order. During disassembly, note the relationship of all parts and springs, and lay them out on the workbench in the order they were removed. By following this procedure you should have no difficulty in reassembly.

TOOLS

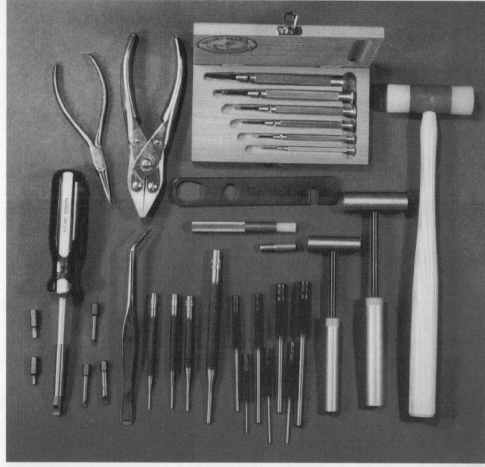

Countless firearms, old and new, bear the marks, burrs and gouges that are the result of using the wrong tools for taking them apart. In the interest of preventing this sort of thing, I am including here a group of tools that are the best types for the disassembly of rifles. Except for the few shop-made tools for special purposes, all of those shown here are available from one of these three sources.

Brownells, Inc.
Route 2, Box 1
Montezuma, Iowa 50171

B-Square Company
P.O. Box 11281
Fort Worth, Texas 76109

Williams Gun Sight Company
7389 Lapeer Road
Davison, Michigan 48423

General Instructions:

Screwdrivers: Always be sure the blade of the screwdriver **exactly** fits the slot in the screw head, both in thickness and in width. If you don't have one that fits, grind or file the tip until it does. You may ruin a few screwdrivers but better them than the screws on a fine rifle.

Slave pins: There are several references in this book to slave pins, and some non-gunsmith readers may not be familiar with the term. A slave pin is simply a short length of rod stock (in some cases, a section of a nail will do) which is used to keep two parts, or a part

and a spring, together during reassembly. The slave pin must be very slightly smaller in diameter than the hole in the part, so it will push out easily as the original pin is driven in to retain the part. When making a slave pin, its length should be slightly less than the width of the part in which it is being used, and the ends of the pin should be rounded or beveled.

Sights: Nearly all dovetail-mounted sights are drifted out toward the right, using a nylon, aluminum, or brass drift punch.

1. The tiniest of these fine German instrument screwdrivers from Brownells is too small for most gun work, but you'll see the rest of them used frequently throughout the book. There are many tight places where these will come in handy.

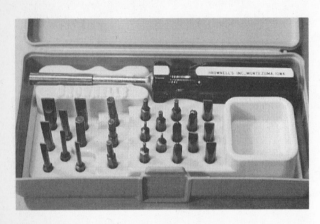

2. When a larger screwdriver is needed, this set from Brownells covers a wide range of blade sizes and also has Phillips- and Allen-type inserts. The tips are held in place by a strong magnet, yet are easily changed. These tips are very hard. With enough force you might manage to break one, but they'll never bend.

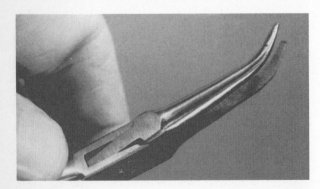

3. You should have at least one good pair of bent sharp-nosed pliers. These, from Brownells, have a box joint and smooth inner faces to help prevent marring.

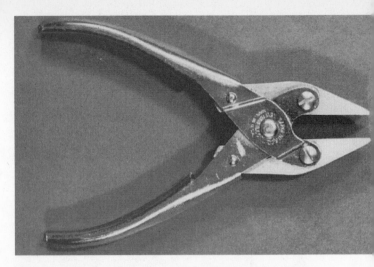

4. For heavier gripping, these Bernard parallel-jaw pliers from Brownells have smooth-faced jaw-pieces of un-hardened steel to prevent marring of parts.

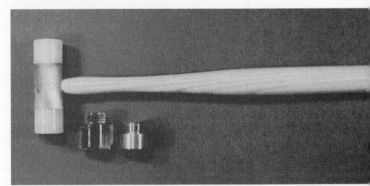

5. For situations where a non-marring rap is needed, this hammer from Brownells is ideal. It is shown with nylon faces on the head, but other faces of plastic and brass are also available. All are easily replaceable.

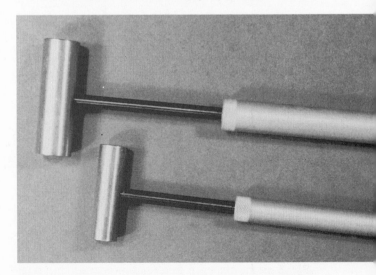

6. For drifting out pins, these small all-metal hammers from B-Square are the best I've seen. Two sizes (weights) are available and they're well worth the modest cost.

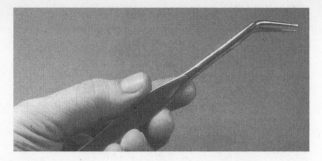

7. For situations where reach and accessibility are beyond the capabilities of sharp-nosed pliers, a pair of large sharp-nosed forceps (tweezers) will be invaluable.

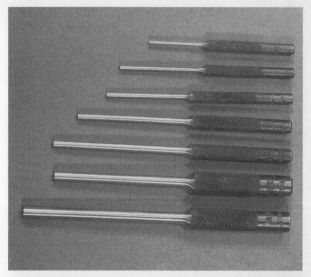

8. One of the most-used tools in my shop is this nylon-tipped drift punch, shown with an optional brass tip in place on the handle. It has a steel pin inside the nylon tip for strength. From Brownells, and absolutely essential.

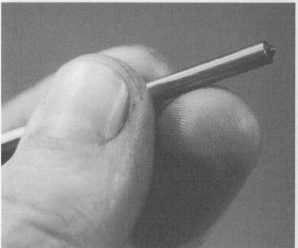

10. These punches by Mayhew are designed specifically for roll pins and have a projection at the center of the tip to fit the hollow center of a roll pin, driving it out without deformation of the ends. From Brownells.

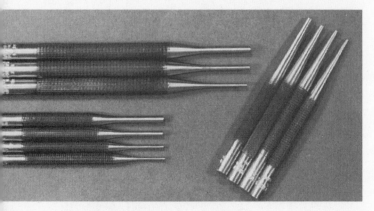

9. A good set of drift punches will prevent a lot of marred pins. These, from Brownells, are made by Mayhew. The tapered punches at the right are for starting pins, the others for pushing them through. Two sizes are available—4 inches or 6 inches.

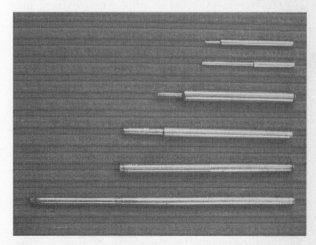

11. Some of the necessary tools are easily made in the shop. These non-marring drift punches were made from three sizes of welder's brazing rod.

12. From Brownells, this wrench is specifically designed for use on the barrel nut on the Winchester 150/250 and 190/290 series.

Rimfire Inner Magazine Tube Disassembly:

With very few exceptions, the disassembly of the inner magazine tube is the same for most rimfire rifles having this type of magazine system. The knurled knob at the end of the tube is retained by a cross pin, with one or both ends of the cross pin protruding to lock the tube in the gun. Most of the pins are driven out toward the non-protruding (or smooth) side. The tube should be supported in a V-block or a slightly opened bench vise during this operation, to avoid deformation of the thin walls of the tube. When the pin is out, the knob can be removed from the end of the tube, and this will release the magazine spring and follower. In some cases, the spring will be slightly compressed, so take care that it doesn't get away, and ease it out. In those cases where the cross pin protrudes on both sides, the pin will be slightly tapered. These should be driven out toward the larger end of the pin. Some box-type magazines can be disassembled, but most of them are of staked construction, and in normal disassembly should not be taken apart.

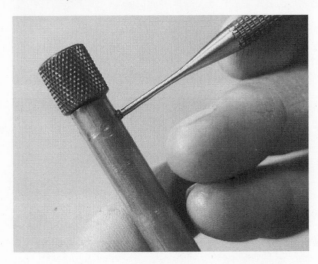

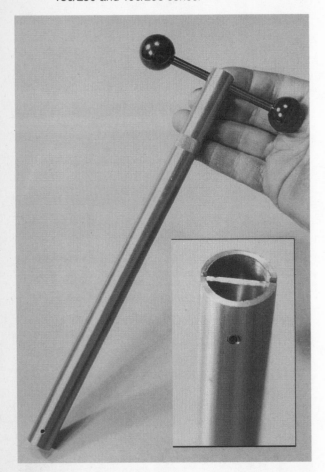

13. The B-Square stock bolt tool automatically centers in the access hole at the rear of the stock, and its wide cross-piece easily "finds" the screw slot. The T-handle gives good leverage. (Inset) This is the end of the B-Square general stock bolt tool, showing the replaceable cross-piece which contacts the screw slot.

Browning A-Bolt 22

Similar/Identical Pattern Guns
The same basic assembly/disassembly steps for the Browning A-Bolt 22 also apply to the following gun:
Browning A-Bolt 22 Gold Medallion

Data:	Browning A-Bolt 22
Origin:	Japan
Manufacturer:	Miroku
Cartridge:	22 Long Rifle
Magazine capacity:	5 rounds
Overall length:	$40^1/_4$ inches
Barrel length:	22 inches
Weight:	5 pounds 9 ounces

The Browning A-Bolt in 22 LR and 22 WMR was also offered in a Gold Medallion version that differs only in fancy stock wood and other embellishments. The standard rifle was introduced in 1986, but fewer than 150 were made in that year. The deluxe model was first made in 1988, and the 22 WMR version in 1989. Among the high-class 22 bolt actions, the A-Bolt ranks as one of the best.

Disassembly:

1. Remove the magazine, open the bolt, and depress the bolt latch. Remove the bolt toward the rear.

2. Remove the stock mounting bolt, located just forward of the magazine well.

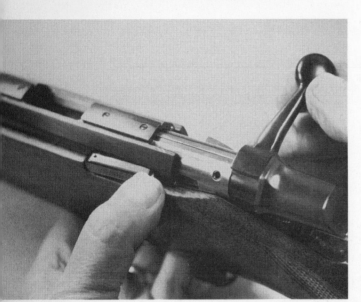

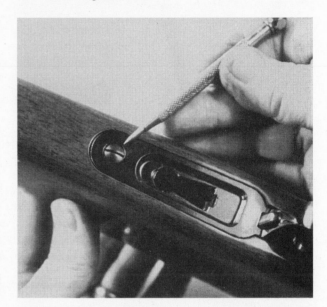

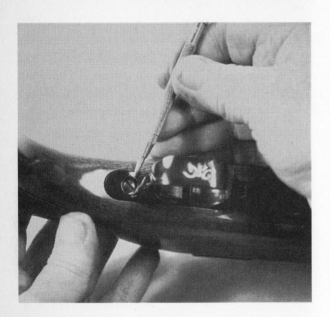

3. Remove the rear stock mounting bolt, located at the rear of the trigger guard unit.

4. Remove the trigger guard assembly downward. The magazine catch and its spring, located in the guard forward of the trigger, are best left in place in normal takedown. If removal is necessary for repair, insert a drift or rod through the loop at the rear of the catch, and draw it back until its side wings align with the exit cuts; then lift it out. Control the spring.

5. Remove the action from the stock, upward.

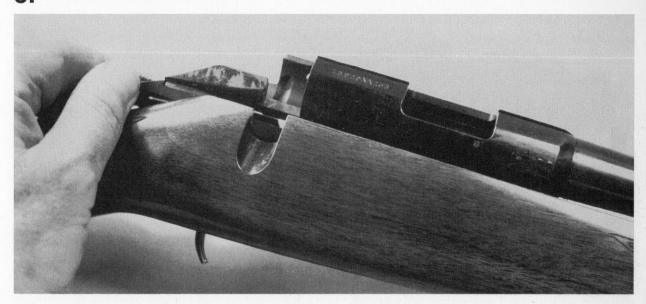

6. Drift out the roll pin at the front of the trigger housing.

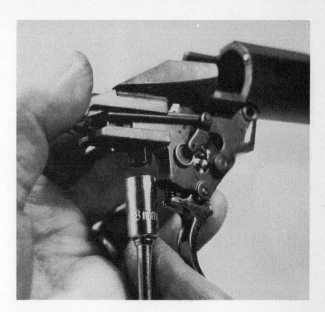

7. Use an 8mm socket to remove the mounting bolt at the rear of the trigger housing. Take care that the lock washer is not lost.

8. Remove the trigger housing downward.

9. The bolt latch can be removed from the left side of the receiver by backing out its retaining and pivot screw. Restrain the latch as the screw is taken out, and ease it off. Remove the spring. In the front of the latch, a vertical roll pin retains the bolt stop/guide pin.

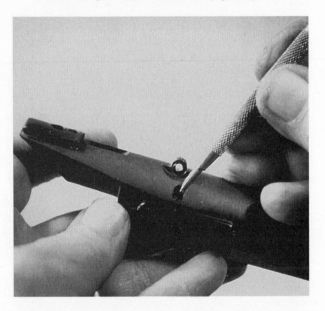

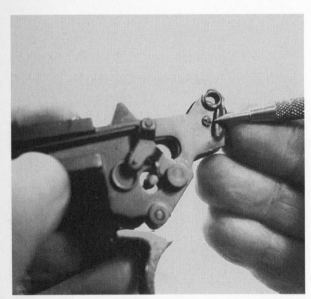

10. Because several of the parts in the trigger group are set or staked at the factory, disassembly of this system should be reserved for repair purposes. The sear pivot, for example, is riveted on both sides, and it is not routinely removable.

11. If necessary, the safety system can be removed. First, pry off the C-clip on the left side of the housing. Control it during removal, as it will snap off when freed.

12. Control the torsion spring, and remove the safety toward the right.

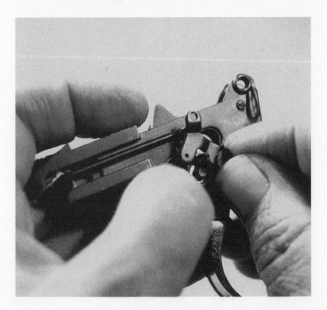

13. Remove the safety spring.

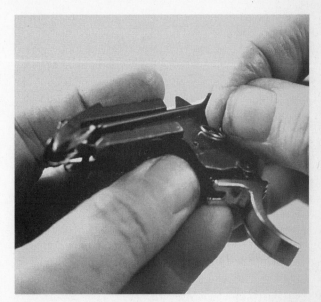

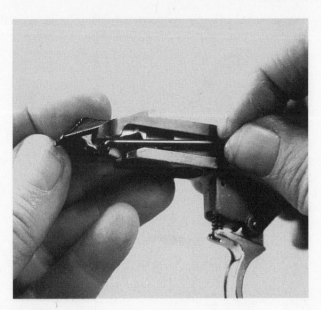

14. Move the connecting rod and the safety button out toward the rear.

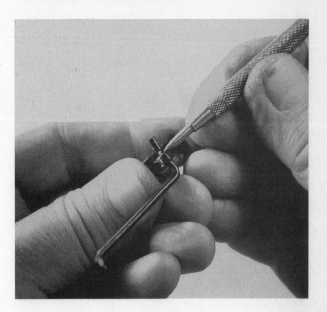

15. The connecting rod is staked on the left side of the button, and these parts are not routinely separated.

16. Unhook the safety-lever spring at the rear to release its tension.

17. Insert a drift in the access hole on the right side, and drift out the safety-lever post toward the left. Remove the lever and spring.

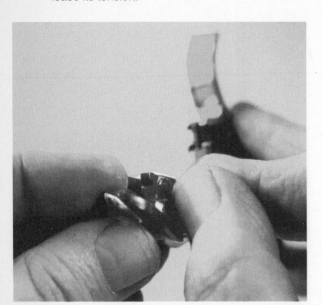

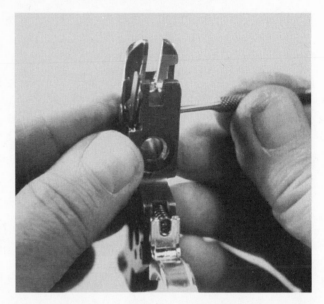

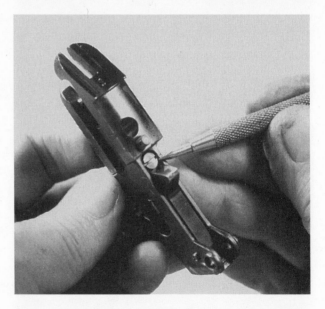

18. In order to remove the safety bolt lock pin, it is necessary to grip its side roll pin with pliers and pull it out. The lock pin is then taken out upward. Damage to the roll pin is likely, so this should not be done in normal takedown.

19. While the sear is not routinely removed, its spring is accessible by removal of the sear limit screw. However, this screw is factory set for proper engagement of the sear contact stud in the top of the trigger. If the screw is disturbed, it must be reset.

20. If the trigger has to be removed for repair, the first step is to unscrew and take out the safety post, shown here.

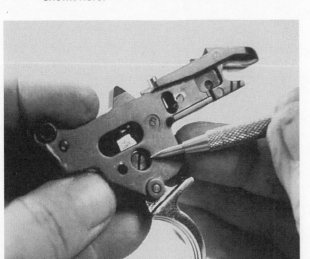

21. After the safety post is removed, drift out the trigger pin and take out the trigger and its spring downward. The sear contact stud in the top of the trigger is a separate part. In normal takedown, this system is best left undisturbed.

22. To remove the extractor, insert a small tool to depress the plunger and spring toward the rear, and lift out the extractor. **Caution:** *Keep the plunger and spring under control and ease them out.*

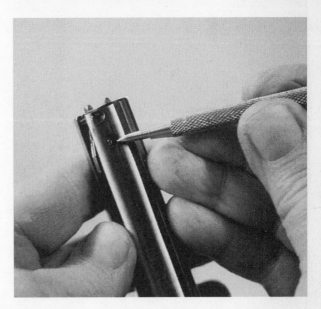

23. The combination ejector and firing pin can be removed by drifting out this roll pin, but the plunger and spring may be difficult to remove without further disassembly of the bolt. It can be done, though, if only this part needs to be replaced in repair. The forward roll pin is a guide only, and it does not have to be removed.

24. Hold the bolt firmly at the front, and turn the handle to lower the striker to fired position, as shown.

25. Restrain the bolt end piece and use an Allen wrench to remove the bolt sleeve retaining screw. **Caution:** *Even in fired mode, the striker spring has some compression, so control the end piece.*

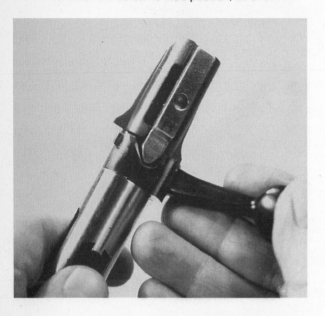

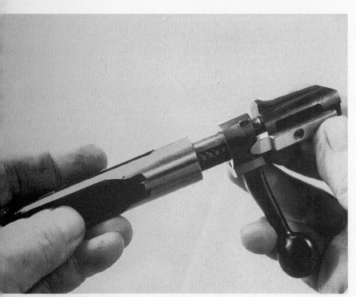

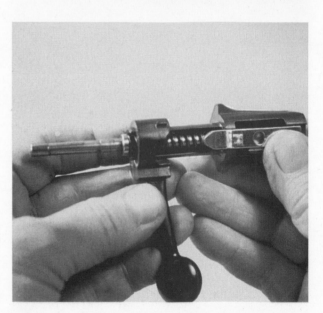

26. Remove the end piece and striker assembly toward the rear.

27. Remove the bolt handle toward the front.

28. With the front of the striker against a firm surface, such as a workbench edge, tip the striker and spring assembly downward, out of the bolt end piece.

29. The striker, its spring, and the collar at the rear can be separated from the cocking piece by drifting out the roll cross pin. **Caution:** *The captive spring is still under tension. Except for repair, this system should be left intact.*

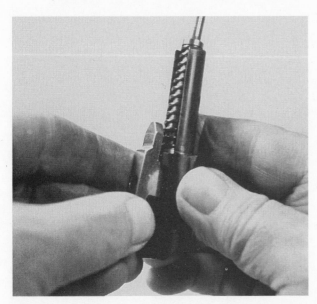

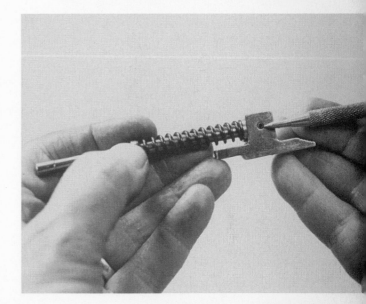

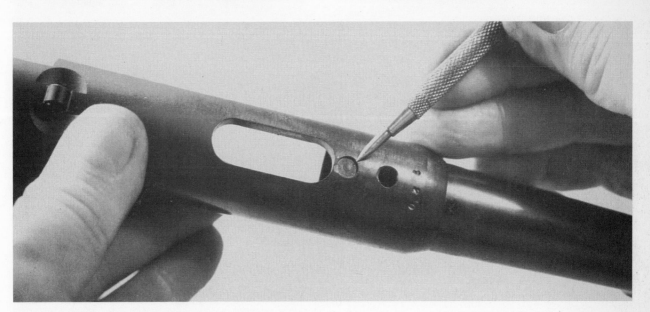

30. The cartridge guide is a separate part, driven into a well in the underside of the receiver. If it is damaged and must be replaced, it can be driven out downward. Replacement requires precise positioning. In normal takedown, even for refinishing, it is best left in place.

Reassembly Tips:

1. When installing the striker assembly in the bolt end piece, place the spring collar against the shoulders in the end piece, and push the assembly back and inward to snap it into place.

2. When replacing the Allen screw, be sure the screw hole is precisely aligned before turning the screw into place.

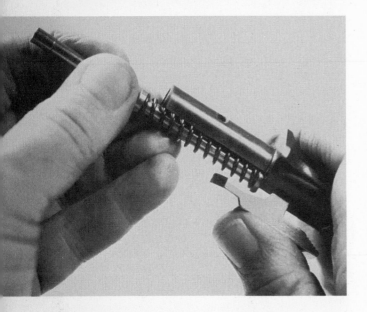

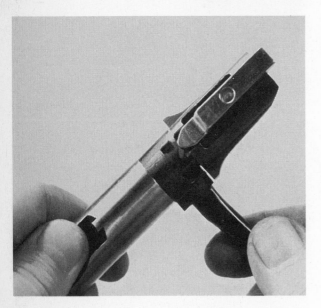

3. Before the bolt can be put back into the receiver, the striker must be in cocked position. Grip the front of the bolt firmly in a shop cloth or a padded vise, and turn the handle until the lug is in the position shown.

4. When installing the safety-lever, be sure its front fork engages the bolt lock side pin, as shown. After the post is drifted into place, remember to rehook the spring under the lever at the rear.

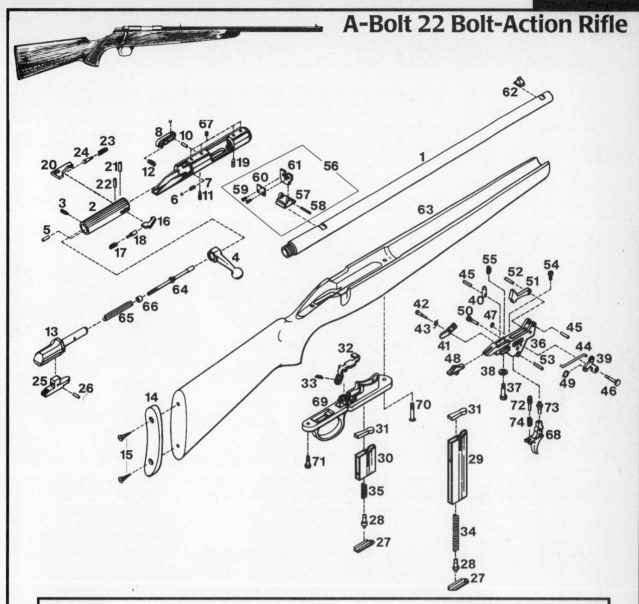

KEY

1 Barrel
2 Bolt
3 Bolt Assembly Screw
4 Bolt Handle
5 Bolt Handle Pin
6 Bolt Handle Stop Ball
7 Bolt Handle Stop Spring
8 Bolt Retainer
9 Bolt Retainer Pin
10 Bolt Retainer Pin Guide
11 Bolt Retainer Screw
12 Bolt Retainer Spring
13 Bolt Shroud
14 Buttplate
15 Buttplate Screws
16 Extractor
17 Extractor Spring
18 Extractor Spring Follower
19 Feed Ramp
20 Firing Pin Ejector
21 Firing Pin Ejector Pin
22 Firing Pin Ejector Relief Pin
23 Firing Pin Ejector Spring
24 Firing Pin Ejector Spring Follower

25 Firing Pin Sear
26 Firing Pin Sear Pin
27 Magazine Base
28 Magazine Base Retainer
29 Magazine Body, 15 Shot
30 Magazine Body, 5 Shot
31 Magazine Follower Guide
32 Magazine Latch
33 Magazine Latch Spring
34 Magazine Spring, 15 Shot
35 Magazine Spring, 5 Shot
36 Mechanism Housing
37 Mechanism Housing Screw
38 Mechanism Housing Screw
     Washer
39 Safety
40 Safety Blocking Pin
41 Safety-Lever
42 Safety-Lever Pin
43 Safety-Lever Spring
44 Safety Link
45 Safety Link Roll Pins
46 Safety Pin
47 Safety Pin Snap Ring
48 Safety Selector
49 Safety Spring

50 Safety Stud
51 Sear
52 Sear Pin
53 Trigger Pin
54 Sear Screw
55 Sear Spring
56 Rear Sight Assembly
57 Sight Base
58 Sight Pin
59 Sight Elevation Screws
60 Sight Elevation Leaf
61 Sight Leaf
62 Front Sight
63 Stock
64 Striker
65 Striker Spring
66 Striker Spring Washer
67 Telescope Mount Filler Screws
68 Trigger
69 Trigger Guard
70 Trigger Guard Screw, Front
71 Trigger Guard Screw, Rear
72 Trigger Pull Adjusting Screw
73 Trigger Sear
74 Trigger Spring

Browning BAR

Data:	Browning BAR
Origin:	Belgium
Manufacturer:	Fabrique Nationale, Herstal, for Browning, Morgan, Utah
Cartridges:	243, 270, 280, 30-06, 308, 7mm Remington Magnum, 300 Winchester Magnum, 338 Winchester Magnum
Magazine capacity:	4 rounds (3 in magnum)
Overall length:	43 and 45 inches
Barrel length:	22 and 24 inches
Weight:	7⅜ and 8⅜ pounds

The factory designation of this gas-operated semi-auto sporter has caused a little confusion, as the famed military selective-fire gun was also called the "BAR." The sleek sporting rifle was introduced in 1967, and it is still in production. The gun has been offered in several grades, the price depending on the extent of stock checkering, carving, engraving, and inlay work. Regardless of the grade, the mechanical details are the same, and the instructions will apply.

Disassembly:

1. With the empty magazine in place, pull back the cocking handle to lock the bolt in open position. With a small wrench or a pair of smooth-jawed pliers, unscrew the front sling swivel base on the underside of the forend near the forward end.

2. Tip the front of the forend downward until firm resistance is felt, then move it forward and off. Do this carefully, and use no extreme force, or the forend will be damaged.

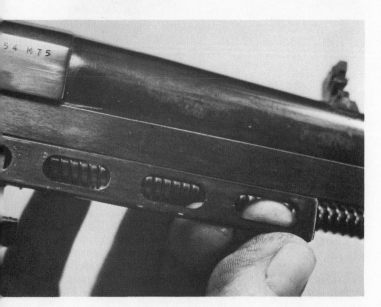

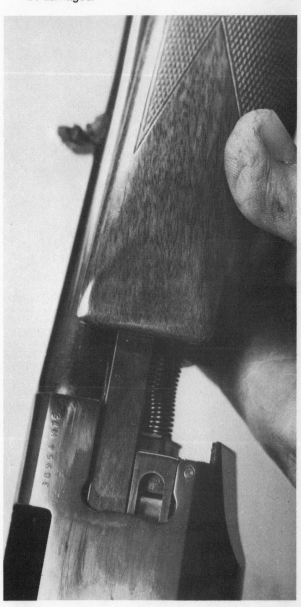

3. Slide the right and left action rod support rails out of the receiver toward the front, and remove them.

4. Disengage the forward ends of the action bars from the studs on the sides of the inertia block, and take the bars out toward the front.

5. Remove the gas regulator from the front end of the gas cylinder. A ⅝-inch open-end wrench will fit the side flats of the regulator, and it is simply unscrewed. Be sure the wrench is properly engaged to prevent marring. Take care not to lose the lock washer behind the gas regulator.

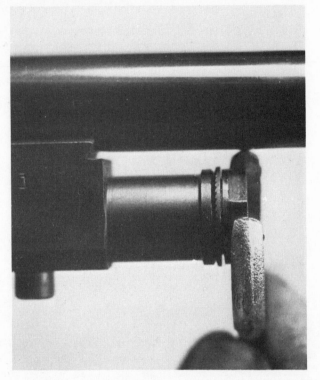

6. Remove the gas piston toward the front. If the piston is very tight, it may have to be nudged from the rear with a drift punch. If this is necessary, be very careful, as any burrs raised will cause the system to malfunction. If the piston won't move with the use of reasonable force, soak it for a time in a good powder solvent or penetrant.

7. Firmly grip the action spring guide at the rear, and lift its rear tip out of its seat in the front of the receiver. Remove the guide, spring, and inertia block toward the rear. **Caution:** *Keep a firm grip on the partially compressed spring, and ease it off.*

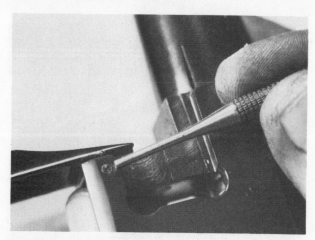

8. Open the magazine floorplate, and insert a small screwdriver at the rear of the magazine to pry it away from the floorplate. Remove the magazine from the floorplate.

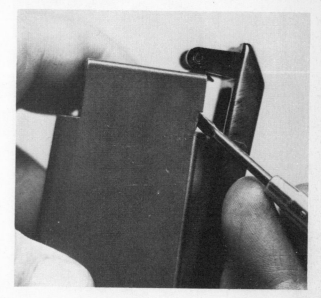

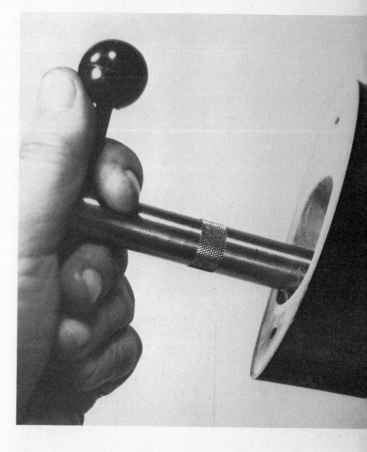

9. The magazine retaining spring is mounted on the end of the floorplate by a cross pin, and is easily removed. The floorplate is attached to the receiver by a cross pin, and the floorplate spring is mounted around the pin. Restrain the spring when drifting out the cross pin, and remove the floorplate downward.

10. Remove the buttplate to give access to the stock mounting bolt. Use a B-Square stock tool or a long screwdriver to remove the stock mounting bolt, and take off the stock toward the rear. If it is very tight, bump the front of the comb with the heel of the hand to start it.

11. Insert a drift punch into the hole in the stock mounting plate at the rear of the receiver, and lift the plate upward, then tip it and remove it toward the rear.

12. Slide the trigger group out of the receiver toward the rear.

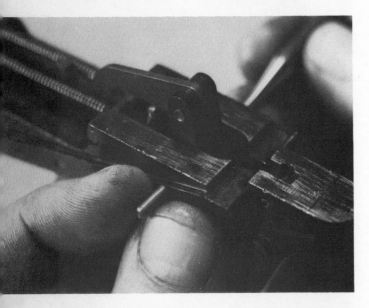

13. Restrain the hammer, pull the trigger, and ease the hammer down to the fired position. Drift out the trigger cross pin.

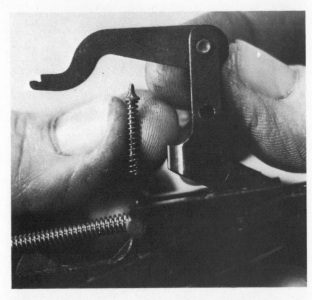

14. Remove the trigger and the attached disconnector upward, and take out the disconnector spring and its plunger. The cross pin that joins the disconnector to the trigger is riveted in place, and should be removed only for repair or replacement purposes.

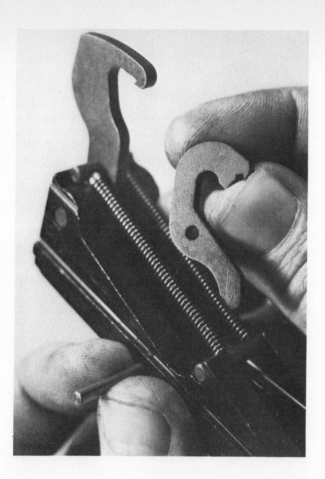

15. Push out the sear cross pin, move the sear forward, then remove it upward.

16. Insert a screwdriver behind the base for the twin hammer springs and lever it forward and upward, out of its seats in the trigger group. **Caution:** *Grip the ends of the base firmly during this operation, and control its movement, as the semi-compressed double springs are quite strong. Remove the spring base, springs, guide rods, and the front base in the hammer.*

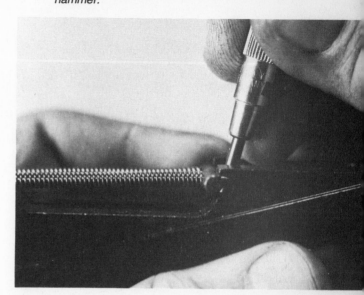

18. The magazine floorplate latch is retained in the receiver by a vertical roll pin, and this pin need not be drifted completely out to free the latch and spring. Just drift it upward enough to clear the latch, and take out the latch and spring toward the front.

17. Push out the hammer cross pin, and take out the hammer upward.

19. A roll cross pin at the rear of the trigger group retains the safety plunger and spring. Restrain the spring at the top when drifting out the pin, and remove the spring and plunger upward. Remove the safety toward either side.

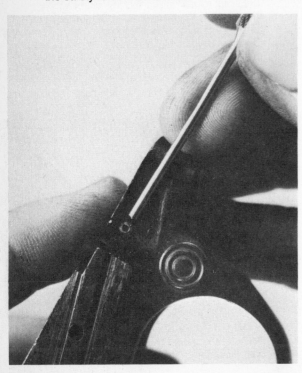

20. Move the bolt so the operating handle is accessible in the ejection port, and insert a small screwdriver to lift the handle latch outward. Move the handle forward, out of its recess in the bolt.

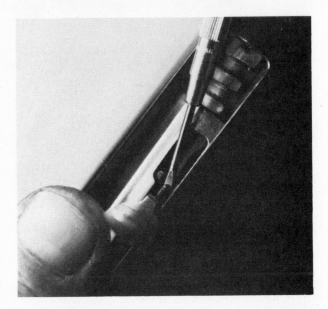

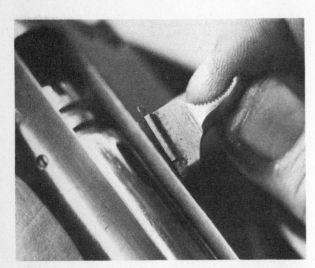

21. Move the operating handle to the wider opening in the bolt cover, and remove the handle toward the right. The latch and spring are retained in the handle by a very small cross pin, and are easily removed. In normal takedown, they are best left in place.

22. After the handle is removed, move the bolt assembly about half-way to the rear, bring it downward from the roof of the receiver, and take it out toward the rear.

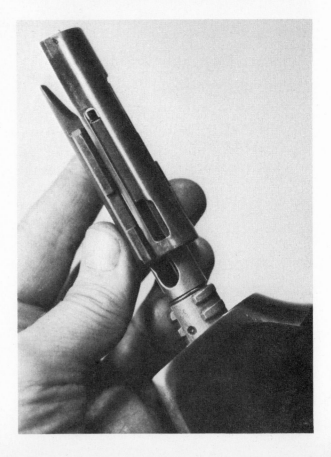

23. Move the bolt cover to the rear of the bolt, and push upward on the right lower edge, tipping it over toward the left, and snapping its guide flange out of the groove on the bolt.

24. Drift out the cross pin in the rear tail of the bolt, and take out the firing pin and its return spring toward the rear. The ends of the cross pin are contoured with the bolt tail, and care should be taken not to deform the ends.

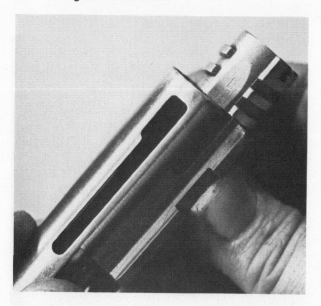

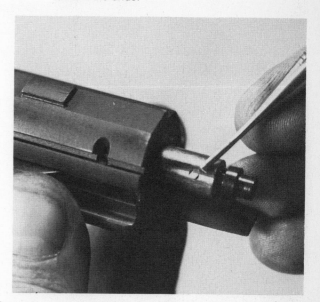

25. Push the cam pin upward out of the bolt sleeve, and remove it.

26. Move the bolt forward out of the bolt sleeve.

27. Drifting out the vertical pin on the left side of the bolt carrier will allow removal of the timing latch toward the left. The pin must be removed upward.

28. The ejector is retained at the front of the bolt by a vertical pin. **Caution:** *Restrain the ejector, and ease it out after removal of the pin, as the ejector spring is compressed.*

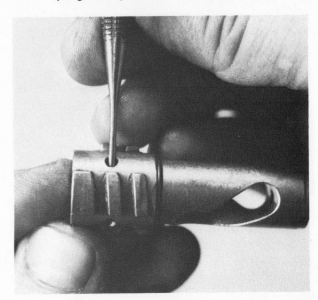

29. Use a small screwdriver to push the extractor spring up out of its groove, and remove the spring toward the rear.

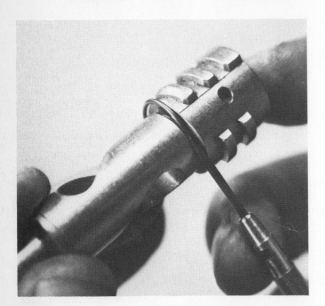

30. After the spring is removed, the extractor can be moved downward, into the bolt face recess, and is taken out toward the front.

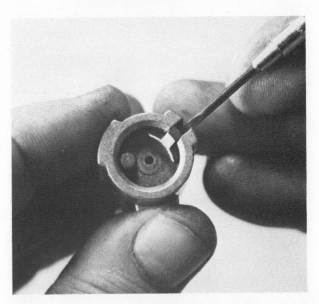

Reassembly Tips:

1. When replacing the bolt in the bolt carrier, be sure the flat between the bolt lugs is on *top*, and the extractor and ejector at upper left and lower right (front view).

2. When replacing the cam pin in the bolt and sleeve, the small hole at the center of the cam pin must be oriented properly for passage of the firing pin.

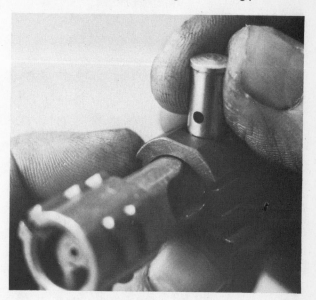

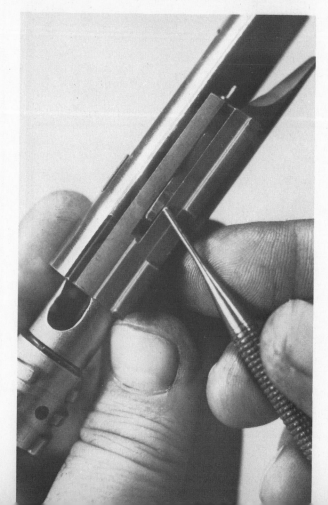

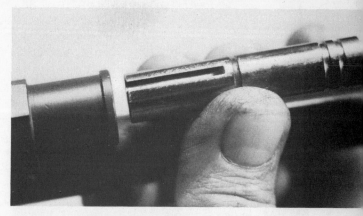

4. When replacing the gas piston, note that there is a guide pin at the lower rear of the gas cylinder, and the piston must be oriented so its rear groove will mate with the pin.

3. When replacing the bolt in the receiver, the bolt must be at its forward position in the sleeve, to allow the timing latch to be retracted.

BAR Standard and Magnum Autoloading Rifle

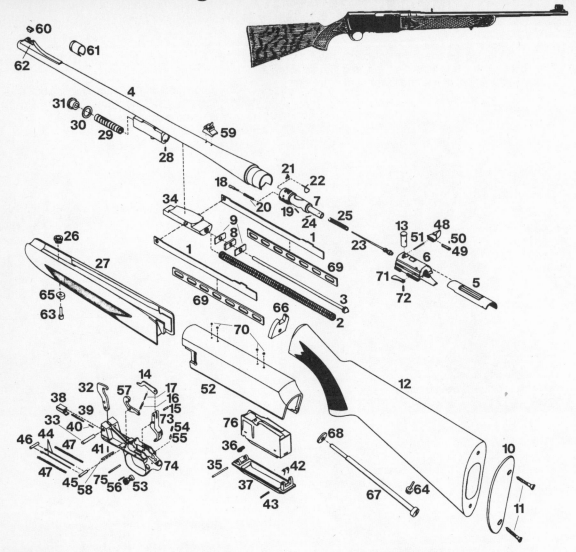

KEY

1	Action Rod
2	Action Spring
3	Action Spring Guide
4	Barrel
5	Bolt Cover
6	Bolt Sleeve
7	Bolt
8	Buffer
9	Buffer Plates
10	Buttplate
11	Buttplate Screws
12	Buttstock
13	Cam Pin
14	Disconnector
15	Disconnector Pin
16	Disconnector Spring
17	Disconnector Spring Plunger
18	Ejector
19	Ejector Retaining Pin
20	Ejector Spring
21	Extractor
22	Extractor Spring
23	Firing Pin
24	Firing Pin Retaining Pin
25	Firing Pin Spring
26	Forend Escutcheon
27	Forend
28	Gas Cylinder
29	Gas Piston
30	Gas Regulator Gasket
31	Gas Regulator
32	Hammer
33	Hammer Pin
34	Inertia Piece
35	Magazine Floorplate Pivot Pin
36	Magazine Floorplate Spring
37	Magazine Floorplate
38	Magazine Latch
39	Magazine Latch Spring
40	Magazine Latch Spring Plunger
41	Magazine Latch Stop Pin
42	Magazine Retaining Spring
43	Magazine Retaining Spring Pin
44	Mainspring Guides
45	Mainspring Pin Hammer
46	Mainspring Pin Trigger Guard
47	Mainsprings
48	Operating Handle
49	Operating Handle Lock
50	Operating Handle Lock Pin
51	Operating Handle Lock Spring
52	Receiver
53	Safety Cross Bolt
54	Safety Spring
55	Safety Spring Plunger
56	Safety Spring Retaining Pin
57	Sear
58	Sear Pin
59	Sight Assembly
60	Sight Bead
61	Sight Hood
62	Sight Ramp
63	Sling Eyelet, Front
64	Sling Eyelet, Rear
65	Sling Eyelet Washer
66	Stock Bolt Plate
67	Stock Bolt
68	Stock Bolt Washer
69	Support Rails
70	Telescope Mount Filler Screws
71	Timing Latch
72	Timing Latch Retaining Pin
73	Trigger
74	Trigger Guard
75	Trigger Pin
76	Magazine Assembly

Browning BLR 81

Similar/Identical Pattern Guns
The same basic assembly/disassembly steps for the Browning BLR 81 also apply to the following guns:
Browning BLR   **Browning BLR Long Action**

Data:	Browning BLR 81
Origin:	Japan
Manufacturer:	Miroku
Cartridges:	222, 223, 22-250, 243, 257 Roberts, 7mm-08, 284, 308, 358; in Long Action: 270, 7mm Remington Magnum, 30-06
Magazine capacity:	4 rounds
Overall length:	39¾ inches
Barrel length:	20 inches
Weight:	6 pounds 15 ounces

Introduced in 1971, the Browning Lever Action Rifle was made at the Fabrique Nationale factory in Belgium during the first year. Since 1972, it has been produced for Browning Arms by Miroku of Japan. A "Long Action" version was introduced in 1991 for cartridges with more length. In 1990 there was a slight modification of the internal portion of the lever system, but this does not affect the takedown sequence.

Disassembly

1. Remove the magazine. Back out the two screws in the recoil pad, and remove it. With a long-shanked screwdriver or a stock tool, as shown, unscrew the stock mounting bolt. Remove the buttstock toward the rear.

2. The housing that contains the hammer spring and its follower is screwed into the receiver at the rear. It is factory-sealed in place, and it is best not to remove it, as the takedown can proceed without disturbing it.

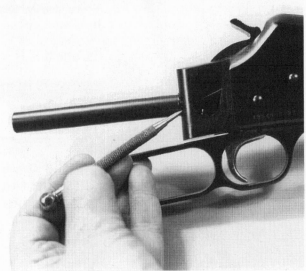

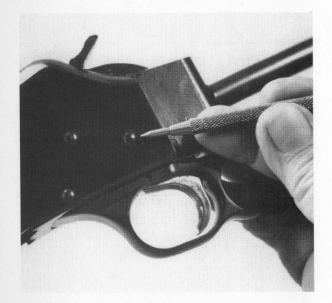

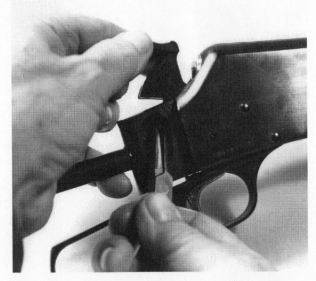

3. The three main cross pins in the receiver are splined at the right tip, and they must be driven out toward the right. These are large pins with domed heads, and a bronze drift of the proper size should be used to avoid marring. Drift out the hammer pivot pin toward the right.

4. Through the frame opening on the right, grip the hammer strut and move it rearward, then turn it upward at the front. Remove the hammer and the strut upward. The hammer spring follower will be stopped by a stud in the bottom of the receiver.

5. Drift out the lever pivot pin toward the right.

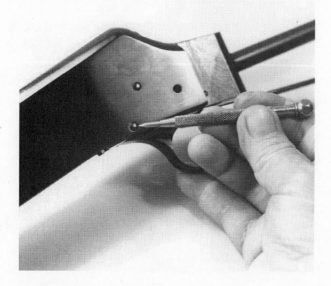

6. Drift out the bolt gear pin toward the right.

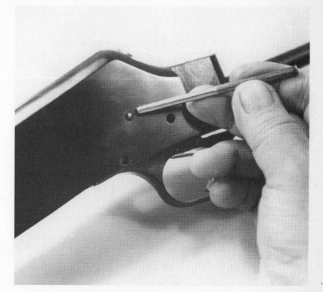

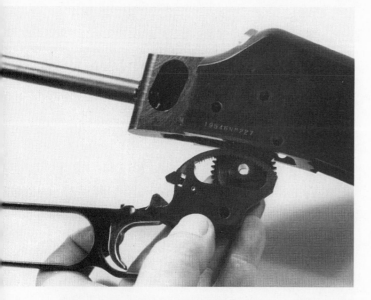

7. Remove the lever and bolt gear assembly downward.

8. Remove the bolt gear spacer disc from the gear.

9. Remove the bolt gear from the lever assembly.

10. The lever latch and its spring are retained in the lever by a roll pin. **Caution:** *The spring is powerful, so control the latch.*

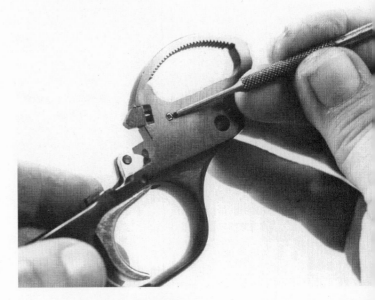

11. A cross pin retains the trigger assembly and the coil trigger spring.

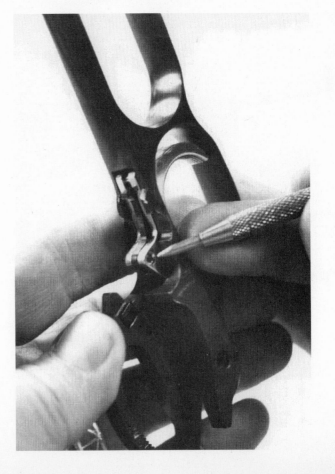

12. The sear connector is retained in the top of the trigger by a cross pin. If necessary for repair, the cross pin and the connector can be removed without taking the trigger out of the lever.

13. There is a trigger adjustment screw in the lever. This is set at the factory, and changes in the adjustment should be done only by an authorized Browning repair station.

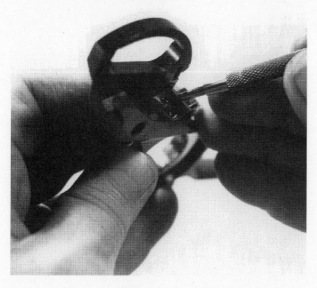

14. Remove the bolt toward the rear.

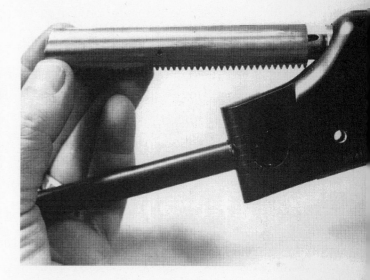

15. Turn the bolt head clockwise (front view) until it stops, and remove it toward the front.

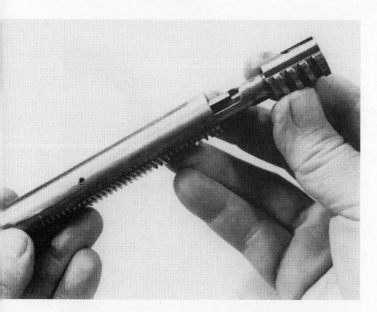

16. Remove the firing pin return spring toward the front.

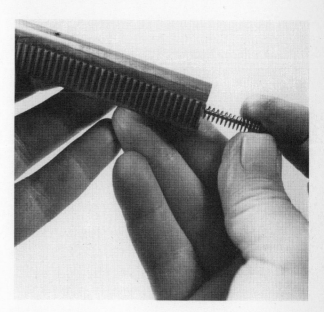

17. A roll pin retains the firing pin in the bolt. The firing pin is removed toward the rear.

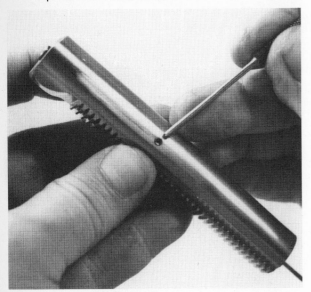

18. Tip the extractor outward for removal.

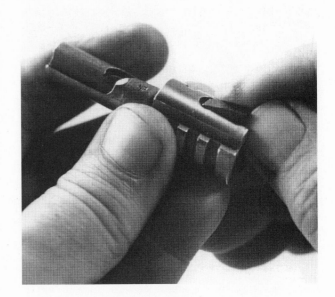

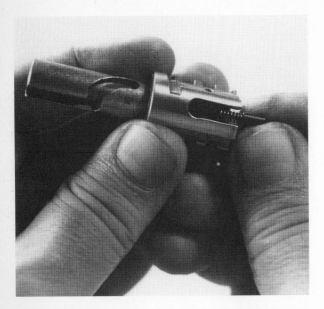

19. Remove the extractor plunger and spring from the bolt head.

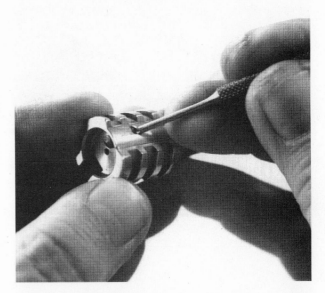

20. The ejector is retained in the bolt head by a cross pin. **Caution:** *As the drift is taken out, control the ejector—the spring is very powerful.*

21. Push out the sear pivot pin.

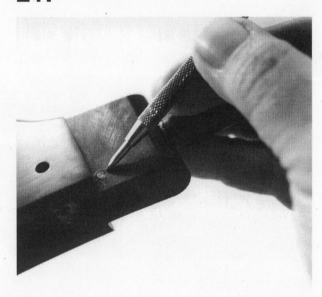

22. Remove the sear and its spring downward.

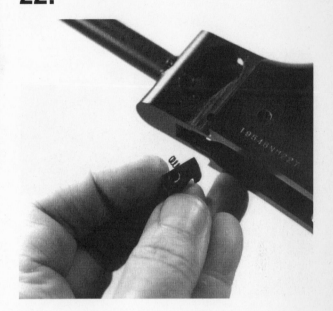

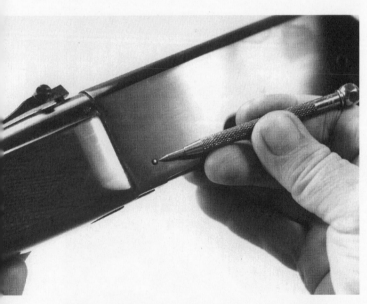

23. Drifting out this cross pin toward the right will release the magazine catch and its spring for removal downward.

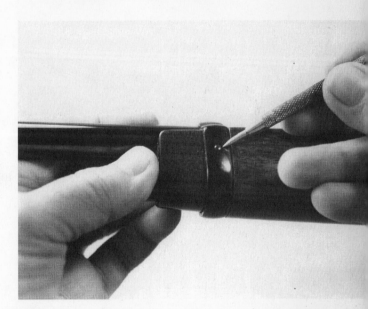

24. Drift out the barrel band cross pin toward the right.

25. Remove the barrel band toward the front.

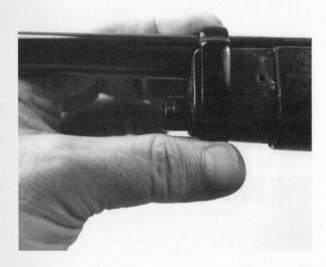

26. Remove the large screw at the front of the forend.

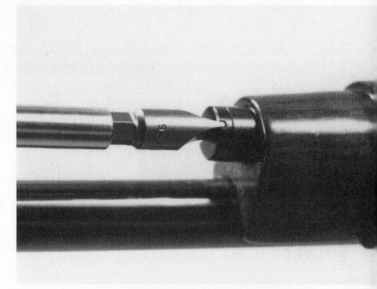

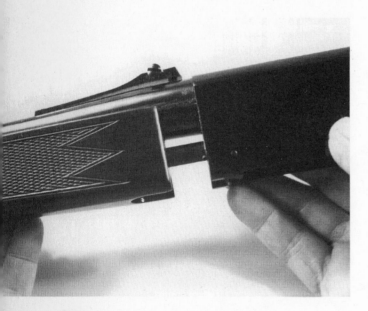

27. Remove the forend toward the front.

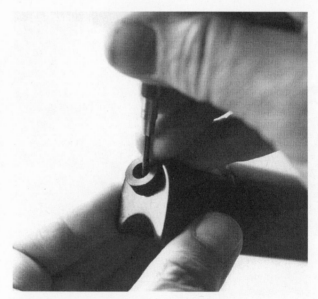

28. The outer spacer ring will usually stay on the forend mounting bolt. If the inner spacer ring needs to be removed, it is easily lifted out of its recess in the forend.

29. The forend mounting rod is retained on a post at the front of the receiver by a roll cross pin.

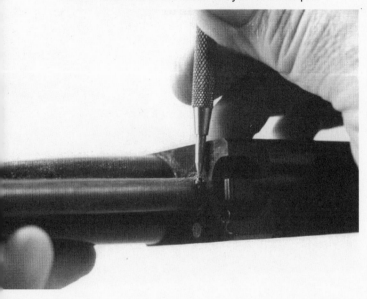

30. The rear sight is retained on top of the barrel by a vertical screw. The front sight may be drifted out of its dovetail toward the right. The front sight ramp is not routinely removable.

Reassembly Tips:

1. When replacing the barrel band, be sure the hole with spline marks is on the right side, and replace the pin accordingly. Be sure all of the cross pins are driven in from right to left, with the splined head on the right side.

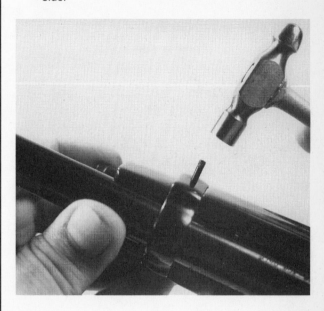

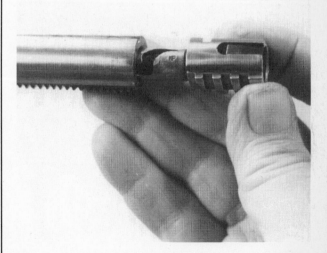

2. When reinstalling the bolt head, be sure the extractor is oriented toward the right side, as shown.

3. Insert the lever assembly with the bolt in fully closed position, and with the bolt gear at the rearmost location in its track, as shown.

4. Insert the gear and lever cross pins, but do not drive them into place until the gear and bolt engagement is correct. There should be a very small space visible at the point indicated with the lever closed. If the space is measurable, as it is here, then the engagement must be readjusted. To do this, pull the lever pin only, and reposition the lever track on the gear until the bolt closure is correct. If it is too tight for full lever travel, back it off by one gear tooth.

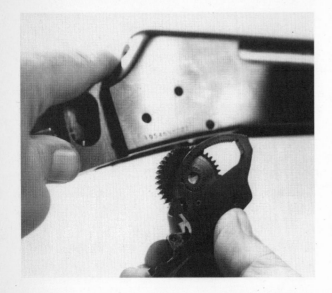

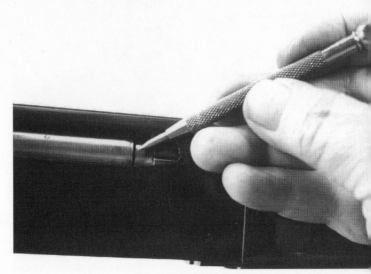

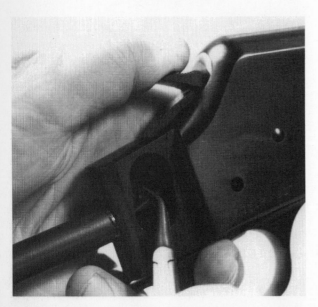

5. As the hammer is reinstalled, the trigger must be pulled fully to the rear for sear clearance, and the strut must be manipulated into proper contact with the hammer and the hammer spring follower. **Important:** *As the hammer pivot pin is reinserted, a tool must be used from the opposite side to depress the lever lock, which uses the hammer pin as a locking surface.*

BLR and Model '81 BLR Lever-Action Rifle

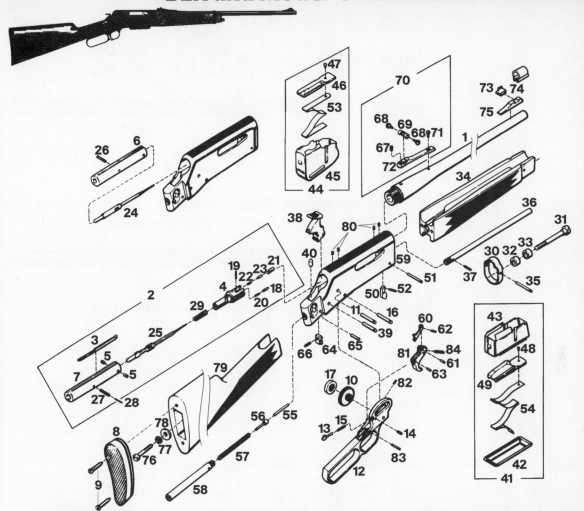

KEY

1 Barrel
2 Bolt Assembly
3 Breech Bolt Guide
4 Breech Bolt Lock
5 Breech Bolt Pins
6 Breech Bolt Slide (BLR)
7 Breech Bolt Slide (M'81)
8 Buttplate
9 Buttplate Screws
10 Cocking Gear
11 Cocking Gear Pin
12 Cocking Lever
13 Cocking Lever Latch
14 Cocking Lever Latch Pin
15 Cocking Lever Latch Spring
16 Cocking Lever Pin
17 Cocking Lever Stop
18 Ejector
19 Ejector Pin
20 Ejector Spring
21 Extractor
22 Extractor Spring
23 Extractor Spring Follower
24 Firing Pin (BLR)
25 Firing Pin (M'81)
26 Firing Pin Retaining Pin
27 Inner Firing Pin Retaining Pin
28 Outer Firing Pin Retaining Pin
29 Firing Pin Spring

30 Forearm Band
31 Forearm Bolt
32 Forearm Bolt Spacer, Inner
33 Forearm Bolt Spacer, Outer
34 Forearm
35 Forearm Pin
36 Forearm Tube
37 Forearm Tube Pin
38 Hammer
39 Hammer Pin
40 Hammer Stop
41 Magazine Assembly (M'81)
42 Magazine Base (M'81)
43 Magazine Body (M'81)
44 Magazine Assembly (BLR)
45 Magazine Body (BLR)
46 Magazine Follower (BLR)
47 Magazine Follower Rivet (BLR)
48 Magazine Follower Rivet (M'81)
49 Magazine Follower (M'81)
50 Magazine Latch
51 Magazine Latch Pin
52 Magazine Latch Spring
53 Magazine Spring (BLR)
54 Magazine Spring (M'81)
55 Mainspring Follower
56 Mainspring Guide
57 Mainspring
58 Mainspring Tube
59 Receiver
60 Sear Link

61 Sear Link Pin
62 Sear Link Spring
63 Sear Link Stop Pin
64 Sear
65 Sear Pin
66 Sear Spring
67 Rear Sight Elevation Adjusting Screw
68 Rear Sight Windage Adjusting Screws
69 Rear Sight Aperture
70 Rear Sight Assembly
71 Rear Sight Base Mounting Screw
72 Rear Sight Base
73 Front Sight
74 Front Sight Hood
75 Front Sight Ramp
76 Stock Bolt
77 Stock Bolt Lock Washer
78 Stock Bolt Washer
79 Stock
80 Telescope Mount Filler Screws
81 Trigger
82 Trigger Adjusting Screw
83 Trigger Pin
84 Trigger Spring

Parts Not Shown
Front Sling Eyelet
Rear Sling Eyelet

Browning Semi-Auto 22

Similar/Identical Pattern Guns
The same basic assembly/disassembly steps for the Browning Semi-Auto 22 also apply to the following guns:

Browning Standard Auto Grade II	**Norinco 22 ATD**
Browning Standard Auto Grade III	**Remington Model 24**
Browning Standard Auto Grade VI	**Remington Model 241**

Data:	Browning Semi-Auto 22
Origin:	Belgium
Manufacturer:	Browning Arms Company, Morgan, Utah (Made for Browning by FN in Belgium)
Cartridge:	22 Long Rifle
Magazine capacity:	11 rounds
Overall length:	37 inches
Barrel length:	$19^{1}/_{4}$ inches
Weight:	$4^{3}/_{4}$ pounds

This neat little semi-auto rifle was first produced in 1914 by Fabrique Nationale in Belgium, and in 1922 the production rights for the U.S. were leased to the Remington company. It was made by them as the Model 24 and Model 241 until 1951. In 1956, an altered version of the original gun was introduced by Browning, and it is still in production. Through all of this time, some 65 years, the internal mechanism has been essentially unchanged. In recent years, the gun has been neatly copied by Norinco of China as the Model 22 ATD. Among all of the different variations, there are minor differences in the extractor and cartridge guide systems, but the instructions will still apply.

Disassembly:

1. The takedown latch is located on the underside of the forend, at its rear edge. Push the latch forward into its recess in the forend.

2. Retract the bolt slightly, and turn the barrel assembly clockwise (rear view) until it stops. Then, remove the barrel assembly toward the front.

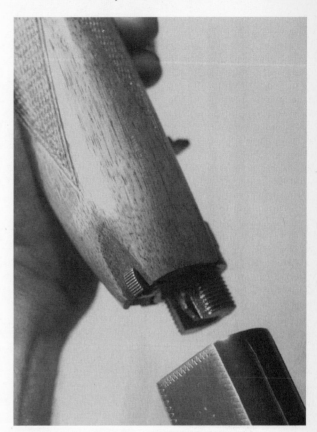

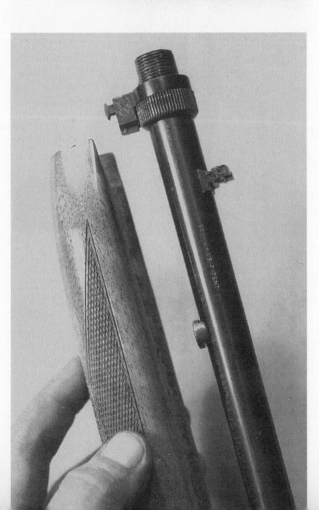

3. Remove the screw on the underside of the forend, and take off the forend downward.

4. Slide the takedown latch forward out of its base at the rear of the barrel. **Caution:** *Two plunger-and-spring assemblies will be released, and must be restrained to prevent loss.* The first will be the positioning plunger and spring at the rear of the latch, and the second will be the wedge-shaped plunger under the latch which bears on the barrel adjustment nut serrations. Ease both of these out, and take care that these small parts aren't lost.

5. Remove the takedown latch base ring toward the rear. Unscrew the knurled barrel adjustment nut and remove it toward the rear.

7. Pull the trigger to release the striker into the bolt, then move the front of the bolt upward out of the guard unit and ease it off forward. **Caution:** *Both the bolt spring and the striker spring are under some tension, so take care that they don't get away.* Remove the springs and their guides from the rear of the bolt.

6. Insert a finger through the trigger guard, place the thumb on the bolt handle, and retract the bolt to the rear while exerting forward pressure on the guard. The trigger group and bolt assembly can now be moved forward together and removed downward.

8. Remove the striker from the rear of the bolt.

9. Drifting out the cross pin at the lower front of the bolt will release the extractor retainer and allow removal of the extractor and its spring downward.

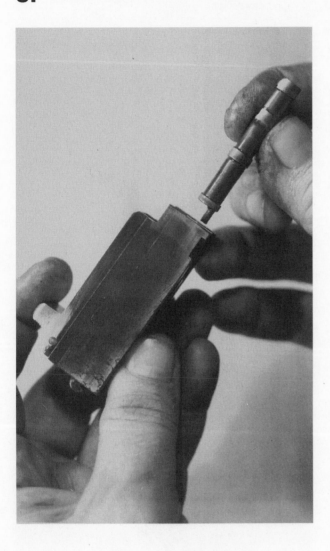

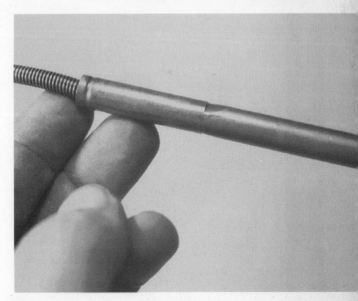

10. To remove the inner magazine tube, pull it out until it stops, then turn it 180 degrees to clear its side steps from the detents in the outer tube and take it out toward the rear.

11. Drifting out the locking cross pin at the head of the inner magazine tube will allow removal of the handle piece, spring, feed cable, and follower.

12. Use a very wide screwdriver or a special shop-made tool to remove the nut at the rear of the buttstock, and its lock washer, and take off the stock toward the rear. The outer magazine tube can now be unscrewed from the rear of the receiver. **Caution:** *Avoid gripping the tube too tightly and deforming it.*

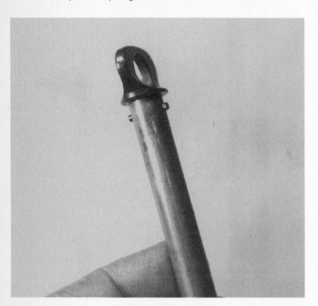

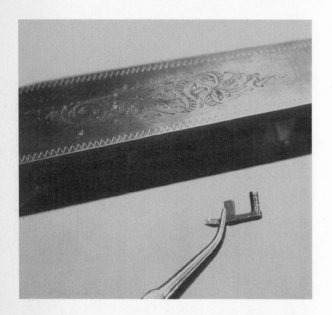

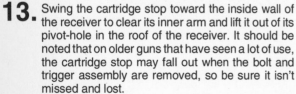

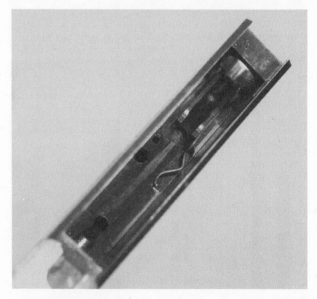

13. Swing the cartridge stop toward the inside wall of the receiver to clear its inner arm and lift it out of its pivot-hole in the roof of the receiver. It should be noted that on older guns that have seen a lot of use, the cartridge stop may fall out when the bolt and trigger assembly are removed, so be sure it isn't missed and lost.

14. Removal of the cartridge guide spring in the top front of the receiver will release the cartridge guide to be taken out toward the front. To remove the spring, use a small tool to pry its rear loop from beneath its flange in the receiver.

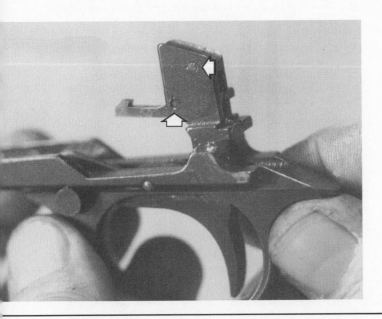

15. Drifting out the small cross pin (upper arrow) at the top of the vertical trigger group extension will release the sear spring and plunger for removal upward. Drifting out the sear pivot pin (lower arrow) will allow the sear to be taken out toward the front. The trigger and disconnector pivot on the same pin, and are removed as a unit, along with the disconnector spring. The disconnector can be separated from the trigger by drifting out the short pin that mounts it in the trigger. To remove the safety, use a small screwdriver to depress the plunger and spring inside, at the center, under the safety, and move the safety out toward the right. **Caution:** *Control the compressed spring and plunger and ease them out.*

Reassembly Tips:

1. When replacing the striker in the bolt, note that the striker has a guide lug on its left side that mates with a track inside the bolt.

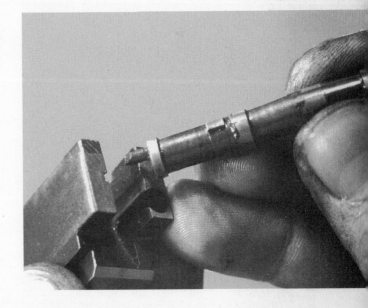

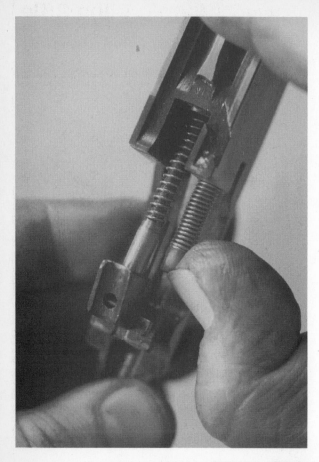

2. When replacing the bolt in the trigger group, carefully compress the recoil spring on its guide, then use a fingertip to hold the spring and guide in place on the bolt while fitting the bolt into place, inserting the tip of the striker spring guide into its hole in the vertical extension. Then, fit the rear bracket of the bolt spring guide onto its lug on the extension. **Caution:** *While the bolt spring is compressed, keep it aimed away from your eyes, in case the finger should slip.*

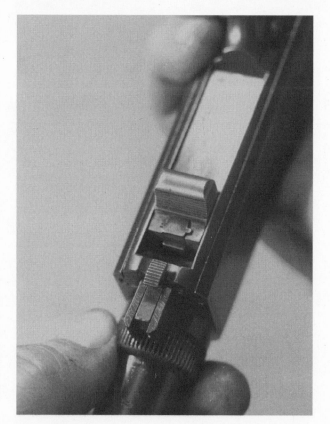

3. When reassembling the takedown latch system, be sure the small wedge-tipped plunger on the underside of the latch is oriented so the wedge tip aligns with the serrations on the adjustment nut. Use a small screwdriver to depress the two plungers alternately as the latch is moved into place.

4. To readjust the barrel nut, install the barrel on the gun before replacing the forend, lock the takedown latch in place, and turn the knurled adjustment nut until the ring is snug against the receiver. Then, reinstall the forend.

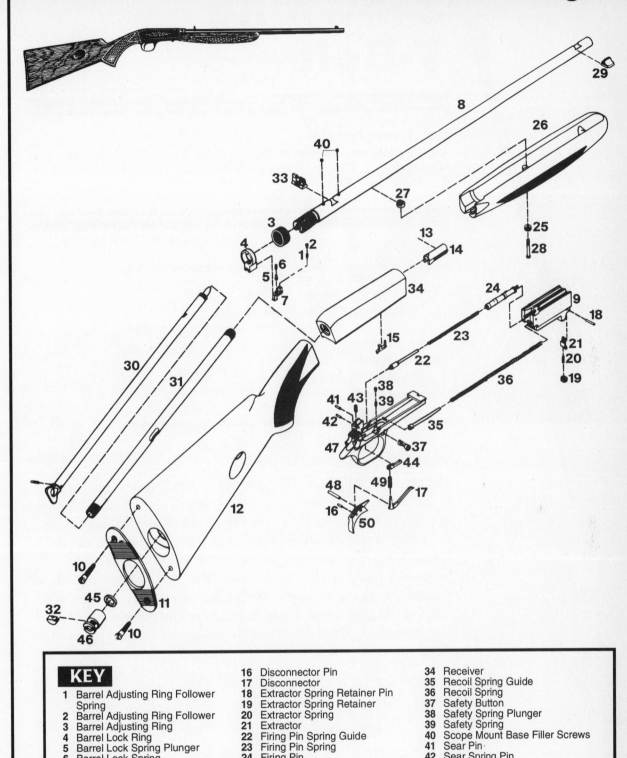

KEY

1 Barrel Adjusting Ring Follower Spring
2 Barrel Adjusting Ring Follower
3 Barrel Adjusting Ring
4 Barrel Lock Ring
5 Barrel Lock Spring Plunger
6 Barrel Lock Spring
7 Barrel Lock
8 Barrel
9 Breechblock
10 Buttplate Screws
11 Buttplate
12 Buttstock
13 Cartridge Guide Spring
14 Cartridge Guide
15 Cartridge Stop

16 Disconnector Pin
17 Disconnector
18 Extractor Spring Retainer Pin
19 Extractor Spring Retainer
20 Extractor Spring
21 Extractor
22 Firing Pin Spring Guide
23 Firing Pin Spring
24 Firing Pin
25 Forend Escutcheon
26 Forend
27 Forend Retainer Stud
28 Forend Screw
29 Front Sight
30 Inner Magazine Tube Assembly
31 Outer Magazine Tube
32 Magazine Tube Stop Spring
33 Rear Sight Assembly

34 Receiver
35 Recoil Spring Guide
36 Recoil Spring
37 Safety Button
38 Safety Spring Plunger
39 Safety Spring
40 Scope Mount Base Filler Screws
41 Sear Pin
42 Sear Spring Pin
43 Sear Spring
44 Sear
45 Stock Nut Washer
46 Stock Nut
47 Trigger Guard
48 Trigger Pin
49 Trigger Spring
50 Trigger

Browning T-Bolt

Similar/Identical Pattern Guns

The same basic assembly/disassembly steps for the Browning T-Bolt also apply to the following gun:

Browning T-2 T-Bolt

Data:	Browning T-Bolt
Origin:	Belgium
Manufacturer:	Fabrique Nationale, Herstal (for Browning Arms Company, Morgan, Utah)
Cartridge:	22 Long Rifle
Magazine capacity:	5 rounds
Overall length:	$39^1/_4$ inches
Barrel length:	22 inches
Weight:	$5^1/_2$ pounds

The unusual "straight pull" bolt of this fine little gun is a masterpiece of good engineering, and works beautifully. Unfortunately, the average American shooter has never been fond of unusual actions, and the T-Bolt was imported for less than ten years, from 1965 to 1973. In addition to the plain T-1 model, a T-2 was offered, with 24-inch barrel and fancy stock. The gun was also available in a left-hand version. An accessory single-shot adapter would allow the use of 22 Short or Long, as well as Long Rifle. Except for the reversal of some directions in the left-hand model, the instructions will apply to all of them.

Disassembly:

1. Remove the magazine, and remove the main stock mounting screw, on the underside just forward of the magazine well. Separate the action from the stock.

2. Removal of the wood screw at the rear of the trigger guard unit will allow the guard to be taken off downward.

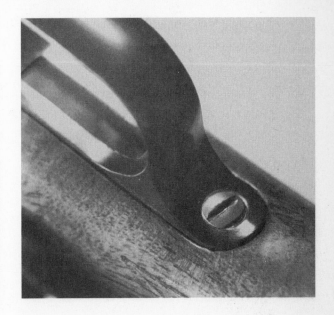

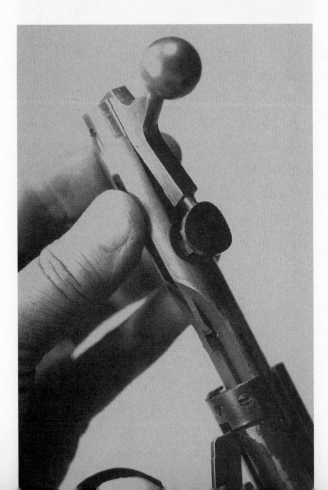

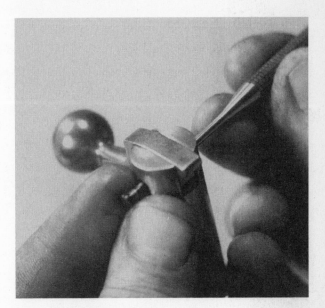

4. With the bolt handle in the closed (locked) position, push the vertical pin at the rear of the bolt upward, and remove it.

3. To remove the bolt, hold the trigger to the rear, and move the bolt out the rear of the receiver.

5. Remove the bolt handle toward the rear.

6. Remove the striker spring and its plunger toward the rear.

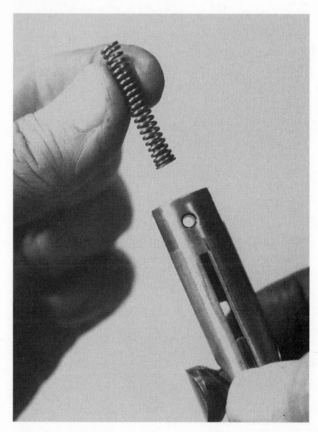

7. Turn the locking block ("cross-bolt") slightly to raise the firing pin out of its inside shoulder, and remove the locking block toward the right.

8. Remove the firing pin from its channel in the top of the bolt.

9. The twin extractors are retained by two vertical roll pins at the front of the bolt. Use a roll pin punch to drift out the pins, and remove the extractors from each side, along with the single transverse coil spring that powers both.

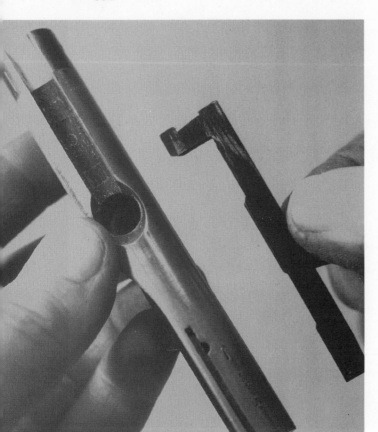

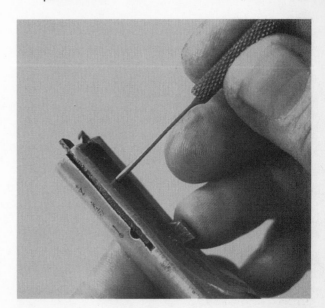

10. Push out the magazine catch cross pin, and remove the magazine catch and its coil spring downward.

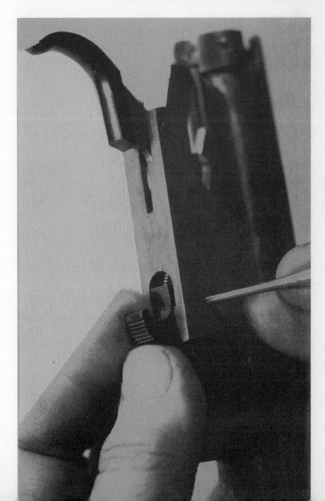

11. Removal of the magazine catch will give access to the magazine housing screw, which is taken out downward.

12. Remove the magazine housing downward.

13. Push out the cross pin at the top of the magazine housing, and remove the sear upward and toward the front.

14. Note the relationship of the trigger and its spring before removal, to aid in reassembly. Push out the cross pin at the lower rear of the magazine housing, and remove the trigger and its spring toward the rear and downward. Take care that the trigger spring isn't lost. Restrain it, and ease it out.

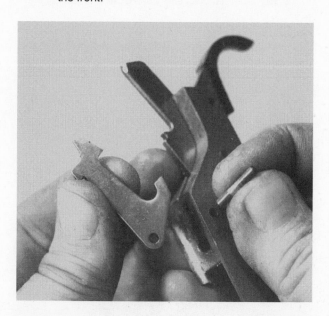

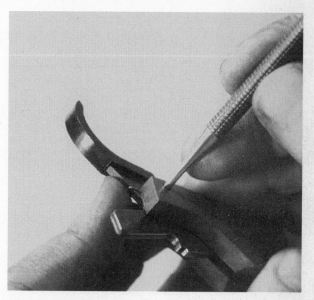

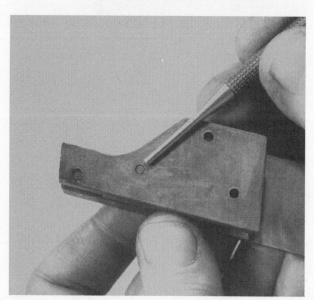

15. The trigger stop pin can also be drifted out, but can be left in place, as it retains no part.

16. The ejector is easily pushed from its slot in the underside of the receiver for removal.

17. Removal of the two screws in the outer band of the safety catch at the rear of the receiver will allow the catch to be taken off. **Caution:** *Removal of the safety will release the safety positioning plunger and spring, so restrain them and ease them out.*

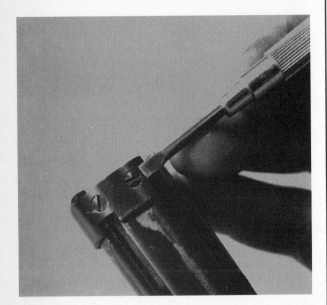

Reassembly Tips:

1. When replacing the ejector in its slot in the underside of the receiver, be sure its vertical face is toward the front, and its angled end toward the rear, as shown.

2. When replacing the trigger and its spring, taking out the trigger stop pin will make this operation easier. Insert the cross pin from the right, just far enough to hold the spring in position, then put in the trigger, and move the cross pin the rest of the way across. Be sure the front arm of the spring is against its shoulder or shelf inside the housing.

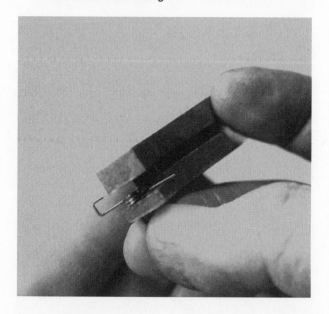

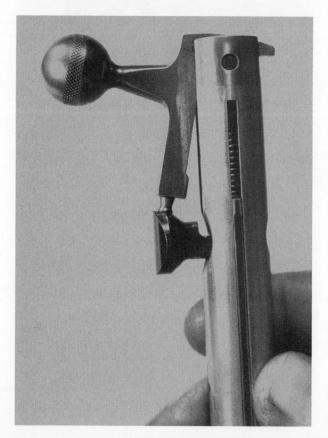

3. When replacing the locking cross bolt in the body of the bolt, note that the face with the deep cut and hole must be oriented toward the rear, and install the locking bolt before the firing pin is returned to its channel.

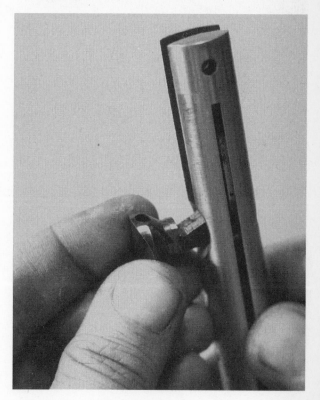

4. When replacing the bolt handle, be sure its front projection enters the hole in the rear face of the locking bolt, and note that the handle must be in the unlocked position, as shown, when the bolt is inserted into the receiver.

T-Bolt Bolt-Action Rifle

KEY

1 Barrel
2 Bolt Assembly
3 Bolt Handle
4 Bolt Handle Pin
5 Breechbolt
6 Buttplate
7 Buttplate Screws
8 Clip Magazine Floorplate
9 Clip Magazine Follower
10 Clip Magazine Follower Spring
11 Cross Bolt
12 Ejector
13 Extractor, Left
14 Extractor Pin
15 Extractor, Right
16 Extractor Spring
17 Firing Pin
18 Firing Pin Spring
19 Firing Pin Spring Follower
20 Loading Ramp
21 Magazine Enclosure
22 Magazine Housing
23 Magazine Housing Screw
24 Magazine Housing Screw Lock Washer
25 Magazine Latch
26 Magazine Latch Pin
27 Magazine Latch Spring
28 Receiver Sight Adjusting Screw, Horizontal
29 Receiver Sight Adjusting Screw Bushing, Horizontal
30 Receiver Sight Assembly Complete
31 Receiver Sight Base
32 Receiver Sight Eyepiece
33 Receiver Sight Eyepiece Adjusting Bushing, Vertical
34 Receiver Sight Eyepiece Housing
35 Receiver Sight Mounting Screw
36 Receiver Sight Mounting Screw Bushing
37 Safety Body
38 Safety Click Pin
39 Safety Click Pin Spring
40 Safety Screws
41 Sear
42 Sear Pin
43 Front Sight Blade
44 Front Sight Ramp
45 Stock T-Bolt
46 Trigger
47 Trigger Guard
48 Front Takedown Screw
49 Rear Trigger Guard Screw
50 Trigger Pin
51 Trigger Spring
52 Magazine Body
53 Magazine Assembly
54 Takedown Screw
55 Receiver

Charter
AR-7 Explorer

Similar/Identical Pattern Guns

The same basic assembly/disassembly steps for the Charter AR-7 Explorer also apply to the following guns:

Armalite AR-7   **Armalite AR-7C**

Armalite AR-7 Custom   **Survival Arms AR-7**

Armalite AR-7S

Data:	Charter AR-7 Explorer
Origin:	United States
Manufacturer:	Charter Arms Corp. Stratford, Connecticut
Cartridge:	22 Long Rifle
Magazine capacity:	8 rounds
Overall length:	35 inches
Barrel length:	16 inches
Weight:	2$\frac{1}{2}$ pounds

In 1959, Armalite, Incorporated of Costa Mesa, California, introduced the AR-7 Explorer, and this little semi-auto carbine instantly became popular with backpackers, fishermen, pilots, and everyone who might eventually be faced with a survival situation. The barrel, receiver, and magazine can be stowed inside the hollow plastic stock, and with the rubber buttplate/cover in place, the whole thing will even float. From 1973 to 1990, the AR-7 was made by Charter Arms. From 1992 to the present, it has been produced by Survival Arms, Incorporated. It remains essentially unchanged from the original guns made by Armalite.

Disassembly:

1. The stock retaining bolt is accessible in a recess at the bottom of the pistol grip portion of the stock, and its head has a raised center piece that is easily grasped with finger and thumb. Turn the bolt counterclockwise until the stock is released from the receiver, and remove the stock down and toward the rear.

2. The barrel is retained by a knurled collar which is threaded onto the front of the receiver. Turn the collar counterclockwise (front view) until it is free of the receiver, and remove the barrel toward the front. Note the guide or key on top of the barrel, which mates with a slot in the top of the receiver extension.

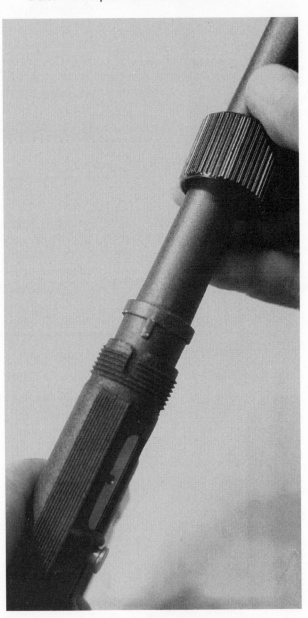

3. The barrel collar can be removed from the barrel only after the front sight is drifted out of its dovetail.

4. Be sure hammer is at rest (in the fired position) and remove the large screw on the left side which retains the sideplate.

Remove the sideplate toward the left. Proceed cautiously, as the left end of the hammer pivot rests in a small hole in the sideplate. If the plate is tight, it may have to be nudged from inside the magazine well and pried gently at the lower rear.

5. After the plate is removed, take note of the relationship of the internal parts before taking them out.

6. Restrain the magazine catch spring to prevent its loss, and remove the catch and spring toward the left.

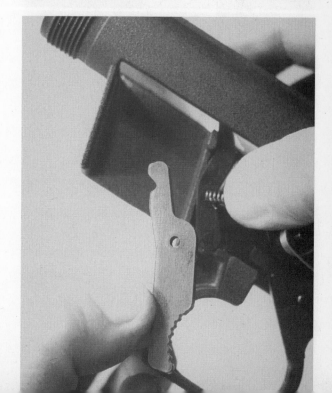

7. Disengage the outside (left) rear arm of the mainspring from its groove in the bearing pin at the rear of the trigger, and swing the spring arm down and forward to relieve its tension.

8. With a small screwdriver, lift the inside (right) rear arm of the mainspring from its groove in the pin at the rear of the trigger, and remove the pin toward the left.

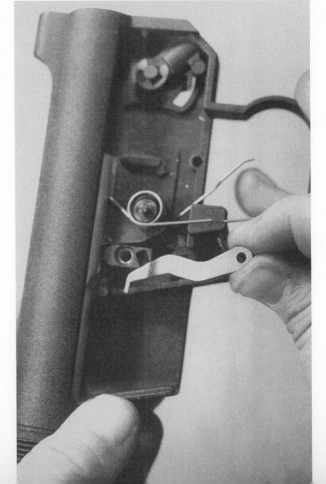

9. Remove the trigger and its pivot pin toward the left.

10. Remove the magazine catch pivot pin toward the left to release the ejector for removal downward.

11. Tip the hammer toward the rear and remove the hammer, spring and pivot assembly toward the left. The spring is easily detached from the hammer. In normal disassembly, the pivot should not be removed from the hammer.

12. Depress the bolt very slightly to align the bolt handle with the enlarged portion of its track in the receiver, and remove the handle toward the right.

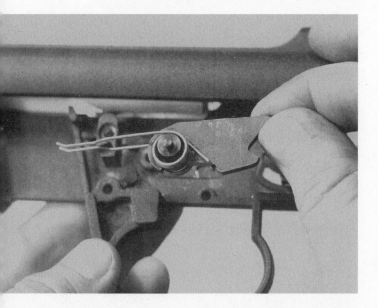

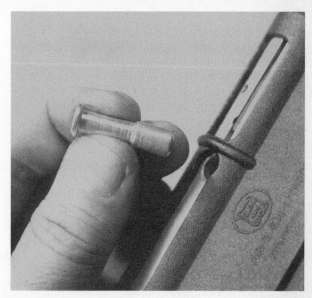

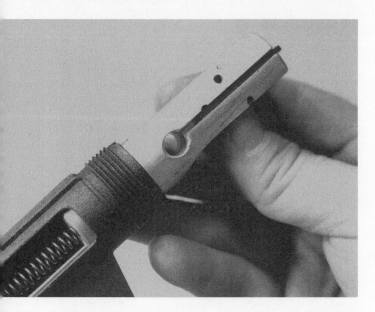

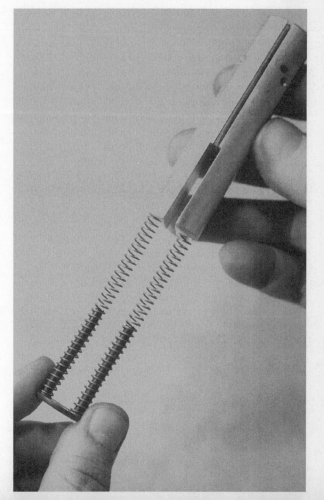

13. Remove the bolt, along with its twin springs and spring guide unit, toward the front.

14. Remove the springs and spring guide unit from the rear of the bolt.

15. Drifting out a horizontal roll pin will release the firing pin for removal from the top of the bolt.

16. Drifting out a vertical roll pin (arrow) on the right side of the bolt will release the extractor and its spring for removal toward the right.

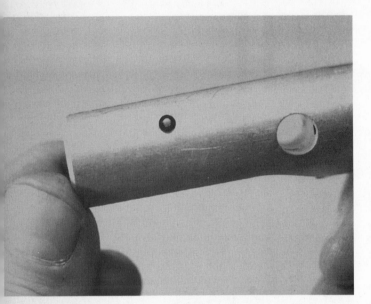

17. The safety is retained by a spring C-clip inside the receiver. After removal of the clip, the safety is removed toward the right.

18. Backing out the screw at the rear of the receiver will release the rear sight for removal.

Reassembly Tips:

When replacing the bolt and bolt spring assembly in the receiver, be sure the two springs are completely seated on the guide, and that the guide is horizontally oriented so the springs will not kink.

Before replacing the trigger in the receiver, swing the inside arm of the mainspring up to the rear and rest it on the inside of the receiver. When the trigger is in place, use a small screwdriver to lift the inner arm of the spring while inserting the spring base pin. Be sure the tip of the spring engages the groove in the pin.

1. When replacing the rear sight, note that the position of the sight plate is adjustable, and any change will affect the point of impact.

2. When replacing the sideplate, be sure the small tip of the hammer pivot is aligned with its hole in the side-plate.

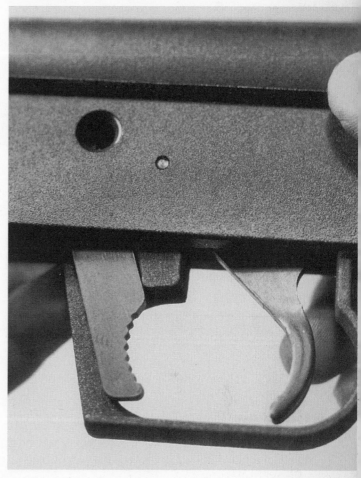

3. When replacing the barrel, be sure the guide key on the top of the barrel enters its slot in the front of the receiver. Tighten the barrel collar firmly, by hand, but do not over-tighten, as both collar and receiver are made of alloy.

AR-7 and AR-7S Explorer Autoloading Rifle

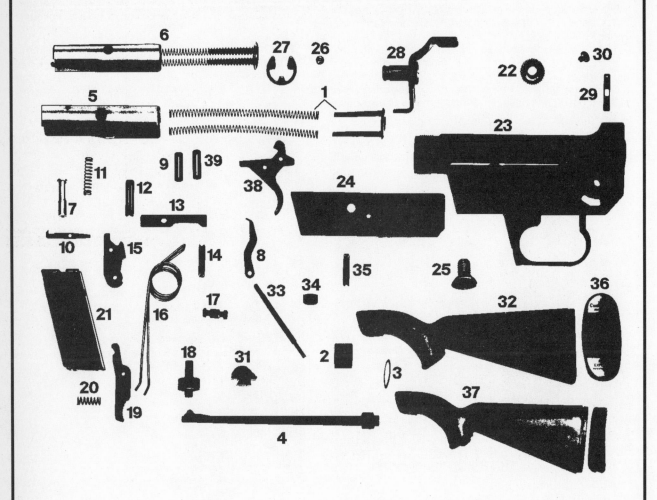

KEY

1 Action Springs and Guide
2 Barrel Nut
3 Barrel Nut Lock Washer
4 Barrel Assembly
5 Bolt
6 Bolt Assembly
7 Charging Handle
8 Ejector
9 Ejector Pin
10 Extractor
11 Extractor Spring
12 Extractor Assembly Pin
13 Firing Pin
14 Firing Pin Assembly Pin
15 Hammer
16 Hammer and Trigger Spring
17 Hammer and Trigger Spring
   Support Pin
18 Hammer Pivot Pin
19 Magazine Latch
20 Magazine Latch Spring
21 Magazine, Complete
22 Rear Sight Press Nut
23 Receiver
24 Receiver Sideplate
25 Receiver Sideplate Screw
26 Safety Detent Ball
27 Safety Snap Ring
28 Safety
29 Sight, Rear
30 Rear Sight Screw
31 Sight, Front
32 Stock
33 Stock Takedown Screw
34 Stock Takedown Screw Nut
35 Stock Takedown Screw Nut Roll
   Pin
36 Stock Outer Buttcap
37 Stock Assembly
38 Trigger
39 Trigger Pivot Pin

Colt AR-15

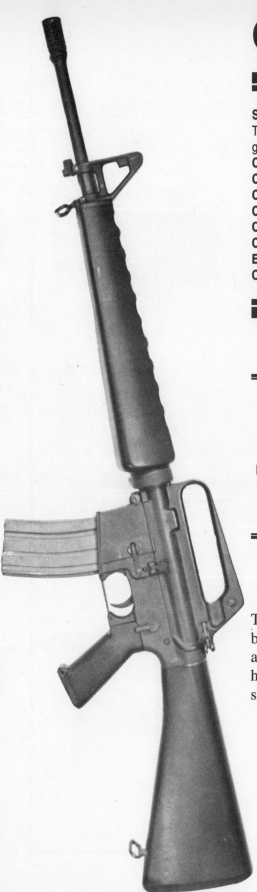

Similar/Identical Pattern Guns

The same basic assembly/disassembly steps for the Colt AR-15 also apply to the following guns:

Colt AR-15 Collapsible Stock Model	Colt AR-15A2 Sporter II
Colt AR-15A2 Carbine	Colt AR-15A2 Delta HBAR
Colt AR-15A2 HBAR	Colt AR-15 Delta HBAR Match
Colt AR-15A2 Government Model Target	Colt AR-15A2 Government Model Carbine
Colt Sporter Lightweight Rifle	Colt Sporter Target Model
Colt Sporter Match Delta HBAR	Colt Sporter Match HBAR
Eagle Arms EA-15	Olympic Arms AR-15 Heavy Match
Olympic Arms AR-15 Service Match	Olympic Arms CAR-15

Data:	Colt AR-15
Origin:	United States
Manufacturer:	Colt Firearms
	Hartford, Connecticut
Cartridge:	223 Remington (5.56mm)
Magazine capacity:	5 and 20 rounds
Overall length:	38⅜ inches
Barrel length:	20 inches
Weight:	7¼ pounds

The original AR-15A1, made from 1963 to 1984, did not have the bolt forward-assist plunger and spring on the right side of the receiver, as on the M-16 military gun. All AR-15A2 rifles, up to the present, have this feature. The plunger is retained by a pin, and removal is a simple operation that will require no additional instructions.

Disassembly:

1. Remove the magazine, and cycle the action to cock the hammer. Push out the takedown pin, located at the upper rear of the grip frame, toward the right.

2. With the takedown pin stopped in pulled-out position, tip the barrel and receiver assembly upward at the rear.

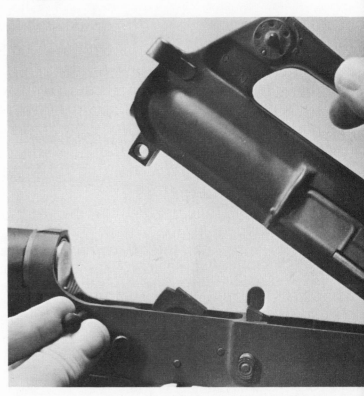

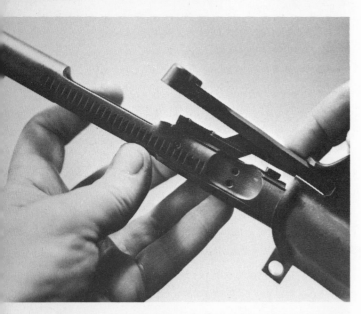

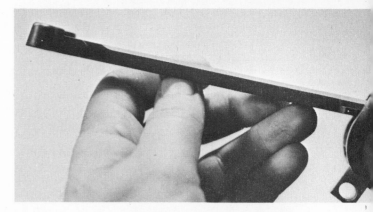

3. Use the charging handle to start the bolt assembly toward the rear, and remove the assembly from the rear of the receiver.

4. Move the charging handle to the rear until it stops, then move it out the rear of the receiver.

5. The charging handle latch and its spring are retained in the handle by a vertical roll pin. In normal takedown, it is best left in place.

6. Use a small tool to pull out the cotter pin on the left side of the bolt carrier, to free the firing pin.

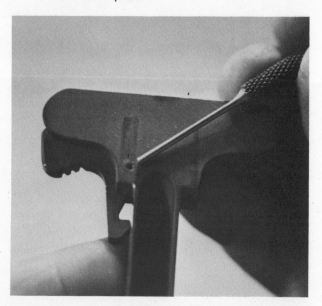

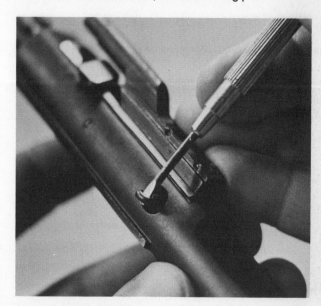

7. Remove the firing pin toward the rear.

8. Rotate the bolt cam pin to clear its flange from beneath the edge of the overhang, and remove the bolt cam pin upward.

9. Remove the bolt from the front of the bolt carrier.

10. The extractor and its coil spring are retained in the bolt by a cross pin which is easily pushed out in either direction.

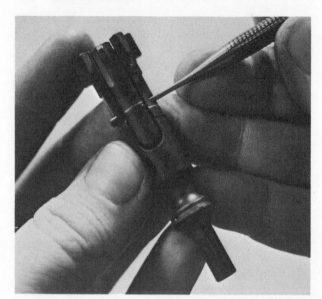

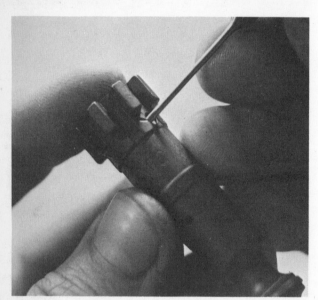

11. The ejector and its spring are also retained by a pin, a small roll pin that crosses the front of the bolt. The ejector spring is quite strong, so restrain the ejector during removal.

12. The gas cylinder is retained by two Allen screws on top of the bolt carrier, and these are heavily staked in place. **CAUTION:** *This unit should be removed only if repair or replacement is necessary.*

13. Remove the cap screw at the left end of the receiver pivot. It will be necessary to stabilize the screw-slotted head of the pivot with another large screwdriver on the right side during removal.

14. Use a slim drift punch that will not damage the interior threads to nudge the receiver pivot out toward the right, and separate the barrel and receiver unit from the stock and grip frame assembly.

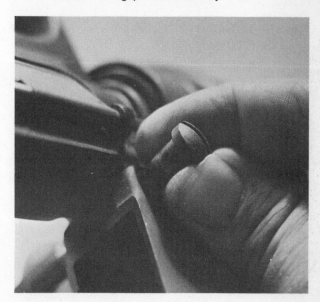

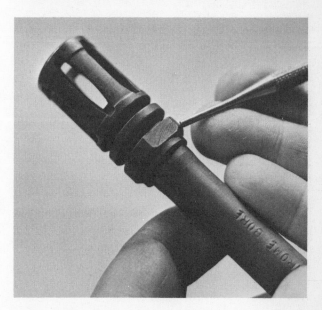

15. Pull back on the grooved slip ring right at the rear of the handguard units, and alternately tip each unit outward at the rear, then remove them rearward.

16. With a wrench of the proper size, unscrew the flash hider from the end of the barrel, and take care not to lose the lock washer behind it.

17. The combination front sight base, gas port unit, and bayonet mount is retained on the barrel by two large cross pins. When these are drifted out toward the right, the unit can be nudged forward off the barrel. During removal, take care that the gas transfer tube is not damaged.

18. The gas conduit is retained in the sight unit by a roll cross pin. In normal takedown, this should not be disturbed.

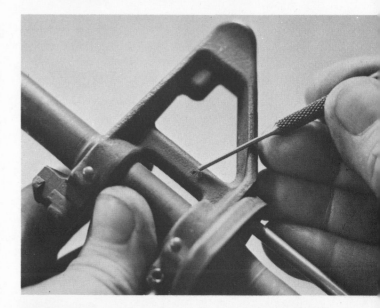

19. Insert a small tool in one of the holes at the top of the large clip-ring at the front of the receiver, and gently pry the ring out of its channel. Moving it rearward will relieve the tension of the circular spring assembly that powers the handguard slip-ring.

20. Move the slip-ring to the rear to give access to the toothed barrel retaining nut, and unscrew the nut counter-clockwise (front view). Take off the retaining nut, slip-ring, spring, and clip-ring toward the front.

21. The long pin which forms the hinge for the ejection port cover is retained by a C-clip in a groove near its forward end. Take off the C-clip, and move the hinge pin out toward the rear. **Caution:** *The cover spring will be released as the pin is cleared, so restrain it. Take care that the very small C-clip is not lost.*

22. Restrain the hammer and pull the trigger to lower the hammer to fired position. Push out the hammer pivot pin toward either side, controlling the hammer against its spring tension.

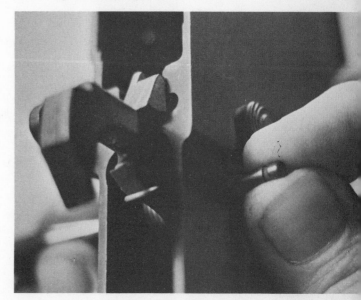

23. Remove the hammer and its spring upward. The spring is easily detached from the hammer.

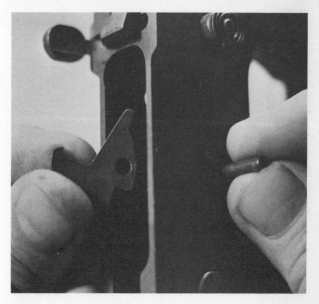

24. Push the trigger pin just far enough toward the right that the disconnector is cleared, and remove the disconnector from the top of the grip frame.

25. Set the safety halfway between its two positions, and use a nylon drift punch on the right side to nudge it toward the left, then remove it.

26. Remove the trigger pin, and take out the trigger assembly upward. The trigger spring and disconnector spring are easily detached from the trigger.

27. The magazine catch is removed by pushing it toward the left beyond its normal magazine release point, then unscrewing the catch piece from the button. The button and spring are then taken off toward the right, and the catch piece toward the left. The catch piece is unscrewed counter-clockwise, left-side view.

28. The hold open device and its spring are retained on the left side of the grip frame by a roll pin, and after removal of the pin they are taken off toward the left.

29. Restrain the recoil buffer against the tension of the recoil spring, and depress the buffer stop plunger. **Caution:** *The spring is strong, so take care to keep it under control.*

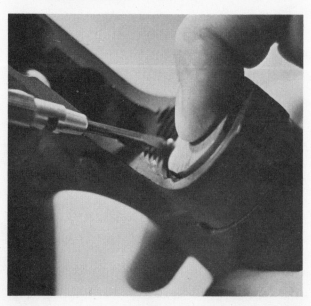

30. Slowly release the tension of the spring, and remove the buffer and spring toward the front.

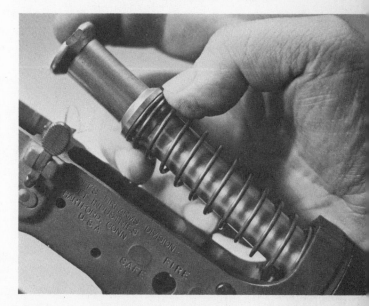

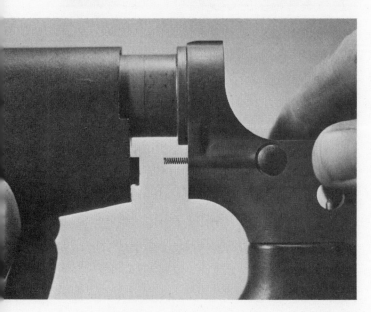

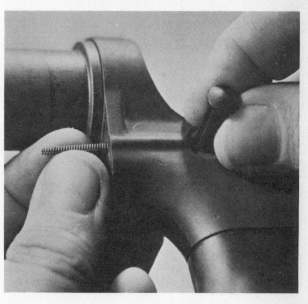

31. Remove the upper screw in the buttplate and remove the buttstock toward the rear. Take care not to lose the takedown pin retaining plunger and its spring at the rear of the grip frame. Removal of the lower screw in the buttplate will give access to the mechanism of the storage compartment cover and its latch.

32. Remove the takedown pin spring and plunger from the rear of the grip frame. The takedown pin can then be removed toward the right.

33. The pistol grip is removed by backing out a screw accessible through the bottom of the grip. Note that this will also release the safety plunger and its spring for removal downward.

34. The lower section of the trigger guard is retained at the rear by a roll cross pin. After this is removed, the section can be swung downward, and a very small roll pin in its forward hinge will be exposed for removal. The hinge pin can then be taken out toward the right, and the lower section removed.

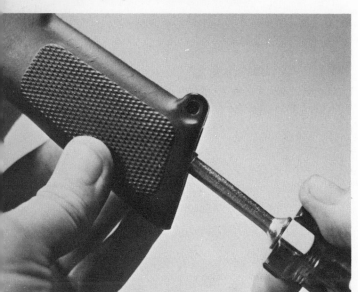

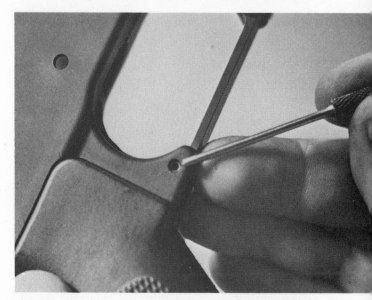

Reassembly Tips:

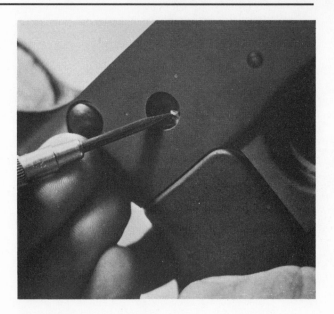

1. When replacing the safety-lever, use a tool on the right side to depress the safety plunger as the safety is pushed into place.

2. When replacing the cocking handle, remember that its forward end must be inserted into the receiver and then moved upward into its track.

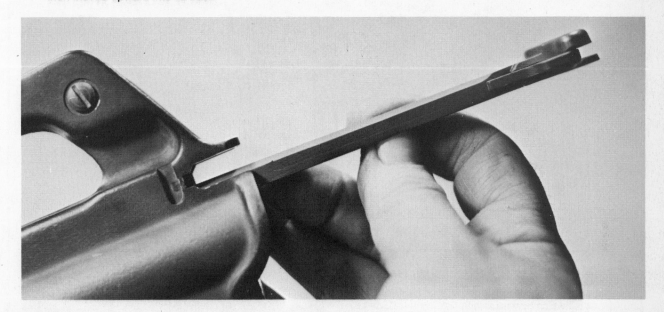

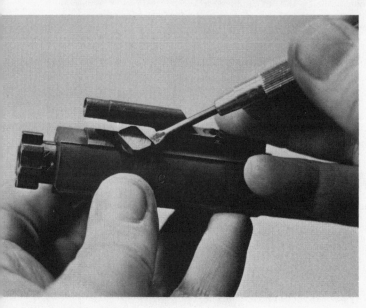

3. When replacing the bolt in the bolt carrier, note that the extractor must be oriented to the upper right, and the ejector to the lower left. Also, remember to turn the bolt cam pin so its flange is beneath the edge of the gas cylinder.

AR15-A2 Autoloading Rifle

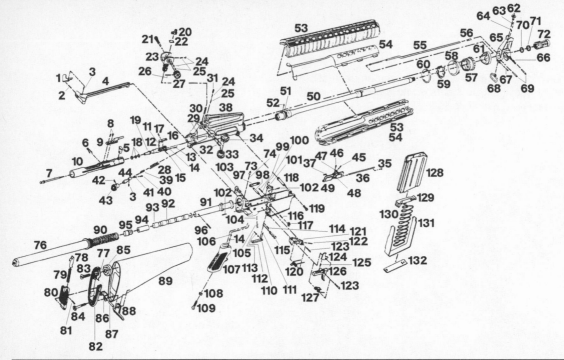

KEY

1	Charging Handle Latch
2	Charging Handle Latch Spring
3	Charging Handle Latch Roll Pin
4	Charging Handle
5	Cam Pin
6	Firing Pin Retaining Pin
7	Firing Pin
8	Socket Head Cap Screws
9	Bolt Carrier Key
10	Bolt Carrier
11	Extractor Spring Insert
12	Extractor Spring
13	Ejector
14	Ejector and Safety Detent Spring
15	Ejector Roll Pin
16	Extractor
17	Bolt Ring
18	Extractor Pins
19	Bolt
20	Rear Sight Aperture
21	Rear Sight Windage Screw
22	Rear Sight Flat Spring
23	Rear Sight Base
24	Rear Sight Ball Bearings
25	Rear Sight Helical Springs
26	Rear Sight Windage Knob Spring Pin
27	Rear Sight Windage Knob
28	Forward Assist Assembly Spring
29	Forward Assist Spring Pin
30	Rear Sight Elevation Spring
31	Index Screw
32	Rear Sight Elevation Spring Pin
33	Rear Sight Elevation Knob
34	Rear Sight Elevation Index
35	Cover Hinge Pin Snap Ring
36	Cover Hinge Pin
37	Cover Spring
38	Upper Receiver
39	Forward Assist Pawl
40	Forward Assist Pawl Detent
41	Forward Assist Detent Spring
42	Forward Assist Cap Pin
43	Forward Assist Cap
44	Forward Assist Plunger
45	Cover Latch Retaining Pin
46	Cover Latch
47	Cover Latch Spring
48	Cover Latch Housing
49	Ejection Slot Cover
50	Barrel
51	Barrel Extension
52	Barrel Indexing Pin
53	Handguard
54	Handguard Liner
55	Gas Tube
56	Gas Tube Plug
57	Barrel Nut
58	Handguard Slip Ring
59	Handguard
60	Handguard Snap Ring
61	Handguard Cap
62	Front Sight Post
63	Front Sight Detent
64	Front Sight Detent Spring
65	Front Sight
66	Gas Tube Roll Pin
67	Front Sling Swivel Rivet
68	Front Sling Swivel
69	Front Sight Taper Pins
70	Compensator Spacer
71	Compensator Spacer
72	Flash Suppressor
73	Buffer Retainer
74	Buffer Retainer Spring
75	Lower Receiver
76	Receiver Extension
77	Buttplate Insert
78	Door Assembly Plunger
79	Door Assembly Plunger Spring
80	Door Assembly Door
81	Door Assembly Door Pin
82	Buttcap
83	Buttcap Screw
84	Rear Swivel Screw
85	Buttcap Spacer
86	Swivel Hinge
87	Rear Swivel Pin
88	Rear Sling Swivel
89	Buttstock
90	Action Spring
91	Buffer Body
92	Buffer Disc
93	Buffer Weight
94	Buffer Spacer
95	Buffer Bumper
96	Buffer Bumper Pin
97	Magazine Catch Plate
98	Magazine Catch Shaft
99	Bolt Catch Plunger
100	Bolt Catch Spring
101	Bolt Catch
102	Bolt Catch Roll Pin
103	Safety Selector Lever
104	Takedown Pin Detent
105	Takedown Pin Spring Detent
106	Safety Detent
107	Pistol Grip
108	Lock Washer
109	Pistol Grip Screw
110	Trigger Guard
111	Roll Pin
112	Trigger Guard Plunger
113	Trigger Guard Spring
114	Trigger Guard Pivot Pin Roll Pin
115	Takedown Pin
116	Magazine Catch Spring
117	Magazine Release Button
118	Receiver Pivot Pin
119	Receiver Pivot Pin Screw
120	Hammer Spring
121	Hammer
122	Hammer Pin Retainer
123	Hammer and Trigger Pin
124	Disconnector
125	Disconnector Spring
126	Trigger
127	Trigger Spring
128	Magazine Box
129	Magazine Follower
130	Magazine Spring
131	Magazine Spacer
132	Magazine Bottom Plate

Harrington & Richardson Model 750

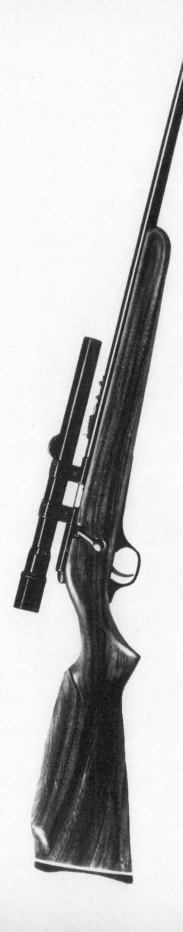

Similar/Identical Pattern Guns

The same basic assembly/disassembly steps for the Harrington & Richardson Model 750 also apply to the following gun:

Harrington & Richardson Model 751

Data:	Harrington & Richardson Model 750
Origin:	United States
Manufacturer:	Harrington & Richardson Gardner, Massachusetts
Cartridge:	22 Short, Long, or Long Rifle
Overall length:	39 inches
Barrel length:	22 inches
Weight:	5 pounds

Introduced in 1954, the Model 750 was named the "Pioneer" like the Model 765 which preceded it. The Model 750 is a good, solid single shot rifle. As a general rule, single shot bolt-action rifles are mechanically very simple, since there are no cartridge feed systems. Each one, though, has a firing mechanism that is unique to its particular manufacturer. There are certain general similarities, however, and the Model 750 H&R is a typical representative of the type. The instructions can also be used for the H&R Model 751.

Disassembly:

1. Back out the large screw on the underside of the stock, forward of the trigger guard, and separate the action from the stock.

2. To remove the bolt, open it and move it toward the rear. Pull the trigger, hold it back, and press the lower lobe of the sear to tip it downward, holding it down while removing the bolt toward the rear.

3. Grip the forward portion of the bolt in a padded vise and turn the bolt handle to allow the striker to move forward to the fired position. The photo shows the striker in the forward position, with the tension of its spring partially relieved.

4. With the front portion of the bolt still gripped in the padded vise, unscrew the domed rear end piece. **Caution:** *The striker spring is quite powerful and has considerable tension, even when at rest. Hold the end piece firmly, control it, and ease the spring tension off slowly.*

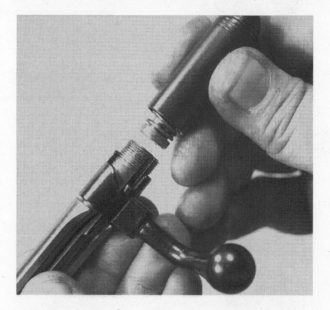

5. Remove the striker spring and its guide from the bolt end piece.

6. Move the bolt handle sleeve off toward the rear, taking with it the striker/firing pin unit.

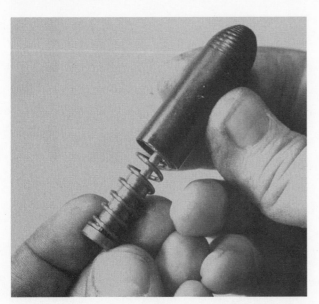

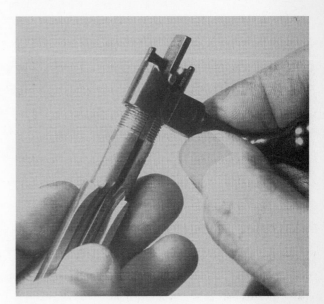

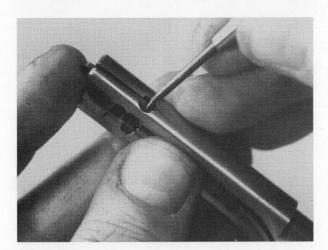

7. To remove the twin extractors, use a small screwdriver to depress the extractor spring plungers, and lift the extractors out of their recesses on each side. **Caution:** *Take care to keep the depressed plungers under control, as the springs can propel them quite a distance if they are released suddenly.* Keep the springs with their respective extractors, as they are not interchangeable.

8. Remove the spring clip on the left side of the trigger housing from the end of the trigger pivot and take out the pivot pin toward the right.

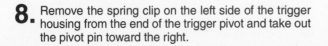

9. As the pivot pin is removed, restrain the trigger against the tension of its spring, and take it off downward. The safety-lever will also be released for removal toward the right. The trigger spring and its plunger are easily removed from their well in the upper rear of the trigger.

10. Remove the spring clip from the left end of the sear pivot and push the pivot pin out toward the right. This will allow removal of the sear and its spring downward, and the safety bar and its spring toward the right. The sear spring is easily removed from its well in the top rear of the sear.

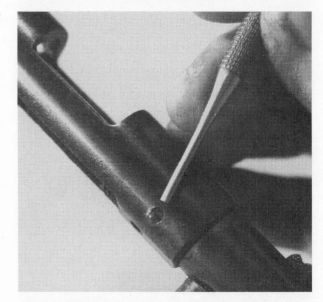

11. The cartridge guide platform with its integral ejector is retained inside the receiver by a screw on the underside, just forward of the trigger housing.

12. The barrel is retained in the receiver by a cross pin, but removal is not recommended in normal disassembly.

Reassembly Tips:

1. When replacing the safety positioning spring, note that the dimple at its center must have its convex side inward, to bear on the recesses in the safety bar.

2. When replacing the safety-lever, be sure the lower turned-in portion of the lever engages its opening in the safety bar.

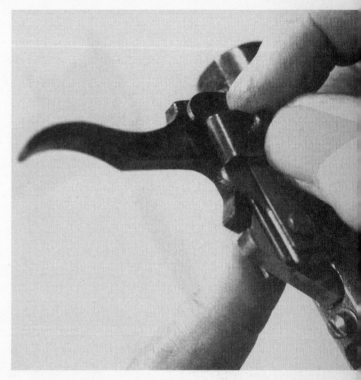

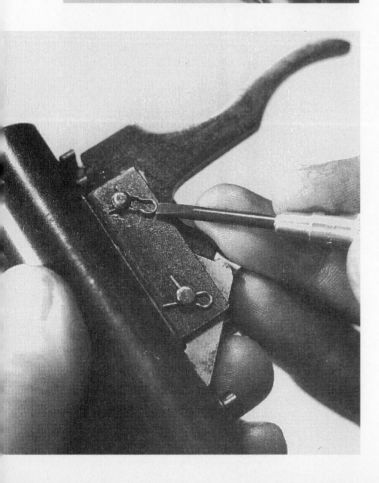

3. When replacing the spring clips on the sear and trigger pins, be sure the pins are turned fully toward the left, so the clips will engage their grooves in the heads of the pins.

4. When replacing the striker/firing pin unit in the bolt, insert it only as far as shown, then install the bolt handle sleeve, and let it carry the striker into the bolt.

5. Replacement of the rear end piece of the bolt, working against the tension of the striker spring, will require that the front portion of the bolt be gripped in a padded vise. Be sure the bolt handle is turned so the striker is in fired position. Be very careful not to cross-thread the end piece. When the end piece is in place, the bolt must be in cocked condition for reinsertion in the receiver. With the bolt still in the padded vise, turn the bolt handle to recock the striker. The photo shows the striker in the cocked position.

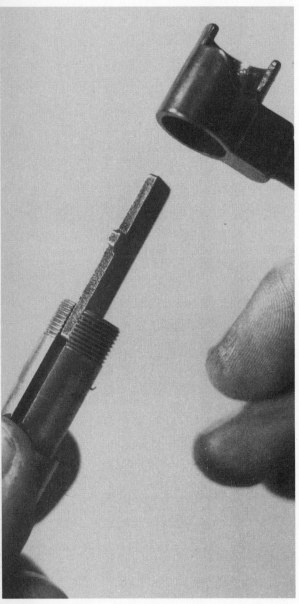

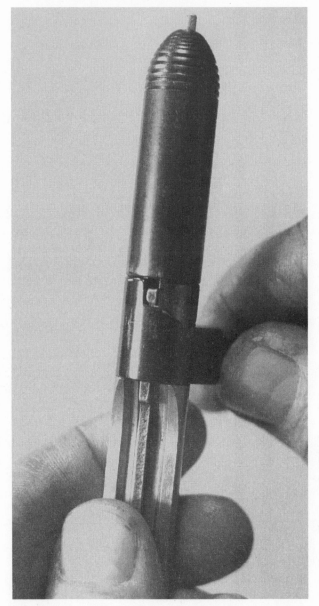

Model 750 and 751 Pioneer Bolt-Action Rifle

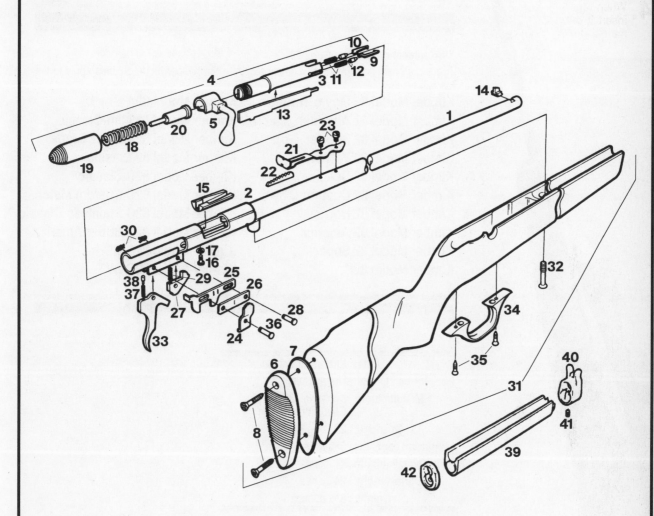

KEY

1 Barrel
2 Barrel and Receiver Assembly
3 Bolt, Front
4 Bolt Assembly, Complete
5 Bolt Cocking Cam Assembly
6 Buttplate
7 Buttplate Filler
8 Buttplate Screws
9 Extractor, Right
10 Extractor, Left
11 Extractor Springs
12 Extractor Spring Plungers
13 Firing Pin

14 Front Sight
15 Loading Platform
16 Loading Platform Screw
17 Loading Platform Screw Washer
18 Mainspring
19 Mainspring Housing
20 Mainspring Plunger with Safety
Pin
21 Rear Sight
22 Rear Sight Elevator
23 Rear Sight Screws
24 Safety-Lever
25 Safety-Lever Slide
26 Safety-Lever Spring
27 Sear

28 Sear Pin
29 Sear Spring
30 Sear and Trigger Pin Clip
31 Stock Assembly, Complete
32 Takedown Screw
33 Trigger
34 Trigger Guard
35 Trigger Guard Screws
36 Trigger Pin
37 Trigger Spring
38 Trigger Spring Plunger
39 Forend
40 Front Sight
41 Front Sight Screw
42 Stock Band

Kimber Model 82

Similar/Identical Pattern Guns

The same basic assembly/disassembly steps for the Kimber Model 82 also apply to the following guns:

Kimber Model 82 Gov't. Target	**Kimber Model 82A Gov't.**
Kimber Model 82 All Amer. Match	**Kimber Model 82 Mini-Classic**
Kimber Model 82 Sporter	**Kimber Model 82 Hunter Grade**
Kimber Model 82 Varminter	**Kimber Model 82 Classic**
Kimber Model 82 Deluxe	**Kimber Model 82C Classic**
Kimber Model 82 Custom Classic	**Kimber Model 82C Custom Match**
Kimber Model 82 Hornet	**Kimber Model 82C Stainless Classic**
Kimber Model 82 America	**Kimber Model 82C Super America**
Kimber Model 82 Super	**Kimber Model 82C HS**
Kimber Model 82B	**Kimber Model 82C SVT**

Data:	Kimber Model 82
Origin:	United States
Manufacturer:	Kimber of Oregon, Inc. Clackamas, Oregon
Cartridge:	22 Long Rifle
Magazine capacity:	5 rounds
Overall length:	41 inches
Barrel length:	24 inches
Weight:	6$\frac{1}{4}$ pounds

Quality and price were both notably high, and the Kimber rifle lasted for about eleven years, from 1980 to 1991. Now, treasured by both shooters and collectors, the original Kimber guns have become difficult to find. The Model 82 was made in several grades and styles, but all were mechanically essentially the same. In recent years, Kimber has again been making rifles, the Model 82C, in various styles, and production continues to the present.

Disassembly:

1. Remove the magazine. Hold the trigger to the rear, open the bolt and remove the bolt toward the rear.

2. Remove the large screw in front of the magazine opening.

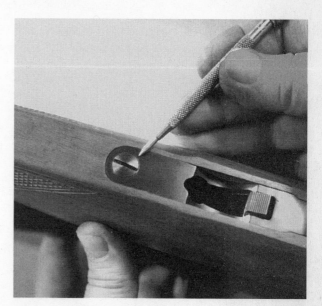

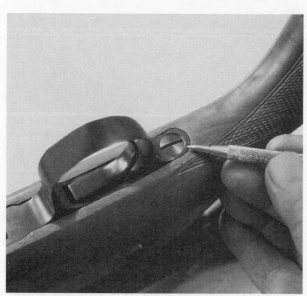

3. Remove the large screw behind the trigger guard. Keep the two screws in order, as they are not interchangeable.

4. Remove the action from the stock.

5. Remove the trigger guard unit from the stock.

6. Hold the front of the bolt firmly with a shop cloth and turn the handle to lower the striker to fired position, as shown.

7. Use an Allen wrench to remove the cocking stud from the striker.

8. Remove the bolt handle unit toward the rear.

9. Insert a tool at the rear to arrest the striker spring and push out the retaining cross pin. **Caution:** *Control the spring.*

10. Remove the striker spring toward the rear.

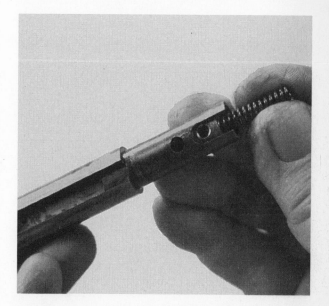

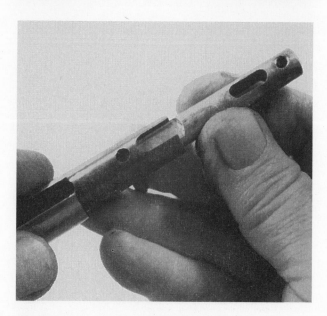

11. Remove the striker toward the rear.

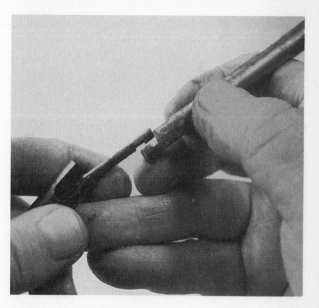

12. As the striker emerges, the firing pin will be released from its hook at the front of the striker.

13. Carefully pry the narrow left arm of the saddle-type spring from its engagement with the left extractor. Control the spring as it is taken off.

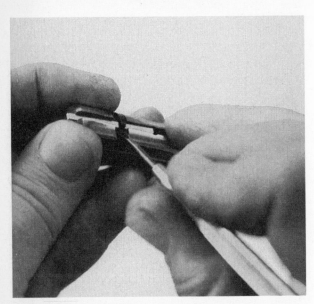

14. The extractors are now easily lifted out of their recesses in the bolt. Keep them in order, as they are not interchangeable.

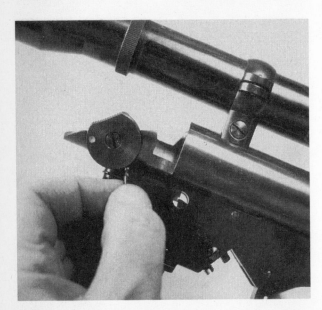

15. Grip the shaft of the safety positioning spring guide and move it downward to disengage its upper tip from the recess in the safety disc. Keep control of the guide and spring and swing them out toward the rear for removal.

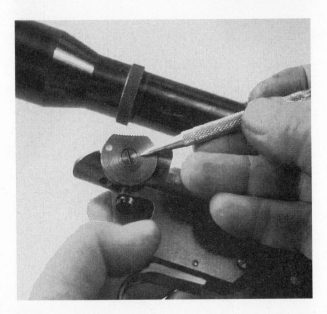

16. The safety disc need not be removed for further disassembly. However, if it is to be taken off, its pivot screw is the retainer.

17. Remove the vertical screw at the front of the trigger and magazine housing. Take care that the lock washer is not lost.

18. Remove the screw and lock washer at the rear of the housing.

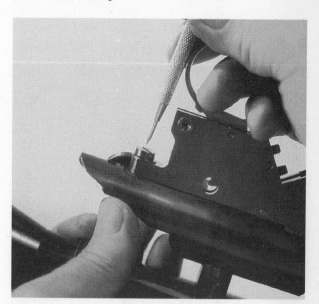

19. Restrain the magazine catch and push out the cross pin.

20. Remove the magazine catch and its spring downward.

21. Remove the center housing screw and its lock washer.

22. Remove the trigger and magazine housing downward.

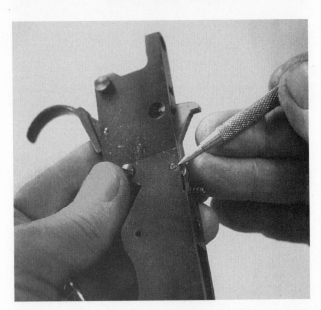

23. The ejector is released internally with removal of the center screw. Retrieve it from inside the action.

24. The sear spring is easily removed from its well in the front of the sear. Drifting out this cross pin will allow removal of the sear upward.

25. Except for repair, removal of the trigger is not advisable, as the original adjustments will be cancelled. However, if it is necessary, the first step is to back out the cinch screw that locks the adjustment screws.

26. The next step is to remove the trigger spring adjustment screw and the spring. The upper screw is the over-travel stop and it can be left in place.

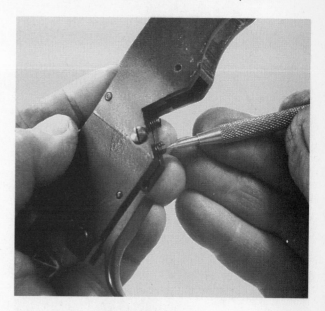

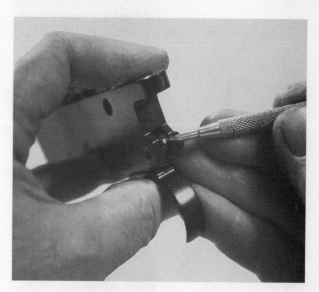

27. If the previous steps have been done, drift out the trigger cross pin and remove the trigger downward.

28. To remove the safety cross-piece, the adjustment screw must first be backed out. Here, again, it is best left in place in normal takedown. If the screw is removed, it will have to be carefully reset for proper bearing on the trigger. Also at the rear of the receiver (not shown) is the bolt handle detent plunger and spring, retained by a small pin in the right side of the receiver. The pin is drifted inward to release the plunger and spring. In normal takedown, leave it in place.

Reassembly Tips:

1. When the ejector is reinstalled, it must be oriented as shown, with the ejector projection at left front. Use a fingertip inside the receiver to hold it in place as the screw is inserted. Before this is done, it is best to put the trigger and magazine housing in place with the front and rear screws.

2. Use a screwdriver blade the same width as the diameter of the striker spring to compress the spring for insertion of the retaining cross pin. This is more easily done with the front part of the bolt in a well-padded vise.

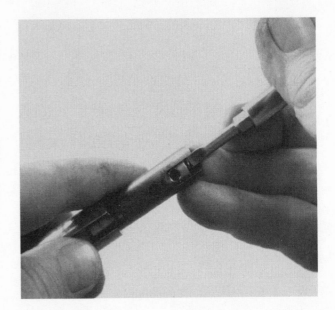

3. Before the bolt can be reinserted in the receiver, the striker must be in cocked position, as shown. Hold the front of the bolt in a shop cloth (or in a padded vise), and turn the handle to recock the striker.

Model 82 U.S. Government Target Bolt-Action Rifle

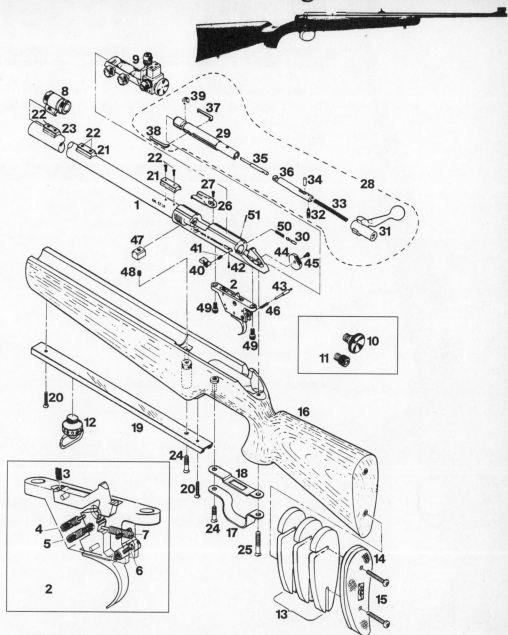

Marlin Model 9

Similar/Identical Pattern Guns
The same basic assembly/disassembly steps for the Marlin Model 9 also apply to the following gun:
Marlin Model 45

Data:	Marlin Model 9
Origin:	United States
Manufacturer:	Marlin Firearms North Haven, Connecticut
Cartridge:	9mm Parabellum
Magazine capacity:	12 rounds
Overall length:	35½ inches
Barrel length:	16½ inches
Weight:	6¾ pounds

This handy "Camp Carbine" was introduced in 1985, and the following year the Marlin company brought out a version in 45 ACP, that one having a seven-round single-row magazine. Except for the dimensional differences to accommodate the larger round, the 45 version is essentially the same as the 9mm, and the instructions will apply.

Disassembly:

1. Remove the magazine. Back out the screws at the front and rear of the magazine housing/trigger guard unit. These are captive screws.

2. Remove the action from the stock.

3. Drift out the cross pins at front and rear, at the lower edge of the receiver. The forward cross pin must be pushed out toward the left.

4. Remove the trigger guard/magazine housing downward. Note that the bolt hold open latch will also be released on the left side at the lower edge of the receiver.

5. Remove the hold open latch spring from its recess in the lower edge of the receiver.

6. Move the bolt slightly to the rear, lift it at the front, and remove the cocking handle.

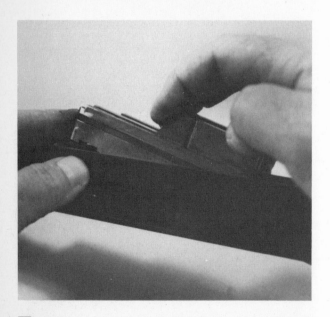

7. Continue lifting the bolt at the front until it will clear, and ease it out toward the front. Control the recoil spring tension.

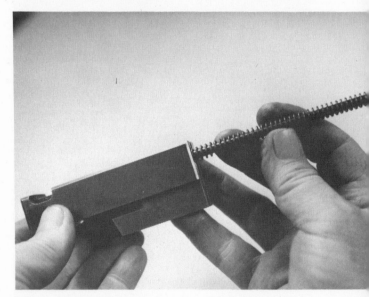

8. Remove the recoil spring and its guide from the rear of the bolt.

9. The firing pin and its return spring are retained in the bolt by a vertical pin which is driven out upward.

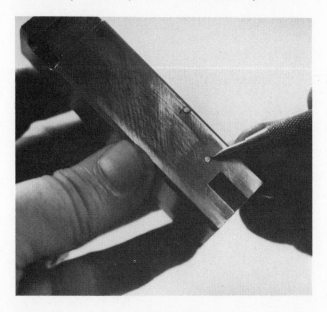

10. The extractor is pivoted and retained by a vertical pin which is driven out upward.

11. Remove the extractor toward the right, and take out the coil extractor spring from its recess.

12. The loaded chamber indicator and its coil spring are also retained and pivoted by a vertical pin which is driven out upward.

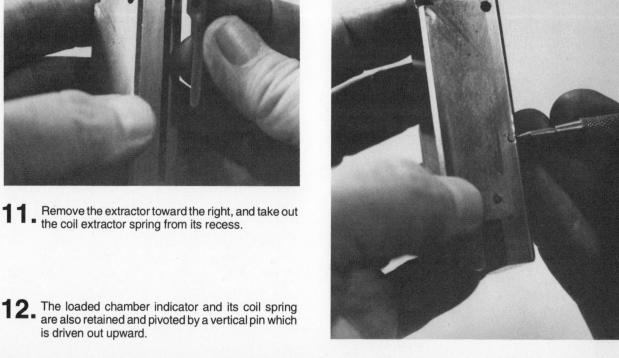

13. If it is necessary to remove the polymer recoil buffer for replacement, it is pried out of its recess toward the front. On the barrel, the rear sight is dovetail-mounted, and the front sight is retained by two vertical screws.

14. Insert a small drift or a paper clip into the hole at the rear of the hammer spring strut, and ease the hammer down to fired position. This will trap the spring on the strut. Note that you will have to temporarily reinsert the magazine to lower the hammer.

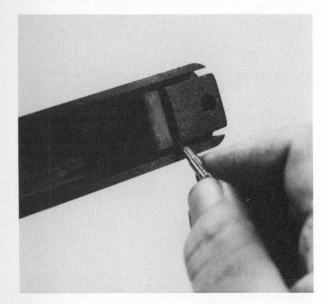

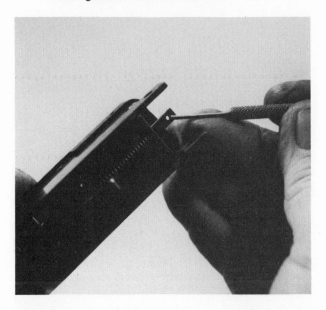

15. Remove the C-clip on the left tip of the hammer pivot.

16. Remove the sideplate.

17. Remove the trapped hammer spring, the strut, and spring base plate. If this unit is taken apart, use caution, as the spring is compressed.

18. Restrain the sear, and push on the hammer pivot to move the right sideplate off.

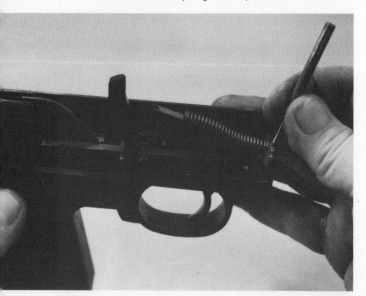

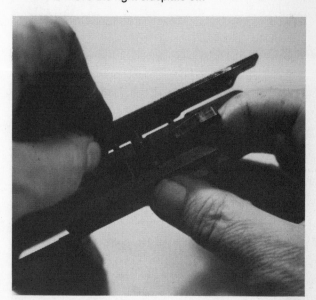

19. Remove the cartridge guide and its spring.

20. Remove the hammer.

21. Remove the sear from the top of the trigger, along with its spring.

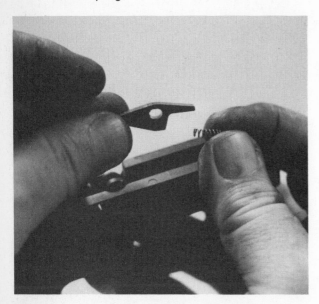

22. Tip the trigger upward at the front, moving it from under its spring at the rear, and remove it.

23. Push the safety out upward for removal. Keep a fingertip over the hole indicated, to arrest the safety positioning ball and spring.

24. Use a magnetized tool to remove the safety ball and spring.

25. Depress the magazine safety at the front, and take out the trigger block lever.

26. The magazine safety and its spring are retained by the forward cross pin of the two ejector mounting pins. In normal takedown, this system is best left in place.

27. The trigger spring can be removed by drifting out its cross pin.

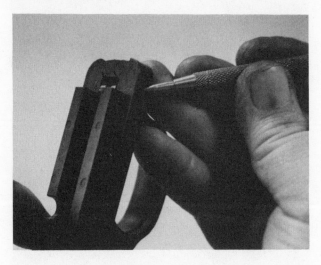

28. The magazine catch can be removed by unscrewing its slotted button. The button is then taken off toward the left, with the spring, and the catch is taken off toward the right.

29. The sear/disconnector trip in the trigger, and its coil spring, can be removed by drifting out a small cross pin.

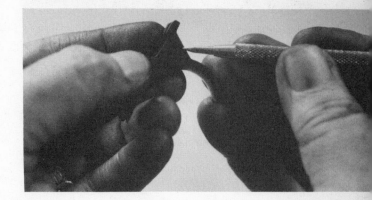

Reassembly tips:

1. When reinstalling the safety, it will be necessary to insert a tool to depress the positioning ball and spring as the safety-lever is moved down into place.

2. When reinstalling the trigger, use a tool at the rear to lift the spring onto the rear of the trigger.

 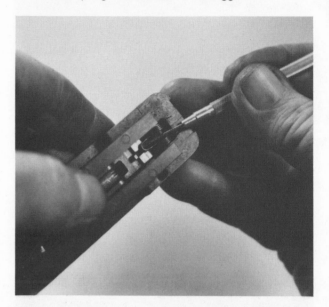

 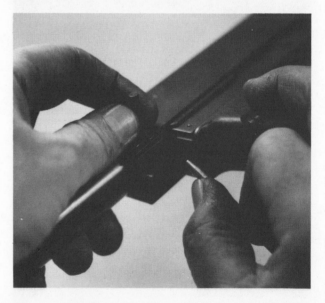

3. Remember that the bolt hold open and its spring must be installed before the lower housing is put back on the receiver.

4. As the trigger and magazine unit is put into place, the cartridge guide must be flexed slightly rearward to clear the edge of the receiver.

When reassembling the trigger unit, the use of slave pins may be a help. However, with patience, it can be done without them.
When replacing the firing pin, extractor, and loaded chamber indicator on the bolt, remember that they are retained by splined pins that are driven in downward.

Model 9 Autoloading Carbine

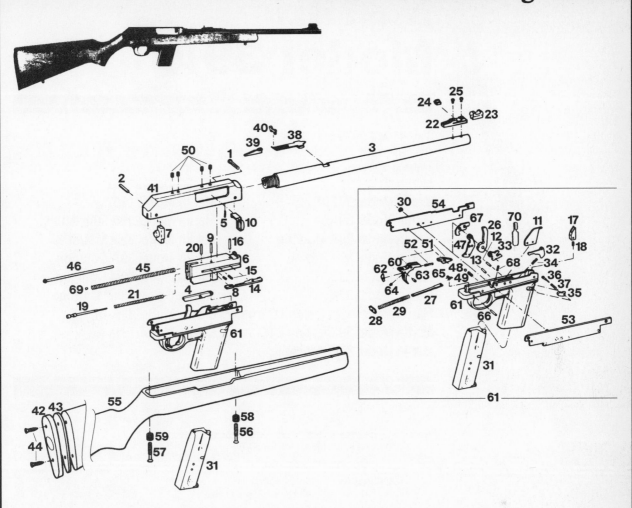

KEY

1 Action Assembly Pin, Front
2 Action Assembly Pin, Rear
3 Barrel
4 Bolt Stop
5 Bolt Stop Spring
6 Breechbolt
7 Buffer
8 Cartridge Indicator
9 Cartridge Indicator Assembly Pin
10 Charging Handle
11 Ejector
12 Ejector/Magazine Disconnector Pin
13 Ejector Pin, Rear
14 Extractor
15 Extractor/Cartridge Indicator Springs
16 Extractor Pin
17 Feed Ramp
18 Feed Ramp Spring
19 Firing Pin
20 Firing Pin Assembly Pin
21 Firing Pin Spring

22 Front Sight Ramp Base
23 Front Sight Ramp Cutaway Hood
24 Front Sight Ramp Red Insert
25 Front Sight Ramp Screws
26 Hammer
27 Hammer Strut
28 Hammer Strut Bridge
29 Hammer Strut Spring
30 Hammer Pivot Pin Retaining Ring
31 Magazine
32 Magazine Disconnector
33 Magazine Disconnector Trigger Block
34 Magazine Disconnector Spring
35 Magazine Latch
36 Magazine Latch Retaining Screw
37 Magazine Latch Retaining Spring
38 Rear Sight Base
39 Rear Sight Elevator
40 Rear Sight Leaf
41 Receiver
42 Recoil Pad
43 Recoil Pad Spacer
44 Recoil Pad Screws
45 Recoil Spring

46 Recoil Spring Rod
47 Safety
48 Safety Plunger Ball
49 Safety Plunger Spring
50 Scope Mount Dummy Screws
51 Sear
52 Sear Spring
53 Sideplate, Right
54 Sideplate, Left
55 Stock
56 Takedown Screw, Front
57 Takedown Screw, Rear
58 Takedown Screw Bushing, Front
59 Takedown Screw Bushing, Rear
60 Trigger
61 Trigger Guard
62 Trigger Disconnector
63 Trigger Disconnector Pin
64 Trigger Disconnector Spring
65 Trigger Return Spring
66 Trigger Return Spring Pin
67 Trigger Block
68 Trigger Block Spring
69 Firing Pin Bushing
70 Manual Hold-Open Lever

Marlin Model 39A

Similar/Identical Pattern Guns

The same basic assembly/disassembly steps for the Marlin Model 39A also apply to the following guns:

Marlin Model 39	Marlin Model 1892
Marlin Model 39TDS	Marlin Model 1897
Marlin Model 39AS	Marlin Model 39A 90th Anniv.
Marlin Model 39A Mountie	Marlin Model 39M Mountie
Marlin Model 39 Carbine	Marlin Model 39A Octagon
Marlin Model 39D	Marlin Model 39M Octagon
Marlin Model 39M	Marlin Golden 39M Carbine
Marlin Model 39M Golden Carbine	Marlin Model 39A-DL
Marlin Model 39 Century LTD	Marlin 39A Article II
Marlin Model 39M Article II	

Data:	Marlin Model 39A
Origin:	United States
Manufacturer:	Marlin Firearms North Haven, Connecticut
Cartridge:	22 Short, Long or Long Rifle
Magazine capacity:	26 Short, 21 Long, 19 Long Rifle
Overall length:	40 inches
Barrel length:	24 inches
Weight:	6$\frac{1}{2}$ pounds

When the Marlin Company introduced the first lever-action, repeating 22 rimfire rifle in 1891, it had one particularly notable feature: It was the first repeating 22 rifle that would feed Short, Long and Long Rifle cartridges interchangeably. The basic gun was slightly redesigned in 1897, 1922 and 1938, finally arriving at the excellent Model 39A that is so popular today. Except for slight manufacturing changes—such as the use of modern round-wire springs—the internal mechanism is basically unchanged from the original 1891 version. With the exception of a shorter barrel and carbine-style, straight-gripped stock, the Mountie model is mechanically identical. The instructions can be used for all of the variants listed above.

Disassembly:

1. Use a coin to start the large, knurled takedown screw on the right side of the receiver. Then use your fingers to back it out until its threads are free. An internal shoulder will keep the screw from coming completely out.

2. Set the hammer on the safety step and bump the left side of the stock with the heel of your hand to force the stock and receiver plate toward the right. Separate the stock and its attached parts from the front portion of the gun.

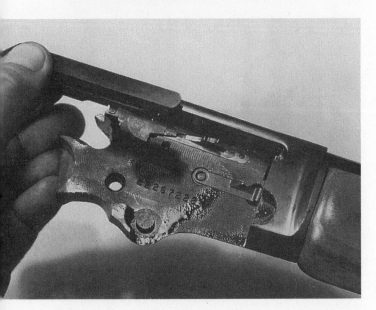

3. Slide the breechblock (bolt) toward the rear until its lower projection stops against the shoulder of the receiver, and then remove the bolt toward the right side of the frame.

4. The firing pin is easily lifted from the top of the breechblock.

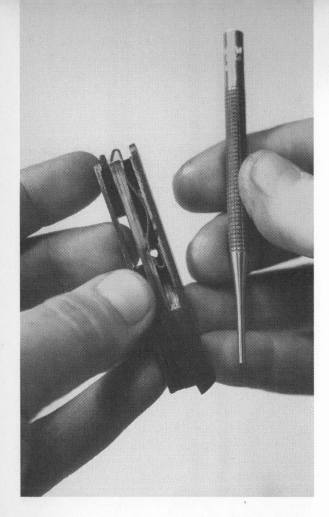

5. Insert a drift punch of the proper size through the small hole in the underside of the breechblock and push the extractor upward and out of its recess in the top of the bolt.

6. The ejector housing is retained on the inside of the receiver by two screws which enter from the outside left of the receiver, near the top. Back out the two screws and remove the ejector assembly toward the right. The ejector spring will be released by removal of the housing, and drifting out a vertical pin will free the ejector for removal. In normal takedown, the ejector lock rivet is not removed. The cartridge stop (arrow), located below the ejector and toward the front, is retained by a single screw which also enters from the outside left of the receiver. Back out this screw and remove the stop and its spacer block toward the right.

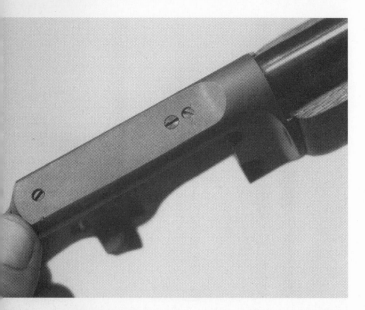

7. The cartridge guide spring, located just above the chamber, is retained by a screw which enters from the top of the receiver. This is the larger screw near the front scope mount screw. The cartridge guide spring is removed downward.

8. Drifting out the small cross pin in the magazine tube hanger will allow removal of the outer magazine tube toward the front. If the inner magazine tube is to be taken apart, drifting out the cross pin which also locks the tube in place will allow removal of the knurled end piece, spring and follower. There is some risk of damage to the thin tube, and in normal takedown the inner tube should be left assembled.

9. Removal of the two screws in the forend cap will allow it to be taken off forward, and the forend cap base can then be driven out of its dovetail toward the right side. When doing this, take care not to damage the screw holes. The forend can now be moved slightly forward and taken off downward.

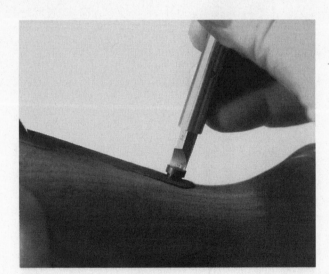

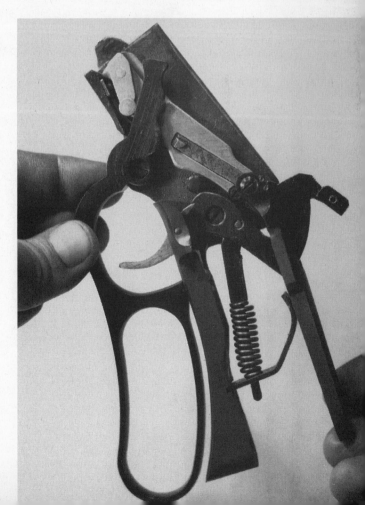

10. Take out the stock mounting bolt—the large screw at the rear tip of the upper tang. The stock can now be removed toward the rear. If the fitting is very tight, it may be necessary to bump the front of the comb with the heel of your hand or a soft rubber hammer.

11. The firing mechanism is shown in proper order, prior to disassembly. Note the relationship of all parts, to aid in reassembly.

12. Grip the upper part of the hammer spring base with pliers and slide it out toward either side, moving its lower end out of its slot in the lower tang. The hammer, of course, must be at rest (in fired position). Remove the base and the spring toward the rear.

13. Take out the hammer pivot screw and remove the hammer from the top of the frame. During this operation, it will be necessary to tilt the attached hammer strut slightly to one side or the other to clear. Proceed carefully, and use no force.

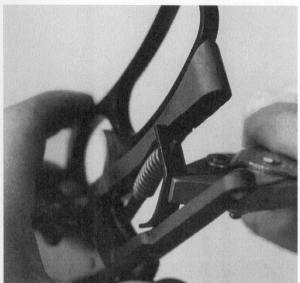

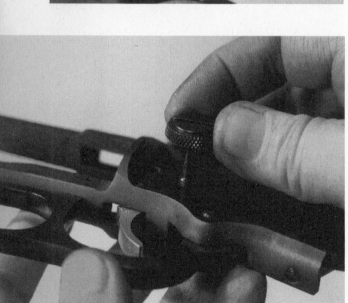

14. Move the takedown screw over until its threads engage the threads in the right side of the receiver, and unscrew it toward the right side for removal.

15. Remove the small screw on the underside of the frame, just forward of the lever, and take out the lever spring from inside the frame.

16. Take out the lever pivot screw and remove the lever toward the left.

17. Take out the carrier pivot screw and remove the carrier assembly toward the front. Taking out the carrier rocker screw will allow removal of the rocker and its spring from the carrier.

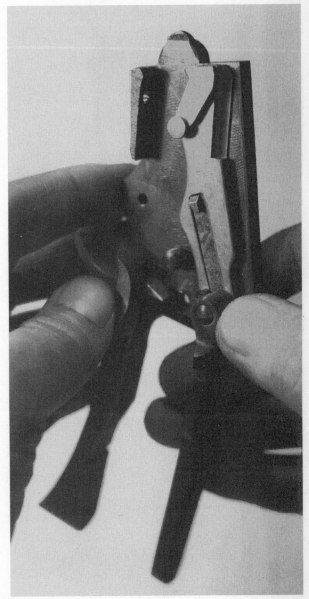

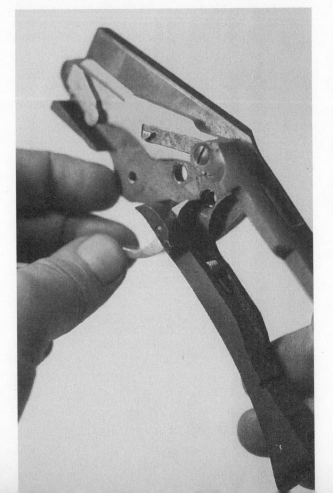

18. Drift out the trigger pin toward the right, and remove the trigger downward. Drift out the trigger spring pin and remove the trigger spring from inside the frame.

Reassembly Tips:

1. When replacing the hammer spring and its base, be sure the hammer is at rest and insert a lower corner of the base into its slot in the lower tang. Then tip the upper part downward and slip it under the upper tang, moving it inward into place.

2. When rejoining the front and rear parts of the gun, be sure the breechblock is all the way forward, the hammer is at full cock or on the safety step, and take care that the front tongue of the sideplate (arrow) is properly engaged with its mating recess in the main frame.

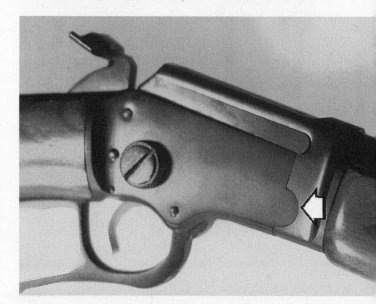

Avoid over-tightening the small screw which holds the cartridge guide spring above the chamber, or the spring may crack. This advice also applies to the cartridge stop screw. Both should be firm and snug, but use no excessive force.

When replacing the extractor in the top of the breechblock, start its rear portion into the recess; then flex the front portion slightly for proper alignment and push it into place.

Model 39A Lever-Action Rifle

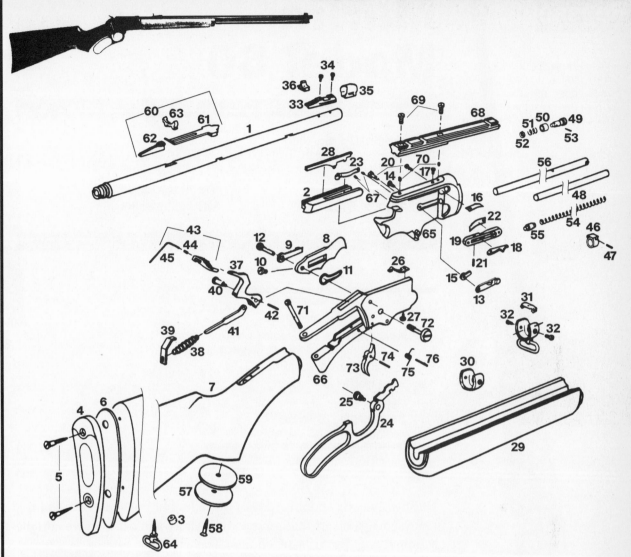

KEY

1	Barrel
2	Breechbolt
3	Bullseye
4	Buttplate
5	Buttplate Screws
6	Buttplate Spacer
7	Buttstock
8	Carrier
9	Carrier Rocker
10	Carrier Rocker Screw
11	Carrier Rocker Spring
12	Carrier Screw
13	Cartridge Cutoff
14	Cartridge Cutoff Screw
15	Cartridge Cutoff Spacer
16	Cartridge Guide Spring
17	Cartridge Guide Spring Screw
18	Ejector
19	Ejector Base with Rivet
20	Ejector Base Screws
21	Ejector Pin
22	Ejector Spring
23	Extractor
24	Finger Lever
25	Finger Lever Screw
26	Finger Lever Spring
27	Finger Lever Spring Screw
28	Firing Pin
29	Forearm
30	Forearm Tip Assembly
31	Forearm Tip Tenon
32	Forearm Tip Tenon Screws
33	Front Sight Ramp Base
34	Front Sight Ramp Base Screws
35	Front Sight Ramp Hood
36	Front Sight Ramp Insert
37	Hammer
38	Hammer Spring
39	Hammer Spring Adjusting Plate
40	Hammer Screw
41	Hammer Strut
42	Hammer Strut Pin
43	Hammer Spur Assembly
44	Hammer Spur Screw
45	Hammer Spur Wrench
46	Magazine Tube Band
47	Magazine Tube Band Pin
48	Magazine Tube, Inside
49	Magazine Tube Plug
50	Magazine Tube Plug Cap
51	Magazine Tube Plug Spring
52	Magazine Tube Plug Bushing
53	Magazine Tube Plug Pin
54	Magazine Tube Spring
55	Magazine Tube Follower
56	Magazine Tube, Outside
57	Pistol Grip Cap
58	Pistol Grip Cap Screw
59	Pistol Grip Cap Spacer
60	Rear Sight
61	Rear Sight Base
62	Rear Sight Elevator
63	Rear Sight Folding Leaf
64	Rear Swivel
65	Receiver
66	Receiver Tang
67	Peep Sight Dummy Screws
68	Scope Adapter Base with Screws
69	Scope Adapter Base Screws
70	Scope Mount Dummy Screws
71	Tang Screw
72	Thumb Screw
73	Trigger
74	Trigger Pin
75	Trigger Spring
76	Trigger Spring Pin

Marlin Model 80

Similar/Identical Pattern Guns
The same basic assembly/disassembly steps for the Marlin Model 80 also apply to the following guns:

Marlin Model 80C

Marlin Model 80E

Marlin Model 80DL

Marlin Model 80G

Data:	Marlin Model 80
Origin:	United States
Manufacturer:	Marlin Firearms Company North Haven, Connecticut
Cartridge:	22 Long Rifle
Magazine capacity:	8 rounds
Overall length:	43 inches
Barrel length:	24 inches
Weight:	$6\frac{1}{2}$ pounds

During my early shooting days I owned a Marlin Model 80, and for many youngsters of that time period who wanted a low-priced bolt action it was the rifle of choice. The gun was offered in several sub-models featuring various options in sights and sling loops. A counterpart tube-magazine rifle, the Model 81, has the same mechanical features, except for the magazine and feed system. The Model 80 was made from 1934 to 1971, when it was replaced in the Marlin line by the Model 780.

Disassembly:

1. Remove the magazine. Open the bolt and hold the trigger to the rear while sliding the bolt out the rear of the receiver. The safety must be in off-safe position, of course.

2. Drift out the cross pin in the bolt, just to the rear of the front section.

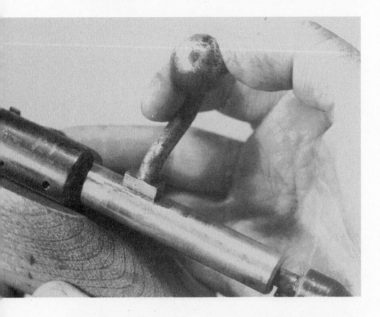

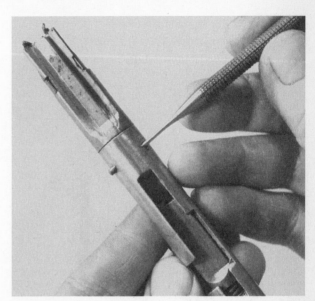

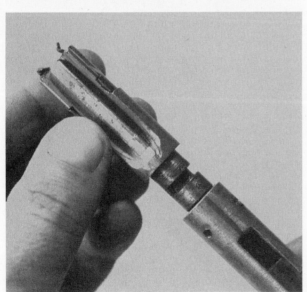

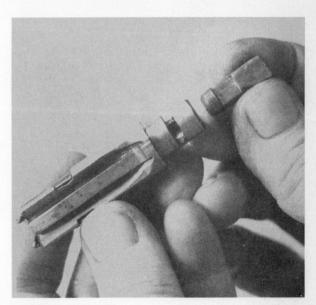

3. Remove the front section of the bolt toward the front.

4. Remove the rear firing pin from the front section.

5. Tap the front section to shake out the front firing pin and its return spring, and remove them toward the rear.

6. Insert a very small screwdriver from the front under the left extractor arm, and lever it outward and over toward the right to remove the twin extractor unit. Be sure to lift it only enough to clear, to avoid deformation or breakage.

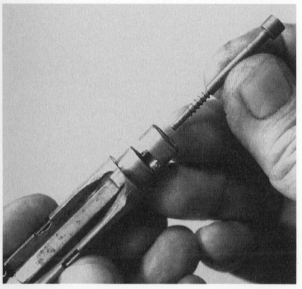

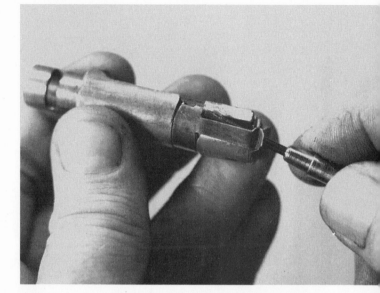

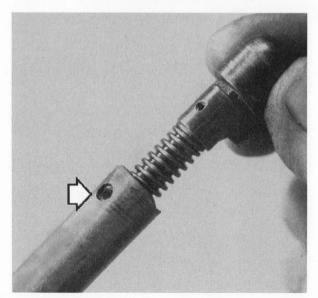

7. Tap the cocking lug pin on the striker knob toward the side, out of its detent notch at the rear of the bolt, to allow the striker to go forward, partially relieving its spring tension. When the striker is forward, it will be in the position shown.

8. Remove the small screw (arrow indicates hole) on the side of the bolt near its rear edge. Remove the striker assembly toward the rear.

9. Grip the forward portion of the striker firmly in a vise, and while keeping pressure on the striker knob, drift out the small cross pin. **Caution:** *The striker spring is under tension, so control it and release the pressure slowly.* Remove the striker knob, sleeve ring and striker spring toward the rear.

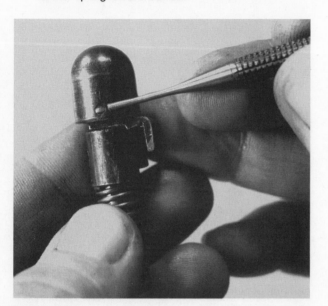

10. Back out the main stock mounting screw, located on the underside at the rear edge of the magazine plate, and separate the action from the stock.

11. The magazine catch hook is retained on the underside of the receiver by a single screw, and is taken off downward.

12. The safety and its positioning spring are retained on the right rear of the receiver by two post screws, and both are removed toward the right.

13. The trigger is mounted on a post below the receiver by a cross pin. When the cross pin is drifted out, the trigger and its spring will be released downward. The spring is under some tension, so control the trigger during removal. As the pin is drifted out, be sure the mounting post is well-supported, to avoid deformation or breakage.

14. After the trigger is removed, the sear pin can be drifted out and the sear and its spring removed downward. The same cautions as in the preceding step should be applied.

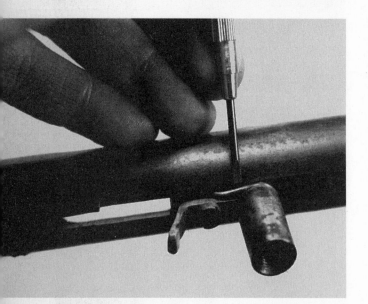

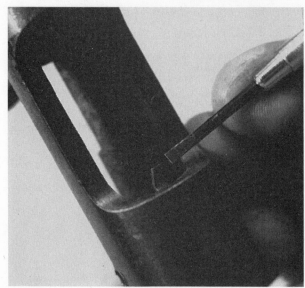

15. The ejector, a part made of round spring-wire, is held in place by the stock screw base, which is threaded into the underside of the receiver. Grip the base firmly with non-marring pliers and unscrew it to release the ejector.

16. Removal of the cartridge guide above the chamber requires removal of the barrel.

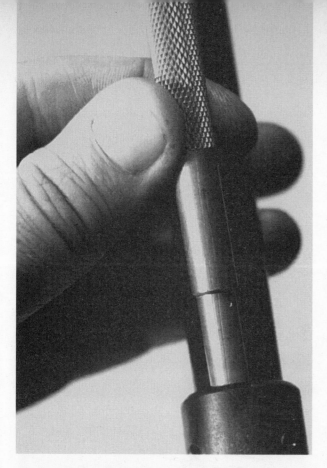

17. A cross pin retains the barrel in the receiver. If the barrel is very tight in the receiver, grip the barrel in a padded vise and use a non-marring drift punch to drive the receiver off the barrel toward the rear. When the barrel is out, the cartridge guide can be lifted from its recess at the top rear of the barrel.

Reassembly Tips:

1. When replacing the striker assembly in the bolt, be sure the threaded hole in the retaining sleeve is aligned with the screw recess in the side of the bolt, and insert a small screwdriver to cam the sleeve into position for insertion of the screw. In this operation, a third hand would be helpful.

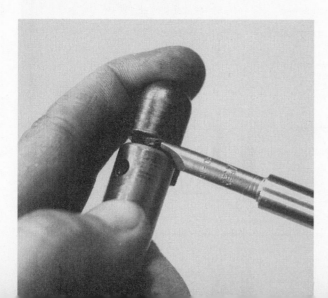

2. When replacing the front section of the bolt, note that the cross-groove in the tail piece and the groove in the rear firing pin must be oriented for passage of the retaining cross pin.

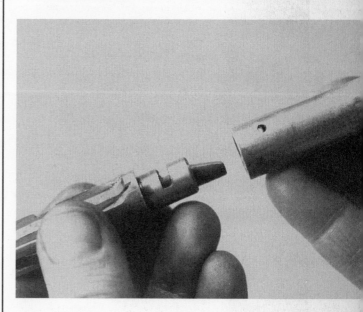

3. Before the reassembled bolt can be reinserted in the receiver, the striker must be recocked. Grip the front section of the bolt in a vise, and turn the bolt handle counterclockwise (rear view) until the cocking lug is in the position shown.

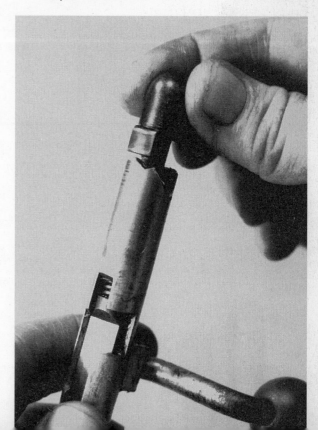

Model 80C and 80DL Bolt-Action Rifle

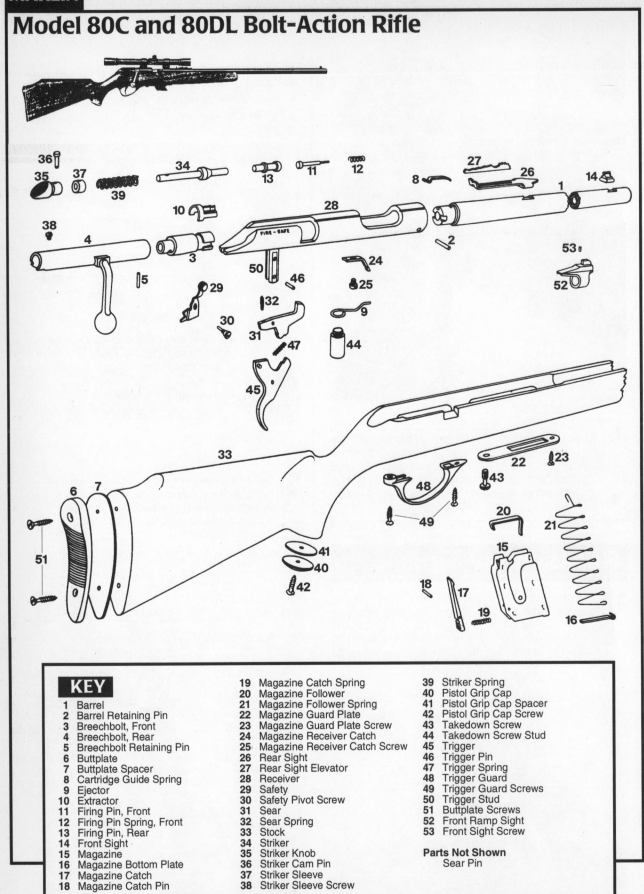

KEY

1 Barrel	
2 Barrel Retaining Pin	
3 Breechbolt, Front	
4 Breechbolt, Rear	
5 Breechbolt Retaining Pin	
6 Buttplate	
7 Buttplate Spacer	
8 Cartridge Guide Spring	
9 Ejector	
10 Extractor	
11 Firing Pin, Front	
12 Firing Pin Spring, Front	
13 Firing Pin, Rear	
14 Front Sight	
15 Magazine	
16 Magazine Bottom Plate	
17 Magazine Catch	
18 Magazine Catch Pin	
19 Magazine Catch Spring	
20 Magazine Follower	
21 Magazine Follower Spring	
22 Magazine Guard Plate	
23 Magazine Guard Plate Screw	
24 Magazine Receiver Catch	
25 Magazine Receiver Catch Screw	
26 Rear Sight	
27 Rear Sight Elevator	
28 Receiver	
29 Safety	
30 Safety Pivot Screw	
31 Sear	
32 Sear Spring	
33 Stock	
34 Striker	
35 Striker Knob	
36 Striker Cam Pin	
37 Striker Sleeve	
38 Striker Sleeve Screw	
39 Striker Spring	
40 Pistol Grip Cap	
41 Pistol Grip Cap Spacer	
42 Pistol Grip Cap Screw	
43 Takedown Screw	
44 Takedown Screw Stud	
45 Trigger	
46 Trigger Pin	
47 Trigger Spring	
48 Trigger Guard	
49 Trigger Guard Screws	
50 Trigger Stud	
51 Buttplate Screws	
52 Front Ramp Sight	
53 Front Sight Screw	

Parts Not Shown
Sear Pin

Marlin Model 99M1

Similar/Identical Pattern Guns
The same basic assembly/disassembly steps for the Marlin Model 99M1 also apply to the following guns:

Marlin Model 99C	**Marlin Model 989M1**
Marlin Model 99DL	**Marlin Model 989M2**
Marlin Model 99	**Marlin Model 989G**
Marlin Model 99G	**Marlin Model 989MC**
Marlin Model 49	**Marlin Model 995**
Marlin Model 49DL	**Marlin Model 990L**

Data:	Marlin Model 99M1
Origin:	United States
Manufacturer:	Marlin Firearms North Haven, Connecticut
Cartridge:	22 Long Rifle
Magazine capacity:	18 rounds in rifle, 9 in carbine
Overall length:	Rifle—42 inches, Carbine—37 inches
Barrel length:	Rifle—22 inches, Carbine—18 inches
Weight:	Rifle—$5^{1}/_{2}$ pounds, Carbine—$4^{1}/_{2}$ pounds

The original Model 99 semi-auto was introduced in 1959 and was soon followed by several sub-models—the 99DL, 99C and 99M1, the carbine shown here. The same basic action was later used in the Model 49 and its sub-models, the 989 and 990 and the current 995 rifles. There have been several minor modifications along the way, but the instructions can be applied generally to all of these. The gun was available in both tubular and box magazine types. The gun in the photos is the 99M1 tubular version.

Disassembly:

1. Remove the barrel band retaining screw, located on the right side of the barrel band, and take off the band toward the front. Remove the inner magazine tube.

2. Remove the two screws at the top rear of the handguard and take off the handguard piece.

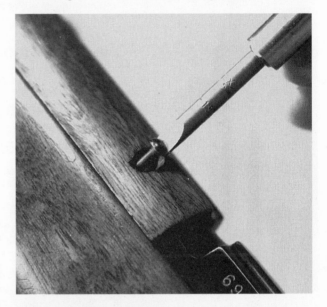

3. Remove the screw on the underside at the rear of the trigger guard—the screw nearest the guard. Remove the main stock mounting screw, located on the underside just forward of the trigger guard, and lift the action out of the stock.

4. Removal of the screws at each end of the trigger guard will allow the guard to be taken off downward. The rear screw is a wood screw, and the front screw has a flat internal nut-plate which may have to be stabilized during removal. The trigger and its spring are retained in the guard unit by a cross pin. Note the position of the spring before removal of the pin, to aid reassembly.

5. Remove the cap screw and screw-slotted post at the rear of the sub-frame below the receiver. If this assembly is very tight, it may require two opposed screwdrivers to immobilize the post while the screw is taken out.

6. Remove the two opposed screws at the front of the sub-frame below the receiver.

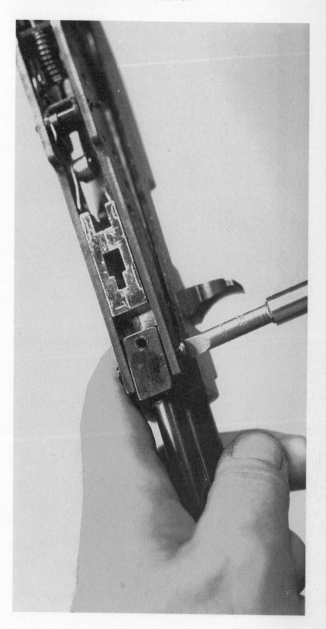

7. Remove the sub-frame downward.

8. Before disassembling the sub-frame, note the relationship of all parts and springs, to aid reassembly. Lower the hammer to the fired position, easing it down. Unhook the right arm of the carrier spring from its resting place on the carrier and ease it downward, relieving its tension. Remove the C-clips from the tips of the hammer/carrier pivot and the sear pivot on the **right** side only, taking care that the small clips are not lost. Depending on its tightness, it may also be necessary to remove the cross pin at the rear of the sub-frame which retains the recoil buffer. Remove the right sideplate of the sub-frame toward the right. This will allow disassembly of all the internal mechanism parts except the disconnector, which is mounted on the left sideplate on a post retained by a C-clip on the left side.

9. Invert the gun and retract the bolt far enough so that a finger or tool can be inserted in front of it. Lift the front of the bolt away from the inside top of the receiver and remove the bolt handle from the ejection port. Continue to lift the bolt, until its front will clear the underside of the receiver, and take out the bolt, bolt spring and follower. **Caution:** *The spring will be compressed. Control it, and ease its tension slowly.*

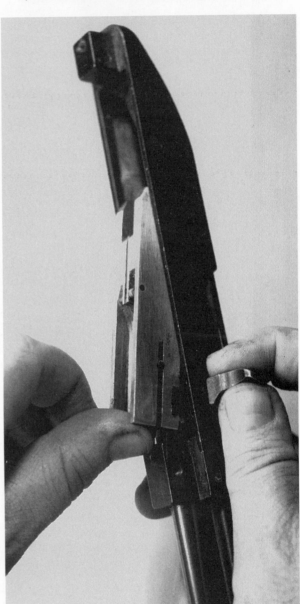

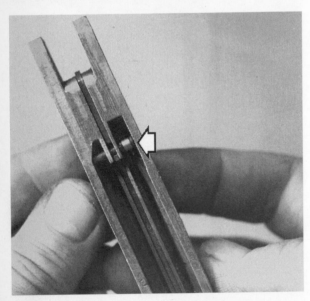

10. The firing pin is retained in the bolt by a cross pin at the lower edge of the bolt. Note that there is also a small roller on the cross pin (arrow), on the right side of the bolt, and take care that this roller isn't lost. When the pin is out, the firing pin can be removed toward the rear.

11. The extractors are retained by vertical pins on each side of the bolt, and these are driven out toward the top. The extractors and their small coil springs are then removed toward each side. **Note:** Keep each spring with its extractor because the springs are not of equal tension. The stronger spring must be put back on the right side.

12. Drifting out the small cross pin in the magazine tube hanger will allow removal of the outer magazine tube toward the front. The hanger can then be driven out of its dovetail cut toward the right. The front sight is retained by a single Allen screw in its top, just to the rear of the sight blade. After the screw is backed out, the sight is removed toward the front. After its large positioning screw on the right side is loosened, the rear sight can be slid off the scope rail in either direction.

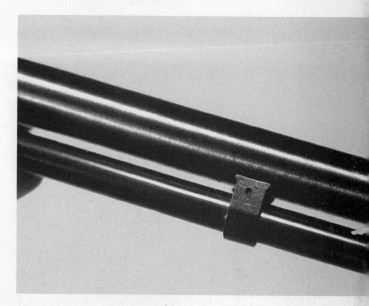

Reassembly Tips:

When replacing the sub-frame in the receiver, be sure the hammer is cocked. There will be some tension from the carrier spring as the sub-frame is pushed into place. Insert the rear screw-post first; then start the two front screws. Do not tighten the screws until all three are in position and started.

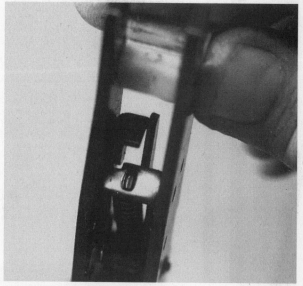

1. When replacing the hammer spring baseplate in the sub-frame, note that there is a notch in one corner of the plate. This must go on the left side at the top, to clear the rear portion of the disconnector.

Model 989M2 Autoloading Carbine

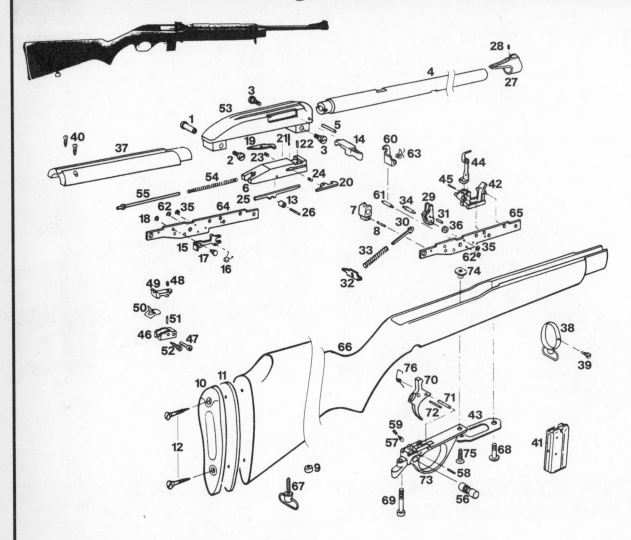

KEY

1	Assembly Post
2	Assembly Post Screw
3	Assembly Screws, Front
4	Barrel
5	Barrel Retaining Pin
6	Breechbolt
7	Buffer
8	Buffer Pin
9	Bullseye
10	Buttplate
11	Buttplate Spacer
12	Buttplate Screws
13	Cartridge Lifter Roller
14	Charging Handle
15	Disconnector
16	Disconnector Spring
17	Disconnector Stud
18	Disconnector Stud Ring
19	Extractor, Left
20	Extractor, Right
21	Extractor Pin, Left
22	Extractor Pin, Right
23	Extractor Spring, Left
24	Extractor Spring, Right
25	Firing Pin
26	Firing Pin Retaining Pin
27	Front Sight Complete
28	Front Sight Binding Screw
29	Hammer
30	Hammer Strut
31	Hammer Strut Pin
32	Hammer Strut Bridge
33	Hammer Spring
34	Hammer Pin
35	Hammer Pin Ring
36	Hammer Spacer
37	Handguard
38	Handguard Band with Swivel
39	Handguard Band Screw
40	Handguard Screws
41	Magazine Complete
42	Magazine Guide
43	Magazine Guard Plate
44	Magazine Latch and Ejector
45	Magazine Latch Pin
46	Rear Sight Base
47	Rear Sight Binding Screw
48	Rear Sight Elevator Screw
49	Rear Sight Leaf
50	Rear Sight Leaf Spring
51	Rear Sight Pin
52	Rear Sight Windage Screw
53	Receiver
54	Recoil Spring
55	Recoil Spring Guide
56	Safety
57	Safety Plunger
58	Safety Plunger Pin
59	Safety Plunger Spring
60	Sear
61	Sear Pin
62	Sear Pin Ring
63	Sear Spring
64	Sideplate, Left
65	Sideplate, Right
66	Stock
67	Swivel, Rear
68	Takedown Screw, Front
69	Takedown Screw, Rear
70	Trigger
71	Trigger Pin
72	Trigger Stop Pin
73	Trigger Guard
74	Trigger Guard Nut, Front
75	Trigger Guard Screw, Front
76	Trigger Spring

Marlin Model 336

Similar/Identical Pattern Guns

The same basic assembly/disassembly steps for the Marlin Model 336 also apply to the following guns:

Marlin Model 30AS

Marlin Model 336L

Marlin Model 336 LTS

Marlin Model 336 Zipper

Marlin Model 336 Marauder

Marlin Model 336 Extra-Range

Marlin Model 336C

Marlin Model 336DL

Marlin Model 336 Sporting Carbine

Marlin Model 336T

Marlin Model 336CS

Data:	Marlin Model 336
Origin:	United States
Manufacturer:	Marlin Firearms Company North Haven, Connecticut
Cartridge:	219 Zipper, 30-30 Winchester, 32 Winchester Special, 307 Winchester, 35 Remington, 356 Winchester, 375 Winchester, 44 Remington Magnum
Magazine capacity:	6 rounds
Overall length:	38½ inches
Barrel length:	20 inches
Weight:	7 pounds

An extensive redesign of the Marlin Model 36 (1936) rifle, the Mod[el] 336 was first offered in 1948. It was initially available in seve[ral] calibers, but in recent years only the 30-30 and 35 Reming[ton] chamberings have been in production. Although most lever-act[ion] guns are generally more complicated than other manually-oper[ated] types, the Model 336 has a relatively easy takedown, with no r[eally] difficult points. Several sub-models of this gun were made, an[d the] instructions will apply to any of these.

Disassembly:

1. Partially open the lever, and take out the lever pivot cross screw. Remove the lever downward.

2. Remove the bolt toward the rear.

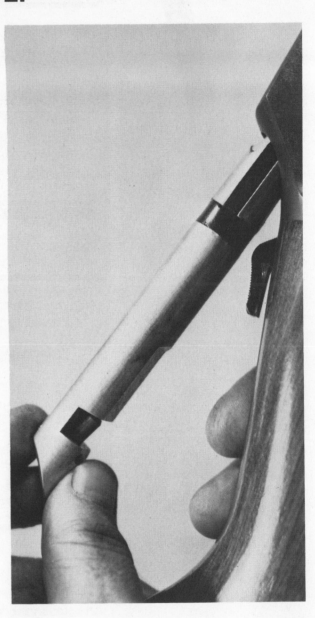

3. Push the ejector mounting stud inward, and remove the ejector from inside the receiver. The ejector spring is staked in place, and removal in normal disassembly is not advisable, except for repair.

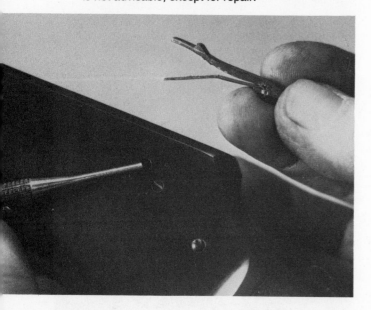

4. Drifting out the vertical roll pin at the rear of the bolt will release the rear firing pin and its spring for removal toward the rear.

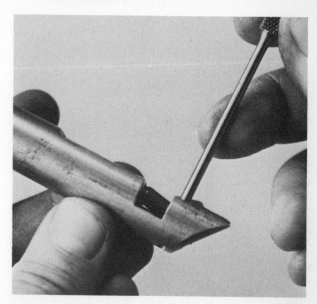

5. Use a small screwdriver to pry the extractor clip off its recess on the front of the bolt, using a fingertip to lift the front of the extractor out of its channel. Removal of the extractor will give access to the vertical pin that retains the front firing pin. After the pin is drifted out, the firing pin is removed toward the rear.

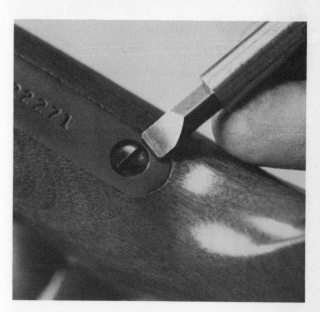

6. Remove the vertical screw at the rear of the upper tang, and take off the stock toward the rear. If the stock is tight, bump the front of the comb with the heel of the hand to start it off.

7. Depress the trigger-block (arrow), on the underside behind the trigger, and gently lower the hammer to the fired position. With smooth-jawed pliers or strong fingers, grip the upper portion of the hammer spring base plate, tilt it forward, and slide it toward the side, moving its lower end out of its groove in the lower tang. Keep a firm grip on the plate, as the spring is under some tension, even when at rest. Remove the plate, and the hammer spring, toward the rear.

8. Remove the hammer pivot screw, and take out the hammer upward. Drifting out the cross pin at the rear of the hammer will release the hammer spring strut, but in normal takedown it is best left in place.

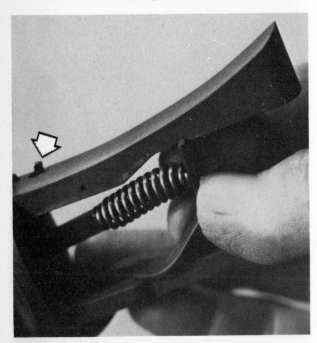

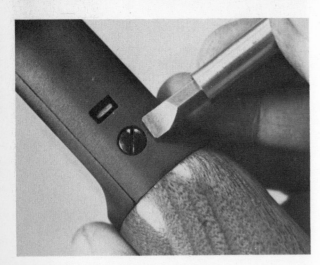

9. Remove the vertical screw on the underside at the forward end of the trigger housing.

10. Remove the screw on the left side of the receiver at lower center.

11. Remove the trigger housing downward and toward the rear. If it is very tight, it may be necessary to tap it with a plastic hammer to start it out.

12. Drifting out the trigger cross pin will allow the trigger and sear to be removed downward. The small pin just forward of the trigger is the contact for the lever latch, and does not have to be removed.

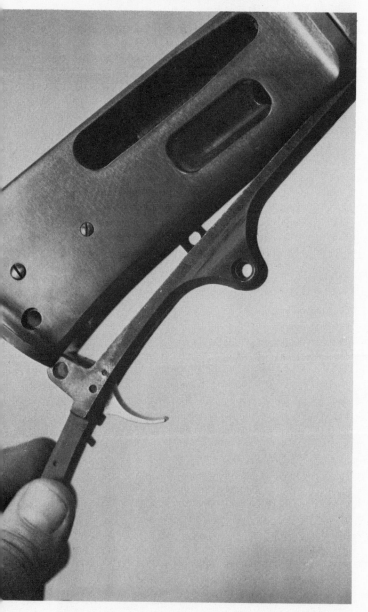

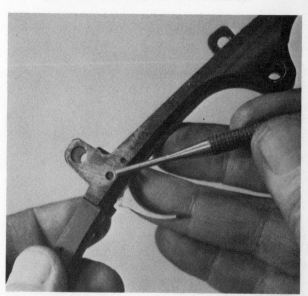

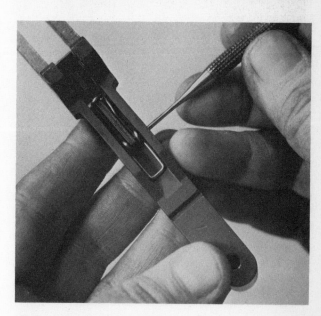

13. A small cross pin in the lower tang portion of the trigger housing retains the trigger safety-block and the combination spring that powers the block and the trigger/sear system. After the pin is drifted out, the block and spring are removed upward. **CAUTION:** *The spring is under tension. Control it, and ease it out.*

14. The lever latch plunger and its spring are retained in the lever by a cross pin, and are removed toward the rear. The short coil spring is quite strong, so control it and ease it out.

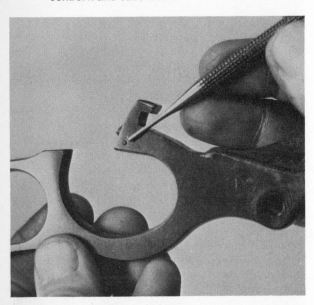

15. After the trigger housing plate is taken off, the bolt locking block can be moved downward out of the receiver.

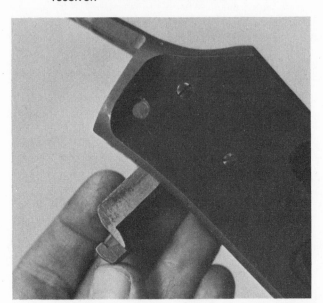

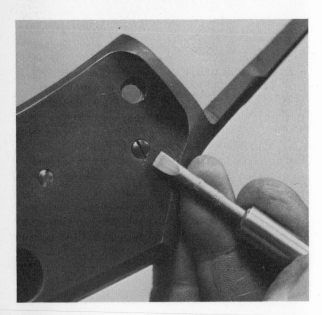

16. Remove the carrier pivot screw, located on the right side of the receiver at center rear.

17. Remove the carrier downward. The carrier rocker and its spring are retained on the left side of the carrier by a vertical pin.

18. Remove the small screw on the right side of the receiver to the rear of the loading port, and take out the loading gate from inside the receiver.

19. Remove the screw on the underside of the magazine tube at its forward end, and take out the tube end piece, magazine spring, and follower. **Caution:** *Some magazine springs are more powerful than others, and all are under some tension. Ease the end piece out, and control the spring.*

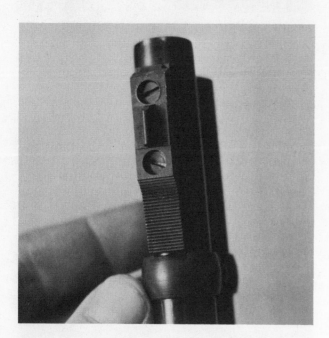

20. Slide the front sight hood off toward the front, remove the two vertical screws in the front sight base, and take off the front sight upward.

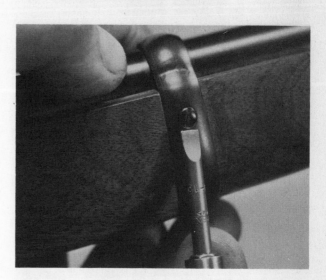

21. Take out the cross screw in the front barrel band. Take out the cross screw in the rear barrel band, and slide the barrel band off toward the front.

22. Move the forend wood forward to free the magazine tube, then slide the magazine tube, forend wood, and front barrel band off toward the front.

Reassembly Tips:

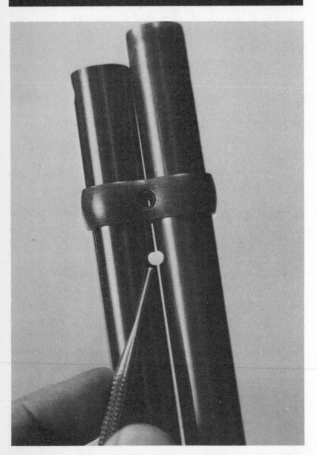

1. When replacing the magazine tube, be sure its rear tip enters the well in the front of the receiver. Be sure it is oriented at the front so its screw groove will align with the hole in the front barrel band.

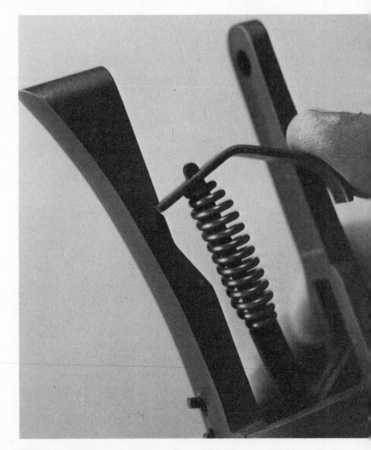

2. When replacing the hammer spring system, hook the lower end of the spring plate in its groove in the lower tang, tip the top of the plate forward, beneath the upper tang, and slide the plate across into place.

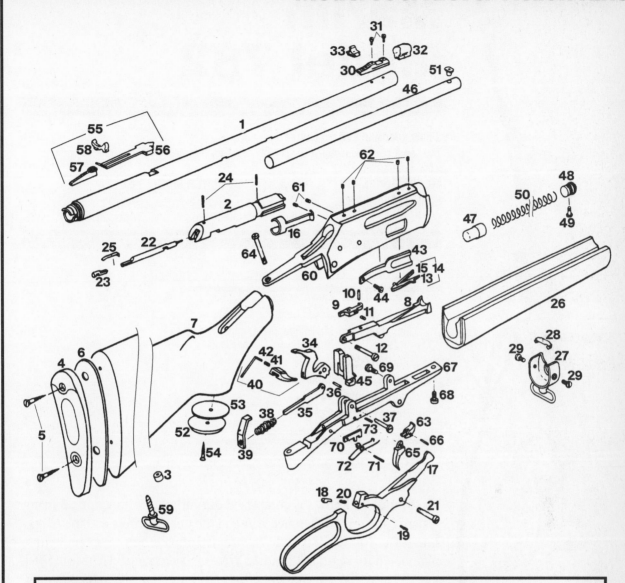

KEY		
1 Barrel	**24** Firing Pin Retaining Pins	**49** Magazine Tube Plug Screw
2 Breechbolt	**25** Firing Pin Spring	**50** Magazine Tube Spring
3 Bullseye	**26** Forearm	**51** Magazine Tube Stud
4 Buttplate with Spacer	**27** Forearm Tip with Swivel	**52** Pistol Grip Cap
5 Buttplate Screws	**28** Forearm Tip Tenon	**53** Pistol Grip Cap Spacer
6 Buttplate Spacer	**29** Forearm Tip Tenon Screws	**54** Pistol Grip Cap Screw
7 Buttstock	**30** Front Sight Base	**55** Rear Sight Assembly
8 Carrier	**31** Front Sight Base Screws	**56** Rear Sight Base
9 Carrier Rocker	**32** Front Sight Hood	**57** Rear Sight Elevator
10 Carrier Rocker Pin	**33** Front Sight Insert	**58** Rear Sight Folding Leaf
11 Carrier Rocker Spring	**34** Hammer	**59** Rear Swivel
12 Carrier Screw	**35** Hammer Strut	**60** Receiver
13 Ejector	**36** Hammer Strut Pin	**61** Peep Sight Dummy Screws
14 Ejector with Spring	**37** Hammer Screw	**62** Scope Mount Dummy Screws
15 Ejector Spring	**38** Hammer Spring	**63** Sear
16 Extractor	**39** Hammer Spring Adjusting Plate	**64** Tang Screw
17 Finger Lever	**40** Hammer Spur	**65** Trigger
18 Finger Lever Plunger	**41** Hammer Spur Screw	**66** Trigger and Sear Pin
19 Finger Lever Plunger Pin	**42** Hammer Spur Wrench	**67** Trigger Guard Plate
20 Finger Lever Plunger Spring	**43** Loading Spring	**68** Trigger Guard Plate Screw
21 Finger Lever Screw	**44** Loading Spring Screw	**69** Trigger Guard Plate Support Screw
22 Firing Pin, Front	**45** Locking Bolt	**70** Trigger Safety Block
23 Firing Pin, Rear	**46** Magazine Tube	**71** Trigger Safety Block Pin
	47 Magazine Tube Follower	**72** Trigger Safety Block Spring
	48 Magazine Tube Plug	**73** Trigger Guard Plate Latch Pin

Marlin Model 782

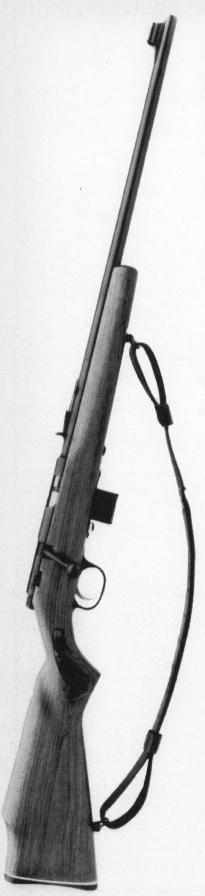

Similar/Identical Pattern Guns

The same basic assembly/disassembly steps for the Marlin Model 782 also apply to the following guns:

Marlin Model 780   **Marlin Model 781**

Marlin Model 783

Data:	Marlin Model 782
Origin:	United States
Manufacturer:	Marlin Firearms Company North Haven, Connecticut
Cartridge:	22 WMR
Magazine capacity:	7 rounds
Overall length:	41 inches
Barrel length:	22 inches
Weight:	6 pounds

The Marlin 780 series is comprised of four guns with identical firing systems, the only difference being in the chamberings and the magazines. The Model 780 and 782 are detachable box magazine guns, chambered for regular 22 and 22 WMR, respectively. The Model 781 and 783 have the same chamberings, with tubular magazine systems. Except for the magazines, takedown and reassembly instructions can be applied to any of the guns in the group. The Model 782 was made from 1971 to 1988.

Disassembly:

1. Remove the magazine. Open the bolt and hold the trigger pulled to the rear while removing the bolt from the rear of the receiver.

2. Turn the end piece counterclockwise (rear view) to drop the striker forward to the fired position. If the end piece can't be turned easily, tap the cam pin out of its engagement with its detent notch at the rear of the bolt.

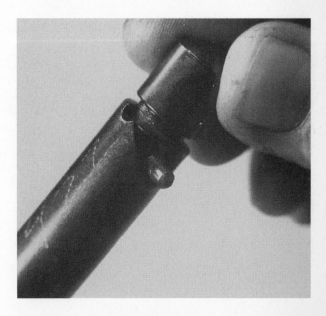

3. Remove the small screw on the side of the bolt near the rear edge. Remove the striker assembly toward the rear.

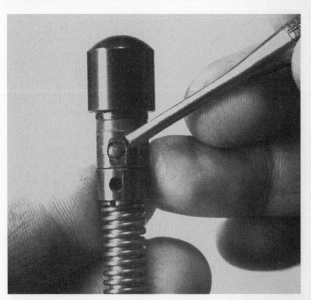

4. Grip the front of the striker firmly in a vise and drive out the striker cam pin from the knob. **Caution:** *Restrain the knob, as the striker sleeve and knob will be forced off when the cam pin is removed. Control them, and ease them off.*

5. Drift out the bolt retaining cross pin.

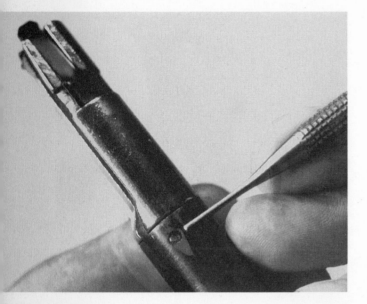

6. Remove the bolt head toward the front.

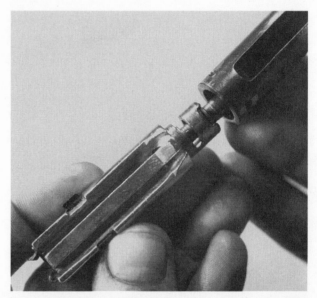

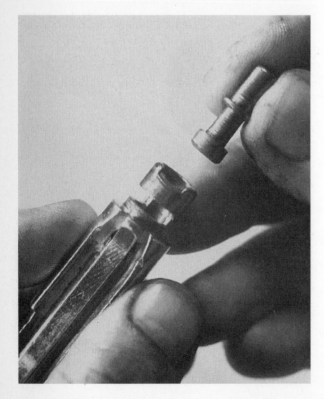

7. Remove the rear firing pin from the bolt head.

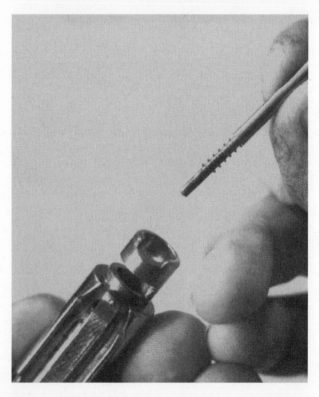

8. Remove the front firing pin and its return spring from the bolt head.

9. Insert a small screwdriver under the left extractor and lift it out of its recess just enough to clear. Turn the screwdriver to lever the extractor clip off the bolt.

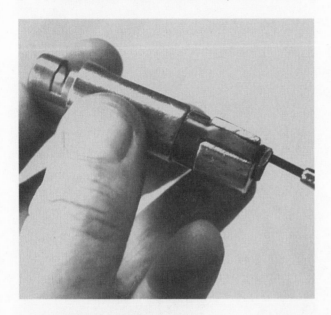

10. Back out the stock mounting bolt, on the underside forward of the magazine plate, and remove the action from the stock. Removal of the small vertical screws at each end of the trigger guard and magazine plate will allow the guard and plate to be taken off downward.

11. Remove the large vertical screw on the underside of the receiver, just to the rear of the magazine guide bar and catch.

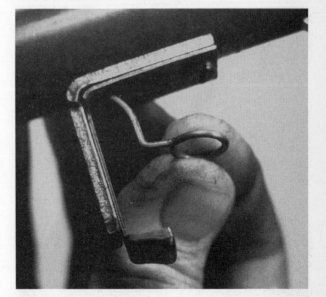

12. Remove the ejector downward and toward the rear.

14. Remove the trigger and its spring downward.

13. Remove the smaller screw, at the rear of the magazine guide bar and catch base. Remove the guide bar and magazine catch downward. Drift out the trigger cross pin, taking care that the trigger post is well supported.

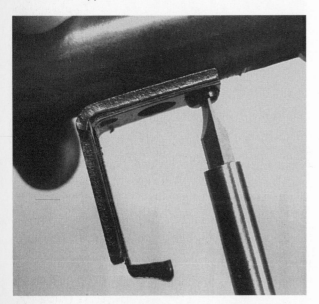

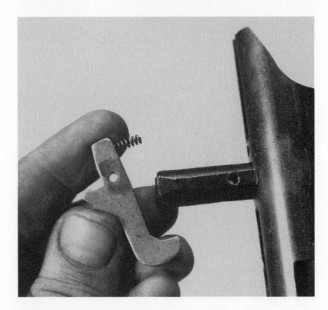

15. Restrain the sear and remove the screw on the right side of the receiver. Remove the safety-lever toward the right.

16. Remove the sear and its spring downward.

Reassembly Tips:

1. When replacing the bolt head, note that it must be oriented with the retaining cut aligned for insertion of the cross pin. Also, the rear firing pin must be pushed forward as the pin is inserted.

2. When replacing the striker assembly, be sure the screw hole in the striker sleeve is at the top, aligned with the screw recess in the bolt body.

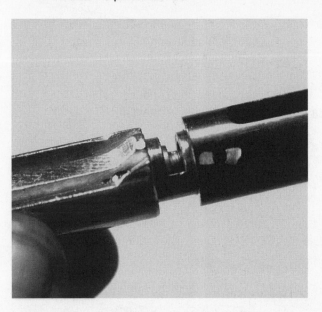

3. The striker must be cocked before the bolt is put back into the receiver. Grip the cam pin with non-marring pliers and turn the bolt clockwise (rear view) until the cam pin engages its notch at the rear of the bolt.

4. Before inserting the bolt, turn the bolt head so its underside aligns with the opening in the bottom of the bolt. Note that there is a guide flange on the left side of the extractor which must mate with a small groove inside the left wall of the receiver.

Model 780 Bolt-Action Rifle

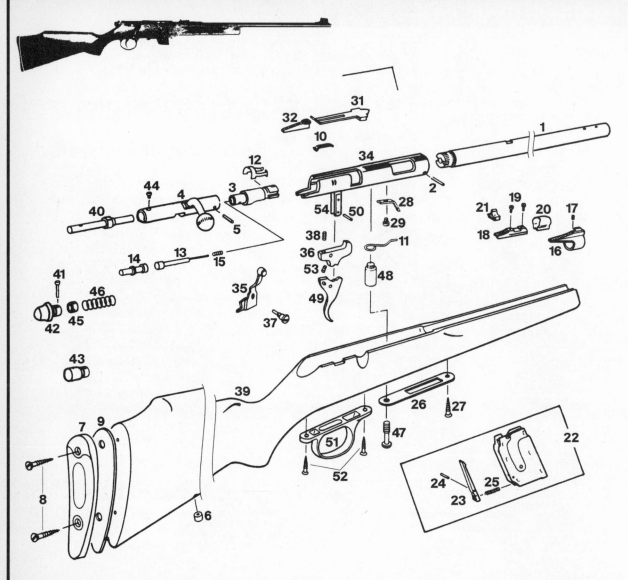

KEY

1 Barrel
2 Barrel Retaining Pin
3 Breechbolt, Front
4 Breechbolt, Rear
5 Breechbolt Retaining Pin
6 Bullseye
7 Buttplate
8 Buttplate Screws
9 Buttplate Spacer
10 Cartridge Guide Spring
11 Ejector
12 Extractor
13 Firing Pin, Front
14 Firing Pin, Rear
15 Firing Pin Spring
16 Front Sight Assembly (Old Style)
17 Front Sight Binding Screw (Old Style)
18 Front Sight Ramp Base
19 Front Sight Ramp Base Screws

20 Front Sight Ramp Hood
21 Front Sight Ramp Insert
22 Magazine Complete
23 Magazine Catch
24 Magazine Catch Pin
25 Magazine Catch Spring
26 Magazine Guard Plate
27 Magazine Guard Plate Screw
28 Magazine Receiver Catch
29 Magazine Receiver Catch Screw
30 Rear Sight Complete (New Style)
31 Rear Sight Base
32 Rear Sight Elevator
33 Rear Sight Folding Leaf
34 Receiver
35 Safety
36 Sear
37 Sear and Safety Pivot Screw
38 Sear Spring
39 Stock
40 Striker
41 Striker Cam Pin

42 Striker Knob (Old Style)
43 Striker Knob
44 Striker Retaining Screw
45 Striker Sleeve
46 Striker Spring
47 Takedown Screw
48 Takedown Screw Stud
49 Trigger
50 Trigger Pin
51 Trigger Guard
52 Trigger Guard Screws
53 Trigger Spring
54 Trigger Stud

Parts Not Shown
Rear Sight (Old Style)
Sear (Old Style)
Sear Spring (Old Style)
Trigger (Old Style)
Trigger Spring (Old Style)

Mauser Model 1898

Similar/Identical Pattern Guns

The same basic assembly/disassembly steps for the Mauser Model 1898 also apply to the following guns:

Argentine Model 1909 Rifle
Argentine Model 1909 Cavalry Carbine
Argentine Model 1909 Engineer Carbine
Brazilian Model 1908 Rifle
Brazilian Model 1908 Short Rifle
Browning High-Power Rifle
Chilean Model 1912
Chinese "Chiang Kai-shek" (Mauser "Standard Model")
Colombian Model 1912 Rifle
Costa Rican Model 1910 Rifle
Czech Model 24 (VZ24)
FN Supreme Mauser
German Model 98a Carbine
German Model 98b Carbine
German Model G33/40 Carbine
Interarms Mark X
Iranian Model 1930 Short Rifle
Iranian Model 1938 Rifle

Iranian Model 1949 Short Rifle
Mauser Model 1904 (Brazil, Chile, China)
Mexican Model 1907
Mexican Model 1910
Mexican Model 1912
Mexican Model 1936
Paraguayan Model 1907 Rifle
Paraguayan Model 1907 Carbine
Peruvian Model 1909 Rifle
Polish Model 98a Carbine
Swedish Model 40
Turkish Model 1903 Rifle
Turkish Model 1905 Carbine
Venezuelan Model 1910 Rifle
Yugoslavian Model 24 Rifle
Yugoslavian Model 48 Rifle

Data:	Mauser Model 1898 (Karabiner 98k)
Origin:	Germany
Manufacturer:	Various government arsenals
Cartridge:	7.92mm Mauser (8x57mm Mauser)
Magazine capacity:	5 rounds
Overall length:	43.6 inches
Barrel length:	23.62 inches
Weight:	9 pounds

The classic Model 1898 was made in both military and sporting versions from 1898 to 1935, when the military rifle was redesigned to become the Model 98k, the famous Karabiner of W W II. After the war, countless numbers of 98k guns were brought into the U.S. as war souvenirs, and large quantities of stored guns are still being sold on the surplus market. The actions have always been popular as the basis for sporting rifles, while the full military guns in top condition are prizes for collectors. Many of today's finest commercial sporting rifles have action designs based on the original Mauser 98 system.

145

Disassembly:

1. Cycle the bolt to cock the striker, and turn the safety-lever up to the vertical position. Open the bolt, and move it toward the rear while holding the bolt stop pulled out toward the left. Remove the bolt from the rear of the receiver.

2. Depress the bolt sleeve lock plunger, located on the left side, and unscrew the bolt sleeve counter-clockwise (rear view), taking care not to trip the safety-lever from its vertical position. Remove the bolt sleeve and striker assembly toward the rear.

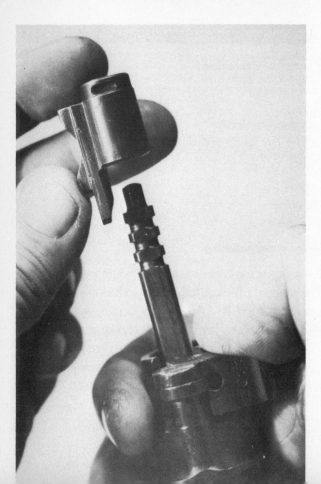

3. If the round takedown bushing is still in the side of the buttstock, insert the firing pin section of the striker shaft into the hole in the center of the bushing to hold the assembly for takedown. If the gun does not have the original stock and bushing, grip the front of the striker in a vise. Either way, take care to exert no side pressure. Holding the bolt sleeve against the tension of the striker spring, turn the safety-lever back to off-safe position, and push the bolt sleeve toward the front until the rear edge of the sleeve clears the front of the cocking piece underlug. Turn the cocking piece a quarter-turn in either direction, and remove it from the rear end of the striker shaft. **Caution:** *Keep a firm grip on the bolt sleeve, holding the compressed striker spring.*

4. Slowly release the spring tension, moving the bolt sleeve off the rear of the striker shaft, and removing the spring toward the rear.

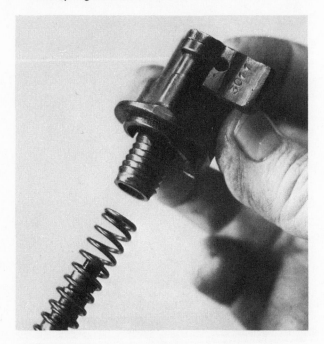

5. Turn the safety-lever over to the right side (clockwise, rear view), and remove it toward the rear.

6. To remove the bolt sleeve lock plunger and its spring, push the plunger inward, and turn it to bring its retaining stud into the exit track. Remove the plunger and spring toward the front.

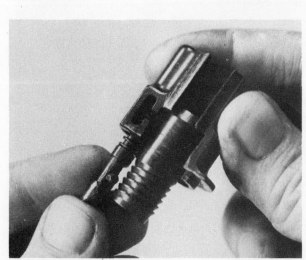

7. If you have the Brownells extractor pliers, use them to raise the front of the extractor just enough to clear the groove at the front of the bolt. A screwdriver inserted beneath the extractor can also do this. With the extractor lifted, turn it clockwise (rear view) until it is aligned with the grooveless area at the front of the bolt.

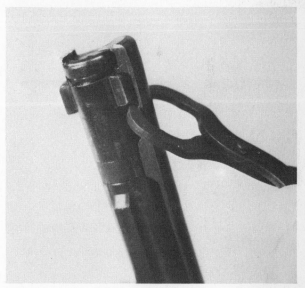

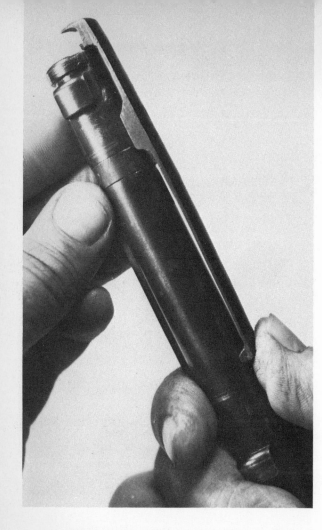

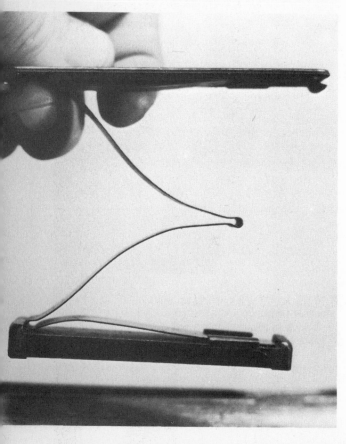

8. Push the extractor straight off toward the front. The mounting ring is not removed from the bolt in normal disassembly.

9. Insert a medium-sized drift punch in the hole at the rear of the magazine floorplate, and depress the floorplate latch. Move the floorplate toward the rear.

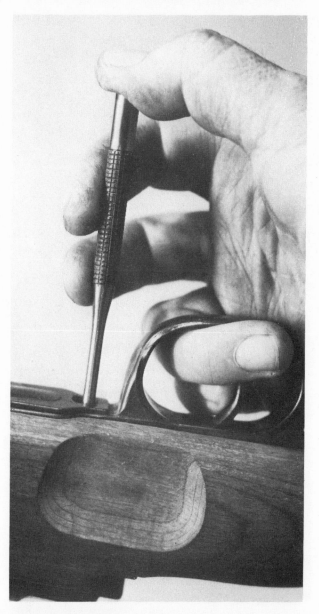

10. Remove the magazine floorplate, spring, and follower downward. The spring is easily detached from the plate and follower.

11. If the end section of cleaning rod is present in the front of the stock, unscrew it and remove it. Depress the front barrel band latch and slide the barrel band off toward the front.

12. The spring latch is now free to be removed from its recess in the stock, and the rear barrel band can be slid off forward and removed. The upper handguard wood can also be taken off at this time.

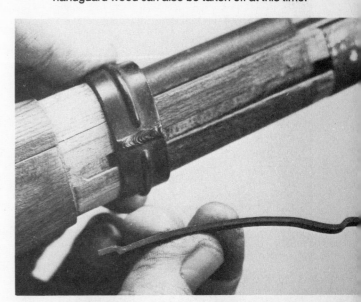

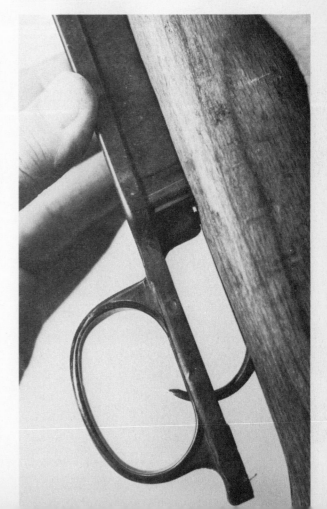

13. Remove the lock screws, and take out the larger vertical screws on the underside of the stock at the front and rear of the trigger guard/magazine housing.

14. Remove the trigger guard/magazine housing downward, and separate the action from the stock.

15. The magazine floorplate latch is retained by a cross pin in the trigger guard/magazine housing, and is removed downward. **Caution:** *This is a very strong spring, so control the plunger and ease it out.*

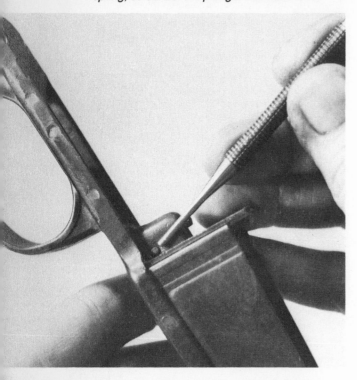

16. Remove the small vertical screw at the left rear of the receiver, the pivot for the bolt stop. Then remove the bolt latch/ejector assembly toward the left side.

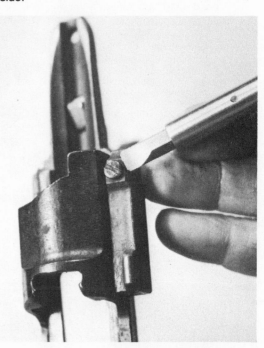

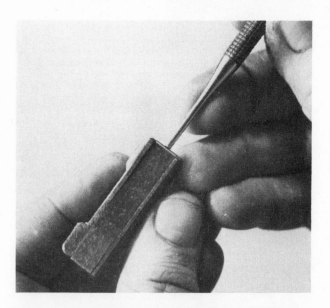

17. Remove the ejector toward the front.

18. To remove the combination bolt latch and ejector spring, set a drift punch against its rear edge, and drive it out toward the front. When the rear tip has cleared the cross piece at the rear of the bolt latch, the tip of the spring will move inward, and can then be levered out toward the front with a screwdriver blade.

19. Drifting out the cross pin that retains the sear will allow removal of the sear, sear spring, and the attached trigger downward. The trigger cross pin can be drifted out to separate the trigger from the sear.

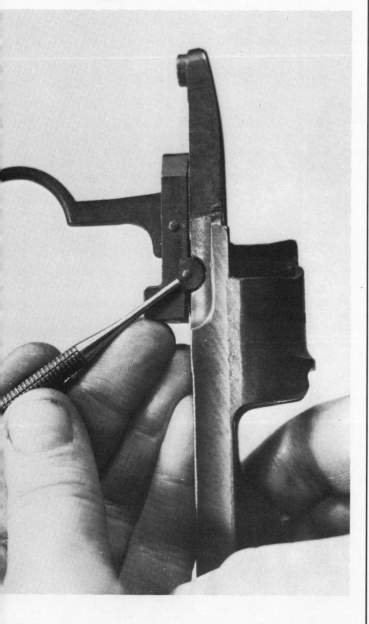

Reassembly Tips:

1. When replacing the combination bolt stop and ejector spring, it will be necessary to insert a screwdriver or some other tool to lift its rear tip onto the cross piece at the rear of the bolt stop, as the spring is driven into place.

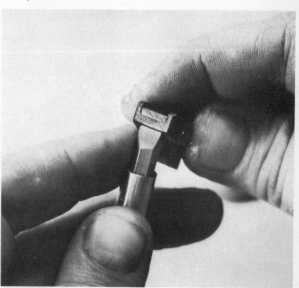

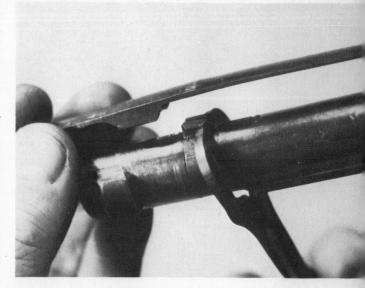

2. When replacing the extractor on the bolt, be sure the mounting ring flanges are aligned with the ungrooved area at the front of the bolt. Use the Brownells pliers or some other tool to compress the ring flanges, and slide the extractor onto the ring.

3. With the extractor pliers or a screwdriver blade, lift the front of the extractor while depressing the center of its tail, to lift the underlug at the front over the edge of the bolt face. When the underlug is aligned with the groove, turn the extractor back toward the left (counter-clockwise, rear view), until it covers the right lug of the bolt.

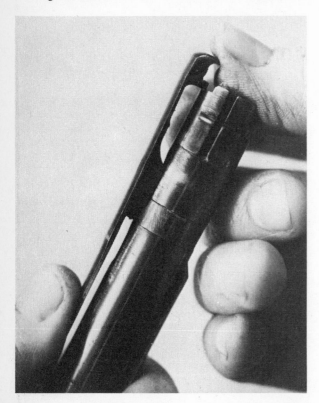

4. Before the bolt sleeve and striker assembly can be put back into the bolt, the striker must be moved to the rear and the safety turned into the vertical on-safe position. As the assembly is turned into place, the sleeve latch plunger must be pushed in twice—once to clear the bolt handle, and again as it enters its locking notch.

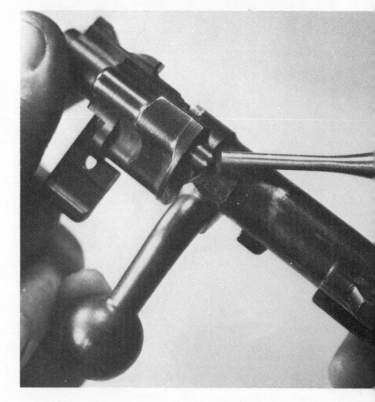

Model 98 Bolt-Action Rifle

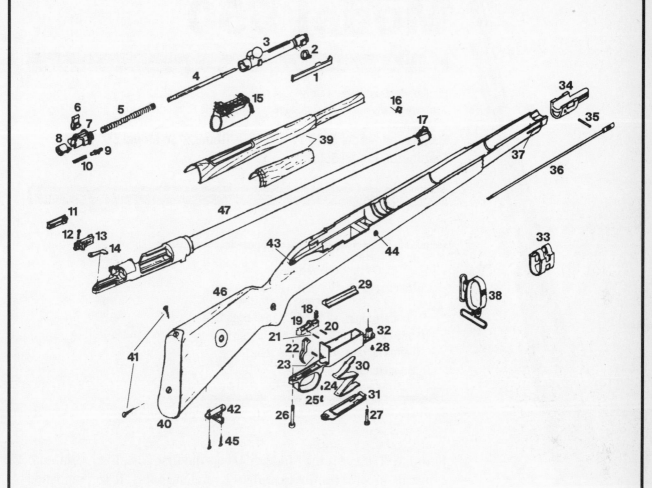

KEY

1 Extractor
2 Extractor Collar
3 Stripped Bolt
4 Firing Pin
5 Firing Pin Spring
6 Safety
7 Bolt Sleeve
8 Cocking Piece
9 Bolt Sleeve Catch
10 Bolt Sleeve Catch Spring
11 Ejector Spring and Bolt Stop
   Assembly
12 Bolt Stop Screw
13 Bolt Stop
14 Ejector
15 Rear Sight Complete
16 Front Sight Blade
17 Front Sight Complete
18 Sear Spring
19 Sear
20 Sear Pin
21 Trigger Pin
22 Trigger
23 Floorplate Catch Pin

24 Floorplate Catch Spring
25 Floorplate Catch
26 Rear Guard Screw
27 Front Guard Screw
28 Lock Screw
29 Follower
30 Magazine Spring
31 Floorplate
32 Trigger Guard
33 Front Band
34 Bayonet Stud
35 Bayonet Stud Pin
36 Cleaning Rod
37 Front Band Spring
38 Lower Band with Side and Bottom
   Swivels
39 Handguard
40 Buttplate
41 Butt Screws
42 Rear Swivel
43 Rear Guard Screw Bushing
44 Recoil Lug Assembly
45 Rear Swivel Screws
46 Stock
47 Barrel

Remington Model 550

Similar/Identical Pattern Guns

The same basic assembly/disassembly steps for the Remington Model 550 also apply to the following guns:

Remington Model 550P   **Remington Model 550-2G**

Remington Model 550A

Data:	Remington Model 550
Origin:	United States
Manufacturer:	Remington Arms Company Bridgeport, Connecticut
Cartridge:	22 Short, Long, or Long Rifle
Magazine capacity:	22 Shorts, 17 Longs, 15 Long Rifles
Overall length:	43$^1/_2$ inches
Barrel length:	24 inches
Weight:	6$^1/_4$ pounds

Introduced in 1941, the Model 550 was the first 22-caliber semi-auto to use all three 22 rimfire cartridges interchangeably. It accomplished this with a unique "floating chamber" which allowed the Short cartridge to deliver the same impact to the bolt as the longer rounds. During its time of production several sub-models were offered—the 550A, 550P, and so on, with different sight options. All of the 550 series guns are mechanically identical, and the same instructions will apply.

Disassembly:

1. Back out the stock mounting screw on the underside of the stock, and separate the action from the stock. If necessary, the stock screw can be removed by moving it out until its threads engage the threads in its escutcheon, and then unscrewing it.

2. Pull the trigger to release the striker, so it will be in the fired position, and unscrew the receiver end cap at the rear of the receiver. If the end cap has been over-tightened, there is a large coin slot at the rear of its dome to aid in starting it. Remove the end cap and its attached spring guide, and the bolt spring and striker spring and guide toward the rear. The springs are under some tension, but not so much that the end cap can't be easily controlled. The springs are easily removed from the guide on the end cap, but the hollow guide is not removable. Take care not to lose the collar at the front of the bolt spring.

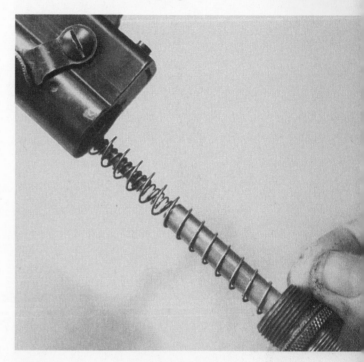

3. Move the bolt all the way to the rear, until the bolt handle aligns with the opening at the end of its track, and remove the bolt handle toward the right.

4. Use a small tool to push the bolt toward the rear, and remove it from the rear of the receiver.

5. Remove the striker (firing pin) from the rear of the bolt.

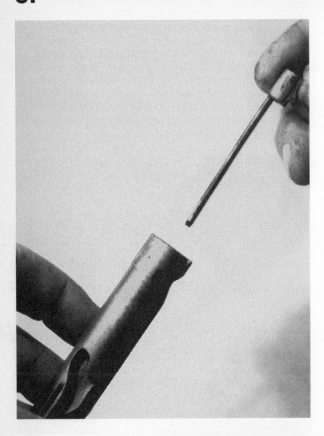

6. Use a small screwdriver to depress the extractor spring plunger, and lift the extractor out of its recess in the bolt. **Caution:** *Take care that the plunger and spring don't get away, as the compressed spring can propel the parts quite a distance.* They are very small and difficult to locate.

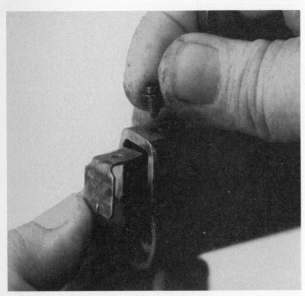

7. Remove the small screw and washer on the underside of the receiver near the rear edge, and take out the L-shaped end cap lockplate.

8. With the safety in the on-safe position, remove the safety screw and take off the safety-lever toward the right. The safety tumbler can then be moved inward and removed toward the rear. As the tumbler is moved inward, the trigger spring will move its plunger upward, so control it and ease its tension slowly. Next, drift out the trigger pin and the trigger limit pin. The trigger will be freed, but can't be removed at this point because of its attached disconnector assembly.

9. Drift out the cross pin in the forward section of the receiver, and remove the carrier assembly and its spring downward. The two leaves of the carrier, the spacer bushing, and the spring are easily separated. This pin also is the sear pivot, and the sear can now be moved forward and taken out downward.

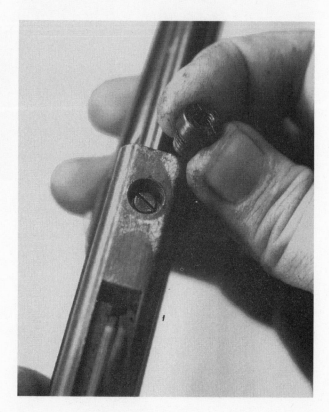

10. Remove the screw-slotted sear spring housing (looks like a large screw head) from the bottom center of the receiver, along with the sear spring it contains. The housing is often found staked in place, and some effort may be required to start it. **Caution:** *Never try to remove the housing while the sear is still in place on its cross pin, or the parts are likely to be damaged.* The trigger assembly may now be moved upward into the receiver, then forward, and out the carrier opening. The disconnector system may be separated from the trigger by drifting out the small cross pin, releasing the disconnector and its spring and plunger. However, the cross pin is usually riveted in place, and during routine disassembly it is best left undisturbed.

11. Removal of the stock mounting base at the lower front of the receiver will give access to a small screw beneath it. Taking out this screw will allow removal of the outer magazine tube toward the front. This will also release the receiver insert—the sub-frame which forms the cartridge guide—and allow it to be pushed out toward the rear. The insert is often tight, and may require the use of a hammer and nylon drift to start it. Take care that it is not deformed during removal. The ejector is staked in place in the left wall of the receiver, and no attempt to remove it should be made during normal disassembly.

Reassembly Tips:

1. When replacing the striker in the bolt, be sure its slim forward portion enters its tunnel in the bolt, and that the striker goes all the way forward. This can be checked on the underside of the bolt, as shown.

3. Before replacing the receiver end cap, be sure the springs are in the proper order, with the striker spring guide in the front of the spring, and the collar on the front of the bolt spring, as shown.

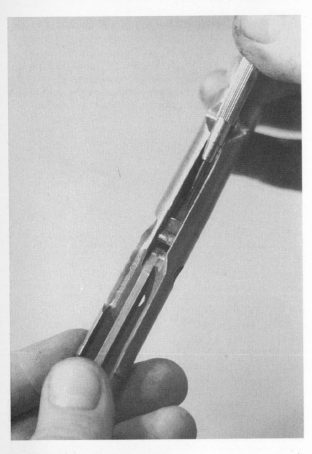

When installing the sear and sear spring system, put the sear and carrier system in place, and insert a smaller diameter rod or drift through the pin hole to keep them in general position. Then install the sear spring housing, being sure the top of the spring enters its recess in the underside of the sear. Next, move the sear downward and toward the rear, engaging its rear lobe with the collar on the housing. When it is in position, insert the cross pin, pushing out the smaller diameter rod or drift. This is the most difficult point in the reassembly of the Model 550.

2. When replacing the bolt handle, be sure the flat inner tip of the handle is at the top, as shown. Also, be sure the carrier is in its raised position (up at the front) before inserting the bolt in the receiver.

Model 550 Autoloading Rifle

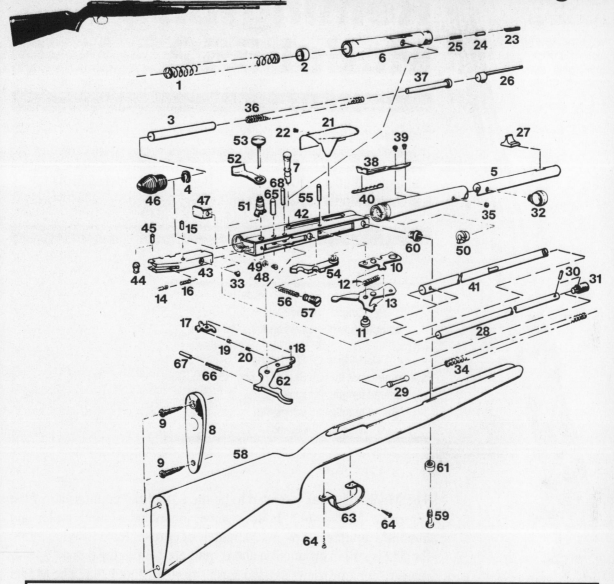

KEY

1	Action Spring
2	Action Spring Bushing
3	Action Spring Guide
4	Action Spring Guide Retainer
5	Barrel
6	Bolt
7	Bolt Handle
8	Buttplate
9	Buttplate Screws
10	Carrier
11	Carrier Spacer Bushing
12	Carrier Tension Spring
13	Cartridge Stop
14	Cartridge Stop Detent
15	Cartridge Stop Detent Pin
16	Cartridge Stop Detent Spring
17	Connector
18	Connector Pin
19	Connector Plunger
20	Connector Spring
21	Deflector
22	Deflector Screw
23	Extractor
24	Extractor Plunger
25	Extractor Spring
26	Firing Pin
27	Front Sight
28	Inner Magazine Tube
29	Magazine Follower
30	Magazine Pin
31	Magazine Plug
32	Magazine Ring
33	Magazine Screw
34	Magazine Spring
35	Magazine Tube Support Screw
36	Mainspring
37	Mainspring Plunger
38	Open Sight Leaf
39	Open Sight Screws
40	Open Sight Step
41	Outer Magazine Tube
42	Receiver Assembly
43	Receiver Insert
44	Receiver Insert Spacer
45	Receiver Insert Spacer Pin
46	Receiver Plug
47	Receiver Plug Retainer
48	Receiver Plug Retainer Screw
49	Receiver Plug Retainer Screw Lock Washer
50	Recoiling Chamber
51	Safety
52	Safety-Lever
53	Safety Screw
54	Sear Assembly
55	Sear Pin
56	Sear Spring
57	Sear Spring Case
58	Stock
59	Takedown Screw
60	Takedown Screw Bushing
61	Takedown Screw Escutcheon
62	Trigger
63	Trigger Guard
64	Trigger Guard Screws
65	Trigger Pin
66	Trigger Spring
67	Trigger Spring Plunger
68	Trigger Stop Pin

Remington Model 552

Similar/Identical Pattern Guns

The same basic assembly/disassembly steps for the Remington Model 552 also apply to the following guns:

Remington Model 552C   **Remington Model 552BDL**

Remington Model 552GS

Data:	Remington Model 552
Origin:	United States
Manufacturer:	Remington Arms Company
	Bridgeport, Connecticut
Cartridge:	22 Short, Long or Long Rifle
Magazine capacity:	20 Short, 17 Long, 15 Long Rifle
Overall length:	42 inches
Barrel length:	25 inches
Weight:	5$\frac{1}{2}$ pounds

The Model 552 was intended to be the 22-caliber counterpart of the centerfire Model 742. It does have somewhat similar looks and handling qualities, though it's lighter, of course. Introduced in 1958, the 552 is still in production and is marketed under the name "Speed-master," a name that was used earlier for the Model 241. The Model 552 has also been offered in a carbine version with a 21-inch barrel (552C), and a Gallery Special gun in 22 Short only chambering. The instructions apply to all of these.

Disassembly:

1. Remove the inner magazine tube and cycle the bolt to cock the hammer. With a non-marring tool such as a brass or bronze drift punch, push out the large cross pin at the rear of the receiver and the smaller cross pin at the center of the receiver. It may be necessary to tap the drift with a small hammer to start the pins out.

2. Remove the trigger group downward and toward the rear.

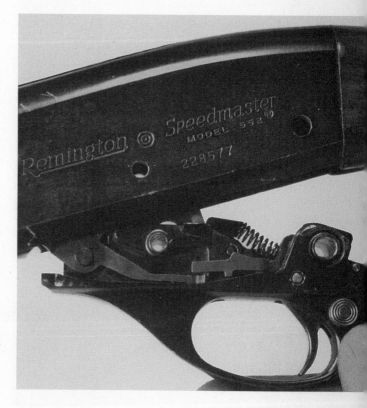

3. Restrain the hammer against the tension of its spring, pull the trigger, and ease the hammer down to the fired position. Remove the small spring clip from the right end of the front cross pin sleeve and push the sleeve out toward the left. This will free the carrier and its spring for removal from the right side of the group. **Caution:** *The carrier spring is strong and is under some tension, so restrain the carrier and ease it off.*

4. Pull the trigger and hold it back to relieve the tension on the rear cross pin sleeve; then push it out toward the left with its spring clip left in place.

5. Removal of the cross pin sleeve will allow the trigger top to move further to the rear, relieving the tension of the trigger/sear spring. Flex the spring away from its stud on the back of the sear and remove the spring upward.

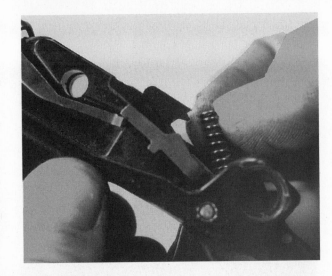

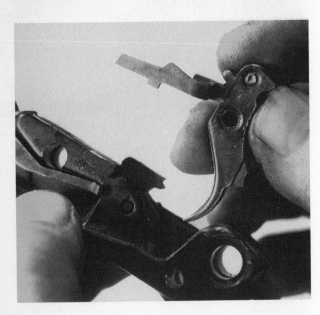

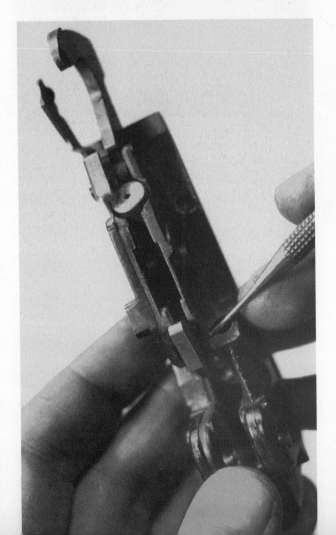

6. Drift out the trigger cross pin and remove the trigger, with its attached connector bar, upward. The two leaves of the connector are riveted at the top of the trigger and removal in normal takedown is not advisable.

7. Insert a small drift punch on the right side of the trigger group, as shown, and push out the sear pivot toward the left. The sear is then removed upward.

8. Push out the small cross pin at the extreme rear of the trigger group and remove the safety spring and ball upward. The safety can then be slid out toward either side. **Caution:** *The spring is under some tension, so hold a fingertip over the top of the hole when removing the drift punch to control it.* If the detent ball can't be shaken out the top after removal of the spring, wait until the safety is taken out, and then insert a small drift punch from the top and push it out into the safety channel. Take care that this small steel ball isn't lost.

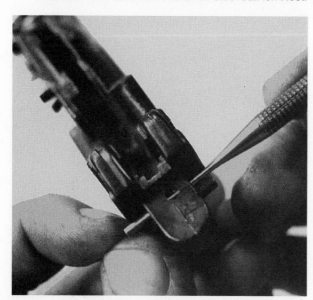

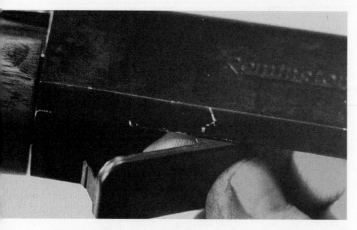

10. Slide the receiver coverplate on the underside about a quarter inch toward the rear, and insert a finger inside the receiver from the rear to tip its front end outward. Pivot it over toward the rear and remove it.

11. With a coin or a specially shaped screwdriver, remove the large screw on the underside of the forend. Move the rear of the forend slightly downward to clear the forward extension of the receiver, and slide the forend forward on the magazine tube. It is not removed at this point.

9. A large cross pin with an enlarged head on the left side pivots and retains both the hammer and the disconnector, and the pin is riveted over a washer on the right side of the trigger group (illus.). Because of the riveting, a drift punch of smaller diameter than the pin body must be used. Be sure the disconnector is well supported when driving out the pin, to avoid damage. **Caution:** *Removal of the disconnector will also release the hammer spring and plunger, so take care to restrain them and ease them out.*

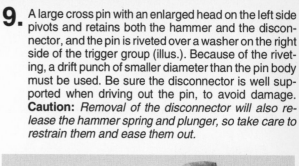

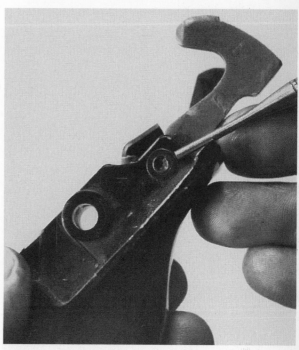

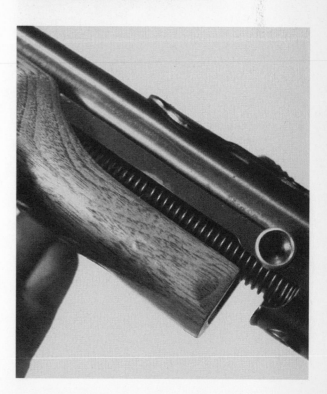

12. Move the barrel assembly forward out of the receiver.

13. Restrain the tension of the bolt spring by holding onto the action bar, and carefully detach the rear vertical lug of the action bar from its recess in the side of the bolt. Remove the bolt toward the rear and ease the action bar forward, relieving the tension of the spring.

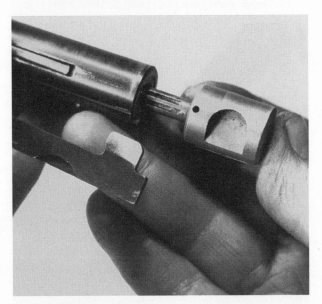

14. Remove the small screw on the underside of the front magazine tube hanger and slide the outer magazine tube out toward the front.

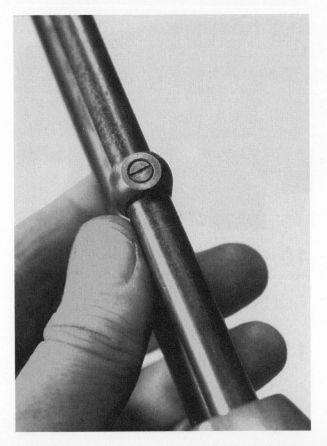

15. Removal of the magazine tube will release the forend piece, action bar and bolt spring to be taken off downward. The front magazine tube hanger has a threaded mounting post and is unscrewed from the underside of the barrel. The steel support piece at the front of the forend can be slid out forward.

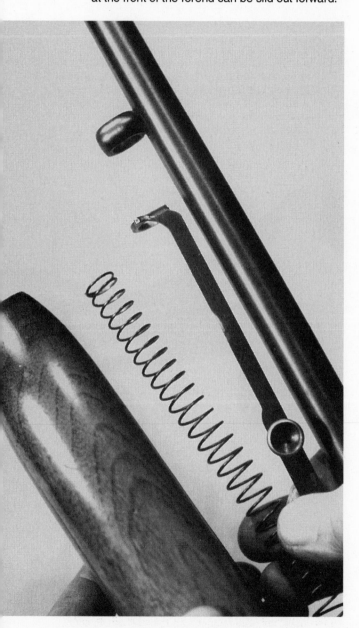

16. The firing pin is retained by a small cross pin in the larger rear portion of the bolt, and after removal of the pin it can be taken off upward.

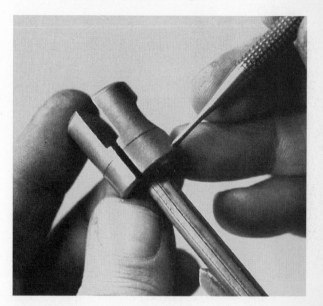

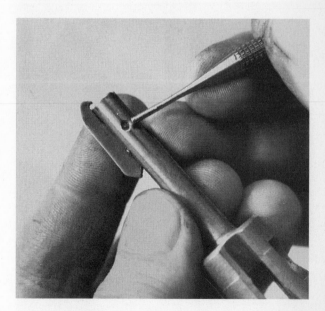

17. After the firing pin is removed, the very short vertical pin that retains the extractor can be driven out, and the extractor and its coil spring can then be taken off toward the right.

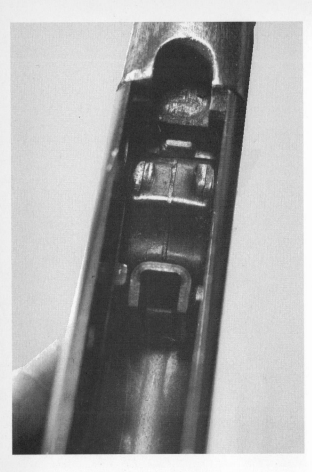

18. Inside the receiver at the rear is a steel bolt buffer and a rubber buffer pad. With the gun inverted, these can be pried upward out of their recess and removed. The stock is retained by a through-bolt from the rear, accessible by removing the buttplate.

19. To remove the ejector, insert a small screwdriver at its rear and move the ejector forward. When its front end can be grasped, tip it outward and remove it toward the left. The rear magazine tube hanger is removed in the same manner as the front one, by simply unscrewing it, and this will release the cartridge ramp that it retains.

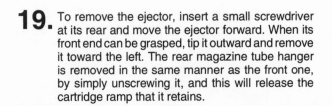

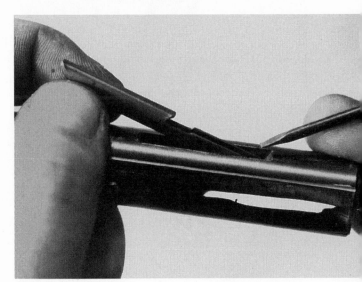

20. The rear sight and the shell deflector are each retained by two small screws. On some Model 552 rifles, the front sight is also retained by two screws. Others have a standard dovetail mount.

Reassembly Tips:

1. When replacing the extractor pivot pin in the slim forward section of the bolt, take care that it does not protrude into the firing pin recess at the top.

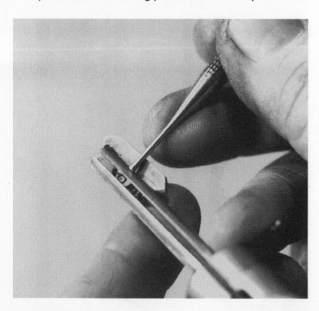

2. When replacing the safety in the trigger group, remember that the side with the red band goes on the left side. When replacing the trigger and its attached connector bars, note that the left connector arm must be installed *above* the rear tip of the disconnector, as shown.

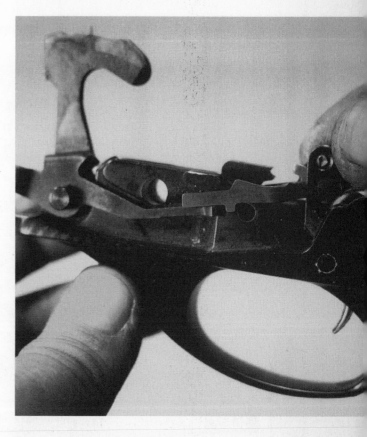

3. Before replacing the barrel assembly in the receiver, put all the components together prior to insertion. The photo shows the proper engagement of the action bar and the bolt. Take care that the lug of the action bar doesn't slip out of its recess in the bolt as the assembly is being slid back into the receiver.

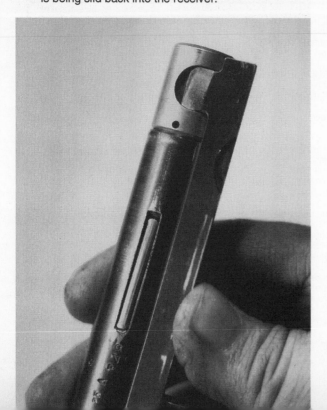

4. To replace the receiver coverplate on the underside, invert the gun and start the plate with its inner surface facing outward. Press it inward, compressing its rear side wings; then swing it over forward until it can be snapped into its retaining grooves.

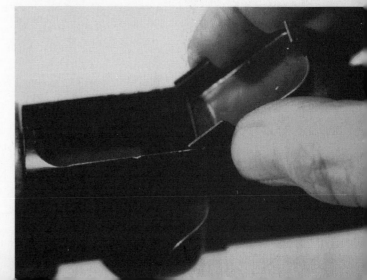

Model 552 Autoloading Rifle

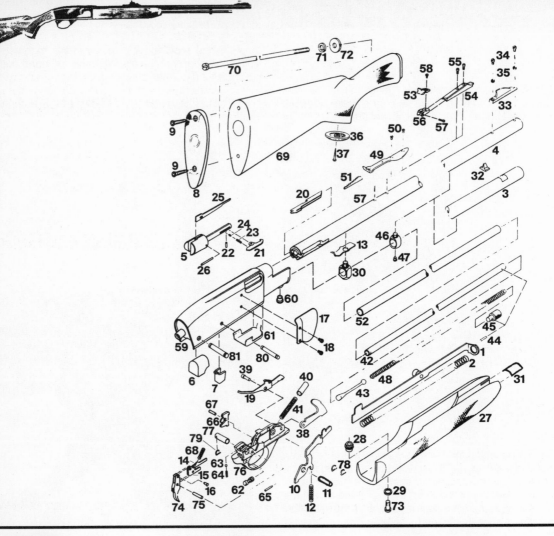

Remington Model 581

Similar/Identical Pattern Guns

The same basic assembly/disassembly steps for the Remington Model 581 also apply to the following gun:

Remington Model 580   **Remington Model 581-S**
Remington Model 582

Data:	Remington Model 581
Origin:	United States
Manufacturer:	Remington Arms Company Bridgeport, Connecticut
Cartridge:	22 Short, Long, or Long Rifle
Magazine capacity:	5 rounds
Overall length:	$42^3/_8$ inches
Barrel length:	24 inches
Weight:	$4^3/_4$ pounds

The Model 581 was introduced in 1967 and was made until 1984. For many shooters it served the same purpose as the 512 and 513 for an earlier generation. The 581 was supplied with a single shot adapter, a useful accessory when teaching youngsters to shoot. It was also available in a left-handed version, the mechanical details being the same.

Disassembly:

1. Remove the magazine, and use a wide, thin-bladed screwdriver to back out the main stock mounting screw, on the underside just forward of the magazine well. Separate the action from the stock. To remove the bolt, open it and move it toward the rear while pushing the safety-lever forward, beyond its normal off-safe position. Withdraw the bolt from the rear of the receiver.

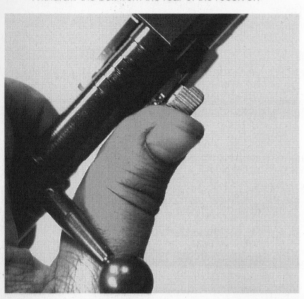

2. Grip the underlug of the striker head, at the rear of the bolt, in a sharp-edged bench vise, and be sure it is firmly held. Push forward on the bolt end piece, against the tension of the striker spring, and unscrew the forward portion of the bolt from the end piece. **Caution:** *The powerful spring is under heavy tension, so control the bolt as the threaded section is cleared.*

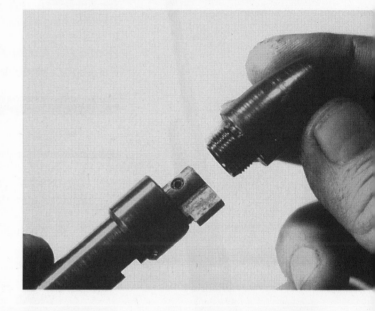

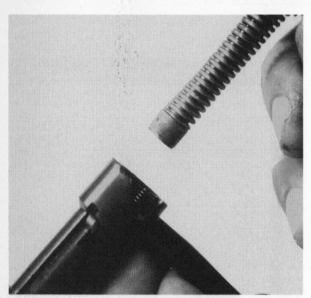

3. Remove the striker and its captive spring assembly from the rear of the bolt. The striker head may be separated from the front portion of the striker by drifting out the roll cross pin. This will release the striker spring with force, so proceed with caution. In normal disassembly, this unit is best left intact. If it is taken apart, take care not to lose the compression washer, located between the spring and the striker head.

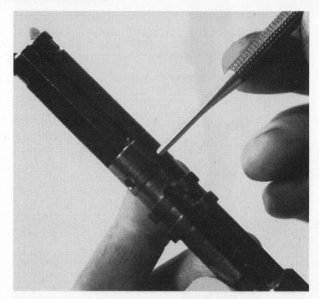

4. A solid cross pin near the forward end of the bolt body retains the breechblock on the front of the bolt. Drifting out the cross pin will allow the breechblock to be taken off toward the front.

5. Use a small screwdriver to gently pry the left end of the semi-circular spring-clip at the front of the bolt upward. Flexing the left extractor very slightly outward will make insertion of the screwdriver tip easier. Take care to lift the clip only enough to slip it off, as it will break if flexed too far.

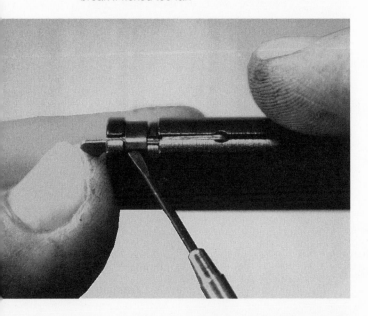

6. After the spring clip has been removed, the extractors are easily removed from their recesses on each side, and the firing pin can be taken out of its slot in the top. Note that the extractors are not identical, and each must be returned to the proper side in reassembly.

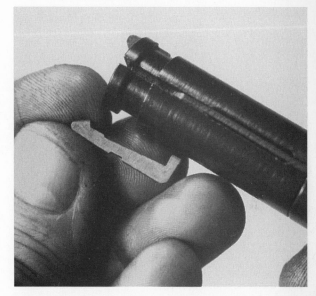

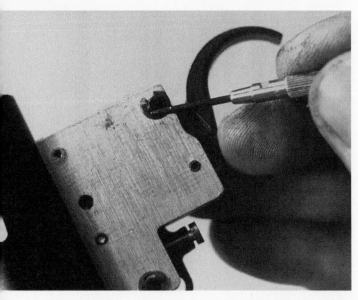

7. The safety-lever is mounted on the trigger housing by its pivot post at the rear and a guide post at the front, and these posts are retained on the left side of the housing by C-clips. Carefully remove the C-clips, guarding against their loss, and take out the two mounting posts toward the right.

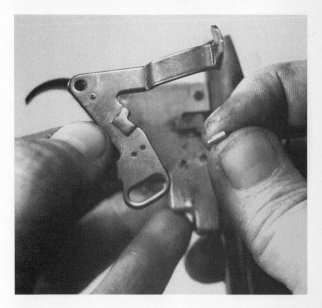

8. Remove the safety-lever toward the right. **Caution:** *As the safety-lever is removed, the safety plunger and spring will be released from their cross-hole in the housing.* Control them during removal, and take them out of the housing. The safety plunger and spring will usually come out of the housing together. If not, it may be necessary to use a small screwdriver to lift out the spring.

9. The large pin at the upper rear of the trigger housing is the sear pivot pin. It is sometimes mistaken for the trigger group retaining pin, and is drifted out in error. This will release the sear within the housing, and the housing must then be removed to replace the sear and its spring in proper order.

10. The trigger housing retaining pin is a roll pin at the upper center of the housing. Drifting out this cross pin will allow the trigger housing to be taken off downward. When the housing is removed, the bolt stop and its spring can be lifted from their well in the top of the housing, and the sear is easily removed by drifting out its cross pin.

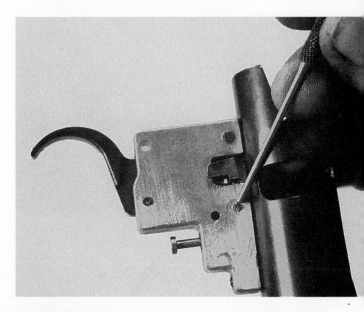

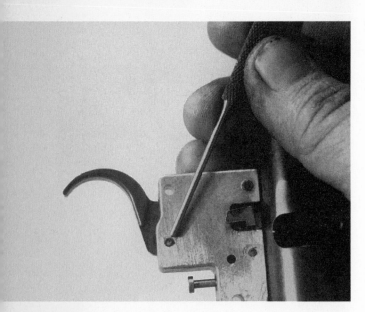

11. The trigger is retained by a roll cross pin at the lower edge of the housing, and is removed downward. The same coil spring powers both the sear and the trigger.

12. The housing tension screw at the extreme front edge of the housing can be backed out if the housing mounting pin is unusually tight, as this will ease tension on the cross pin.

13. Backing out the single screw at the rear of the magazine catch will allow removal of the magazine catch and magazine guide downward. The ejector is an integral part of the magazine guide.

14. Removal of the large screw just forward of the rear sight will allow the sight and sight base to be taken off upward.

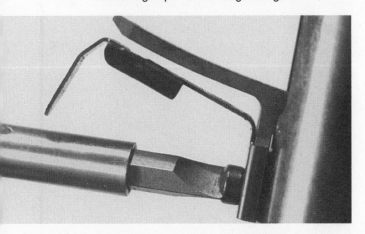

Reassembly Tips:

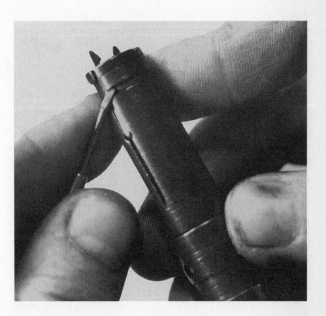

1. When replacing the safety-lever, seat the tip of the safety spring plunger in the larger, dished-out recess on the inside of the lever while pushing the safety into place. In this position, the plunger will be less likely to slip out during installation.

2. When replacing the semi-circular spring clip at the front of the bolt that retains and powers the extractors, note that the small central projection at its top must go toward the front, and its split wing toward the left. Use a small screwdriver to guide its lower end over the extractor as it is pushed into place.

When replacing the extractors, note that the one with the sharp break must be placed on the right.

Model 580, 581 and 582 Bolt-Action Rifle

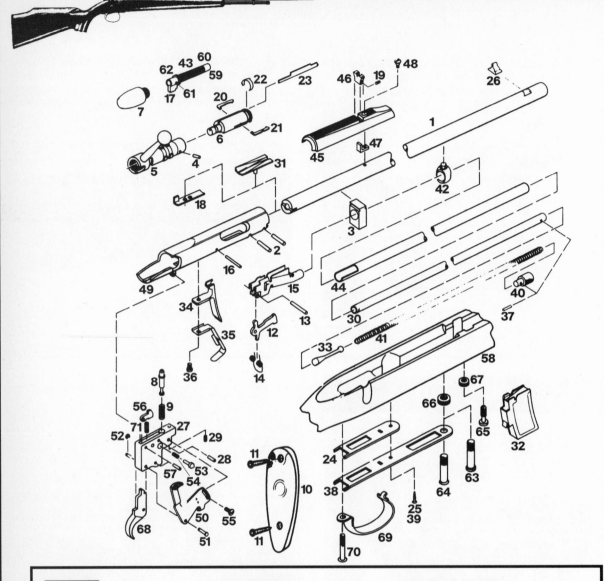

Remington Model 600

Similar/Identical Pattern Guns

The same basic assembly/disassembly steps for the Remington Model 600 also apply to the following guns:

Remington Mohawk 600   **Remington Model 660**

Data:	Remington Model 600
Origin:	United States
Manufacturer:	Remington Arms Company Bridgeport, Connecticut
Cartridges:	222, 223, 243, 6mm Remington, 308, 35 Remington, 6.5mm Remington Magnum and 350 Remington Magnum
Magazine capacity:	4, 5 or 6 rounds, depending on caliber
Overall length:	37¼ inches
Barrel length:	18½ inches
Weight:	5½ pounds

This handy little carbine, and its counterpart the Model 660, did not stay long on the scene. The Model 600, with its distinctive ventilated barrel rib, was made from 1964 to 1967. The successor, the Model 660, was made from 1968 to 1971. During this time, a version called the "Mohawk 600" was produced, a gun very similar to the Model 660, but without the barrel rib. Mechanically, these three are virtually identical, and the same instructions will apply.

Disassembly:

1. Open the bolt and move it part-way to the rear. Use a small tool to depress the bolt stop, located at the left rear of the receiver on the inside, next to the bolt. Hold the stop down, and remove the bolt toward the rear. As the bolt emerges from the receiver, it must be lifted to clear its right lug over the safety.

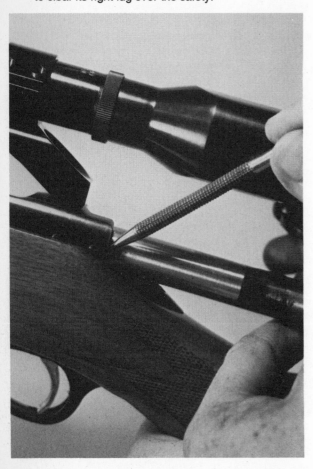

2. Grip the underlug of the cocking piece firmly in a vise and pull the bolt forward until a gap appears between the front of the cocking piece and the rear of the bolt end piece. Insert a thin piece of steel plate between the cocking piece and the bolt end piece. Note that on some models, such as the one shown, a slot is provided on the side of the cocking piece for the insertion of the plate. Release the spring tension, and the plate will trap the striker at the rear.

3. Taking care not to dislodge the plate, unscrew the bolt end piece from the rear of the bolt. The factory advises against further disassembly of the striker system, since reassembly can be difficult without special tools. I will note here that the cocking piece is retained on the rear of the striker shaft by a cross pin.

4. The ejector is retained in the front of the bolt by a cross pin. Restrain the ejector when drifting out the pin, and remove the ejector and spring toward the front.

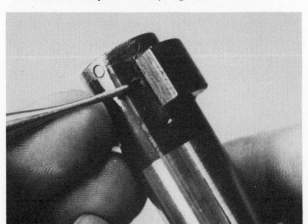

5. The extractor is retained inside the bolt face recess by a small rivet, and if unbroken, it should not be removed. If removal is necessary, the rivet is driven inward. The ejector must first be removed.

6. Remove the large screw on the underside at the front of the trigger guard/magazine housing. Remove the screw on the underside at the rear of the trigger guard, and separate the action from the stock. The trigger guard unit can be taken off downward.

7. The magazine box is easily detached from the underside of the receiver, and the spring and follower can be taken out of the box.

8. Position the safety snap washer so its opening is aligned with the stud on the detent spring, and push off the snap washer upward. Take off the detent spring, and take care not to lose the small steel ball in the side of the safety-lever beneath the spring.

9. Push out the safety pivot toward the left, and remove the safety toward the rear and downward.

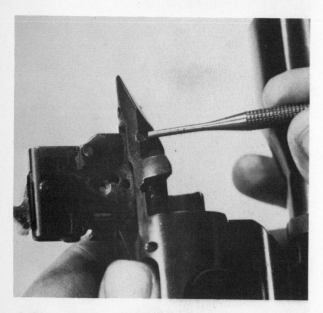

10. Drift out the rear trigger housing cross pin toward the left, while restraining the sear at the top. When the pin is out, the sear spring will push the sear upward.

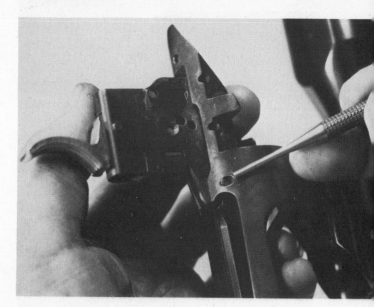

11. Drift out the front trigger housing cross pin, and remove the trigger housing downward.

13. The trigger housing should not be disassembled beyond this point in normal takedown. There are three trigger adjustment screws, two at the front and one at the rear, which are set and sealed with lacquer at the factory, and these should not be disturbed. A cross pin retains the trigger and its connector, but removal requires that the two front screws be backed out.

12. Remove the sear and sear spring from the top of the trigger housing.

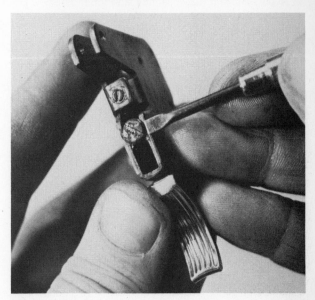

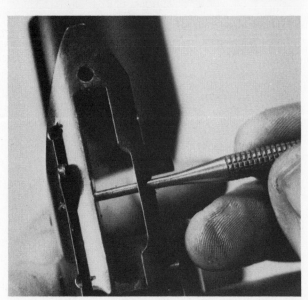

14. Removal of the bolt stop requires that its short pin be drifted out toward the left, and there is an access hole on the right side of the receiver through which a drift punch can be inserted to drive out the pin. The bolt stop and its spring are removed downward.

Reassembly Tips:

1. When replacing the trigger housing, start the two cross pins in from the left, and be certain that the holes in the housing are aligned with the pins, to avoid deforming the housing. When the pins are just into the housing, but not into the center space, insert the sear from the rear, align its hole with the front cross pin, and drive the pin across. Be sure the left tip of the cross pin is clear of the bolt stop slot.

2. Insert the sear spring, being sure it is properly positioned to engage its recess on the underside of the sear, and swing the sear downward, keeping it depressed while the rear cross pin is driven across.

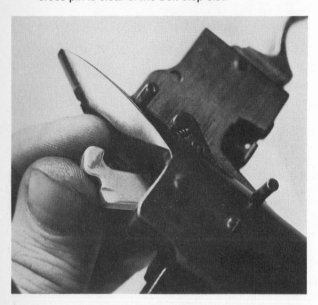

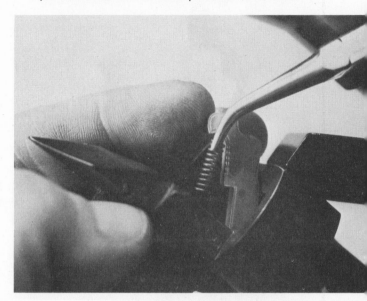

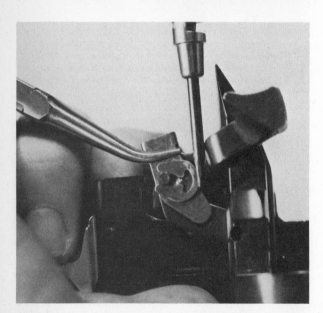

3. When replacing the safety system, be sure the pivot post is all the way through to the right when installing the detent spring and snap washer. Use pliers to compress the detent spring, and be sure the inside surfaces of the washer engage the groove in the top of the pivot post.

4. When removing the steel plate holding the striker, position the bolt end piece as shown, so the released striker cocking piece will be in cocked position, and the bolt will be ready for reinsertion in the receiver.

Model 600 Bolt-Action Carbine

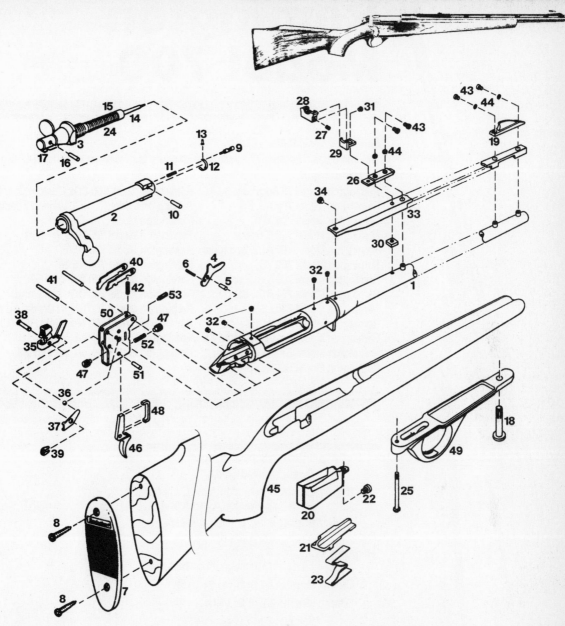

KEY

1 Barrel	**18** Front Guard Screw	**37** Safety Detent Spring
2 Bolt Assembly	**19** Front Sight Assembly	**38** Safety Pivot Pin
3 Bolt Plug	**20** Magazine	**39** Safety Snap Washer
4 Bolt Stop	**21** Magazine Follower	**40** Sear Safety Cam
5 Bolt Stop Pin	**22** Magazine Housing Screw	**41** Sear Pins
6 Bolt Stop Spring	**23** Magazine Spring	**42** Sear Spring
7 Buttplate	**24** Mainspring	**43** Sight Screws
8 Buttplate Screws	**25** Rear Guard Screw	**44** Sight Washers
9 Ejector	**26** Rear Sight Base	**45** Stock
10 Ejector Pin	**27** Rear Sight Elevation Screw	**46** Trigger
11 Ejector Spring	**28** Rear Sight Eyepiece	**47** Trigger Adjusting Screws
12 Extractor	**29** Rear Sight Leaf	**48** Trigger Connector
13 Extractor Rivet	**30** Rear Sight Nut	**49** Trigger Guard
14 Firing Pin	**31** Rear Sight Windage Screw	**50** Trigger Housing
15 Firing Pin Assembly	**32** Receiver Plug Screws	**51** Trigger Pin
16 Firing Pin Cross Pin	**33** Rib	**52** Trigger Spring
17 Firing Pin Head	**34** Rib Screw	**53** Trigger Stop Screw
	35 Safety Assembly	
	36 Safety Detent Ball	

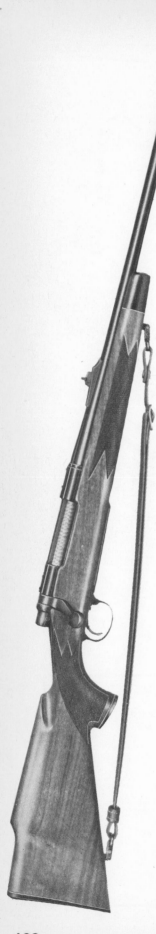

Remington Model 700

Similar/Identical Pattern Guns

The same basic assembly/disassembly steps for the Remington Model 700 also apply to the following guns:

Remington Model 78 Sportsman	Remington Model 700 BDL Custom Deluxe
Remington Model 700 AS, FS	Remington Model 700 BDL Varmint Special
Remington Model 700 ADL	Remington Model 700 Classic
Remington Model 700 C Grade	Remington Model 700 VLS Varmint
Remington Model 700 ADL Synthetic	Remington Model 700 AWR
Remington Model 700 VS	Remington Model 700 VS SF
Remington Model 700 Sendero	Remington Model 700 Sendero SF
Remington Model 700 BDL SS	Remington Model 700 BDL Left Hand
Remington Model 700 LSS	Remington Model 700 Safari Grade, Custom KS
Remington Model 700 APR	Remington Model 700 Mountain Rifle, Custom KS
Remington Model Seven, Custom KS	Remington Model Seven Youth
Remington Model Seven FS	Remington Model Seven Custom MS
Remington Model Seven SS	

Data:	Remington Model 700
Origin:	United States
Manufacturer:	Remington Arms Company Bridgeport, Connecticut
Cartridges:	Most popular calibers from 222 to 458
Magazine capacity:	4 rounds (3 in magnum calibers)
Overall length:	41½ to 44½ inches
Barrel length:	22 or 24 inches
Weight:	7 to 7½ pounds

When Remington discontinued the Model 721, 722, and 725 rifles in 1962, the successor was the excellent Model 700. Although the basic mechanical features were essentially the same, there were a number of small mechanical improvements. Since its introduction, the Model 700 has been offered in several sub-models, each having various special features. From a takedown viewpoint, the only notable difference would be the version with a blind magazine, lacking a separate magazine floorplate. Otherwise, the same instructions will apply.

Disassembly:

1. Open the bolt, and push upward on the bolt release, located inside the trigger guard, just forward of the trigger. Remove the bolt toward the rear.

2. Grip the underlug of the cocking piece firmly in a vise, and pull the bolt body toward the front to clear the front projection of the cocking piece from the rear of the bolt. Unscrew the bolt from the sleeve and striker assembly counter-clockwise (front view).

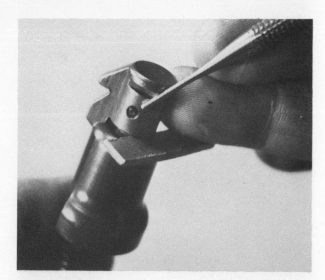

3. Grip the front portion of the striker firmly in a vise, taking care to exert no side pressure, and push the sleeve forward until a small piece of steel (at least 1/16-inch thickness) can be inserted between the front of the cocking piece and the rear of the sleeve. Grip the cocking piece in a vise, hold firmly to the striker and spring, and drift out the cross pin in the cocking piece. **Caution:** *The striker spring is fully compressed and is quite strong, so keep it under control.* When the pin is out, slowly release the spring tension and remove the striker, spring, and bolt sleeve toward the front.

4. Drifting out the cross pin at the front of the bolt will release the ejector and its spring for removal toward the front. **Caution:** *The ejector spring is partially compressed, even when at rest. Control it, and ease it out.*

5. The extractor is retained inside the cartridge head recess in the front face of the bolt by a tiny rivet, and removal in normal disassembly is definitely not recommended, as this will usually break the extractor. If removal is necessary to replace a broken extractor, use a small-diameter drift punch to drive the rivet inward. Note that the ejector must be removed before this is done.

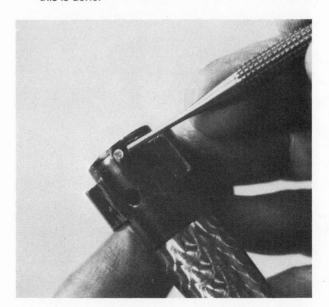

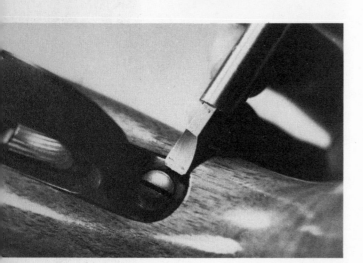

6. Remove the large vertical screw at the rear of the trigger guard. Remove the large vertical screw on the underside of the stock, forward of the trigger guard. Remove the vertical screw at the front of the trigger guard, and take the action out of the stock upward. The trigger guard can be taken off downward.

7. The magazine spring and follower will be released for removal as the action is taken out of the stock. The magazine box is retained by a small vertical screw through a tab at the rear, on the right underside of the receiver.

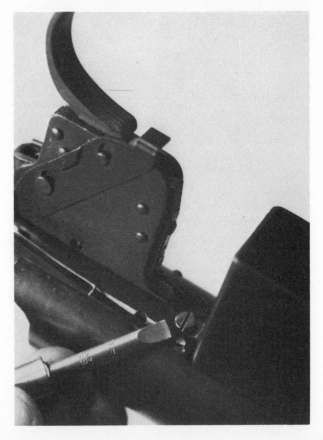

8. Drift out the front trigger housing cross pin toward the right.

9. Note that the rear trigger housing cross pin is also the retainer and pivot for the bolt stop and its spring, and the spring should be restrained while the pin is drifted out.

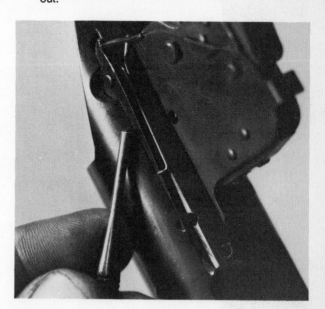

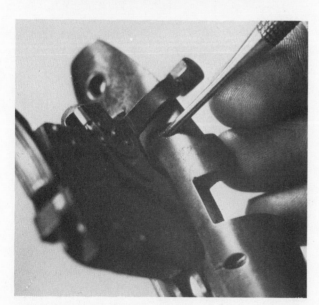

10. Set the safety-lever in the on-safe position, and drift out the rear trigger housing cross pin. Remember that the bolt stop and its spring will be released as the pin clears their position.

11. Remove the trigger assembly downward.

12. Remove the bolt stop and its spring.

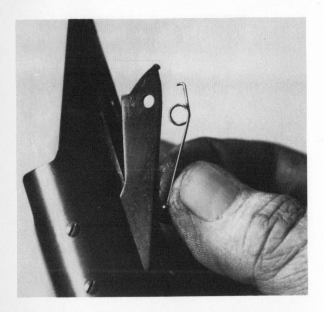

13. Remove the sear and its spring from the top of the trigger housing.

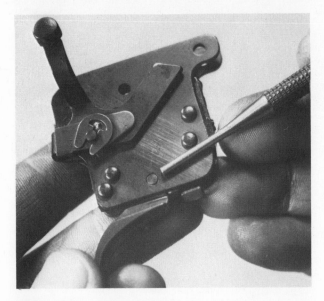

14. Remove the C-clip from the end of the safety pivot post on the right side of the housing, and take out the pivot post toward the left. The safety detent spring can then be pivoted downward and removed. Take care not to lose the small detent ball, which will be released as the spring is removed. The safety can now be moved out toward the rear. Removal of the pivot post will also free the bolt stop release from the left side of the housing.

15. Drifting out the trigger cross pin will release the trigger and trigger connector for removal. The other four cross pins hold the housing together, and are riveted in place. Removal of these pins is not recommended.

Reassembly Tips:

1. Before the bolt can be replaced in the receiver, the striker must be in the cocked position, as shown.

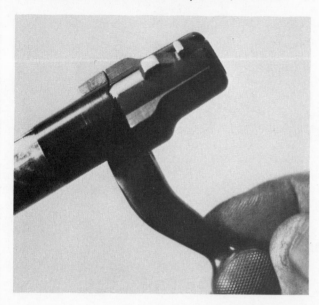

2. If a broken extractor is being replaced, a new extractor rivet should be used. Clinching the new rivet is difficult, as its inner head must be well supported while the outer tip is peened and spread. With a tool from B-Square, shown in the photo, the job is much less difficult.

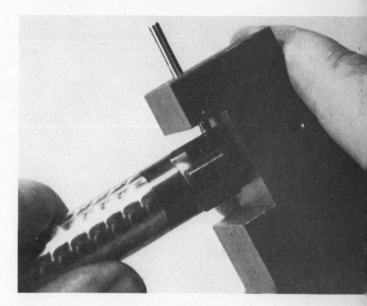

Model 700 Bolt-Action Rifle

KEY

1 Barrel Assembly
2 Bolt Assembly
3 Bolt Plug
4 Bolt Stop
5 Bolt Stop Pin
6 Bolt Stop Spring
7 Buttplate
8 Buttplate Spacer
9 Buttplate Screws
10 Center Guard Screw
11 Ejector
12 Ejector Pin
13 Ejector Spring
14 Extractor
15 Firing Pin
16 Firing Pin Assembly
17 Firing Pin Cross Pin
18 Floorplate Latch

19 Floorplate Latch Pin
20 Floorplate Latch Spring
21 Floorplate Pivot Pin
22 Front Guard Screw
23 Front Guard Screw Bushing
24 Front Sight
25 Front Sight Ramp
26 Front Sight Ramp Screws
27 Front Sight Hood
28 Front Swivel Bushing
29 Front Swivel Screw
30 Magazine
31 Magazine Follower
32 Magazine Spring
33 Mainspring
34 Rear Guard Screw
35 Rear Sight Aperture
36 Rear Sight Base
37 Rear Sight Base Screws
38 Rear Sight Slide

39 Elevation Screw
40 Rear Swivel Screw
41 Receiver Plug Screws
42 Sear Pin
43 Sling Strap Assembly
44 Stock Assembly
45 Swivel Assembly
46 Trigger Assembly
47 Trigger Guard
48 Trigger Guard Assembly
49 Windage Screw

Parts Not Shown
  Grip Cap
  Grip Cap Screw
  Grip Cap Spacer
  Magazine Tab Screw
  Stock Reinforcing Screw
  Stock Reinforcing Screw Dowel

Remington Model 742

Similar/Identical Pattern Guns

The same basic assembly/disassembly steps for the Remington Model 742 also apply to the following guns:

Remington Model 74 Sportsman	**Remington Model 740**
Remington Model 742 BDL	**Remington Model 742 Carbine**
Remington Model 7400	**Remington Model 7400 Carbine**
Remington Model Four	

Data:	Remington Model 742
Origin:	United States
Manufacturer:	Remington Arms Company Bridgeport, Connecticut
Cartridges:	6mm Remington, 243 Winchester, 280 Remington, 308 Winchester, 30-06 Springfield
Magazine capacity:	4 rounds
Overall length:	42 inches
Barrel length:	22 inches
Weight:	7½ pounds

The original version of this gun, the Model 740, was first offered in 1955, and was made for only five years. It was redesigned in 1960 to become the Model 742. A carbine version was also available, with an 18½-inch barrel. In 1982, a slight redesign created the Model 7400 and the Model Four. In 1985, a no-frills version was called the Model 74 Sportsman. The last two named were discontinued in 1987. In the later models, the extractor is not riveted to the bolt. Otherwise, the instructions will apply.

Disassembly:

1. Remove the magazine, and cycle the action to cock the internal hammer. Push the safety across to the on-safe position. Use a drift punch to push out the two cross pins in the receiver.

2. Move the trigger group forward, then take it off downward.

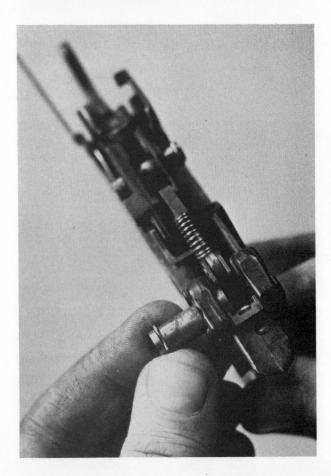

3. Push the safety to the off-safe position. Restrain the hammer, pull the trigger to release it, and ease it forward. Keeping the trigger pulled to the rear, push out the rear cross pin sleeve toward the left.

4. Removal of the pin sleeve will allow the top of the trigger to move further toward the rear, easing the tension of the combination sear and trigger spring. This spring can now be flexed off its stud on the rear of the sear, and removed upward.

5. Drift out the trigger cross pin toward the right.

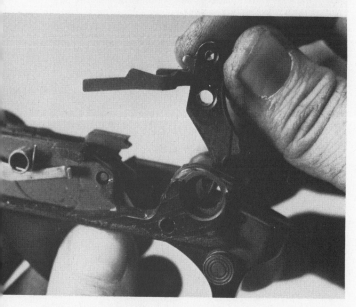

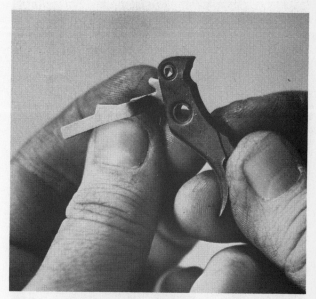

6. Remove the trigger assembly upward, turning it slightly to allow its left connector arm to clear the shelf on the trigger housing.

7. If necessary for repair, the right and left connector arms can be detached from the trigger by drifting out the cross pin. However, its left tip is semi-riveted on the left side, and in normal disassembly it is best left in place. If removal is necessary, the pin must be drifted out toward the right, and take care that the parts are well supported, to avoid deforming the top wings of the trigger.

8. Push out the small cross pin at the upper rear of the trigger housing toward the right, holding a fingertip over the hole on top to restrain the released safety spring.

9. Remove the safety spring from its hole in the top, and, if possible, the detent ball beneath it. If the ball can't be shaken out at this time, it can be removed after the safety is taken out. Push out the safety toward either side, and if the detent ball has not been previously removed, insert a small drift into the hole at the top, and push the ball downward, into the safety tunnel. Take care to catch it as it rolls out.

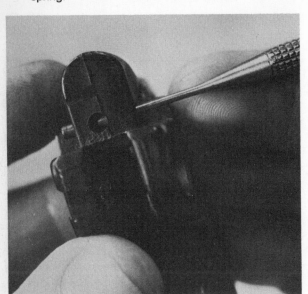

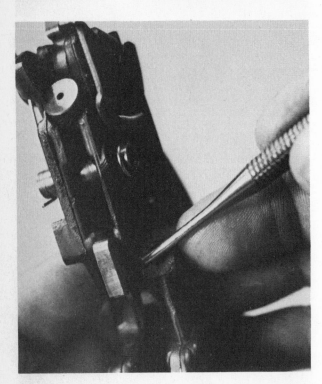

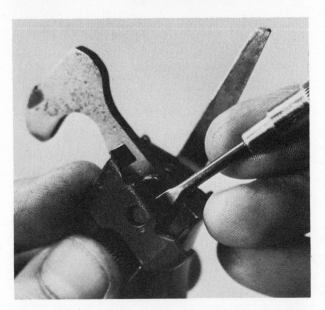

11. The magazine catch is moved off its post on the trigger housing toward the right for removal. **Caution:** *The catch spring is compressed even when at rest, so control it during removal. If the catch is very tight, it may have to be pried gently off its post.*

10. The sear pivot pin is accessible on the right side of the trigger housing by angling a small drift punch as shown. After it is started out, it can be removed toward the left. The sear is then taken out upward.

12. Unhook the disconnector spring from its slot in the left end of the front cross pin sleeve, and push out the sleeve toward the right.

13. Pull the hammer back to slightly depress the hammer spring plunger, and relieve tension on the disconnector, and push the hammer and disconnector pivot pin toward the right, just far enough to clear the disconnector.

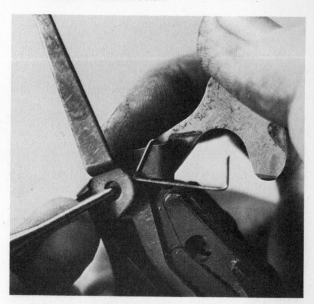

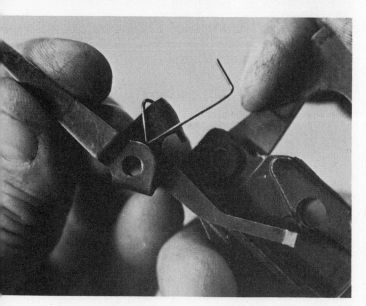

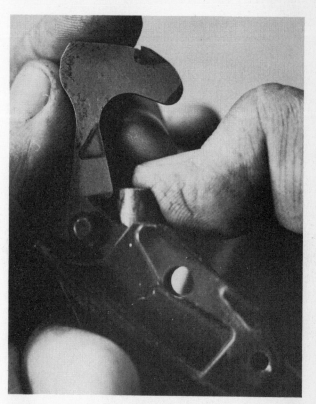

14. Remove the disconnector and its spring. Keep a firm grip on the hammer during this operation, with its spring plunger slightly depressed. The disconnector spring is easily separated from the disconnector after the part is removed.

15. Ease the hammer forward while holding and restraining the plunger, slowly releasing the tension of the spring.

16. Push the hammer pivot pin out toward the right, and take off the hammer. Remove the hammer plunger and spring from their recess in the trigger housing.

17. The buttstock is retained by a through-bolt from the rear, accessible by taking off the buttplate. Use a B-Square stock tool or a large screwdriver to unscrew the bolt, and remove the stock toward the rear. Take care not to lose the stock bearing plate, mounted between the stock and the receiver. The forend is retained by a large screw in its forward tip. Remove the screw, and take off the forend cap. The forend can then be slid forward and off.

18. Use a roll pin punch to drift out the action tube support pin, the large cross pin in the gas tube housing.

19. Draw the bolt all the way to the rear, and move the action tube support bracket back off the gas tube housing. Tip the action tube downward, and slide it toward the front when it has cleared the lower edge of the gas tube housing. Take care not to release the bolt at this time, as it is very important to avoid damage to the gas tube.

20. Release the bolt very slowly as the action tube is withdrawn, easing the tension of the recoil spring. Remove the recoil spring from the rear of the action bar sleeve. It will still have some tension, so control it and ease it out.

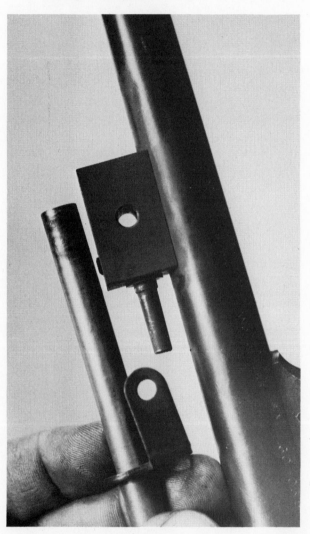

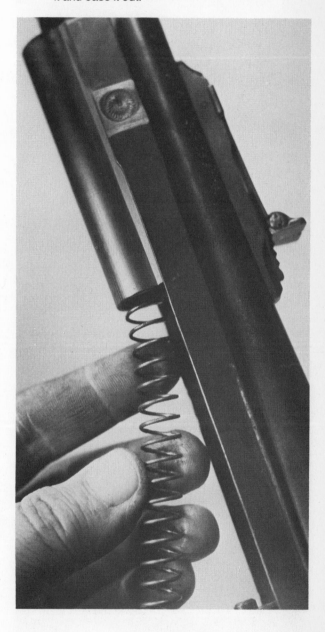

21a. With a Brownells wrench, as shown, or an open-end wrench of the proper size, turn the barrel nut counter-clockwise (front view) and remove it. Take off the forend stabilizer spring, mounted behind the nut.

21b. If the barrel nut has never been removed, it will be quite tight, and it may be necessary to rap the wrench handle with a hammer to start the nut.

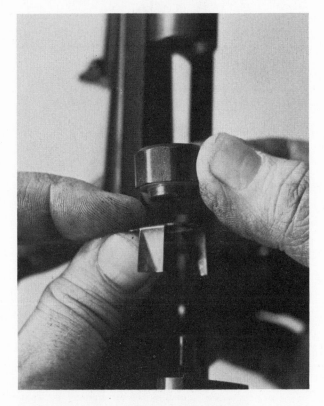

22. Move the bolt partially toward the rear to clear its locking lugs from the barrel, and move the barrel forward out of the receiver. Move the bolt back to the front to allow space between the action bars, and turn the barrel at a right angle to the receiver to clear its underlug projections from the action bars. Lift the barrel straight up and out of the action bars.

23. Position the bolt handle and the ejection port cover to give access to the bolt handle retaining pin, and drive out the pin downward. Remove the bolt handle toward the right.

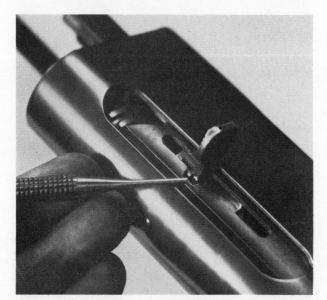

24. Remove the bolt and action bar assembly toward the front, taking off the ejection port cover as it emerges from the receiver.

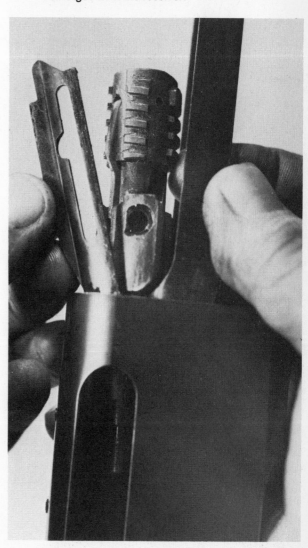

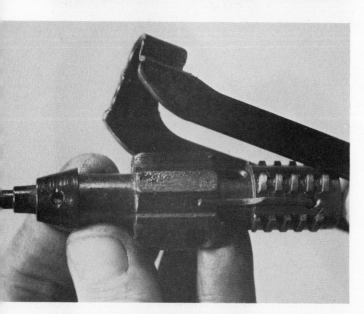

25. The bolt is easily detached from the action bar assembly by moving it downward, turning it slightly, and taking it off toward the rear.

26. The firing pin is retained in the bolt by a cross pin at the rear, and the firing pin and its return spring are removed toward the rear.

27. Insert a small screwdriver into the cam pin track at the front to lift the cam pin out of its hole in the bolt carrier. The bolt can then be separated from the carrier.

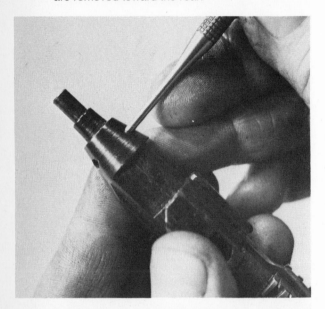

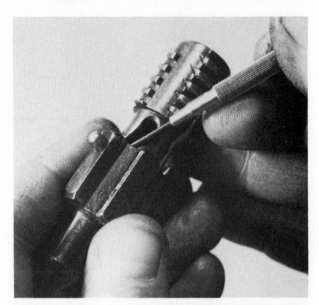

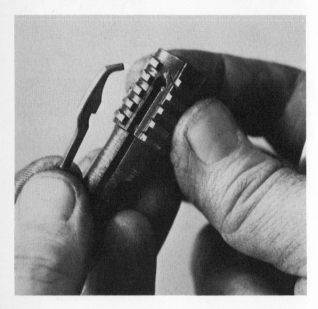

28. The bolt latch can now be moved toward the rear and upward for removal. Take care that the bolt latch pivot and plunger, and their springs, are not lost from their holes beneath the bolt latch—these are very small parts.

29. The ejector is removed by drifting out its cross pin near the front of the bolt. **Caution:** *The ejector spring is quite strong, so restrain the ejector during removal, and ease it out.*

30. The extractor is mounted inside the cartridge head recess at the front of the bolt, and is held in place by a small rivet on the left side. Except for replacement of a broken extractor, this assembly should not be disturbed, as attempted removal will almost always break the extractor.

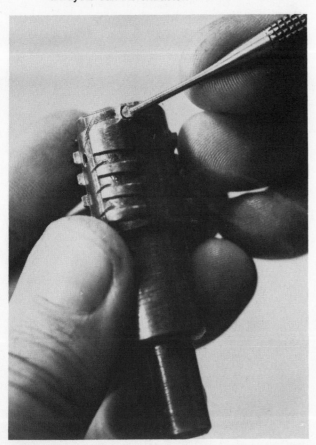

Reassembly Tips:

1. If the extractor has been removed for replacement of a broken one, installing and setting the new rivet can be very difficult, unless a tool such as the one shown is used. Available from B-Square, it is designed specifically for this job on all of the guns from Remington that have an extractor of this type.

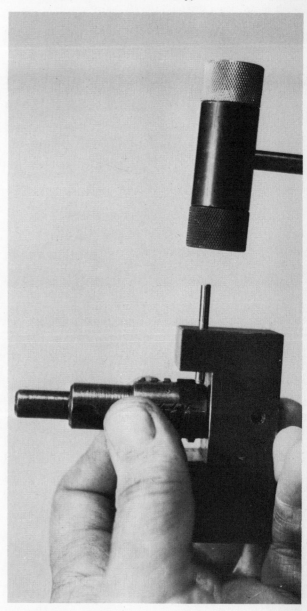

2. When replacing the bolt carrier on the rear of the bolt, note that there is a notch on the carrier which must align with the tail of the bolt latch. The bolt latch must be depressed slightly as the parts are rejoined.

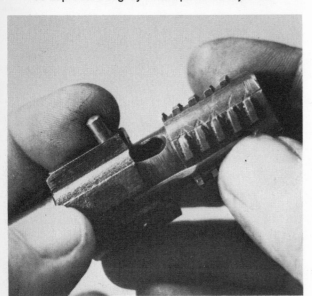

3. When replacing the bolt handle retaining pin, note that it has lengthwise stake marks at one end, and the opposite end should be inserted. Grip the pin with sharp-nosed pliers, insert it from inside the receiver, and drive it upward into place. Be sure the bolt handle is fully in place, and properly aligned with the hole, before driving in the pin.

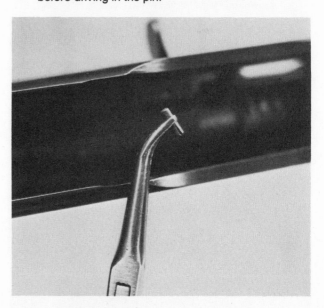

4. When replacing the barrel nut and forend stabilizer spring, be sure they are installed as shown, with the outer flanges of the stabilizer at the top, and the rebated nose of the barrel nut toward the rear.

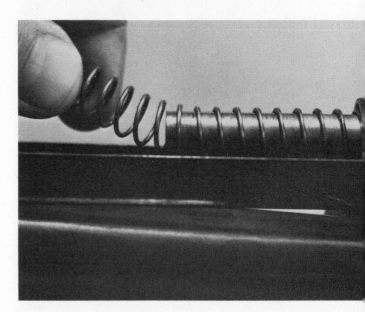

5. When replacing the recoil spring, partially insert the action tube, and slip the spring onto it from the rear, compressing the spring until its rear tip can be lifted onto its stud at the center of the barrel nut bolt. Then, push the action tube all the way to the rear. Once again, take care that the projecting gas tube is not damaged during replacement of the tube and its support bracket.

6. When replacing the front trigger group cross pin sleeve, note that it must be oriented with its slot in the left end on the underside, so the disconnector spring can be hooked into the slot.

7. When replacing the safety spring, use a small screwdriver to depress the spring while inserting the cross pin, pointed end first.

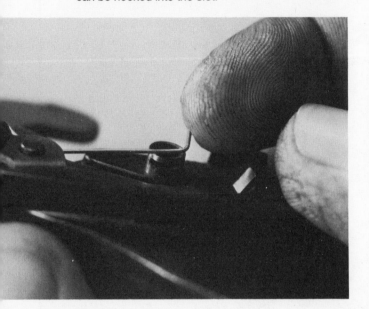

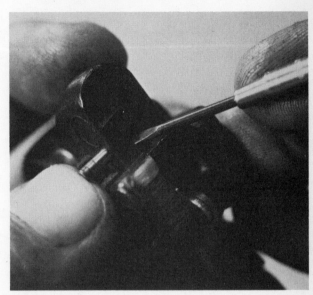

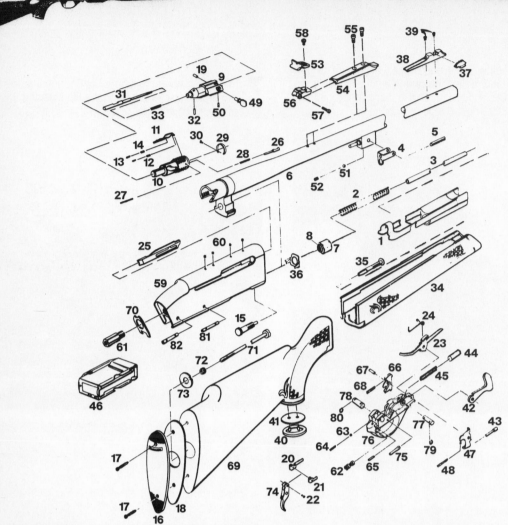

KEY

1 Action Bar Assembly
2 Action Spring
3 Action Tube
4 Action Tube Support
5 Action Tube Support Pin
6 Barrel Assembly
7 Barrel Takedown Nut
8 Barrel Takedown Nut Washer
9 Bolt Carrier
10 Breechbolt Assembly
11 Bolt Latch
12 Bolt Latch Pivot
13 Bolt Latch Springs
14 Bolt Latch Spring Plunger
15 Breech Ring Bolt
16 Buttplate
17 Buttplate Screws
18 Buttplate Spacer
19 Cam Pin
20 Connector, Left
21 Connector, Right
22 Connector Pin
23 Disconnector
24 Disconnector Spring
25 Ejector Port Cover
26 Ejector
27 Ejector Retaining Pin

28 Ejector Spring
29 Extractor
30 Extractor Rivet
31 Firing Pin
32 Firing Pin Retaining Pin
33 Firing Pin Retractor Spring
34 Forend Assembly
35 Forend Screw
36 Forend Spring
37 Front Sight
38 Front Sight Ramp
39 Front Sight Ramp Screws
40 Grip Cap
41 Grip Cap Spacer
42 Hammer
43 Hammer Pin
44 Hammer Plunger
45 Hammer Spring
46 Magazine Assembly
47 Magazine Latch
48 Magazine Latch Spring
49 Operating Handle
50 Operating Handle Retaining Pin
51 Orifice Ball
52 Orifice Screw
53 Rear Sight Aperture
54 Rear Sight Base
55 Rear Sight Base Screws
56 Rear Sight Slide

57 Elevation Screw
58 Windage Screw
59 Receiver Assembly
60 Receiver Plug Screws
61 Receiver Stud
62 Safety
63 Safety Detent Ball
64 Safety Spring
65 Safety Spring Retaining Pin
66 Sear
67 Sear Pin
68 Sear Spring
69 Stock
70 Stock Bearing Plate
71 Stock Bolt
72 Stock Bolt Lock Washer
73 Stock Bolt Washer
74 Trigger
75 Trigger Pin
76 Trigger Plate
77 Trigger Plate Pin Bushing, Front
78 Trigger Plate Pin Bushing, Rear
79 Trigger Plate Pin Detent Spring, Front
80 Trigger Plate Pin Detent Spring, Rear
81 Trigger Plate Pin, Front
82 Trigger Plate Pin, Rear

Remington Nylon 66

Similar/Identical Pattern Guns

The same basic assembly/disassembly steps for the Remington Nylon 66 also apply to the following guns:

F.I.E. Model GR-8

Magtech Model MT-66

Remington Nylon 66GS

Remington Nylon 66MB

Remington Nylon 66 Bicentennial

Data:	Remington Nylon 66
Origin:	United States
Manufacturer:	Remington Arms Company Bridgeport, Connecticut
Cartridge:	22 Long Rifle
Magazine capacity:	14 rounds
Overall length:	$38^1/_2$ inches
Barrel length:	$19^5/_8$ inches
Weight:	4 pounds

Around 1959, when the Remington Nylon 66 first arrived on the scene, many firearms traditionalists sneered at its DuPont Zytel stock/receiver, stamped-steel parts and expansion-type springs. Over the years, though, they found that it works, and keeps working, uncleaned, mistreated, and abused—a tribute to Wayne Leek and the design team at Remington. For those not familiar with its mechanism, though, the Nylon 66 can be a disassembly/reassembly nightmare. The Nylon 66 was discontinued by Remington in 1988, but has been made in South America since then. This later version was marketed for a short time by the now-defunct Firearms Import & Export (F.I.E.) as the GR-8, and by Magtech Recreational Products as their MT-66.

Disassembly:

1. Remove the inner magazine tube from the stock. Grip the bolt handle firmly and pull it straight out toward the right.

2. Back out the two cross-screws, located near the lower edge of the receiver cover, and remove them toward the right.

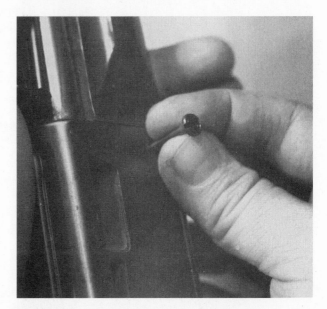

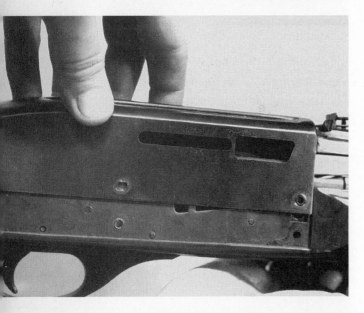

3. Remove the receiver cover assembly upward. The internal cartridge guide spring and the rear sight base are riveted on the cover, and removal is not advisable in normal disassembly.

4. Remove the ejector from its recess in the left side of the receiver.

5. Loosen the large cross-slotted screw on the underside of the stock, just forward of the trigger guard; then push it upward to raise the barrel retaining piece until its upper cross bar clears its recess on top of the barrel. Slide the barrel out toward the front.

6. The front sight is retained on top of the barrel by two screws, one at each end.

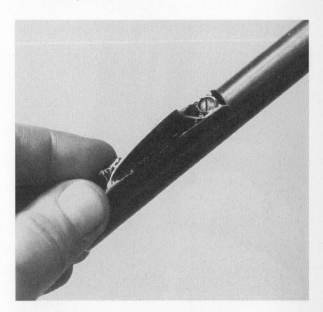

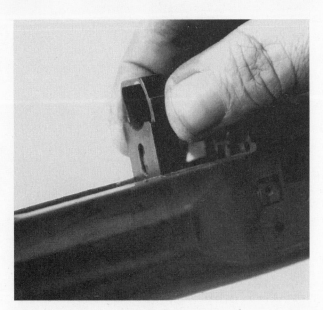

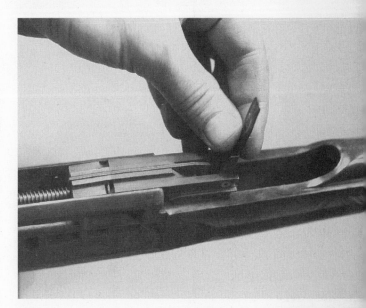

7. Take out the cross-slotted screw from the bottom of the stock, and lift the barrel retainer and its front plate out of their recess in the top of the stock.

8. Be sure the hammer is in its cocked position (at the rear), and the safety in the on-safe position. Grasp the cartridge guide, and move the bolt forward out of its tracks in the receiver. Remove the bolt spring and its guide toward the front.

9. Move the safety to the off-safe position, restrain the hammer against the tension of its spring, and pull the trigger to release the hammer. Ease the spring tension slowly, and move the hammer forward out of its tracks in the receiver. Remove the hammer spring and its guide.

10. Push out the cross pin located in the receiver just above the forward end of the trigger guard (arrow). Tip the trigger guard downward at the front, disengage its rear hook from inside the receiver, and remove the guard downward.

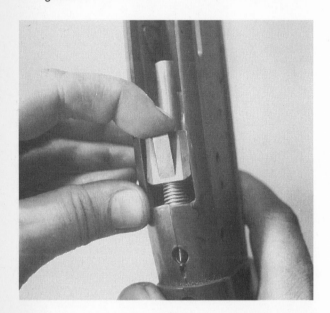

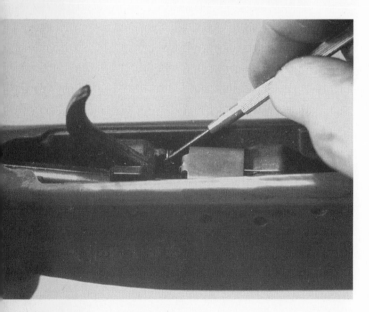

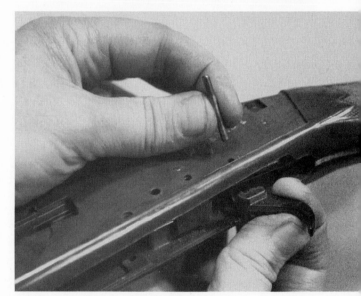

11. Use a small tool to unhook the trigger spring from its groove on the front of the trigger.

12. Push out the trigger cross pin, and remove the trigger downward.

13. Push out the cross pin just below the ejector recess (arrow), and remove the cartridge stop and its flat spring from the bottom of the receiver.

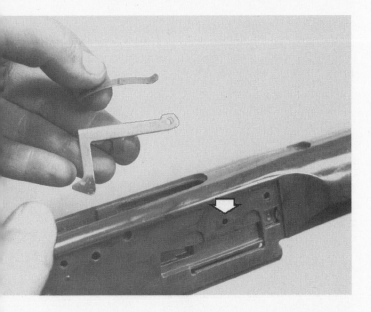

14. Use a tool to push the front of the cartridge feed throat (insert) downward, and tip it out of its recess for removal from the bottom of the receiver.

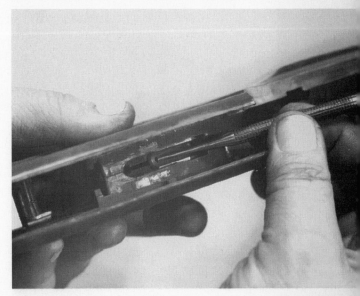

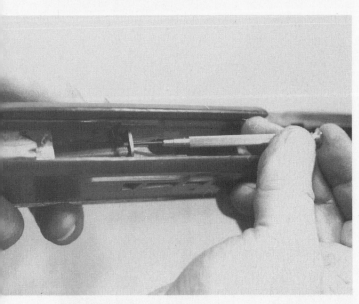

15. Use a small tool to lift the magazine tube retainer from its recess inside the receiver, and remove it from the top. Take out the magazine tube toward the rear.

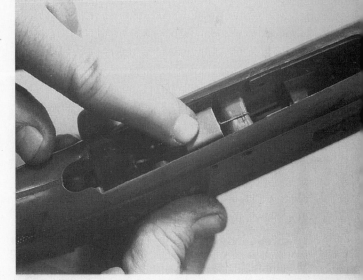

16. Restrain the sear at the top of the receiver against its spring tension, and push the disconnector pivot at the bottom of the receiver to release the sear. Allow the sear to pivot upward, slowly releasing the tension of its spring.

17. Use a tool to disengage the hook of the disconnector pivot spring from the receiver cross-piece at the bottom.

18. Push out the disconnector pivot points, one on each side of the receiver. After one has been removed, the other may be pushed out from the inside, using one of the other cross pins already removed or a drift punch.

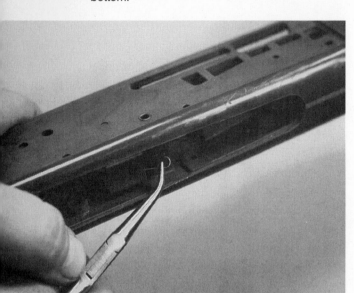

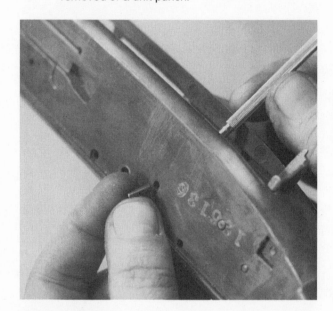

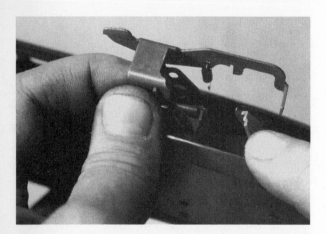

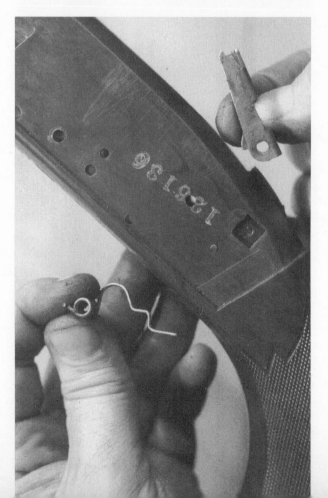

19. Depress the sear slightly to clear the rear arm of the disconnector, and remove the disconnector assembly from the top of the receiver. The disconnector is easily separated from its pivot by squeezing the sides of the pivot inward just enough to detach the lugs from the holes in the disconnector. The springs are also easily detached by turning their ends out of the holes in the parts.

20. Push out the sear pivot pin, and remove the sear and its spring from the top of the receiver (actually, the spring will usually fall from the bottom as the pin is taken out).

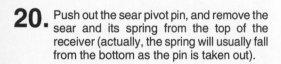

21. Push out the safety-lever cam pin, the last cross pin at the rear of the receiver. This will allow the safety-lever to drop, and the safety and its attached lever can then be removed upward.

22. Use a fingernail or a small tool to move the safety detent spring retaining pin out toward the rear. The pin has a groove at its rear tip to aid removal. The detent spring is not under heavy tension, but it can flip the pin as it is removed, so restrain it with a fingertip during removal. Take out the detent spring and the ball bearing from their hole in the top of the receiver, and take care that the bearing isn't lost.

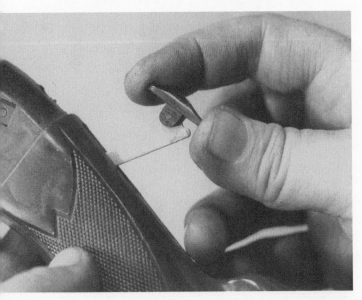

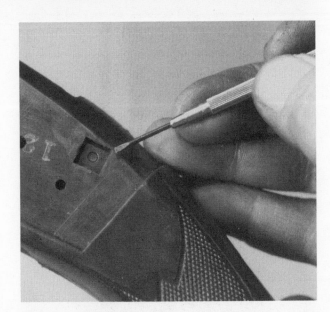

23. The two internal cross screws with square nuts on the left side do not retain parts, and their removal is neither necessary nor advisable during normal takedown.

24. The firing pin is retained in the bolt by a cross pin on top, near the rear of the bolt. The retaining pin is bent down on each side to lock it in place, and one end must be pried upward before the pin is drifted out. The firing pin is then removed toward the rear.

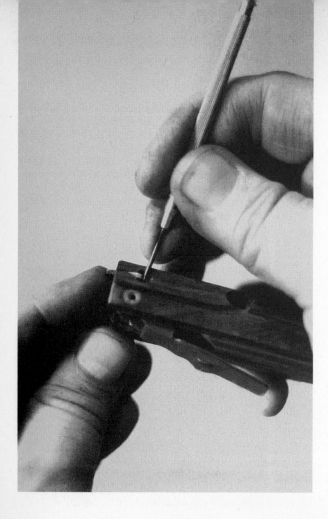

25. Insert a small screwdriver between the rear of the extractor and its plunger, and depress the plunger while lifting the extractor out of its recess. **Caution:** *The spring is under compression, so take care it doesn't get away.* Ease it out, and remove the plunger and spring.

26. A roll pin across the top front of the bolt retains the cartridge guide. Drifting out the pin will release the guide for removal. Be sure to use a roll pin punch to avoid deforming the pin.

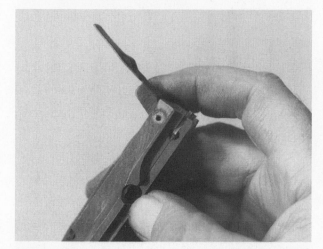

Reassembly Tips:

1. When replacing the disconnector assembly, remember that the sear (arrow) must be tipped forward to allow the rear arm of the disconnector to go behind the sear.

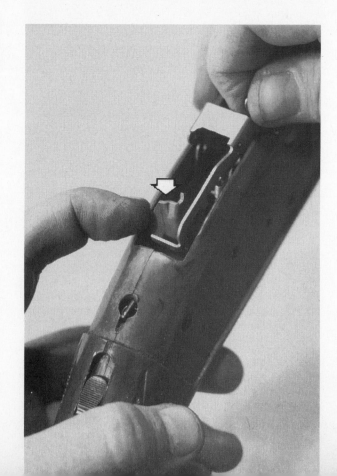

2. Remember that the cartridge feed throat ("cartridge insert") must be put in from below. Insert its rear tip first; then swing its front wings upward into the recesses while holding the rear tip in place with a tool, as shown. When the cartridge feed throat is in place, invert the gun so the feed throat will not fall back into the stock before installation of the cartridge stop (the front tip of the stop spring holds the feed throat in place). Installation of the cartridge feed throat is the single most difficult point in the reassembly of the Nylon 66.

3. Do not attempt to install the cartridge stop and its flat spring at the same time. Install the stop, then insert the spring, with its forward end going under the pin (remember, the gun is inverted), and push the spring forward until its indented catch locks on the front edge of the cartridge stop.

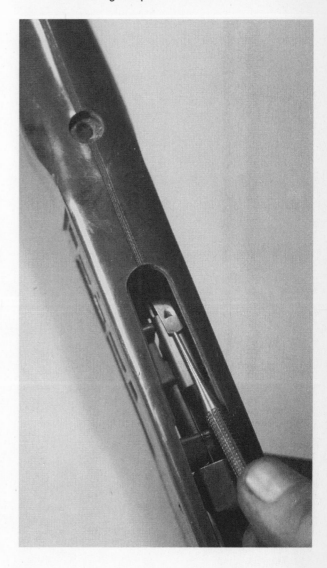

4. When properly installed, the front lip of the sear (arrow) should be under the front cross-piece of the disconnector, as shown.

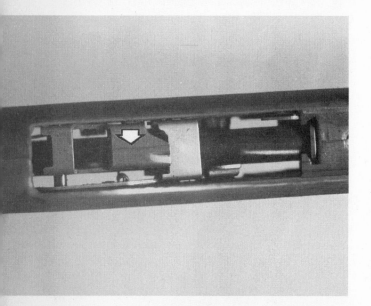

When reinstalling the hammer assembly, it is necessary to use a small tool to depress the sear while holding the trigger back, allowing the hammer to move to the rear. When the hammer is moved back to the cocked position, set the safety in the on-safe position to prevent release of the hammer while the bolt is installed.

When installing the barrel retainer, note that the front plate goes at the front of the retainer, and that the plate has an oblong slot which mates with a stud on the retainer.

Before replacing the receiver cover, be sure the ejector is in place in its recess on the left side. This part is often left out during reassembly, or drops off if the gun is tilted toward the left during replacement of the cover.

Before replacing the cover, be sure the cartridge guide is flipped over forward, to lie on top of the barrel.

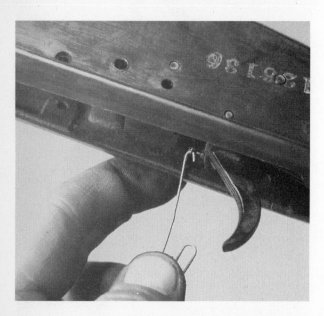

5. It is very difficult to reattach the trigger spring to the front of the trigger without a small hooked tool. The one shown was made from an opened paper clip.

Nylon 66 Autoloading Rifle

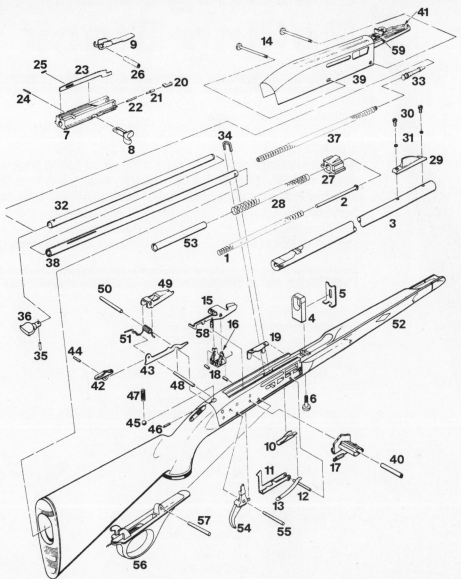

KEY

1 Action Spring	**20** Extractor	**41** Rear Sight Rivet
2 Action Spring Plunger	**21** Extractor Plunger	**42** Safety
3 Barrel	**22** Extractor Spring	**43** Safety-Lever
4 Barrel Bracket	**23** Firing Pin	**44** Safety-Lever Pin
5 Barrel Support	**24** Firing Pin Retaining Pin	**45** Safety Detent Ball
6 Barrel Lock Screw	**25** Firing Pin Retractor Spring	**46** Safety Detent Retaining Pin
7 Bolt	**26** Firing Pin Stop Pin	**47** Safety Detent Spring
8 Bolt Handle	**27** Firing Pin Striker	**48** Safety-Lever Cam Pin
9 Cartridge Feed Guide	**28** Firing Pin Striker Spring	**49** Sear
10 Cartridge Feed Insert	**29** Front Sight	**50** Sear Assembly Pin
11 Cartridge Stop	**30** Front Sight Screws	**51** Sear Spring
12 Cartridge Stop Pin	**31** Front Sight Washers	**52** Stock Assembly
13 Cartridge Stop Spring	**32** Inner Magazine Tube	**53** Striker Spring Sleeve
14 Cover Screws	**33** Magazine Follower	**54** Trigger Complete
15 Disconnector	**34** Magazine Lock	**55** Trigger Assembly Pin
16 Disconnector Pivot	**35** Magazine Pin	**56** Trigger Guard
17 Disconnector Pivot Spring	**36** Magazine Plug	**57** Trigger Guard Assembly Pin
18 Disconnector Pivot Pins	**37** Magazine Spring	**58** Trigger Spring
19 Ejector	**38** Outer Magazine Tube	**59** Windage Screw
	39 Receiver Cover Assembly	
	40 Rear Cover Screw Bushing	

Remington Rolling Block

Similar/Identical Pattern Guns

The same basic assembly/disassembly steps for the Remington Rolling Block also apply to the following guns:

Navy Arms Rolling Block	Navy Arms Rolling Block Buffalo Rifle
Navy Arms Rolling Block Buffalo Carbine	Navy Arms Rolling Block Baby Carbine
Navy Arms Rolling Block Creedmoor Target	Remington No. 1 Rolling Block Creedmoor
Remington No. 2	Remington No. 3
Remington No. 4	Remington No. 5
Star Rolling Block Carbine	Uberti Rolling Block Baby Carbine

Data:	Remington Rolling Block
Origin:	United States
Manufacturer:	Remington Arms Company, Ilion, New York, Springfield Armory, and armories in several foreign countries
Cartridges:	50 U.S., 45 Danish Remington, 43 Spanish, 7x57, many others
Overall length:	46 inches (carbine, 35⅝ inches)
Barrel length:	30 inches (carbine, 20½ inches)
Weight:	8½ pounds (carbine, 7 pounds)

Note: Weights and measurements are for the 7mm model of 1897-1902, used mainly in Central and South America

In 1866, Joseph Rider redesigned the Remington-Geiger action, and the rolling block was born. In the years between 1870 and 1900, this gun became the official military arm of a large number of countries, and was also used by the U.S. Navy. Its ingenious "rolling" breechblock made the action a very strong one, and its simplicity made it ideal for military use. The era of the bolt-action repeater ended its military career, but Remington made it as a sporting rifle up to 1933. In more recent times, European-made reproductions of the rolling block have been offered by several importers. All are mechanically the same as the originals.

Disassembly:

1. Back out the vertical screw at the rear of the upper tang, and remove the buttstock toward the rear. If the stock is very tight, bump the front of the comb with the heel of the hand to start it.

2. If the gun is equipped with a saddle ring, back out the ring bar screw, and swing the bar upward. Remove the ring. The bar is threaded into the side of the receiver, and is not removed at this time.

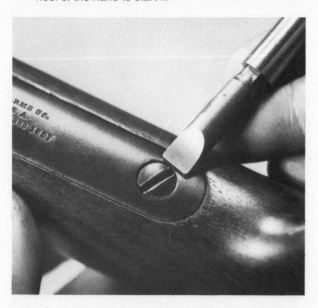

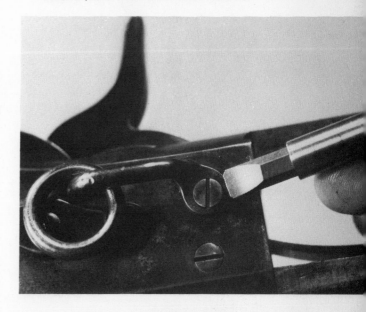

3. Remove the screw at the center of the lock plate, located between the two large pins on the left side of the receiver (Note: Remington called the lock plate the "button"). Take off the lock plate toward the left.

4. Cock the hammer, and push out the breechblock pivot pin toward the left. If the pin is tight, use a non-marring nylon or brass drift punch to start it.

5. Remove the small screw on the left side of the receiver, just below the breechblock pivot hole.

6. Remove the breechblock assembly, including the ejector, upward and toward the rear.

7. The ejector is easily detached from the left side of the breechblock.

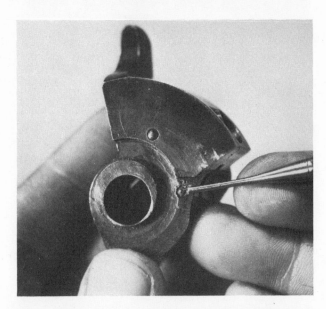

8. Drifting out the lower cross pin in the breechblock will allow the firing pin retractor to be taken out downward, and removal of the upper cross pin will free the firing pin, which is taken out toward the rear.

9. Restrain the hammer, pull the trigger, and ease the hammer down beyond its normal full forward position. Push out the hammer pivot toward the left.

10. Remove the hammer upward.

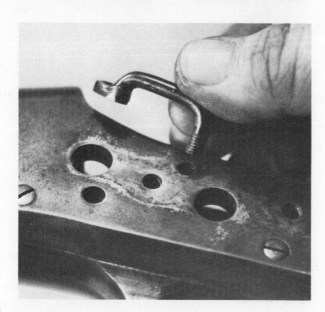

11. If the gun has a saddle ring bar, it can now be unscrewed from the left side of the receiver and taken off. When unscrewing it, lift its free end slightly during the first few turns, to avoid marring the receiver.

12. Remove the cross screw at the lower front of the receiver.

13. Remove the cross screw at the lower rear of the receiver.

14. Remove the trigger guard assembly downward and toward the rear.

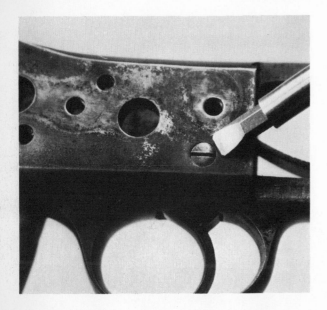

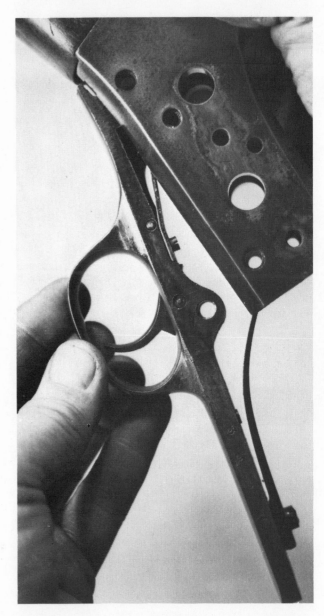

15. Remove the hammer spring screw, and take off the hammer spring upward.

16. Remove the trigger spring screw, and take out the trigger spring upward.

17. Drift out the trigger cross pin, and remove the trigger upward.

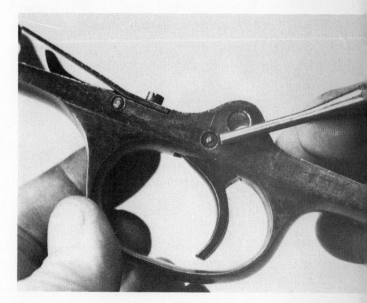

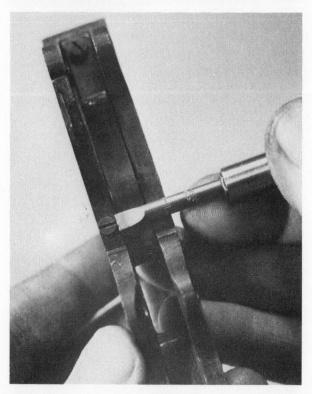

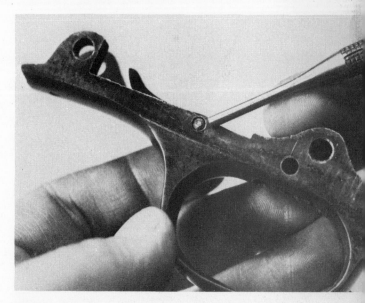

19. Drift out the cross pin at the front of the guard, and remove the breechblock locking lever upward. **Caution:** *This pin is very near the upper edge of the guard frame, so take care that the edge is not broken during removal.*

18. Remove the ejector spring screw, and take off the ejector spring upward.

20. Remove the vertical screw at the front of the guard unit, and take out the locking lever spring upward.

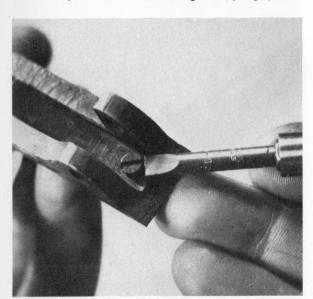

21. If the gun is a full-length rifle, there will be three barrel bands to be removed. On the carbine, as shown, remove the single band by depressing its spring latch and sliding it off toward the front. The forend wood can now be taken off downward.

22. Before the upper handguard wood can be removed, the rear sight must be taken off by backing out its two screws, at the front and rear of the sight base.

Reassembly Tips:

1. After the hammer is installed on its pivot in the receiver, insert a tool from the rear to depress the front of the hammer spring, to insure that the tip of the spring engages the spring lobe on the rear of the hammer.

2. When replacing the breechblock assembly in the receiver, you must exert downward pressure on the assembly while inserting the pivot pin, to slightly compress the lock lever and the ejector spring.

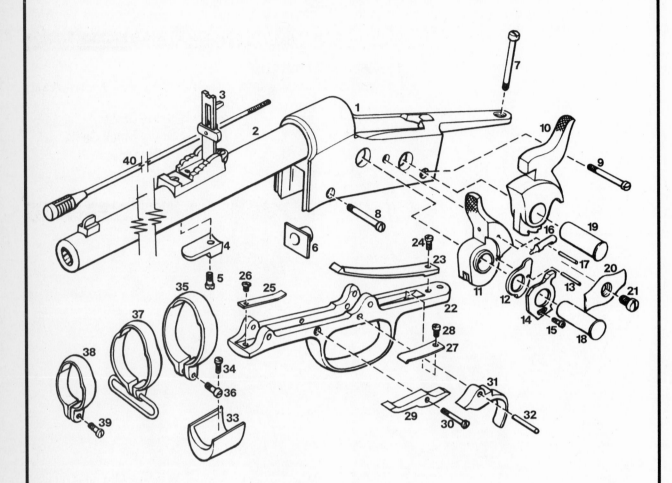

KEY

1 Receiver
2 Barrel
3 Rear Sight
4 Recoil Stud
5 Recoil Stud Screw
6 Ramrod Stop
7 Tang Screw
8 Front Guard Plate Screw
9 Rear Guard Plate Screw
10 Hammer
11 Breechblock
12 Firing Pin Retractor
13 Retractor Pin
14 Extractor
15 Extractor Screw

16 Firing Pin
17 Firing Pin Limit Pin
18 Breechblock Pin
19 Hammer Pin
20 Button
21 Button Screw
22 Guard Plate
23 Mainspring
24 Mainspring Screw
25 Lever Spring
26 Lever Spring Screw
27 Trigger Spring
28 Trigger Spring Screw
29 Locking Lever
30 Locking Lever Screw
31 Trigger
32 Trigger Pin

33 Stock Tip
34 Stock Tip Screw
35 Rear Band
36 Rear Band Screw
37 Middle Band and Screw
38 Front Band
39 Front Band Screw
40 Ramrod

Parts Not Shown
Buttstock
Buttplate
Buttplate Screws
Rear Stock Swivel
Rear Stock Swivel Screws

Ruger 10/22

Similar/Identical Pattern Guns

The same basic assembly/disassembly steps for the Ruger 10/22 also apply to the following guns:

Ruger 10/22 Sporter

Ruger 10/22 International

Ruger 10/22 Deluxe Sporter

Ruger K10/22RP All-Weather

AMT Lightning 25/22

AMT Lightning Small Game

Ruger 10/22T Target

Data:	Ruger 10/22
Origin:	United States
Manufacturer:	Sturm, Ruger & Company Southport, Connecticut
Cartridge:	22 Long Rifle
Magazine capacity:	10 rounds
Overall length:	$36^3/_4$ inches
Barrel length:	$18^1/_2$ inches
Weight:	$5^3/_4$ pounds

Since its introduction in 1964, the 10/22 has established an enviable record of reliability. Over the past fifteen years, I have repaired only one of these guns, and that one had been altered by its owner. Originally offered in Carbine, Sporter and International models, the latter with a full Mannlicher-style stock was discontinued for many years. The gun is again available in those three styles, plus two others, the only differences being in the stock, barrel band and steel. The instructions will generally apply to any of the 10/22 guns.

Disassembly:

1. Loosen or remove the cross-screw at the lower end of the barrel band, and take off the barrel band toward the front. If the band is tight, applying slight downward pressure on the barrel will make it move off more easily.

2. Remove the magazine, and cycle the action to cock the internal hammer. Back out the main stock screw, located on the underside just forward of the magazine well.

3. Center the safety halfway between its right and left positions so it will clear the stock on each side, and move the action upward out of the stock.

4. When the action is removed from the stock, the bolt stop pin, the large cross pin at the rear of the receiver, will probably be loose and can be easily taken out at this time.

5. Drift out the front and rear cross pins (arrows) that hold the trigger group on the receiver. Then remove the trigger group downward.

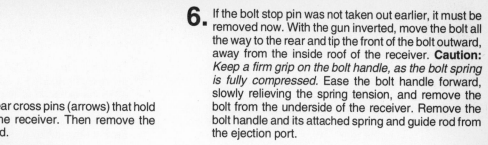

6. If the bolt stop pin was not taken out earlier, it must be removed now. With the gun inverted, move the bolt all the way to the rear and tip the front of the bolt outward, away from the inside roof of the receiver. **Caution:** *Keep a firm grip on the bolt handle, as the bolt spring is fully compressed.* Ease the bolt handle forward, slowly relieving the spring tension, and remove the bolt from the underside of the receiver. Remove the bolt handle and its attached spring and guide rod from the ejection port.

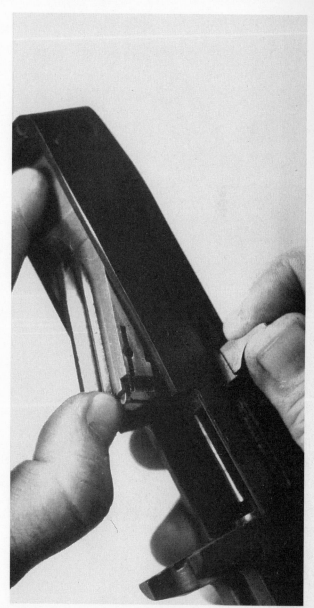

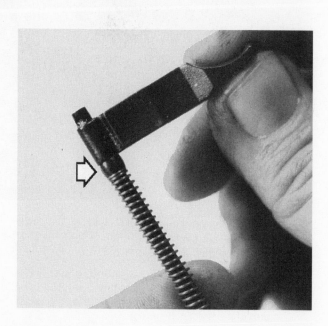

7. The bolt spring guide rod is staked at the forward end, ahead of the bolt handle, and if the stake lumps are filed off for disassembly, a new guide rod may be required. In normal disassembly, this unit is best left intact. If it is taken apart, be careful not to lose the small spacer (arrow) between the spring and the handle at the forward end.

8. The firing pin is retained by a roll cross pin at the upper rear of the bolt. Use a roll-pin punch to drift out the cross pin, and remove the firing pin and its return spring toward the rear.

9. To remove the extractor, insert a small screwdriver to depress the extractor spring plunger, and hold it in while the extractor is lifted out of its recess. **Caution:** *Take care that the screwdriver doesn't slip, as the plunger and spring can travel far if suddenly released.* Ease them out slowly, and remove them from the bolt.

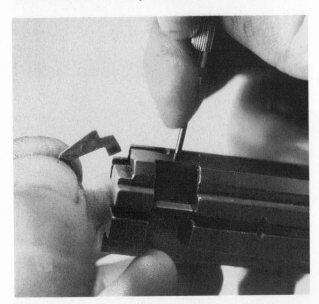

10. Restrain the hammer against the tension of its spring, pull the trigger, and ease the hammer forward beyond its normal fired position. The hammer spring assembly can now be moved forward and upward, out of the trigger group. The hammer spring assembly can be taken apart by compressing the spring and sliding the slotted washer off the lower end of the guide. Proceed with caution, as the spring is under tension.

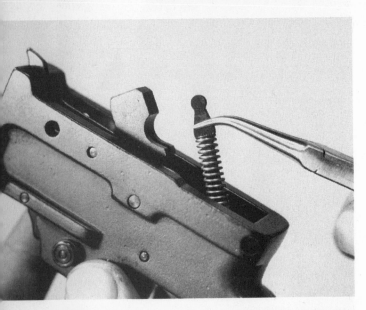

11. Before going any further with disassembly of the trigger group, carefully note the relationship of all parts and springs, to aid in reassembly. Tip the front of the ejector out of its slot in the front of the trigger group, push out the cross pin at the rear of the ejector, and remove the ejector upward. Note that removal of the cross pin will also release the upper arm of the bolt latch spring.

12. A cross pin at the lower front of the trigger group pivots and retains the bolt latch and the magazine catch lever. The bolt latch is removed upward. Restrain the magazine catch plunger with a finger-tip, remove the catch lever downward, and ease the plunger and its spring out toward the front.

13. Hold the trigger back to remove sear tension from the hammer, and push out the hammer pivot cross pin. Remove the hammer assembly upward. The bolt latch spring encircles the hammer bushing on the right side, and the two hammer pivot bushings are easily removed from the hammer.

14. Note the position of the sear and disconnector in the top of the trigger before disassembly. Push out the trigger pivot cross pin, and remove the trigger/sear/disconnector assembly upward. As the trigger is moved upward, the trigger spring and plunger will be released at the rear of the trigger guard. Ease them out, and remove them downward and toward the front.

15. The sear is removed from the trigger toward the front, along with the combination sear and disconnector spring. Drifting out the cross pin at the upper rear of the trigger will release the disconnector for removal.

16. Grip the safety firmly with a thumb and finger at each end, and give it a one-quarter turn toward the front; then push it out toward the left. **Caution:** *Insert a fingertip inside the trigger group, above the safety, to arrest the safety plunger and spring, as they will be released as the safety is moved out.*

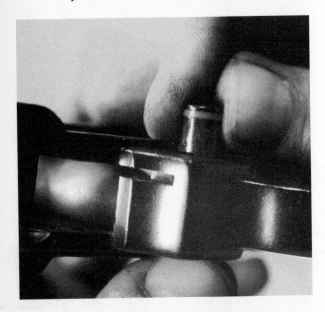

17. In normal takedown, removal of the barrel is not advisable. If necessary, however, use an Allen wrench to back out the two large screws that secure the barrel retainer block and take out the barrel toward the front. If the barrel is tight, grip the barrel in a padded vise and use a nylon hammer to tap the receiver off toward the rear.

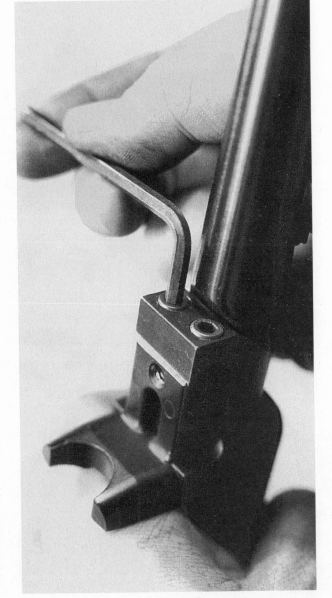

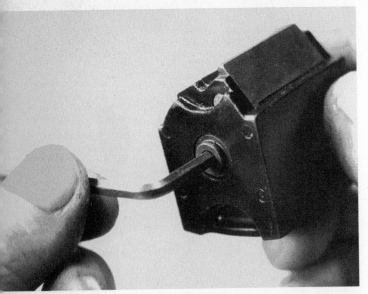

18. Magazine disassembly is not recommended in normal takedown. If it becomes necessary, removal of the screw at the front of the magazine will allow the backplate to be taken off, and the internal parts can then be taken out toward the rear. **Caution:**—*Don't remove the spring from the rotor.* Carefully note the relationship of all parts to aid in reassembly.

Reassembly Tips:

1. When replacing the trigger/sear/disconnector assembly in the trigger group, use a slave pin to hold the three parts and the spring in position for reinsertion. The photo shows the parts in place and the slave pin in the pivot hole.

2. When replacing the hammer, its pivot bushings and the bolt latch spring, note that the spring must be on the right side of the hammer, as shown. Be sure the lower arm of the spring engages its notch in the cross-piece of the bolt latch. The upper arm of the spring goes below the cross pin that retains the ejector.

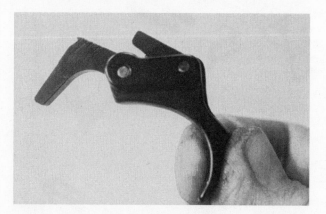

4. When replacing the bolt in the receiver, remember that the bolt handle must be fully to the rear, with the spring compressed, before the bolt can be tipped back into engagement with the handle at the front.

When replacing the action in the stock, be sure the safety is again set between its right and left positions to clear the interior as the action is moved into place.

If the magazine has been disassembled, insert the screw in the magazine body and place the rotor and spring on the screw, with the longer hub of the rotor toward the front. Replace the feed throat, being sure the larger end stud enters its recess at the front. Put the backplate back on the magazine body and hold it in place. Insert the front of the hexagonal-headed magazine nut into the rear of the spring, and be sure the hooked tip of the spring engages the hole in the nut. Turn the nut clockwise (rear view) until the rotor stops turning; then give it an additional $1^{1}/_{4}$ turns to properly tension the spring. Move the nut into its recess and tighten the magazine screw, taking care not to over-tighten.

3. When replacing the magazine catch system, remember that the bolt latch must be in place before the catch lever, plunger, and spring are installed. Insert the magazine catch plunger and spring first; then put in the catch lever from below. The upper arm of the lever will hold the plunger and spring in place while the cross pin is inserted. Be sure the cross pin passes through the bolt latch and the magazine catch.

10/22 Autoloading Rifle

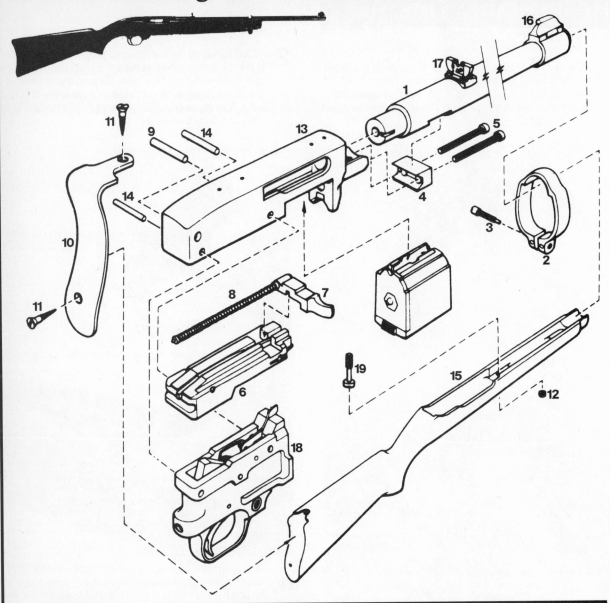

Ruger 44 Carbine

Similar/Identical Pattern Guns
The same basic assembly/disassembly steps for the Ruger 44 Carbine also apply to the following guns:

Ruger 44RS Carbine

Ruger 44 Sporter Deluxe Carbine

Ruger 44 International Carbine

Data:	Ruger 44 Carbine
Origin:	United States
Manufacturer:	Sturm, Ruger & Company Southport, Connecticut
Cartridge:	44 Magnum
Magazine capacity:	4 rounds
Overall length:	36 inches
Barrel length:	18½ inches
Weight:	5¾ pounds

When the Ruger 44 Autoloading Carbine arrived in 1961, it was the first rifle chambered for this round. It gained much popularity as a close-range gun for medium game, and the ballistics of its cartridge are comparable to the old 30-30. Like all of Bill Ruger's creations, it is an engineering masterpiece. It is not unnecessarily complicated, but an inter-dependency of certain parts makes takedown and reassembly an endeavor best left to the professional. The 44 Carbine was discontinued in 1985.

Disassembly:

1. Pull back the operating handle to lock the bolt open. Remove the cross screw at the bottom of the barrel band, and take off the band toward the front.

2. Lift the action at the front, and disengage its rear hook from the recoil block in the stock. Take out the action upward and toward the front.

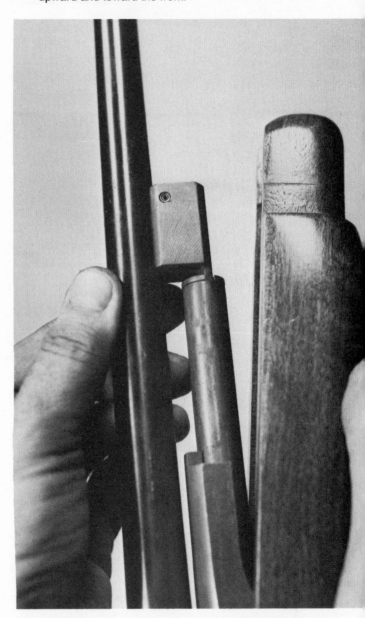

3. If necessary, the recoil block can be removed by taking off the buttplate and backing out the through-bolt which enters the block from the rear. The block is then removed forward and upward.

4. Push the lifter latch, and ease the bolt to closed position. Drift out the cross pin at the rear of the receiver.

5. Move the trigger housing toward the rear, and take it off downward.

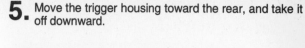

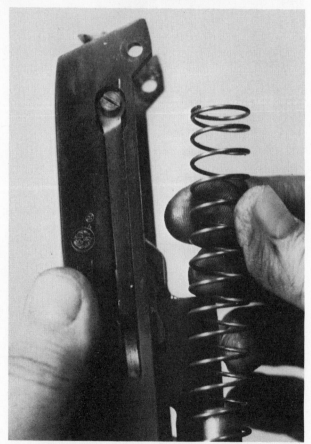

6. With the gun inverted, grip the rear of the recoil spring firmly, and lift the action slide away from the bottom of the receiver. As soon as the rear end of the spring has cleared the edge of the receiver, slowly release the spring and remove it toward the rear.

7. Remove the bolt handle from its slot in the action slide, and take it off toward the right.

8. Remove the action slide and magazine tube together from the bottom of the receiver. Separate the magazine tube from the action slide.

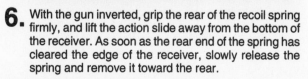

9. Drifting out the roll pin at the front of the magazine tube will allow removal of the tube end piece, magazine spring, and follower. **Caution:** *The spring is under tension, so control the end piece and ease it out.*

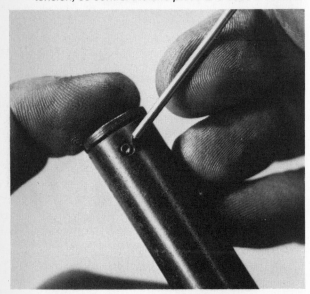

10. Remove the screw at the left rear of the receiver, and take off the ejector toward the left.

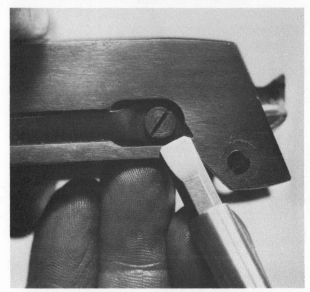

11. Insert a finger through the ejection port to turn the bolt and free its locking lugs, then move it toward the rear about half-way. Lift the bolt out of the underside of the receiver.

12. The gas piston is usually easy to remove from the rear of the gas cylinder. If it is tight because of powder residue, tap the rear flange of the cylinder with a plastic hammer to nudge it out.

13. The piston block plug at the front of the gas cylinder is retained by two concentric roll pins, and is removed toward the front. In normal takedown, it is best left in place.

14. The firing pin is retained in the bolt by a pin at the rear, and the firing pin and its return spring are taken out toward the rear.

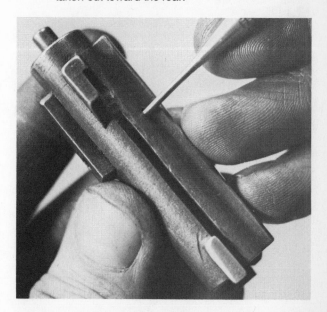

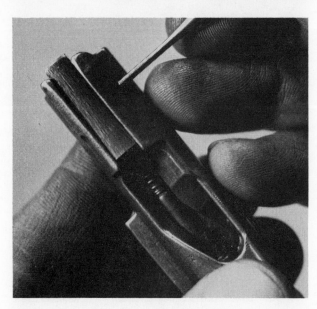

15. The extractor is retained by a vertical pin at the front of the bolt, and this pin must be driven out upward. The extractor and its coil spring are then removed toward the right.

16. Restrain the hammer, pull the trigger, and ease the hammer down to the fired position. Unhook the outer arms of the hammer spring, on each side of the housing, from the grooved ends of the hammer pivot pin, partially relieving the tension of the springs. **Caution:** *Use pliers to disengage the springs, as they are under heavy tension.*

17. When the spring arms are turned downward, the hammer spring pin can be pushed out and removed. After removal of the pin, the springs will be loose, but they are not taken out at this time.

18. Push out the hammer pivot pin toward either side. Remove the hammer upward.

19. Drift out the cross pin that retains the lifter latch.

20. Raise the lifter at the front, and take out the lifter latch downward. The plunger and spring are easily detached from the rear of the lifter latch.

21. Move the front of the lifter back to its lowered position to relieve tension on the cam spring, and push out the lifter cam pin toward the left.

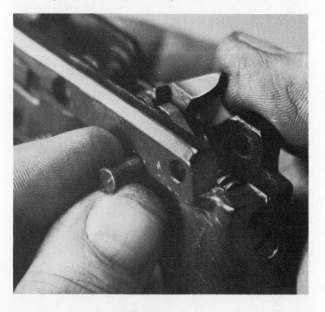

22. Insert an angled drift punch through the lifter cam pin hole, and lever the lifter cam slightly toward the rear. Raise the front of the lifter, and remove the cam and its spring upward and toward the front.

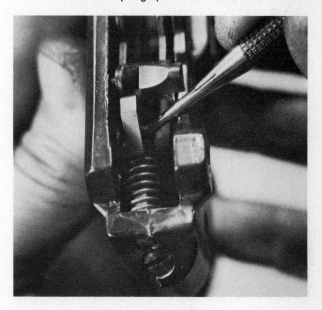

23. Insert a small screwdriver on the left side at the rear tip of the carrier, and push the lifter dog pin out toward the right until it can be grasped with pliers and pulled out. Remove the lifter dog upward.

24. Squeeze the rear arms of the carrier (lifter) together, to move the side studs from their holes in the sides of the housing, and remove it upward and toward the rear.

25. Push out the trigger pin, and move the twin hammer springs out to each side to clear the trigger and sear assembly.

26. Remove the trigger, sear, and disconnector assembly upward, and remove the sear spring from its well in the housing.

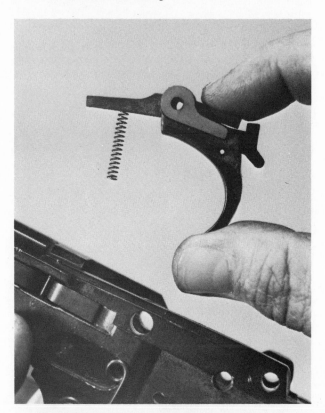

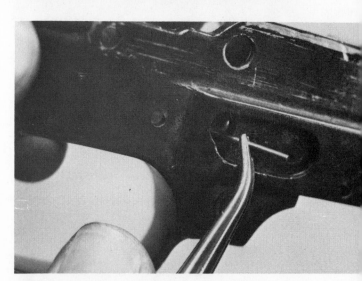

27. Remove the trigger plunger and spring from their hole at the rear of the trigger guard.

28. Move the hammer springs inward, one at a time, tip the outer arms outward, and push the springs into the interior of the trigger housing for removal.

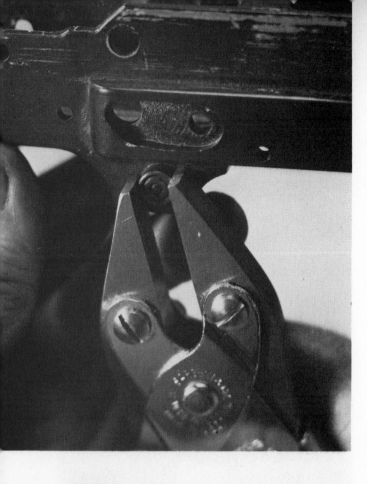

29. Grip the safety with smooth-jawed parallel pliers, and give it one-quarter turn clockwise (right side view). Remove the safety toward the left. **Caution:** *The safety plunger and spring will be released as the safety clears, so insert a screwdriver into the housing to restrain them.*

30. The flat cartridge stop spring is retained on the left side of the trigger housing by a vertical pin which is in a blind hole. Use a small screwdriver to nudge it upward until it can be grasped with pliers and taken out. The flat spring is then removed toward the left.

31. After the flat spring is removed, take out the rear-most of the two coil springs from its hole in the trigger housing.

32. The cartridge stop and flapper pivot pin is also in a blind hole, and is removed in the same way as the previous one. Note that the cartridge stop spring will be released when the pin is out, so control it.

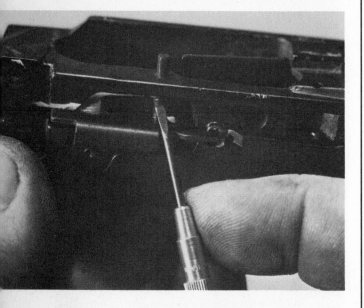

33. Remove the cartridge stop and its spring toward the left, and move the flapper inward and take it out toward the top of the housing.

Reassembly Tips:

1. When replacing the cartridge stop system, note that the cartridge stop spring and the flapper spring are of unequal length. Remember that the shorter spring goes at the front, under the tail of the cartridge stop.

2. When replacing the flat cartridge stop spring, it is necessary to lay the housing on its right side on a firm surface, and use a small drift punch to depress the spring at its pin dip to allow passage of the pin.

3. It is possible to install the sear/trigger/disconnector system by just holding them in place, but the use of a slave pin to hold the parts together will make it much easier. Be sure the lower end of the sear spring enters its hole inside of the trigger housing, and be sure the rear tail of the disconnector goes in front of the trigger spring plunger at the rear.

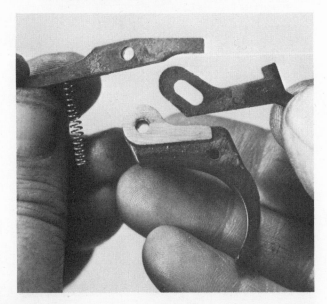

4. When replacing the hammer springs, they must be reinserted from inside the trigger group. When the long arm of the spring is protruding to the outside, insert a drift punch into the center of the spring, and tilt the drift toward the front of the housing, levering the spring into its hole.

5. Installing the hammer is perhaps the most difficult of reassembly operations. Be sure the short inner arms of both hammer springs engage the underside of the small roller at the lower rear of the hammer. Push the hammer straight downward, and insert a drift punch through the hammer pivot hole to hold it in place for insertion of the cross pin. Be sure the spring ends are not allowed to slip from beneath the roller during installation of the pin. Remember to replace the spring cross pin, and re-hook the spring arms onto the hammer pivot pin.

6. When replacing the magazine tube, note that the slot in the tube end piece is offset, and must fit onto the flange at the rear of the gas piston housing. The larger area of the end piece goes toward the barrel, as shown.

7. When replacing the magazine tube and recoil spring assembly, note that at the rear the spring must bear against the receiver, and must not extend into the recess for the rear tip of the magazine tube, as shown.

8. When properly assembled, the spring and tube will be as shown.

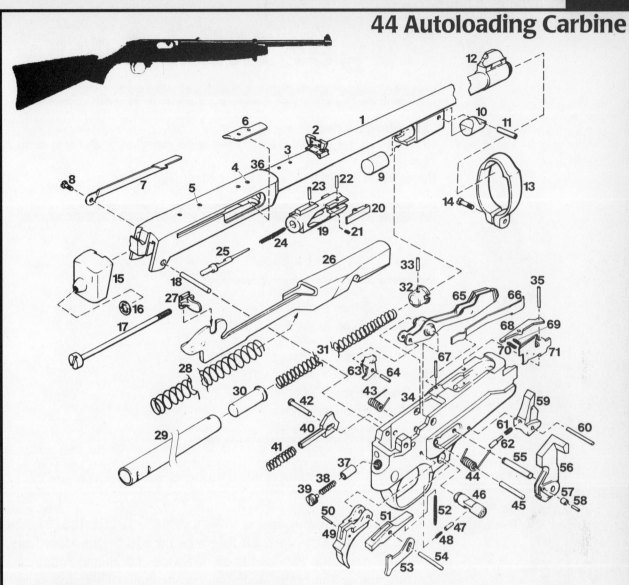

KEY

1 Barrel	
2 Rear Sight	
3 Scope Mount Filler Screws	
4 Ejector Screws	
5 Scope Mount Filler Screws	
6 Ejector	
7 Cartridge Guide Plate	
8 Cartridge Guide Plate Screw	
9 Piston	
10 Piston Block Plug	
11 Piston Block Plug Retaining Pin	
12 Front Sight	
13 Barrel Band	
14 Barrel Band Screw	
15 Recoil Block	
16 Recoil Block Bolt Washer	
17 Recoil Block Bolt	
18 Receiver Cross Pin	
19 Bolt	
20 Extractor	
21 Extractor Spring	
22 Extractor Pivot Pin	
23 Firing Pin Retaining Pin	
24 Firing Pin Retaining Spring	
25 Firing Pin	

26 Slide	
27 Slide Handle	
28 Slide Spring	
29 Magazine Tube	
30 Magazine Follower	
31 Magazine Spring	
32 Magazine Plug	
33 Magazine Plug Cross Pin	
34 Trigger Guard and Housing	
35 Cartridge Stop Pivot Pin	
36 Receiver	
37 Disconnector Plunger	
38 Disconnector Plunger Spring	
39 Disconnector Plunger Spring Screw	
40 Lifter Cam	
41 Lifter Cam Spring	
42 Lifter Cam Pin	
43 Hammer Spring, Left	
44 Hammer Spring, Right	
45 Hammer Spring Retaining Pin	
46 Safety	
47 Safety Detent Plunger	
48 Safety Detent Plunger Spring	
49 Trigger	
50 Trigger Cross Pin	
51 Sear	
52 Sear Spring	

53 Disconnector	
54 Trigger Pivot Pin	
55 Hammer Pivot Pin	
56 Hammer	
57 Hammer Roller	
58 Hammer Roller Pivot Pin	
59 Lifter Latch	
60 Lifter Latch Pivot Pin	
61 Lifter Latch Spring	
62 Lifter Latch Plunger	
63 Lifter Dog	
64 Lifter Dog Pivot Pin	
65 Lifter Assembly	
66 Cartridge Stop Flat Spring	
67 Retaining Pin	
68 Cartridge Stop	
69 Flapper Spring	
70 Cartridge Stop Coil Spring	
71 Flapper	

Parts Not Shown
Buttstock
Buttpad
Screws
Forend

Ruger Mini-14

Data:	Ruger Mini-14
Origin:	United States
Manufacturer:	Sturm, Ruger & Company Southport, Connecticut
Cartridge:	223 Remington (5.56mm)
Magazine capacity:	5 rounds
Overall length:	37¼ inches
Barrel length:	18½ inches
Weight:	6.4 pounds

While externally it may appear to be a miniature of the U.S. M-14 service rifle, the Mini-14 is all Ruger on the inside. Introduced in 1973, this neat little carbine has gained wide acceptance both as a sporting gun and in police and guard applications. There has been one small change in the original design—a bolt hold-open button was added on the top left side of the receiver, and all guns of more recent manufacture will have this feature. The Ruger Mini Thirty in 7.62x39 and the Ruger Ranch Rifle are mechanically the same.

Disassembly:

1. Remove the magazine, and cycle the action to cock the internal hammer. Push the safety back to the on-safe position, and insert a non-marring tool through the hole at the rear of the trigger guard to spring the guard downward at the rear. Swing the guard toward the front until it stops.

2. Remove the trigger housing downward.

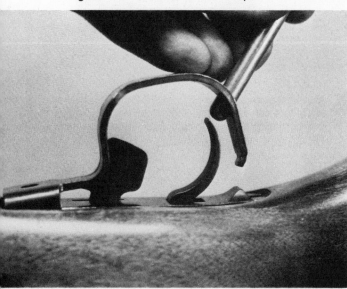

3. Tip the rear of the action upward out of the stock, and remove it toward the front.

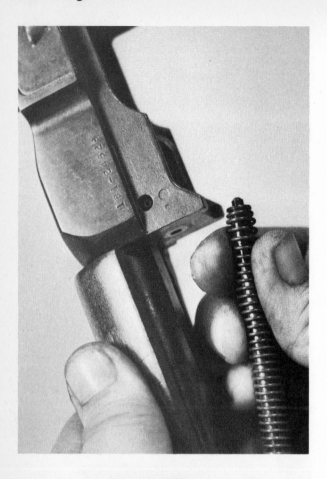

4. Grasp the recoil spring firmly at the rear, where it joins the receiver, and lift the tip of the guide out of its hole in the front of the receiver. **Caution:** *This is a strong spring, so keep it under control.* Tilt the spring and guide upward, slowly release the tension, and remove the spring and guide toward the rear.

5. Move the slide assembly toward the rear until its rear lug aligns with the exit cut in the slide track, and move the operating handle upward and toward the right. Remove the slide assembly.

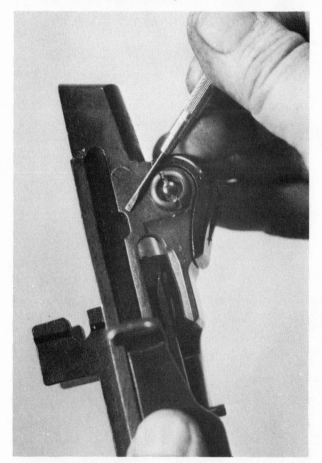

6. Move the bolt forward to the position shown, and remove it upward and toward the right. The bolt must be turned to align the underlug of the firing pin with the exit cut in the bottom of the bolt track.

7. In normal takedown, the gas block assembly should not be removed. If it is necessary, use an Allen wrench to remove the four vertical screws, separating the upper and lower sections of the gas block. The gas port bushing will be freed with removal of the lower block, so take care that it isn't lost.

8. Slide the bolt hold-open cover downward out of its slots in the receiver and remove it.

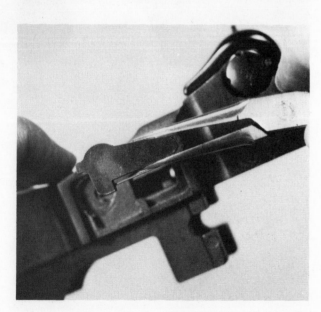

9. Depress the bolt latch plunger on top of the left receiver rail, and lift the bolt lock out of its recess toward the left. **Caution:** *The bolt latch retains the plunger, so control the plunger and ease it out upward, along with its spring.*

10. The front magazine catch, located in the front of the receiver below the barrel, is retained by a roll cross pin, accessible through holes on each side. Drift out the cross pin, and remove the catch toward the front.

11. Insert a small screwdriver beside the extractor plunger, and turn and tip the screwdriver to depress the plunger. Move the extractor upward out of its recess. **Caution:** *As the extractor post clears the ejector it will be released, so restrain the ejector and ease it out toward the front. Also, take care to keep the extractor plunger under control, and ease it out.* Removal of the extractor will also free the firing pin to be taken out toward the rear.

12. Close and latch the trigger guard, and insert a piece of rod or a drift punch through the hole in the rear tip of the hammer spring guide.

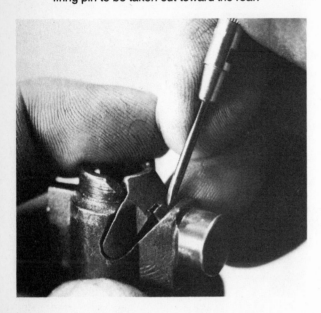

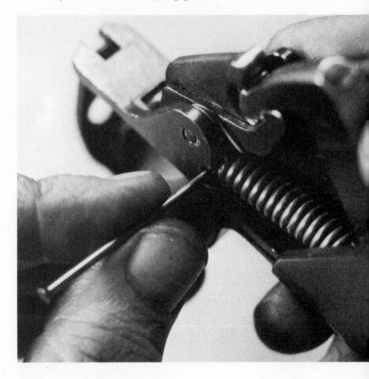

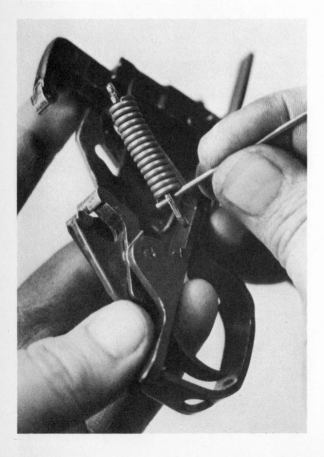

13. Restrain the hammer, move the safety to the off-safe position, and pull the trigger to release the hammer. The rod will trap the hammer spring on the guide. Tip the front of the guide upward, out of its recess at the rear of the hammer, and remove the guide assembly toward the right. If the spring is to be taken off the guide, proceed with care, as the spring is fully compressed.

14. Push out the hammer pivot, and remove the hammer upward and toward the right.

15. Move the safety back to the on-safe position, and take off the trigger guard downward and toward the rear.

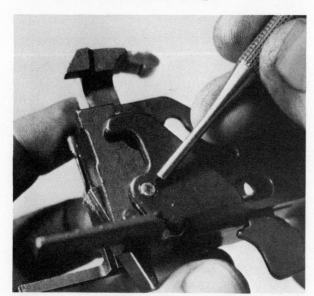

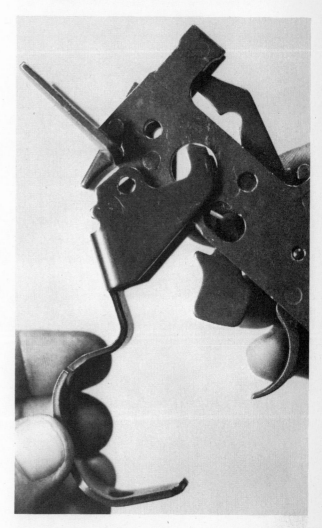

16. Drift out the safety spring pin toward the left, ease the spring tension slowly, and move the spring toward the rear, unhooking it from the safety. Remove the spring toward the right rear.

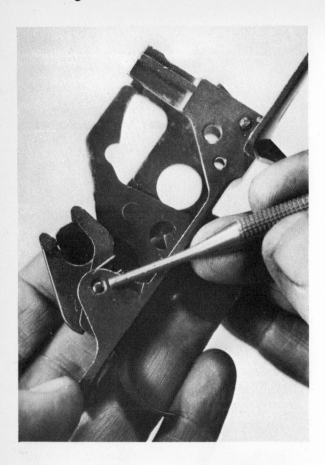

17. Restrain the trigger and sear assembly, and drift out the trigger cross pin.

18. Remove the trigger and sear assembly upward.

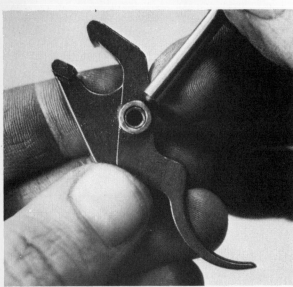

19. The trigger spring is easily detached from the trigger, and the pivot bushing can be drifted out to free the secondary sear and its coil spring from the top of the trigger. **Caution:** *Use a roll pin punch to avoid damaging the bushing, and take care to restrain the sear against the tension of its spring.*

20. Tip the upper portion of the safety catch toward the right, moving its pivot stud out of its hole in the trigger housing, and remove the safety upward.

21. The main magazine catch is retained by a cross pin at the front of the trigger housing, and the pin must be drifted out toward the left. **Caution:** *The strong magazine catch spring will also be released when the pin is removed, so insert a shop cloth into the housing behind the spring to catch it. This spring is rather difficult to reinstall, so if removal is not necessary for repair, the catch is best left in place.*

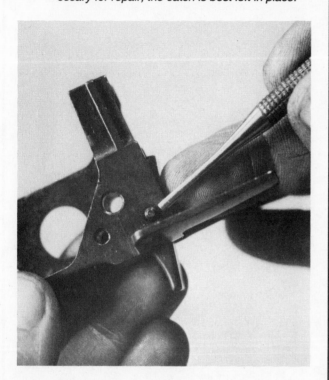

Reassembly Tips:

1. When installing the trigger and sear assembly, tilt the assembly forward, and be sure the front hooks of the trigger spring engage the top of the cross piece in the housing. Push the assembly downward and toward the rear until the cross pin can be inserted.

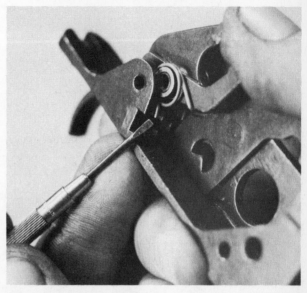

When replacing the safety spring, be sure that its front arm goes on the right side of the rear arm of the magazine catch spring. Otherwise, the safety spring pin cannot be fully inserted.

Mini-14 Autoloading Rifle (181-184 Prefix)

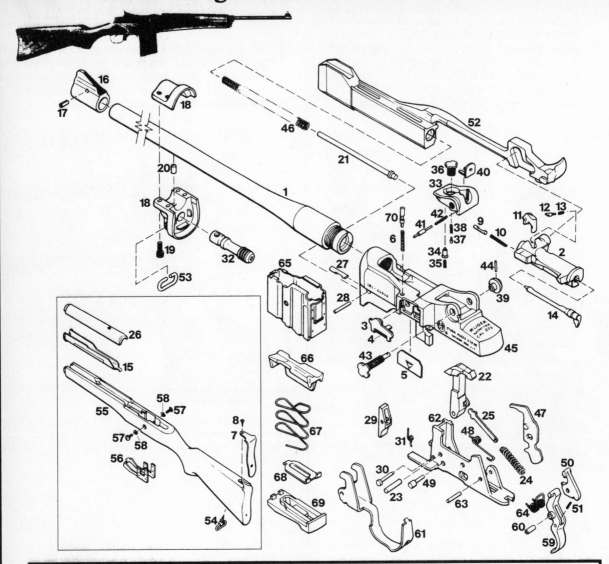

KEY

1 Barrel
2 Bolt
3 Bolt Lock Assembly
4 Bolt Lock Buffer Spring
5 Bolt Lock Cover Plate
6 Bolt Lock Plunger Spring
7 Buttplate
8 Buttplate Screws
9 Ejector
10 Ejector Spring
11 Extractor
12 Extractor Plunger
13 Extractor Spring
14 Firing Pin
15 Forend Liner and Stock Cap Assembly
16 Front Sight
17 Front Sight Cross Pin
18 Gas Block
19 Gas Block Screws
20 Gas Port Bushing
21 Guide Rod
22 Hammer
23 Hammer Pivot Pin

24 Hammer Spring
25 Hammer Strut
26 Handguard
27 Magazine Catch, Front
28 Magazine Catch Retaining Pin
29 Magazine Latch
30 Magazine Latch Pivot Pin
31 Magazine Latch Spring
32 Piston (Gas Pipe)
33 Rear Sight Base
34 Rear Sight Elevation Detent Plunger
35 Rear Sight Elevation Detent Spring
36 Rear Sight Elevation Screw
37 Rear Sight Elevation Plunger
38 Rear Sight Elevation Plunger Spring
39 Rear Sight Nut
40 Rear Sight Peep
41 Rear Sight Windage Detent Plunger
42 Rear Sight Windage Detent
43 Rear Sight Windage Screw
44 Rear Sight Windage Screw Pin
45 Receiver

46 Recoil Spring
47 Safety Assembly
48 Safety Detent Spring
49 Safety Spring Retaining Pin
50 Secondary Sear
51 Secondary Sear Spring
52 Slide Assembly
53 Sling Swivel, Front
54 Sling Swivel Assembly, Rear
55 Stock
56 Stock Reinforcement
57 Stock Reinforcement Screws
58 Stock Reinforcement Lock Washers
59 Trigger
60 Trigger Bushing
61 Trigger Guard
62 Trigger Housing
63 Trigger Pivot Pin
64 Trigger Spring
65 Magazine Box
66 Magazine Follower
67 Magazine Spring
68 Magazine Spring Retainer
69 Magazine Floorplate
70 Bolt Lock Plunger

Ruger Model 77

Similar/Identical Pattern Guns
The same basic assembly/disassembly steps for the Ruger Model 77 also apply to the following guns:

Ruger Model 77R, RS Magnum　　**Ruger Model 77RL**
Ruger Model 77RLS　　　　　　　**Ruger Model 77RSI International**
Ruger Model 77V Varmint　　　　 **Ruger Model 77R Mark II**
Ruger Model 77 Mark II　　　　　 **Ruger Model 77 Mark II Magnum**
Ruger Model 77 Mark II All-Weather　Ruger Model 77 Mark II Express
Ruger Model 77VT Target

Data:	Ruger Model 77
Origin:	United States
Manufacturer:	Sturm, Ruger & Company Southport, Connecticut
Cartridges:	Most popular calibers from 22-250 to 458
Magazine capacity:	3 to 5 rounds
Overall length:	42 to 44 inches
Barrel length:	22 to 26 inches
Weight:	6¾ pounds (Standard)

With some elements of the classic Mauser/Springfield rifle, in 1968 Bill Ruger created a gun that includes the best points of the old and new. Internally, the Model 77 is all modern, with several Ruger innovations, such as the angled front action mounting screw which pulls the action not only down in the stock, but also back, snugging the recoil lug against the interior of the stock. The firing mechanism is uncomplicated, and takedown and reassembly are not difficult. On the Model 77 Mark II, introduced in 1989, the safety has three positions, and the ejector is a spring-and-plunger type. These features will cause no difficulty in takedown.

Disassembly:

1. Open the bolt and move it to the rear, while holding the bolt stop pulled out toward the left. Remove the bolt from the rear of the receiver.

2. Insert a small piece of rod (or a drift punch) at the lower rear of the cocking piece, into the hole provided. This will lock the striker in rear position. Unscrew the striker assembly counter-clockwise (rear view).

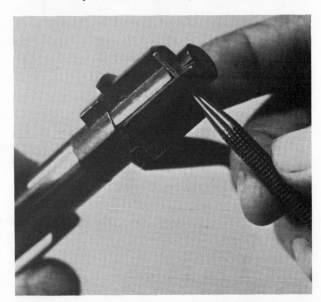

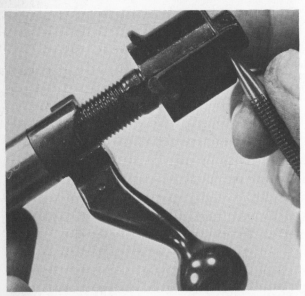

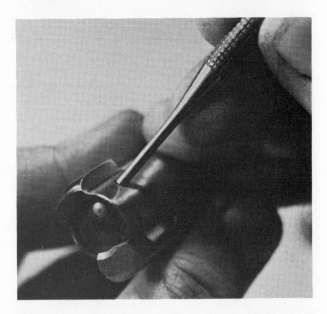

3. Remove the striker assembly from the rear of the bolt. It is possible to grip the front of the striker in a vise and push the bolt end piece forward to expose a cross pin in the cocking piece, and drifting out this pin would release the parts of the striker assembly. There is, however, no reasonably easy way to do this without special tools, and the factory cautions against taking this assembly apart.

4. Drifting out the vertical pin at the front of the bolt will release the ejector and its spring toward the front. **Caution:** *The spring is compressed, so restrain the ejector and ease it out.*

5. Turn the extractor counter-clockwise (rear view) until it is aligned with the base of the bolt handle, then use the Brownells extractor pliers or a small screwdriver blade to lift the front underlug of the extractor out of its groove at the front of the bolt, and push the extractor off the flanges of the mounting ring toward the front.

6. Open the magazine floorplate, and slide the magazine spring out of its slots. The follower can be removed from the spring in the same way.

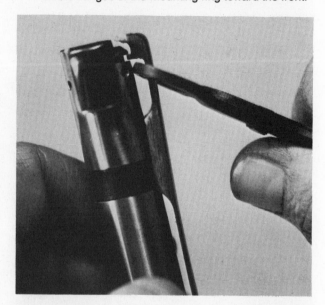

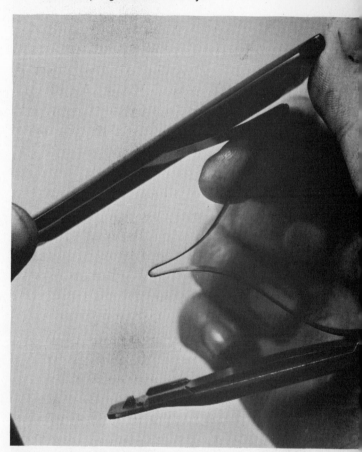

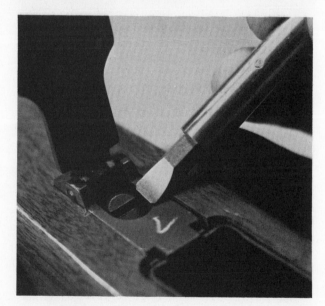

7. Remove the large angled screw inside the front of the magazine floorplate base.

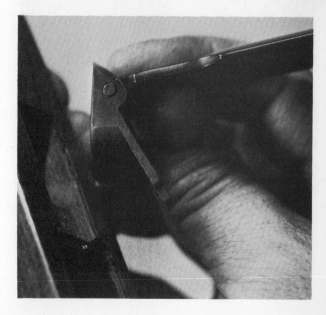

8. Remove the magazine floorplate and its base downward. Pushing out the hinge pin will allow separation of the floorplate and its base.

9. Remove the vertical screw at the front of the trigger guard. Remove the vertical screw at the rear of the trigger guard, and take off the trigger guard downward. Separate the action from the stock.

10. Drifting out the cross pin in the front of the trigger guard will allow removal of the magazine floorplate latch and its spring.

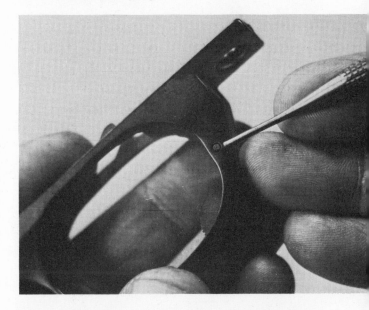

11. The magazine box is a press fit in its recess in the bottom of the receiver. Insert a tool in the openings on each side at the upper rear of the box, and gently pry it away from the receiver.

12. The bolt stop is removed by backing out its mounting screw toward the left.

13. As the screw is backed out, the bolt stop plunger will drop from the edge of the screw head to the internal bushing, and the stud screw is then easily removed.

14. Drifting out the vertical roll pin at the front of the bolt stop will allow removal of the spring and plunger toward the front, and the bushing from the rear opening.

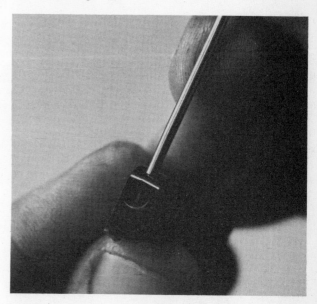

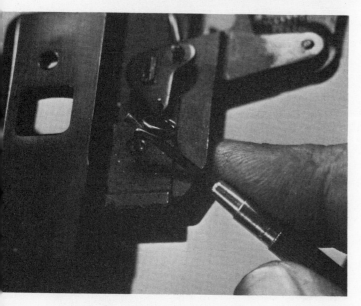

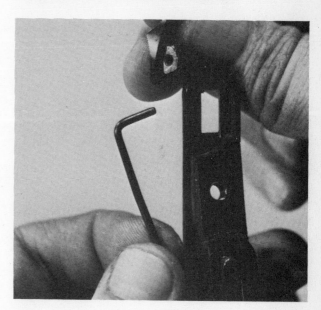

15. With the safety in the on-safe position, use a small screwdriver to lift the front arm of the safety positioning spring out of the center of the trigger housing roll pin. When it is clear, swing it downward, and unhook it from the hole in the edge of the safety shaft plate.

16. Move the rear tip of the safety link out of its cross hole in the underside of the safety button, and unhook its forward end from the safety plate. The safety button can now be removed.

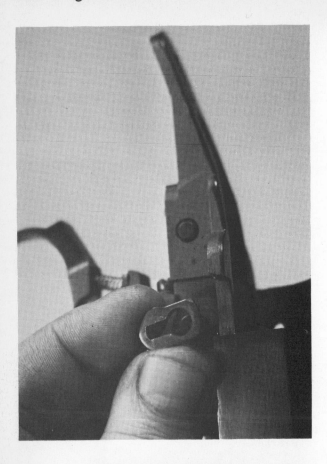

17. After the link rod is removed, push the safety plate toward the right, moving the right tip of its shaft slightly out of the right side of the housing. The safety bolt lock can then be slid off the shaft downward, then removed toward the right.

18. Remove the safety shaft and its attached plate toward the left.

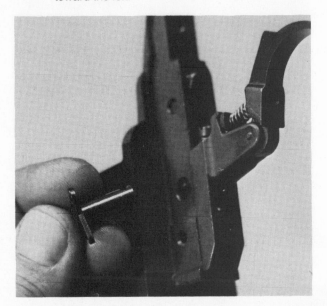

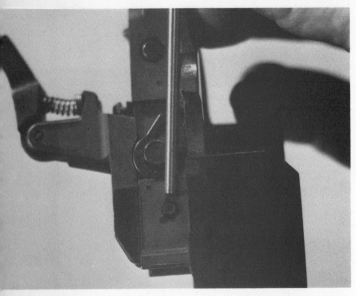

19. Drift out the trigger housing cross pin toward the left, using a roll pin punch. It is important that the ends of this pin are not deformed, as the safety positioning spring must be remounted inside the pin.

20. Remove the trigger housing downward.

21. Move the trigger spring base out of its seat at the rear of the housing, and remove the spring toward the rear. **Caution:** *The spring is under tension.*

22. Pushing out the trigger pin will release the trigger from the housing. The trigger adjustment screws should not be disturbed.

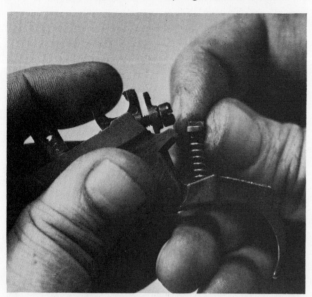

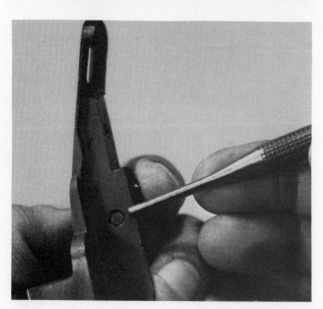

23. Restrain the sear against its spring tension, and push out the sear pin toward the right side. Remove the sear and its spring downward.

Reassembly Tips:

1. When replacing the safety shaft, the trigger must be pulled to clear the shaft tunnel for insertion.

2. When replacing the safety button, note that its longer slope goes toward the front.

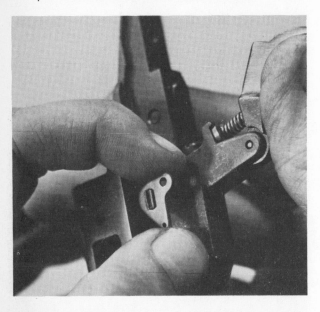

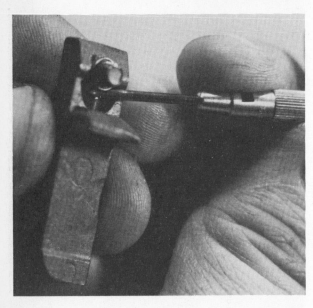

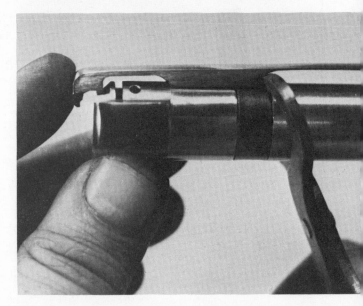

3. Before replacing the bolt stop on the receiver, insert a small screwdriver to jump the plunger back onto the edge of the post screw. During installation, take care that the plunger doesn't slip off the edge.

4. When replacing the extractor on the bolt, use the Brownells extractor pliers to compress the mounting ring flanges while sliding the extractor onto them. After it is well started into the flanges, use the pliers to lift the underlug at the front of the extractor onto the front edge of the bolt. Take care to lift the front of the extractor no more than is absolutely necessary for clearance.

Model 77 Bolt-Action Rifle

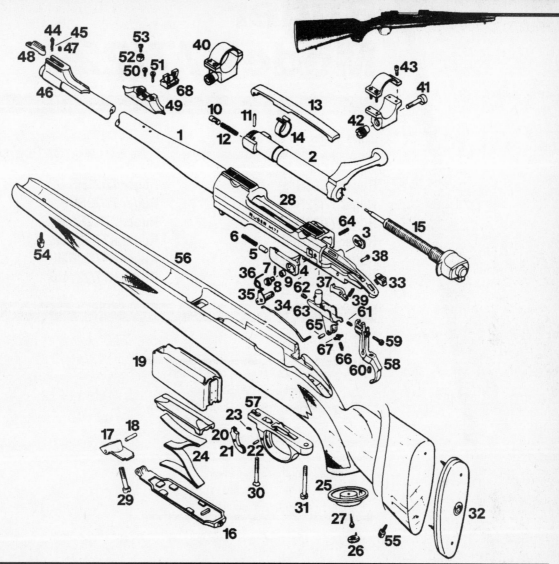

KEY

1	Barrel	**24**	Magazine Spring	**50**	Rear Sight Base Center Screw
2	Bolt Body	**25**	Pistol Grip Cap	**51**	Rear Sight Base Rear Screw
3	Bolt Lock	**26**	Pistol Grip Cap Medallion	**52**	Williams Gib Lock
4	Bolt Stop	**27**	Pistol Grip Cap Screw	**53**	Williams Gib Lock Screw
5	Bolt Stop Plunger	**28**	Receiver	**54**	Sling Swivel Front Screw with Nut
6	Bolt Stop Plunger Spring	**29**	Receiver Mounting Screw, Front	**55**	Sling Swivel Rear Mounting Stud
7	Bolt Stop Plunger Spring Retaining Pin	**30**	Receiver Mounting Screw, Center	**56**	Stock
8	Bolt Stop Screw Stud	**31**	Receiver Mounting Screw, Rear	**57**	Trigger Guard
9	Bolt Stop Stud Bushing	**32**	Recoil Pad	**58**	Trigger
10	Ejector	**33**	Safety Button	**59**	Trigger Engagement Screw
11	Ejector Retaining Pin	**34**	Safety Link	**60**	Trigger Weight of Pull Screw
12	Ejector Spring	**35**	Safety Shaft Assembly	**61**	Trigger Over Travel Screw
13	Extractor	**36**	Safety Spring	**62**	Trigger Over Travel Set Screw
14	Extractor Band	**37**	Sear	**63**	Trigger Housing
15	Firing Pin Assembly	**38**	Sear Pivot Pin	**64**	Trigger Housing Cross Pin
16	Floorplate	**39**	Sear Spring	**65**	Trigger Pivot Pin
17	Floorplate Hinge	**40**	Scope Ring Assembly	**66**	Trigger Return Spring
18	Floorplate Pivot Pin	**41**	Scope Ring Clamp	**67**	Trigger Return Spring Seat
19	Magazine Box	**42**	Scope Ring Nut	**68**	Rear Sight Blade
20	Magazine Follower	**43**	Scope Ring Screw		
21	Magazine Latch	**44**	Front Sight Plunger		**Parts Not Shown**
22	Magazine Latch Pin	**45**	Front Sight Plunger Spring		Forend Escutcheons
23	Magazine Latch Spring	**46**	Front Sight Base		Stock Cross Bolt
		47	Front Sight Base Set Screw		Stock Cross Bolt Nut
		48	Front Sight Blade		Stock Reinforcement Assembly
		49	Rear Sight Base		Stock Reinforcement Screw

Ruger Model 77/22

Similar/Identical Pattern Guns

The same basic assembly/disassembly steps for the Ruger Model 77/22 also apply to the following guns:

Ruger 77/22R	**Ruger 77/22RS**
Ruger 77/22RP	**Ruger 77/22RSP**
Ruger 77/22RM	**Ruger 77/22RSM**
Ruger K77/22RP	**Ruger K77/22RSP**
Ruger K77/22RSMP	**Ruger K77/22RMP**
Ruger K77/22VBZ	**Ruger K77/22VMB**

Data:	Ruger Model 77/22
Origin:	United States
Manufacturer:	Sturm, Ruger & Company Southport, Connecticut
Cartridge:	22 Long Rifle
Magazine capacity:	10 rounds
Overall length:	39³/₄ inches
Barrel length:	20 inches
Weight:	5³/₄ pounds

The original blued-steel and wood-stocked version of the Model 77/22 was introduced in 1983. Six years later, in 1989, the gun was offered in stainless steel with an optional synthetic stock, and also in a 22 WMR version. A beautifully-engineered bolt action, the Model 77/22 uses the same magazine and barrel-mounting system as the Ruger 10/22 autoloader.

Disassembly:

1. Remove the magazine and open the bolt. Depress the bolt stop, located at the left rear of the receiver, and remove the bolt toward the rear.

2. Insert a drift through the hole in the underlug of the striker end piece and turn the bolt headpiece to the position shown.

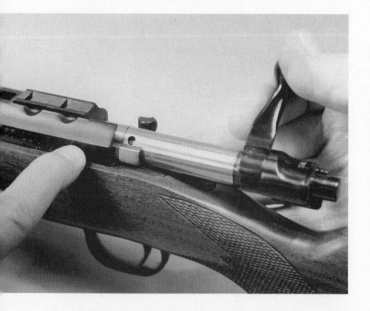

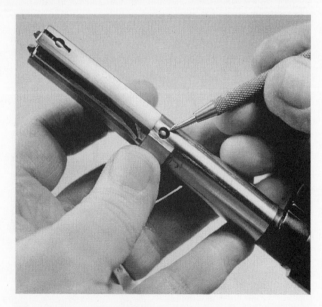

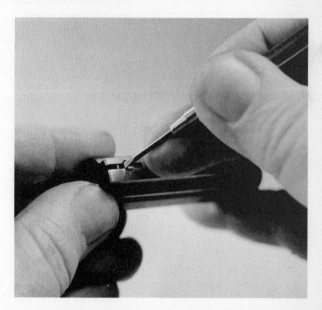

3. After the headpiece is turned, the head of the breech-block pin will be visible in this opening. Use a drift in the aperture on the other side, and push the breech-block pin out. Remove the breechblock toward the front.

4. The extractors can be removed by using a small tool to push their plungers toward the rear. **Caution:** *Control the plunger and spring on each side, and ease them out.* Keep the extractors separate—they are not interchangeable.

5. Using the drift in the hole in the striker underlug, unscrew the striker assembly from the bolt body. Remove the assembly toward the rear. Note that the firing pin can be detached from its hook at the front of the shaft as it emerges.

6. While it is possible to use a vise and special jigs to further disassemble the striker system, the factory advises against this. In normal takedown, it is best left intact.

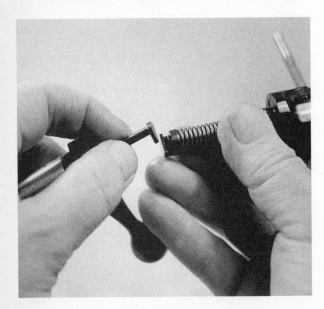

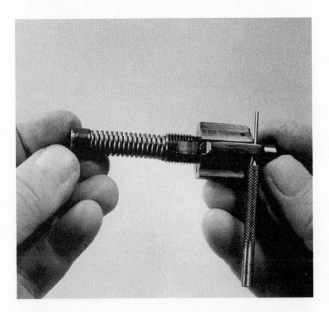

7. Remove the large screw in front of the magazine opening and take off the forward plate.

8. Remove the large screw behind the trigger guard. Tip the trigger guard unit outward to unhook it from the receiver and remove it. Carefully lift the action out of the stock.

9. Restrain the magazine catch plunger and push out the catch lever cross pin.

10. Remove the catch lever downward.

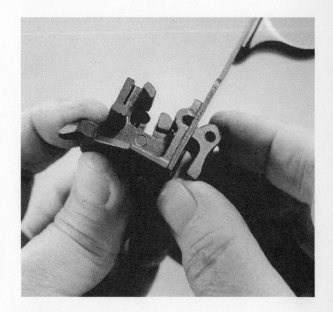

11. Ease the spring tension and remove the plunger and spring toward the front.

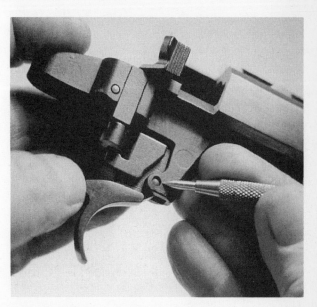

12. Restrain the trigger and push out the trigger cross pin.

13. Remove the trigger downward, along with its spring.

14. Push out the sear cross pin.

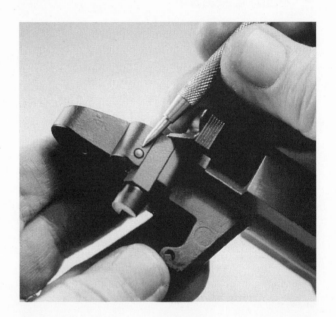

15. Move the sear forward and take it out upward.

16. Turn the safety-lever until it is in the position shown, over the bolt track.

17. Holding the safety in place at top and bottom, push the safety housing upward. **Caution:** *Keep control of the safety, as the detent plunger and spring will force it outward.*

18. Ease the spring tension slowly and remove the safety toward the right.

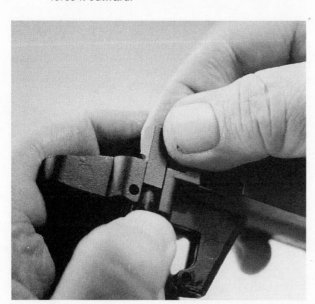

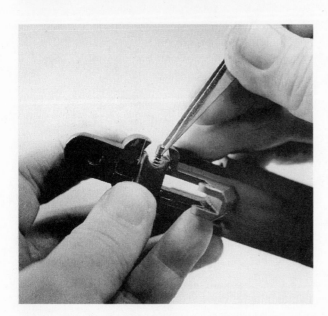

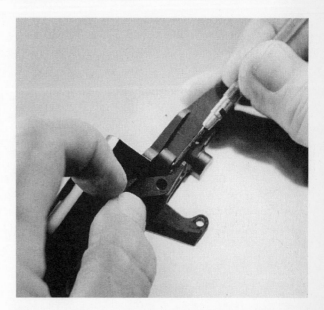

19. Remove the safety plunger and spring.

20. To remove the bolt stop, use a tool to depress the plunger and spring upward and take off the bolt stop toward the left. **Caution:** *Keep the plunger and spring under control, and ease them out.*

Reassembly Tips:

21. If barrel removal is necessary, remove the two Allen screws at the front of the receiver, take off the block and remove the barrel toward the front. The front and rear sights are dovetail-mounted.

1. When installing the safety housing, be sure the recess for the sear cross pin is at the rear, as shown.

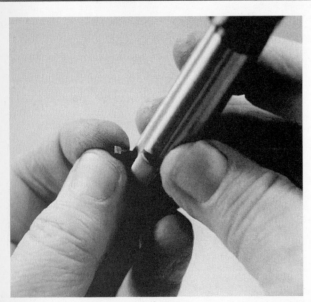

2. When installing the breechblock pin, note that the flats on its head must be oriented to front and rear. Properly installed, the head of the pin must be recessed below the outer surface of the bolt body.

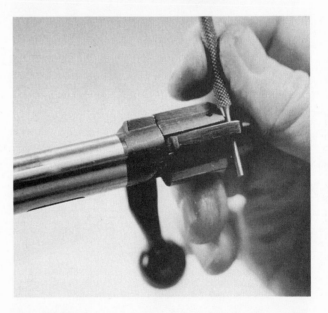

3. Remember to turn the bolt head back to cocked position, as shown, before the bolt is reinserted in the receiver.

Model 77/22 Bolt-Action Rifle

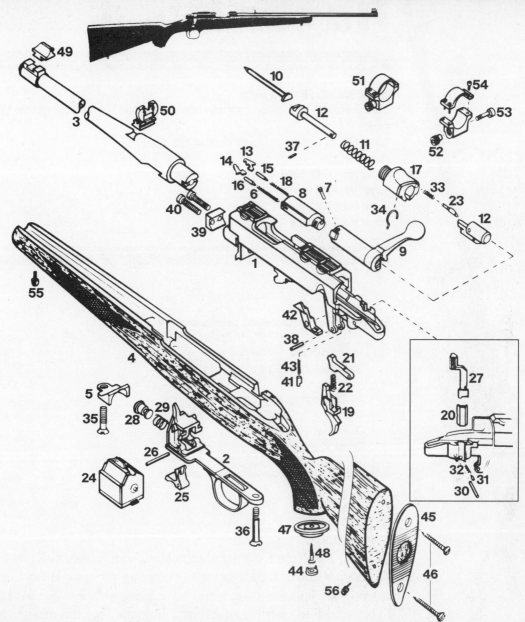

KEY

1	Receiver	19	Trigger	39	Barrel Retainer
2	Trigger Guard Assembly	20	Safety Selector Retainer	40	Barrel Retainer Screws
3	Barrel	21	Sear	41	Bolt Stop Plunger
4	Stock	22	Trigger/Sear Spring	42	Bolt Stop
5	Magazine Well Liner	23	Bolt Lock Plunger	43	Bolt Stop Plunger Spring
6	Cartridge Support Spring	24	Magazine Complete	44	Pistol Grip Cap Medallion
7	Breechblock Retainer	25	Magazine Latch	45	Buttplate
8	Breechblock	26	Magazine Latch Pivot Pin	46	Buttplate Screws
9	Bolt	27	Safety Selector	47	Pistol Grip Cap
10	Firing Pin	28	Magazine Latch Plunger	48	Pistol Grip Cap Screw
11	Striker Spring	29	Magazine Latch Plunger Spring	49	Front Sight
12	Striker/Cocking Piece Assembly	30	Sear Pivot Pin	50	Rear Sight
13	Extractor	31	Safety Selector Detent	51	Scope Ring
14	Cartridge Support	32	Safety Selector Detent Spring	52	Scope Ring Nut
15	Extractor Plunger	33	Bolt Lock Plunger Spring	53	Scope Ring Clamp
16	Cartridge Support Plunger	34	Bolt Lock Plunger Retainer	54	Scope Ring Screw
17	Bolt Sleeve	35	Front Mounting Screw	55	Sling Swivel Front Screw with Nut
18	Extractor Spring	36	Rear Mounting Screw	56	Sling Swivel Rear Mounting Stud
		37	Striker Cross Pin		
		38	Trigger Pivot Pin		

Ruger No. 1

Similar/Identical Pattern Guns
The same basic assembly/disassembly steps for the Ruger No. 1 also apply to the following guns:
Ruger No. 1A Light Sporter, 1S Medium Sporter
Ruger No. 1B
Ruger No. 1H Tropical Rifle
Ruger No. 1RSI International
Ruger No. 1V Varmint
Ruger No. 3 Carbine

Data:	Ruger No. 1
Origin:	United States
Manufacturer:	Sturm, Ruger & Company Southport, Connecticut
Cartridges:	Most popular calibers from 22-250 to 458
Overall length:	42 inches
Barrel lengths:	22, 24 and 26 inches
Weight:	8 pounds

In 1967, Bill Ruger recreated the classic single shot rifle, and over the years it has proved to be an outstanding success. The action and some other features of the gun have some relationship to the old Fraser and Farquharson rifles from England, but the mechanism is pure Ruger, and superior to any other gun of this type, before or since. Also, in contrast to the older guns of this type, the takedown and reassembly operations are not difficult. A plainer carbine version, the No. 3, was made from 1972 to 1987.

Disassembly:

1. Remove the angled screw on the underside of the forend and take off the forend forward and downward.

2. Remove the forend takedown nut, and set it aside to prevent loss.

3. Cycle the action to cock the hammer, and insert a small piece of rod through the transverse hole in the front tip of the hammer spring strut. Pull the trigger to release the hammer.

4. Move the hammer spring assembly slightly toward the rear, tip the front of the assembly downward, and remove it toward the front. If the assembly is to be taken apart, proceed with caution, as the spring is compressed.

5. Remove the cap screw on the lever pivot, and push out the pivot toward the opposite side. The action should be opened while this is done. If the screw is very tight, the lever pivot head has a screw slot, and it can be held with another screwdriver.

6. Remove the hammer downward.

7. Push the breechblock back upward, close the lever, then open the lever about half way, and remove the lever and breechblock assembly downward out of the receiver as a unit.

8. Detach the breechblock from the lever arm, and remove the ejector roller from the left side of the breech-block

9. Holding the breechblock with its left side downward, reach into the underside of the block and work the hammer transfer block back and forth until its pivot pin protrudes from the left side enough to be caught with a fingernail or small screwdriver and pulled out. The pin has a cannelure at its left tip for this purpose.

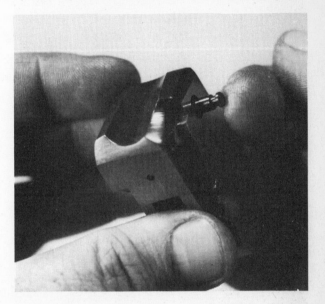

10. Remove the hammer transfer block from the bottom of the breechblock. The firing pin and its return spring can now be taken out from inside the breech-block.

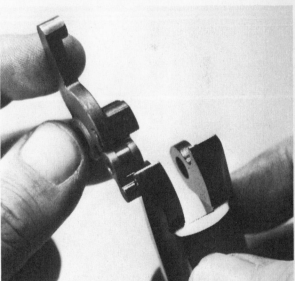

11. The breechblock arm and the lever links are easily separated from each other. Note that the links are joined by a roll pin, and this should be left in place unless removal is necessary for repair

12. Backing out the cross screw in the tail of the lever will allow removal of the lever latch and its spring.

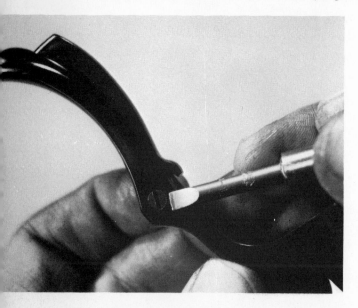

13. Remove the ejector downward, and take care not to lose the plunger and spring mounted in its side.

14. The plunger and spring are easily removed from the side of the ejector.

15. Tip the ejector lever (ejector cam) downward, and take off its spring and guide assembly downward. Note that the guide is two separate parts.

16. Drifting out its pivot pin will allow removal of the ejector cam lever toward the front.

17. The buttstock is retained by a through-bolt from the rear. Take off the buttplate, and use a B-Square stock tool or a large screwdriver to back out the stock bolt. Remove the stock toward the rear. If it is very tight, bump the front of the comb with the heel of the hand to start it.

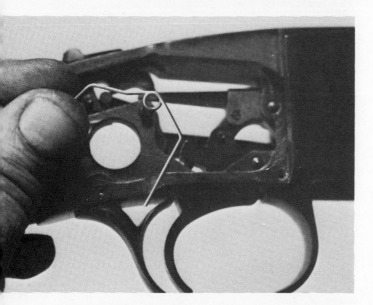

18. Unhook the upper arm of the safety positioning spring from its stud on the safety, and remove the spring from its mounting post toward the right.

19. Removal of the safety button requires the drifting out of two roll pins in its underlug, just below the upper tang.

20. Drifting out this post from the opposite side (from right to left) will release the safety arm and safety bar as a unit to be moved toward the rear and taken out toward the side. This is the same post that is the mounting stud for the safety positioning spring.

21. The trigger guard is retained by two roll pins at the front and rear, crossing the lower tang of the receiver. When these are drifted out, the guard is removed downward.

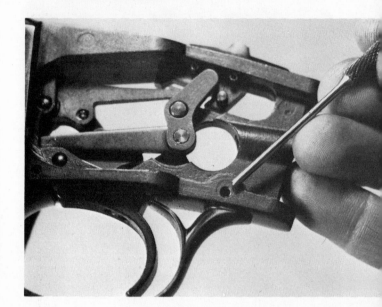

22. The trigger and sear are retained by cross pins, and are joined by a link. After the pins are removed, the trigger and sear are moved slightly toward the rear, then are taken out downward, with their attendant springs.

Reassembly Tips:

1. This view of the right side of the receiver with the stock removed shows the internal parts in their proper order. The safety is shown in the on-safe position.

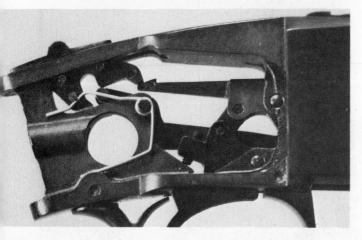

2. This view of the left side of the receiver shows the safety in the off-safe position.

3. After the firing pin spring is in place inside the breech-block, grip the firing pin with forceps or very slim pliers, and set the firing pin point into the spring.

4. When replacing the hammer transfer block, note that the concave area in its lower extension goes toward the rear.

5. When replacing the hammer spring assembly, note that the down-turned neck at the rear of the strut goes in that position—downward.

No. 1 Single Shot Rifle

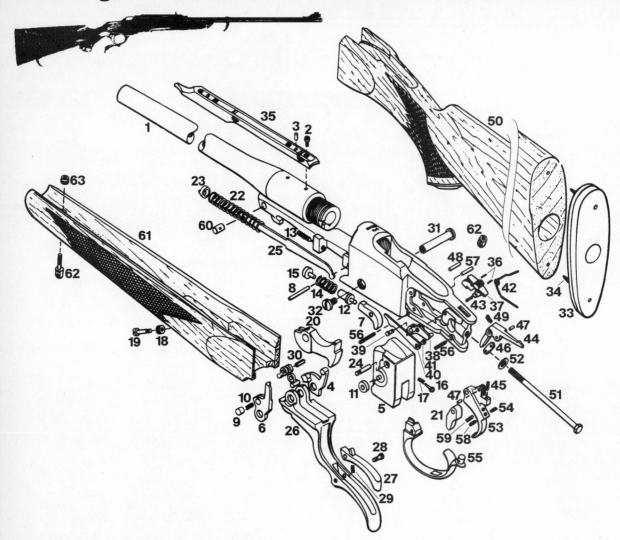

KEY

1	Barrel
2	Barrel Rib Screws
3	Barrel Rib Dowels
4	Breechblock Arm
5	Breechblock
6	Ejector
7	Ejector Cam
8	Ejector Cam Pivot Pin
9	Ejector Plunger
10	Ejector Plunger Spring
11	Ejector Roller
12	Ejector Strut
13	Ejector Strut Adjusting Screw
14	Ejector Strut Spring
15	Ejector Strut Swivel
16	Firing Pin
17	Firing Pin Spring
18	Forend Escutcheon
19	Forend Takedown Screw
20	Hammer
21	Hammer Transfer Block
22	Hammer Spring
23	Hammer Spring Retaining Washer
24	Hammer Transfer Block Pivot Pin
25	Hammer Strut
26	Lever
27	Lever Latch
28	Lever Latch Pivot Pin
29	Lever Latch Spring
30	Lever Link and Pin Assemblies
31	Lever Pivot Pin
32	Lever Pivot Screw
33	Recoil Pad
34	Recoil Pad Screws
35	Rib
36	Roll Pins for Safety Thumb-Piece
37	Safety
38	Safety Arm
39	Safety Arm Pivot Pin
40	Safety Bar
41	Safety Bar Pivot Pin
42	Safety Detent Spring
43	Safety Detent Spring Pin
44	Sear
45	Sear Adjustment Screw
46	Sear Link
47	Sear Link Pins
48	Sear Pivot Pin
49	Sear Spring
50	Buttstock
51	Stock Bolt
52	Stock Bolt Washer
53	Trigger
54	Trigger Adjustment Spring
55	Trigger Guard
56	Trigger Guard Retaining Pins
57	Trigger Pivot Pin
58	Trigger Spring Adjustment Screw
59	Trigger Stop Screw
60	Forend Takedown Nut
61	Forend
62	Sling Swivel Screws
63	Sling Swivel Escutcheon

Parts Not Shown
Front Sight Base
Front Sight Base Set Screw
Front Sight Blade
Front Sight Plunger Spring
Front Sight Retaining Plunger
Lever Pilot Groove Pin
Medallion
Pistol Grip Cap
Pistol Grip Cap Screw
Rear Sight

Russian SKS (Simonov)

Similar/Identical Pattern Guns

The same basic assembly/disassembly steps for the Russian SKS (Simonov) also apply to the following guns:

Chinese Type 56   **Yugoslavian Model 59/66**

Data:	Russian SKS (Simonov)
Origin:	Russia
Manufacturer:	Russian arsenals, and factories in China and other satellite nations
Cartridges:	7.62x39mm Russian
Magazine capacity:	10 rounds
Overall length:	40.2 inches
Barrel length:	20.47 inches
Weight:	8.5 pounds

Introduced in 1945, the Samozaryadnyi Karabin Simonova (SKS) was the first rifle chambered for the then-new 7.62mm "short" cartridge. The gun was made in large quantity, and it has been used at some time by every communist country in the world. Versions of it have been made in China, Yugoslavia, and elsewhere. While some of these variations may be different in small details, the mechanism is the same, and the instructions will apply.

Disassembly:

1. Cycle the action to cock the internal hammer. Turn the takedown latch up to vertical position, and pull it out toward the right until it stops. Take off the receiver cover toward the rear.

2. Move the bolt and recoil spring assembly back until it stops, and lift it off the receiver.

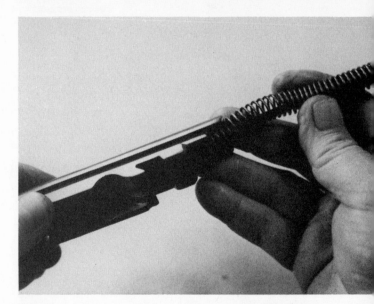

3. The bolt will probably be left in the receiver when the carrier and recoil spring unit are removed. If not, the bolt is simply lifted out of the carrier.

4. The captive recoil spring assembly is removed from the bolt carrier toward the rear.

5. If it is necessary to dismantle the spring assembly, rest the rear tip on a firm surface, pull back the spring at the front, and move the collar downward until it clears the button and take it off to the side. **Caution:** *Control the spring.*

6. Push out the firing pin retainer toward the right.

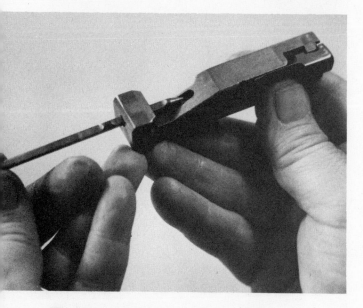

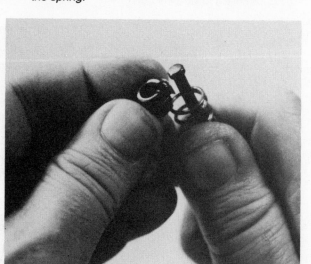

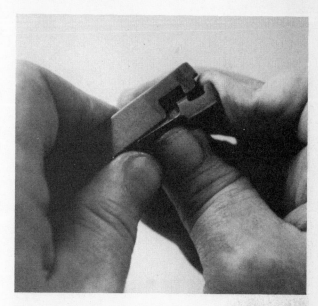

7. Remove the firing pin toward the rear.

8. Push the extractor toward the rear, and tip it out toward the right for removal. The spring is mounted inside the rear of the extractor, and it will come off with it.

9. The takedown latch is retained by an internal cross pin. In normal takedown, it is best left in place. To get the latch out of the way for the remainder of takedown, push it back into its locked position.

10. Insert a drift through the hole in the head of the cleaning rod, lift it out of its locking recess, and remove it toward the front.

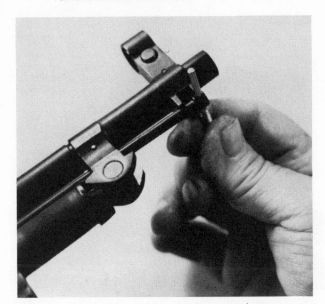

11. The bayonet hinge is often riveted in place. If removal is not necessary for repair, it is best left in place.

12. Be sure the internal hammer is in cocked position, and set the manual safety in on-safe position. Use a bullet tip or a suitable tool to push the guard latch forward.

13. When the latch releases, the guard will jump out slightly. Tip the guard away from the stock, move it toward the rear, and remove the guard unit.

14. Release the safety. Depress the disconnector, at the front of the hammer, about half way. Control the hammer, and pull the trigger. Ease the hammer down to fired position. **Caution:** *The hammer spring is powerful.*

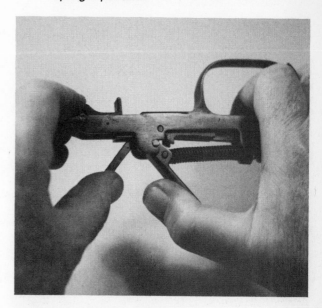

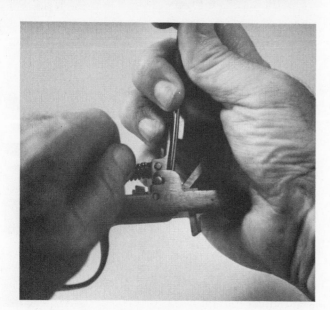

15. Insert a sturdy drift in front of the hammer, and lever it toward the rear until its pivot studs are clear of the hooks on the unit. **Caution:** *Keep a good grip on the hammer.* When it is clear, take off the hammer and its spring and guide. Another method is to grip the unit in a padded vise and use a bar of metal to apply pressure to the front of the hammer.

16. The trigger spring can be removed by gripping a forward coil with sharp-nosed pliers and compressing it slightly rearward, then tipping it out.

17. Pushing out the cross pin will free the disconnector for removal upward.

18. Removal of this cross pin will allow the rebound disconnector to be taken out.

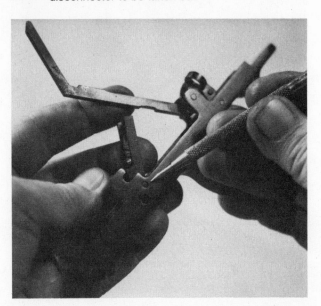

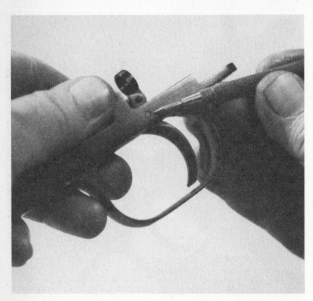

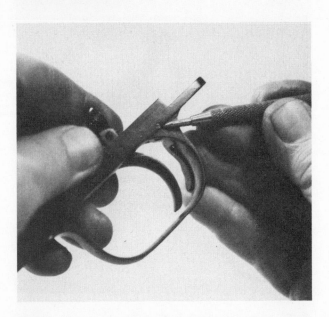

19. Drift out the trigger cross pin, and take out the trigger upward. The safety spring will also be freed for removal.

20. Drift out the safety-lever pin, and remove the safety.

21. This cross pin at the front of the trigger guard assembly retains the magazine catch, the combination spring, and the sear.

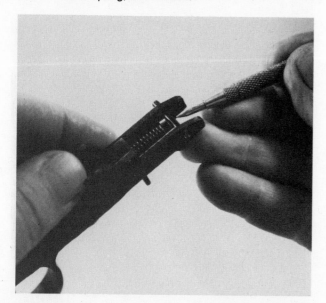

22. The trigger guard spring can be lifted out of its well in the stock.

23. With a bullet tip or a non-marring tool, turn the handguard latch upward until it is stopped by its lower stud in the track. Lift the handguard and gas cylinder assembly at the rear, and remove it.

24. Remove the gas piston from the cylinder.

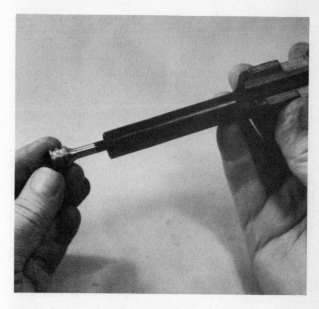

25. The gas port unit is retained on the barrel by a cross pin. In normal takedown, it is left in place.

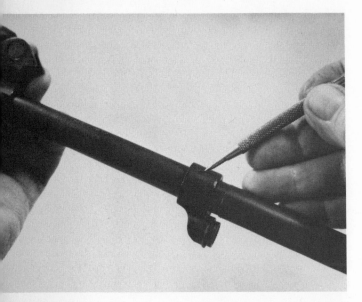

26. Drift out the stock end cap cross pin. Use a non-marring tool to nudge the end cap slightly forward.

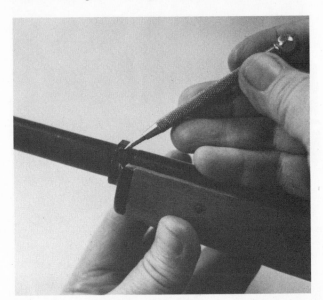

27. Grip the magazine assembly, and pull it rearward and downward for removal.

28. Remove the action from the stock.

29. The rear sight assembly is retained on the barrel by a cross pin, and is driven off toward the front. In normal takedown, the unit is left in place.

30. Drifting out this cross pin will allow removal of the bolt hold-open latch and its coil spring downward.

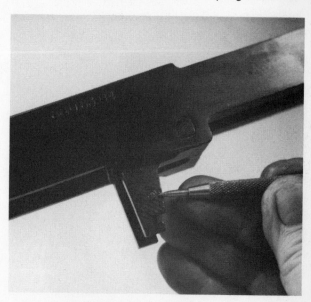

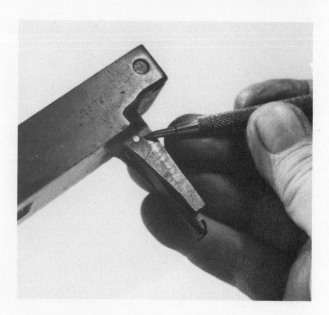

31. The trigger guard latch, which is its own spring, is retained by a cross pin. After removal of the pin, the latch is driven out downward.

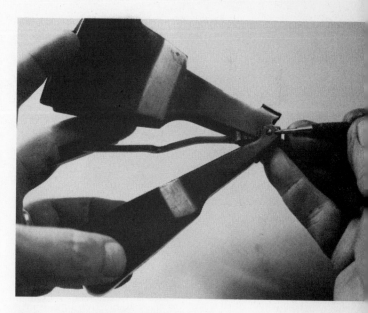

32. The magazine, the follower and its spring, and the magazine cover are joined by a cross pin at the front. The pin is riveted on both sides, and removal should be only for repair.

Reassembly tips:

1. When the stock end piece has been nudged back into position, insert a drift to align the hole with the barrel groove.

2. For those who have disassembled the trigger group, here is a view of that unit with all of the parts properly installed.

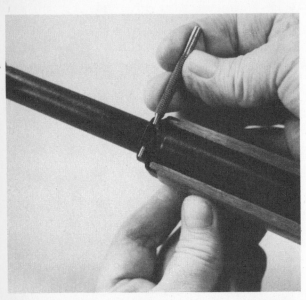

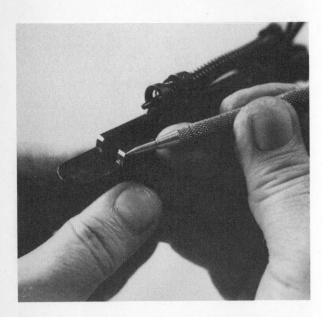

3. When replacing the trigger group in the gun, extremely sharp shoulders at the rear of the sub-frame may cause a seating problem. These can be easily beveled, as shown, with a file. Note: For installation of the trigger group, the manual safety must be in on-safe position. Rest the top of the receiver on a firm surface as the guard unit is pressed into place.

4. When replacing the firing pin in the bolt, be sure the retaining shoulder is on top. Also, be sure the retainer is oriented to fit into its recess on the right side.

7.62x39mm Autoloading Carbine

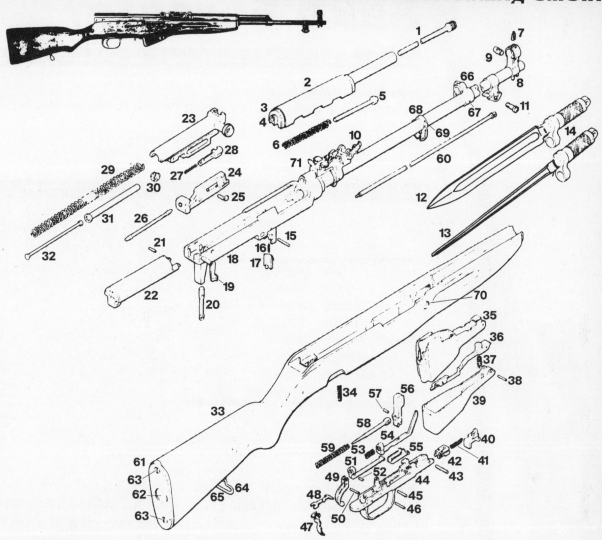

KEY

1 Piston	**25** Firing Pin Retainer	**51** Trigger Bar
2 Handguard and Gas Cylinder	**26** Firing Pin	**52** Trigger Bar Pin
3 Handguard Ferrule	**27** Extractor Spring	**53** Trigger Spring
4 Handguard Ferrule Pin	**28** Extractor	**54** Disconnector
5 Piston Extension	**29** Recoil Spring	**55** Rebound Disconnector
6 Piston Return Spring	**30** Spring Retainer	**56** Hammer
7 Front Sight	**31** Large Spring Guide	**57** Hammer Strut Pin
8 Front Sight Base and Bayonet Lug	**32** Small Spring Guide	**58** Hammer Strut
9 Front Sight Seat	**33** Stock	**59** Hammer Spring
10 Handguard Catch	**34** Trigger Guard Spring	**60** Cleaning Rod
11 Bayonet Screw	**35** Magazine	**61** Buttplate Assembly
12 Bayonet, Blade	**36** Magazine Follower	**62** Buttplate Trap Door Assembly
13 Bayonet, Spike	**37** Magazine Follower Spring	**63** Buttplate Screws
14 Bayonet Handle	**38** Hinge Pin	**64** Rear Swivel
15 Hold-Open Latch Pin	**39** Magazine Cover	**65** Rear Swivel Screws
16 Hold-Open Latch Spring	**40** Cover Latch	**66** Gas Cylinder Front Bracket
17 Hold-Open Latch	**41** Latch Spring and Sear Spring	**67** Gas Cylinder Bracket Pin
18 Receiver and Barrel Assembly	**42** Sear	**68** Stock Ferrule
19 Takedown Latch	**43** Latch Stop Pin	**69** Stock Ferrule Pin
20 Trigger Guard Latch	**44** Trigger Guard	**70** Recoil Lug Assembly
21 Latch Pin	**45** Disconnector Hinge Pin	**71** Rear Sight Assembly
22 Rear Housing	**46** Trigger Pin	
23 Bolt Carrier	**47** Safety Catch	**Parts Not Shown**
24 Bolt, Stripped	**48** Safety Catch Spring	Front Sight Base Pin, Front
	49 Trigger	Front Sight Base Pin, Rear
	50 Safety Catch Pin	Bayonet Spring

Sako Forester

Similar/Identical Pattern Guns
The same basic assembly/disassembly steps for the Sako Forester also apply to the following guns:

Sako Finnbear   **Sako Vixen**
Sako Model 72

Data:	Sako Forester
Origin:	Finland
Manufacturer:	Oy Sako, A.B., Riihimaki
Cartridges:	22-250, 243, 308
Magazine capacity:	5 rounds
Overall length:	42 inches
Barrel length:	23 inches
Weight:	6½ pounds

A redesign of the original L-57 Forester of 1958 was done in 1960. It was designated the Model L-579, and was still called the Forester. In two varmint chamberings and one for medium game, it became very popular in its time, and is still treasured for the smoothness of its action. One of the reasons for this feature is a full-length guide on the bolt, mounted on a pivot-ring in the style of the old Mauser extractor. All Sako rifles are of outstanding quality in both materials and workmanship. The Finnbear and Model 72 are essentially the same and the instructions will generally apply.

Disassembly:

1. Open the bolt and move it toward the rear, while pushing in the bolt stop, located at the left rear of the receiver. Remove the bolt from the rear of the receiver.

2. Grip the underlug of the cocking piece firmly in a vise, and pull the bolt body forward to clear the lug from the bolt sleeve. Turn the bolt until the lug on the bolt sleeve is aligned with the exit track on the bolt body, and separate the body from the sleeve and striker assembly.

3. Back out the striker shaft lock screw, located on the underside of the cocking piece at the rear.

4. With a firm grip on the bolt sleeve and the striker spring, use a screwdriver to turn the screw-slotted rear tip of the striker shaft clockwise (rear view) until the striker is free from the cocking piece. The spring is under tension, so keep it under control.

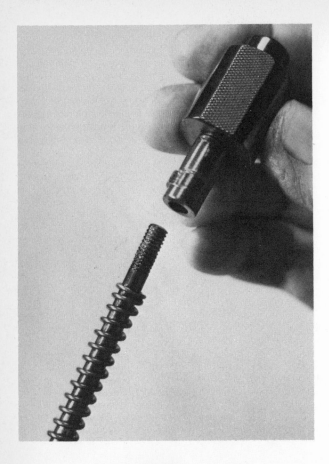

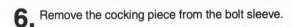
5. Remove the cocking piece, bolt sleeve, and spring from the striker shaft toward the rear.

6. Remove the cocking piece from the bolt sleeve.

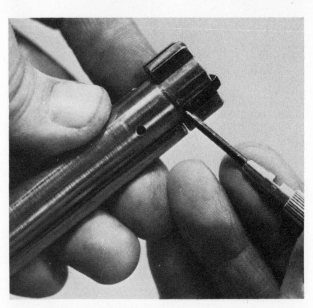

7. A small cross pin retains the bolt guide on the side of the bolt. The mounting ring is not removed in normal takedown. If the guide is removed, take care not to lose the guide rib stop and spring, mounted inside the rib at the front.

8. Insert a small screwdriver between the extractor and its plunger, and depress the plunger toward the rear, lifting the extractor out of its recess. **Caution:** *The spring is compressed, and can send the plunger quite a distance, so control the plunger and ease it out.*

9. Release the magazine floorplate latch, located in the front of the trigger guard, and open the floorplate. Flex the magazine spring away from the plate at the rear, and slide it rearward and out of its mounting slots. The magazine follower can be taken off the spring in the same manner.

10. Close and latch the floorplate, and remove the large vertical screws at the front of the magazine housing and at the rear of the trigger guard. Lift the action out of the stock.

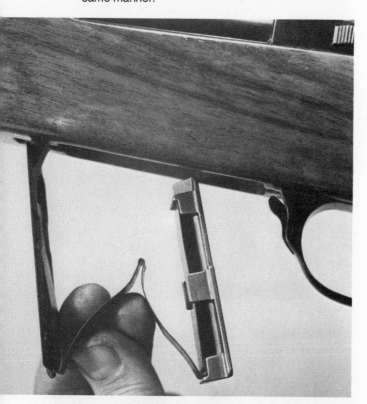

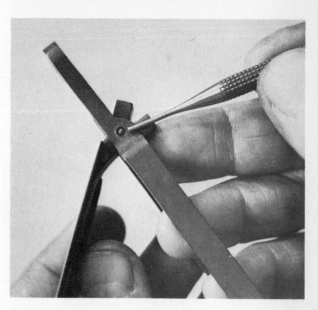

11. The trigger guard/magazine assembly can now be removed downward. When this unit is removed, take care not to lose the steel spacer plates at the front and rear, inside the stock.

12. The magazine floorplate can be removed by drifting out its hinge cross pin.

13. A small cross pin at the front of the trigger guard retains the magazine floorplate latch and its spring. **Caution:** *The spring is very strong. Restrain the latch, and ease it off.*

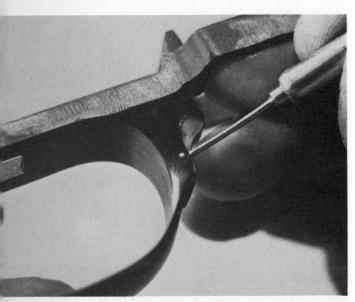

14. The magazine box is easily detached from its recess on the underside of the receiver.

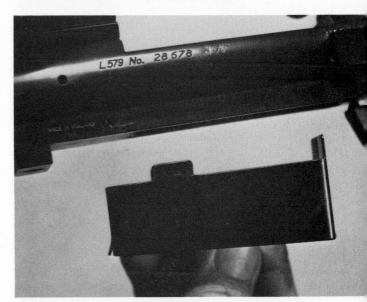

15. The bolt stop is retained by two screws on the left rear of the receiver, and is removed toward the left, along with its torsion spring. The bolt stop is also the ejector, and is pivoted inside its housing by a vertical pin. Drifting out the pin upward will free the stop/ejector and spring for removal.

16. Drift out the cross pin at the upper front of the trigger housing.

17. Remove the trigger assembly downward. Removal of this assembly will not disturb the trigger adjustment settings. Backing out the two screws on the right side of the housing will allow removal of the safety-lever toward the right. **Caution:** *Removal of the safety will release the positioning ball and spring.* See the next step.

18. The safety ball and spring are mounted across the unit, and backing out this small headless screw on the left side will allow separate removal of the ball and spring.

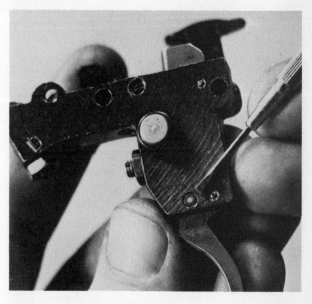

19. After the safety is removed, driving out this cross pin will allow the sear to be taken out upward.

20. Drifting out the trigger cross pin, and the small stop pin behind it, will allow the trigger to be taken out downward. Unless the process of adjustment is known, the trigger adjustment nuts and screws should not be disturbed.

21. The safety cross bolt is retained by a C-clip on the left side, and after its removal the safety bolt is taken out toward the right.

2. The degree of protrusion of the firing pin point from the breech face is governed by the level to which the striker shaft is turned on its threads during reassembly. Generally speaking, the rear tip of the striker shaft should be level with the rear of the cocking piece. To be more precise, the protrusion of the firing pin point at the front should be .055-inch, if you have a means of measuring this.

1. Note that the sides of the striker shaft at the rear have deep grooves lengthwise in the screw threads, and one of these must be aligned with the lock screw.

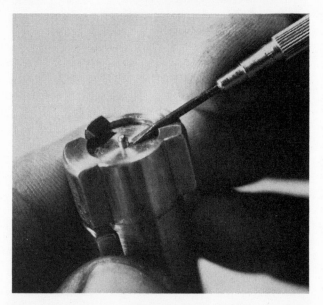

3. To properly check the protrusion, the bolt sleeve/striker assembly must be installed in the bolt. The photo shows an adjustment that has *far too much protrusion*. Adjustment can be made with the bolt fully assembled. After adjustment, be sure to tighten the lock screw securely. Note that the striker must be recocked before the bolt is put back in the gun.

Forester Bolt-Action Rifle

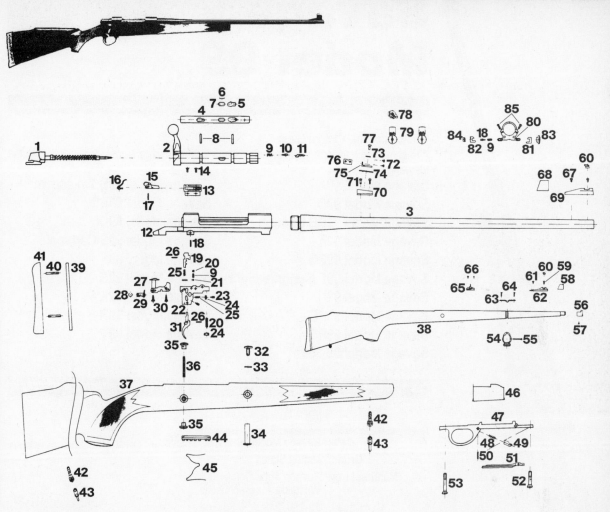

KEY					
1 Firing Pin Assembly	**28** Stop Ring	**57** Muzzle Cap Screw
2 Bolt	**29** Safety Shaft Assembly	**58** Front Sight Hood
3 Barrel	**30** Knob Plate Screws	**59** Front Mounting Screw
4 Bolt Guide	**31** Trigger	**60** Beads
5 Bolt Guide Stop Plate	**32** Recoil Lug Screw, Front	**61** Rear Mounting Screw
6 Bolt Guide Stop Plate Spring	**33** Recoil Lug Spacer	**62** Sight Base
7 Bolt Guide Stop Spring	**34** Recoil Lug Nut, Front	**63** Connecting Plate
8 Bolt Guide Mounting Rings	**35** Recoil Lug Nuts, Rear	**64** Connecting Plate Screws
9 Springs	**36** Recoil Lug Screw, Rear	**65** Rear Sight
10 Extractor Plunger	**37** Stock Complete, Rifle	**66** Rear Sight Mounting Screws
11 Extractor	**38** Stock Complete, Carbine	**67** Sight Base Mounting Screws
12 Receiver	**39** Buttplate Base	**68** Front Sight Hood
13 Bolt Stop Body	**40** Mounting Screws	**69** Front Sight Base
14 Bolt Stop Mounting Screws	**41** Buttplate	**70** Rear Sight Base
15 Bolt Stop	**42** Swivel Screws	**71** Mounting Screws
16 Bolt Stop Spring	**43** Swivels	**72** Sight Body Mounting Screws
17 Bolt Stop Pin	**44** Magazine Follower	**73** Washer
18 Pins	**45** Magazine Spring	**74** Covering Plate
19 Cocking Piece	**46** Magazine Box	**75** Sight Body
20 Set Screws	**47** Trigger Guard	**76** Sight Blade
21 Ball	**48** Floorplate Catch Spring	**77** Mounting Screw
22 Trigger Mechanism Body	**49** Floorplate Catch	**78** Peep Sight Complete
23 Adjusting Screw	**50** Spring Pin	**79** Scope Mount Complete
24 Hexagon Nut	**51** Floorplate	**80** Scope Mount Base
25 Trigger Spring	**52** Front Fastening Screw	**81** Scope Mount Locking Piece
26 Spring Pin	**53** Rear Fastening Screw	**82** Scope Mount Adjusting Piece
27 Knob Plate	**54** Stock Band	**83** Tightening Screw
	55 Stock Band Screw	**84** Tightening Screw
	56 Muzzle Cap	**85** Fastening Screws

Savage Model 99

1

Similar/Identical Pattern Guns

The same basic assembly/disassembly steps for the Savage Model 99 also apply to the following guns:

Savage Model 99A	**Savage Model 99B Takedown**
Savage Model 99C	**Savage Model 99CD**
Savage Model 99DE Citation	**Savage Model 99DL**
Savage Model 99E	**Savage Model 99E Carbine**
Savage Model 99EG	**Savage Model 99F**
Savage Model 99F Featherweight	**Savage Model 99G**
Savage Model 99H	**Savage Model 99K**
Savage Model 99PE	**Savage Model 99R**
Savage Model 99RS	**Savage Model 99T**
Savage Model 99-358	

Data:	Savage Model 99
Origin:	United States
Manufacturer:	Savage Arms Company Westfield, Massachusetts
Cartridges:	22-250, 243, 250 Savage, 300 Savage, 308 Winchester
Magazine capacity:	5 rounds
Overall length:	39¾ to 41¾ inches
Barrel length:	22 and 24 inches
Weight:	6¾ to 7 pounds

In 1899, Arthur W. Savage modified his original design of 1895, and the Model 99 rifle was born. Today, some 80 years later, this gun is still in production. It has been offered in a number of versions or sub-models in the past, and at the present time only one model is currently available. Two calibers, the 303 Savage and 30-30, are no longer made. The Model 99C has a detachable box magazine. The unique Savage rotary magazine was discontinued around 1984. The Model 99A, which replaced the original Model 99 in 1922, is the example shown here.

Disassembly:

1. Remove the buttplate to give access to the stock mounting bolt. Use a long screwdriver to remove the stock bolt, and take off the stock toward the rear. If the stock is tight, bump the front of the comb with the heel of the hand to start it.

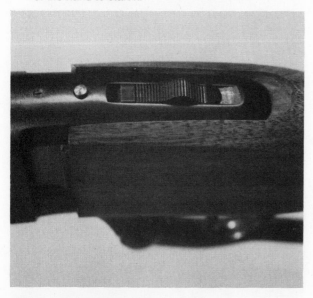

2. Remove the vertical screw at the left rear of the lower receiver extension, and take off the bolt stop.

3. Open the action slowly, and restrain the cartridge cutoff, which will be released toward the right as the bolt clears it. Remove the cutoff and its spring toward the right.

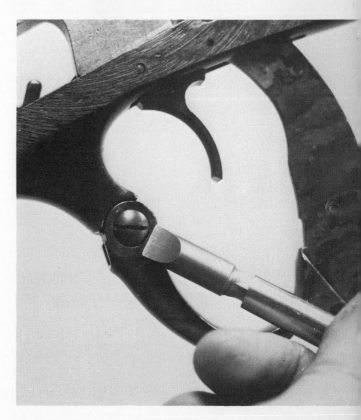

4. Remove the cap screw from the lever pivot. Remove the lever pivot toward the right.

5. Remove the front of the lever from its pivot loop and turn the rear arch slightly to clear its inner lug from the bolt. Remove the lever downward.

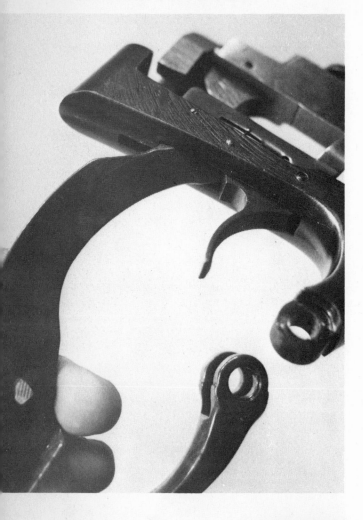

6. Move the bolt all the way to the rear, and pull the trigger to release the sear. Tip the sear to clear the bolt, and remove the bolt toward the left rear. Turn the lower rear of the breechblock (bolt) out toward the left to clear the receiver as the bolt is removed.

7. Remove the hammer and bushing screw from the left side of the bolt at the rear. Note that the screw is usually staked in place, and may require some effort in removal.

8. Remove the hammer and striker assembly toward the rear. Take care not to lose the hammer rebound spring, which will be released as the assembly is moved out to the rear.

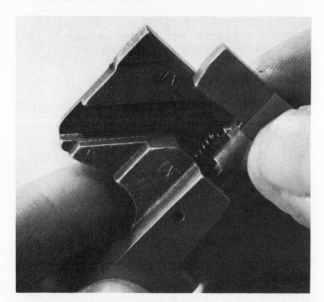

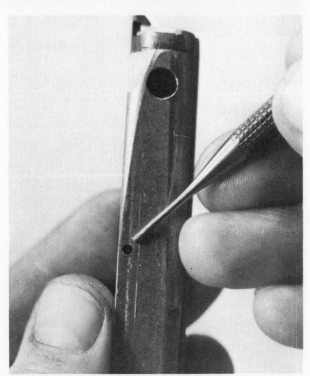

9. A vertical pin in the rear of the firing pin retains it on the front of the hammer shaft. Drifting out the pin will release the firing pin, hammer spring, and hammer bushing for removal toward the front. The pin is contoured at its ends to match the outside surface of the firing pin, and removal should be done only for repair purposes, not in normal takedown. If this unit is disassembled, proceed with caution, as the powerful hammer spring will be released.

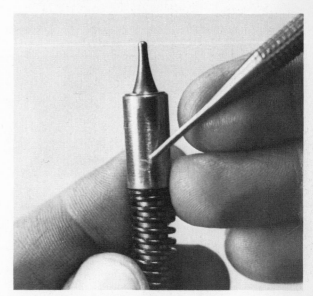

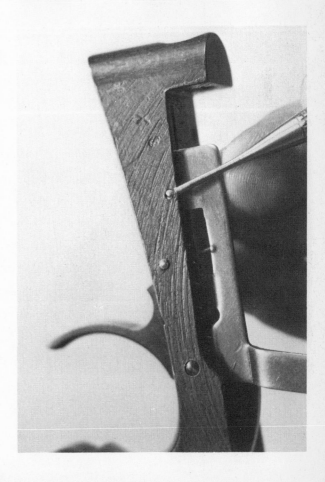

10. The extractor is its own spring, and is retained by a vertical pin on the right side of the bolt. The pin is driven out upward, and the extractor is taken off toward the right.

11. A small cross pin at the rear of the lower receiver extension retains the safety slide. There is an access hole on the left side which allows the pin to be drifted out toward the right.

12. Move the safety slide all the way to the rear, and tip it downward at the front and upward at the rear for removal.

13. Move the safety button all the way to the rear, and remove it from the top of the receiver.

14. The safety positioning spring is retained by a short cross pin, and there is an access hole on the left side of the receiver which allows the pin to be drifted out toward the right. Remove the spring upward.

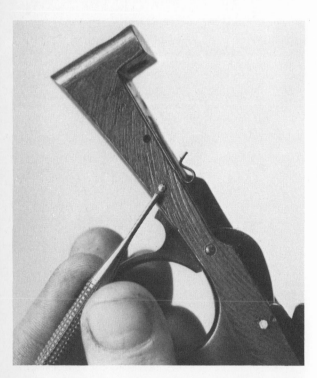

15. Drift out the trigger cross pin, and remove the trigger downward and toward the rear. **Caution:** *The trigger spring is under tension, so control it and ease it out.*

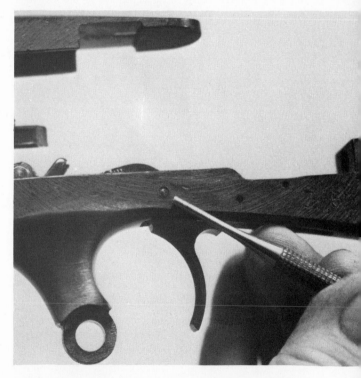

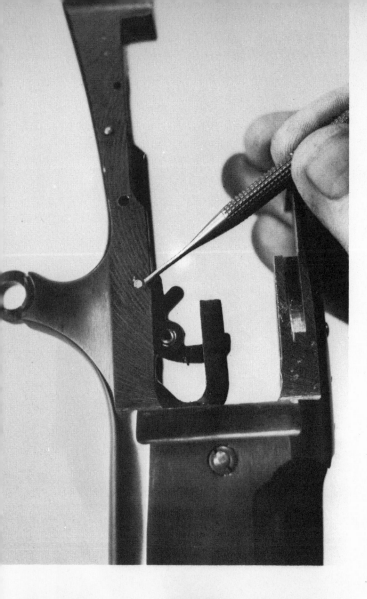

16. Drift out the short pin at the lower rear of the sear bracket. There is no access hole for this pin, so it is necessary to angle a drift punch to start the pin out, then remove it toward the right.

17. Removal of the sear bracket cross screw and nut will require a special twin-pointed tool, easily made by cutting away the center of a screwdriver tip. If the screw is tight, it will be necessary to stabilize the slotted screw head on the opposite side with a regular screwdriver as the nut is removed.

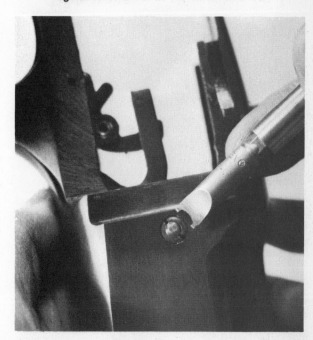

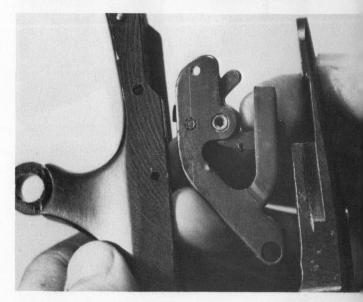

18. After the nut is removed, the screw must be unscrewed from the receiver and taken out toward the left.

19. Move the sear bracket assembly upward, out of its slot in the receiver, then remove it toward the rear.

20. Unhook the lower arm of the sear spring from its groove on the stop stud, and allow it to swing around to the rear, relieving its tension. Remove the spring from the sear post.

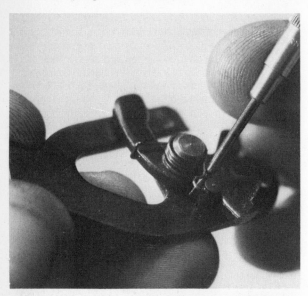

21. The sear is factory-riveted to the sear bracket, and should not be removed except for repair.

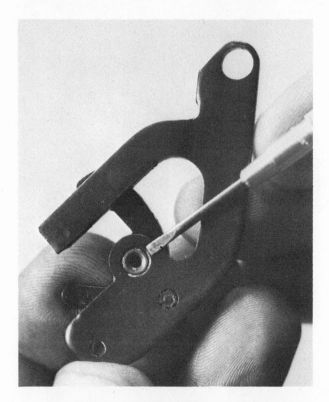

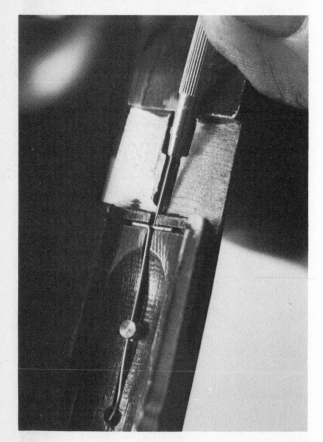

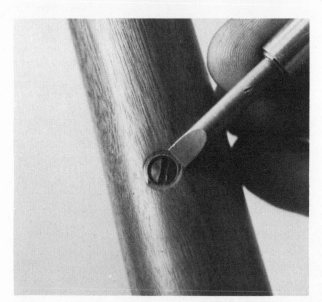

22. The hammer indicator can be removed from the top of the receiver by using a very small tool to lift the rear "T" of the indicator spring from its recess. Take out the spring toward the rear, and remove the indicator upward.

23. The forend is retained by a single vertical screw on its underside, and is taken off toward the front and downward.

24. The same twin-pointed tool used to remove the sear bracket nut can also be used to take off the carrier spindle nut. **Caution:** *Disassembly of the magazine system of the Model 99 is not recommended unless this is necessary for repair, as reassembly is difficult for those not familiar with it.* If disassembly is unavoidable, begin by removing the spindle nut.

25. The carrier spindle head screw is located on the left side of the receiver near the front edge. Restrain the carrier spindle head against rotation, and remove the screw toward the left. Slowly release the tension of the carrier spring, allowing the head to rotate. The spindle head, carrier, and spring can now be removed toward the front, and the carrier spindle and spindle bracket are taken out toward the rear.

27. The cartridge guide is retained by two vertical pins in the lower edge of the ejection port, and is not removed in normal takedown. If necessary, the pins are driven downward and retrieved from inside the receiver, and the guide is taken off toward the left and upward.

Reassembly Tips:

1. When replacing the safety slide, be sure the tip of the positioning spring engages its recess on the underside of the safety slide.

2. When replacing the hammer and striker assembly in the bolt, remember to insert the rebound spring below the assembly just before pushing it into place for insertion of the retaining screw.

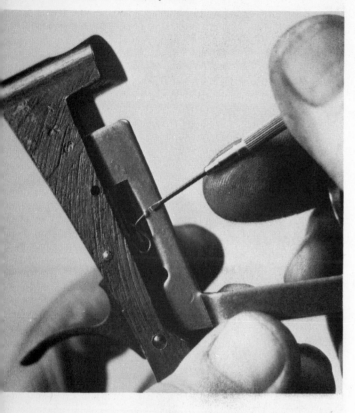

3. When replacing the lever pivot, note that there is a lug beneath its head on the left side that must be oriented to engage a recess in the lever loop on the receiver.

If the magazine has been dismantled, the carrier spring must be retensioned during reassembly by turning the spindle head before reinsertion of the cross screw. The number of turns required depends on the strength of the spring, so this can't be specified here.

Model 99 Lever-Action Rifle

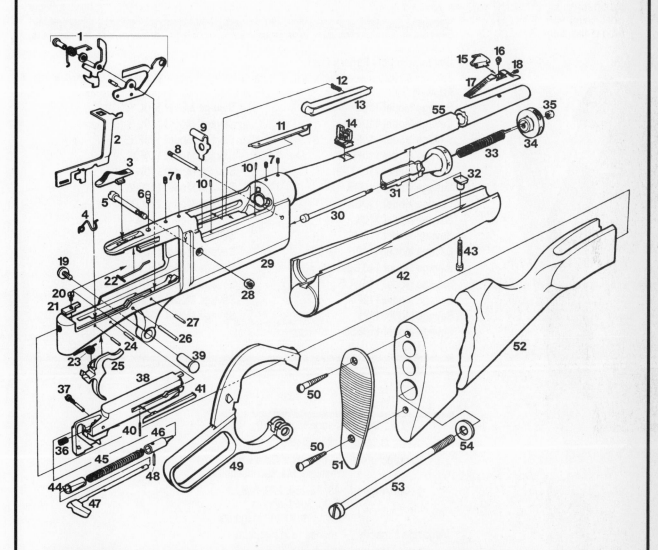

KEY

1 Sear Bracket Assembly
2 Safety Slide
3 Safety Button
4 Safety Slide Spring
5 Sear Screw
6 Hammer Indicator
7 Dummy Screws
8 Carrier Spindle Head Screw
9 Carrier Spindle Support
10 Cartridge Guide Pins
11 Cartridge Guide
12 Automatic Cutoff Spring
13 Automatic Cutoff
14 Rear Sight
15 Front Sight
16 Front Sight Screw
17 Front Sight Base

18 Front Sight Adjusting Screw
19 Lever Bushing Screw
20 Breechbolt Stop Screw
21 Breechbolt Stop
22 Hammer Indicator Spring
23 Trigger Spring
24 Safety Slide Spring and Stop Pins
25 Trigger
26 Trigger Pin
27 Sear Bracket Pin
28 Sear Screw Nut
29 Receiver
30 Carrier Spindle
31 Carrier
32 Barrel Stud
33 Carrier Spring
34 Carrier Spindle Head
35 Carrier Spindle Nut
36 Hammer Retractor Spring

37 Hammer Bushing Screw
38 Breechbolt
39 Lever Bushing
40 Extractor Pin
41 Extractor
42 Forend
43 Forend Screw
44 Hammer Bushing
45 Mainspring
46 Firing Pin
47 Hammer
48 Firing Pin Securing Pin
49 Lever
50 Buttplate Screws
51 Buttplate
52 Stock
53 Stock Bolt
54 Stock Bolt Washer
55 Barrel

Savage Model 110

Similar/Identical Pattern Guns

The same basic assembly/disassembly steps for the Savage Model 110 also apply to the following guns:

Savage Model 110B	Savage Model 110CY
Savage Model 110D	Savage Model 110E
Savage Model 110F	Savage Model 110FNS
Savage Model 110FP	Savage Model 110FX
Savage Model 110FXP3	Savage Model 110G
Savage Model 110GB	Savage Model 110GV
Savage Model 110GX	Savage Model 110GXP3
Savage Model 110K	Savage Model 110M
Savage Model 110MC	Savage Model 110P
Savage Model 110PE	Savage Model 110S
Savage Model 110 Sporter	Savage Model 110V
Savage Model 110WLE	Savage Model 111 Chieftan
Savage Model 112FV	Savage Model 112R
Savage Model 112V	Savage Model 114CU Classic Ultra
Savage Model 116FSS	

Data:	Savage Model 110
Origin:	United States
Manufacturer:	Savage Arms Company Westfield, Massachusetts
Cartridges:	243, 22-250, 270, 308, 30-06, 300 Magnum, 7mm Remington Magnum
Magazine capacity:	4 rounds (3 in magnums)
Overall length:	43 inches
Barrel length:	22 inches
Weight:	7 to 8⅝ pounds

Since its introduction in 1958, the Model 110 has been offered in a wide variety of sub-models, and several of these are still in production. This is one of the few rifles that is also available in a left-handed action, and the moderate price of the Model 110 has made it very popular. Recent additions to the line include a version with a detachable magazine. The instructions can be applied to all of the sub-models.

Disassembly:

1. Open the bolt, pull the trigger, and push down the sear lever on the right side of the receiver. Hold it down, and remove the bolt toward the rear.

2. With a coin or a large screwdriver, unscrew the large knob at the rear of the bolt. Once it is started, its knurled edge will allow it to be turned by hand. Remove the knob toward the rear.

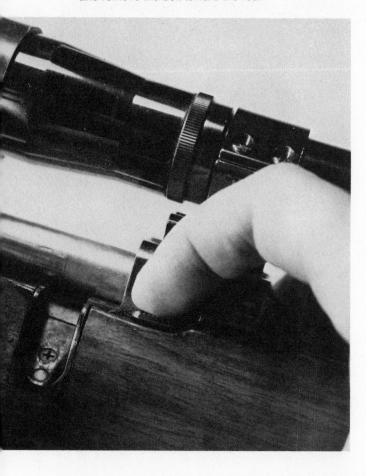

3. The attached cocking piece sleeve will come out with the knob as it is removed.

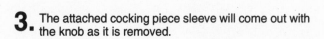

4. Remove the bolt handle toward the rear.

5. Remove the rear baffle piece toward the rear. If necessary, the two detent balls and spring can be removed from the baffle by pushing the inner ball outward until it aligns with the hole at the bottom of the baffle. The spring will then force both balls out. In normal disassembly, these parts are best left in place.

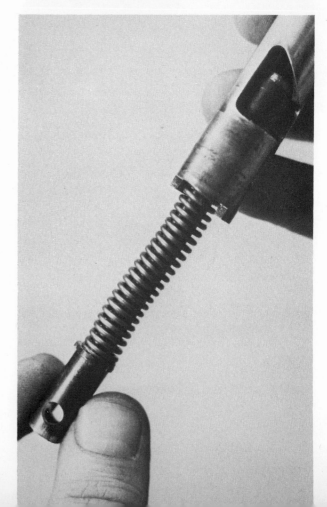

6. Remove the cocking piece pin from its hole in the side of the striker assembly.

7. Remove the striker assembly from the rear of the bolt.

8. Grip the front of the striker firmly in a vise, insert a punch through the hole in the cocking piece, and unscrew the cocking piece from the rear tip of the striker shaft. **Caution:** *The striker spring is partially compressed, so control the parts and ease the tension slowly.* Take care not to disturb the striker stop nut at the front, as it controls the protrusion of the firing pin point at the bolt face. If the striker system does not need repair, it's best not to disassemble it.

9. Drift out the bolt head retaining pin.

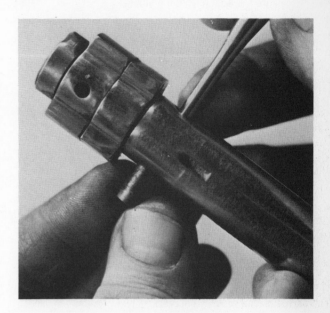

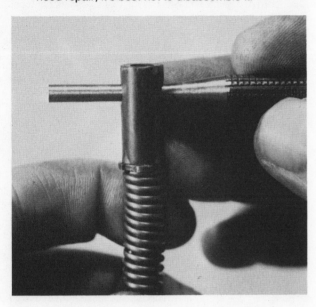

10. Remove the bolt head, baffle and friction washer toward the front. The front baffle is easily taken off the bolt head toward the rear.

11. Insert a small screwdriver under the end of the extractor nearest the ejector slot, and twist the screwdriver toward the left, levering the extractor out of its groove and toward the front of the bolt.

12. Remove the large vertical screw on the underside at the front of the magazine floorplate. Remove the large vertical screw at the front of the trigger guard, in the rear tip of the magazine floorplate. Remove the floorplate and magazine insert downward, and take out the magazine spring and follower. Separate the action from the stock.

13. Depress the combination magazine latch and ejector housing upward, tip its lower end away from the magazine box, and remove the latch/housing, spring, and ejector downward.

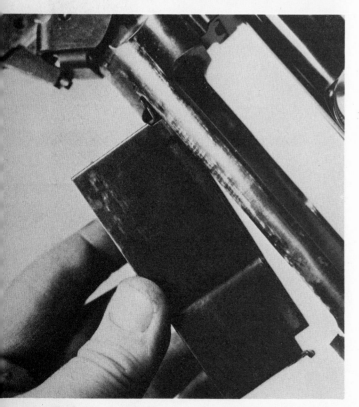

14. The magazine box can now be moved toward the rear, tipped down at the front, and removed forward and downward.

15. While restraining the sear spring, push out the sear pin toward the left.

16. Remove the sear downward and toward the front, along with its spring and bushing. Take care that the small bushing isn't lost.

17. Tip the trigger housing down at the front, and unhook its rear lip from the underside of the receiver. Remove the trigger housing downward. After the housing is taken off, the small spring steel trigger pull screw cover can be slid to the rear of its slot at the rear of the receiver, and removed. Remove the safety bearing pin from the housing.

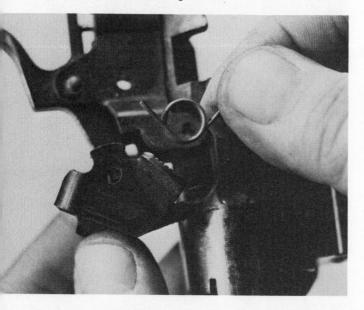

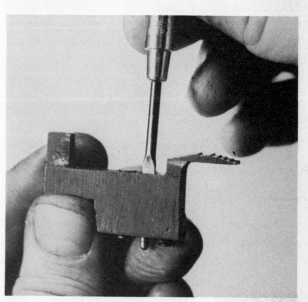

19. The trigger adjustment screws in the safety-block need not be disturbed. The one at top center retains the trigger spring and its plunger, and can be taken out to allow removal of the spring and plunger upward.

18. Lift the safety-block from the top of the trigger housing.

20. Drifting out the trigger cross pin will allow removal of the trigger from the housing. Note that this pin is held at center by a ball and spring in the front of the trigger, retained by a screw at the front. This screw should not be disturbed.

21. The barrel is retained in the receiver by a large grooved nut which also holds the recoil lug on the front of the receiver. In normal takedown, the barrel is best left in place.

Reassembly Tips:

1. When replacing the sear system, insert the sear cross pin from the left, and stop it short of crossing the spring recess. Insert the spring from the rear, and insert a drift punch into the spring bushing from the right to lever the bushing and spring into position for the cross pin to be pushed through to the right.

2. When replacing the bolt head assembly, note that there is a recess in the rear tail of the bolt head and a depression and inside welt on the inside of the bolt body, and these must be aligned.

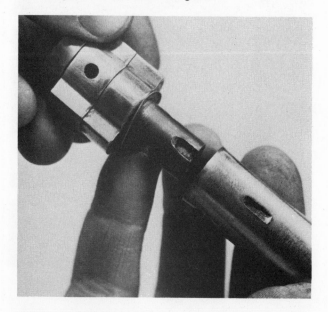

3. When replacing the bolt head retaining cross pin, note that there is a hole at its center for passage of the firing pin, and this hole must be properly oriented as the cross pin is installed.

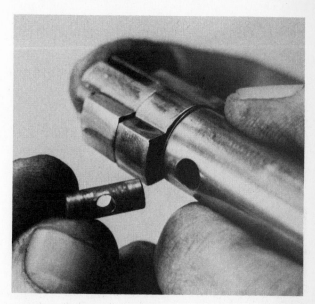

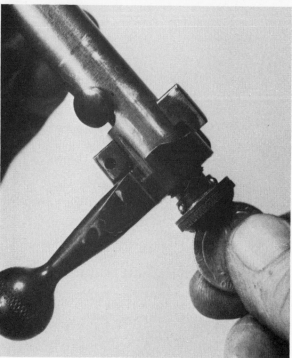

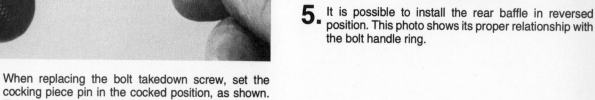

5. It is possible to install the rear baffle in reversed position. This photo shows its proper relationship with the bolt handle ring.

4. When replacing the bolt takedown screw, set the cocking piece pin in the cocked position, as shown. This will make tightening the screw a bit stiffer, but will leave the action cocked for reinsertion of the bolt into the receiver.

Model 110B, 110C, 110D and 110E Series J and K Bolt-Action Rifle

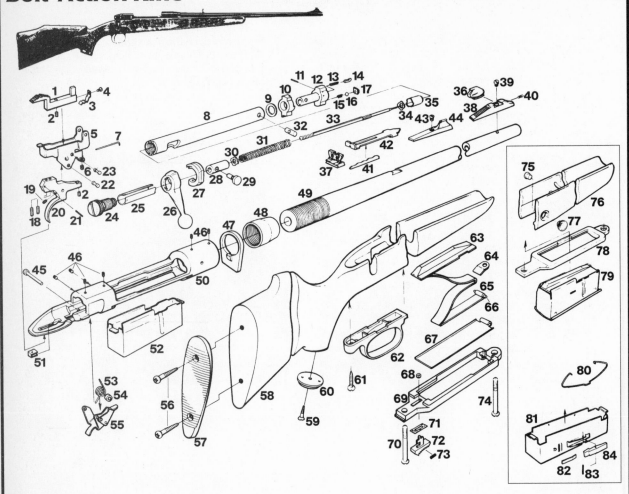

KEY

1 Safety
2 Trigger Pull Adjusting Screw
3 Safety Detent Spring
4 Safety Detent Spring Screw
5 Trigger Bracket
6 Trigger Pull Adjusting Screw
7 Trigger Pull Adjusting Spring
8 Bolt Body
9 Front Baffle Friction Washer
10 Front Baffle
11 Ejector Retaining Pin
12 Bolt Head Assembly
13 Ejector Spring
14 Ejector
15 Extractor Spring
16 Steel Ball
17 Extractor
18 Trigger Travel Adjusting Screws
19 Trigger Pin Retaining Screws
20 Trigger
21 Trigger Spring Pin
22 Trigger Pin
23 Safety Bearing Pin
24 Bolt Assembly Screw
25 Cocking Piece Sleeve
26 Bolt Handle
27 Rear Baffle Assembly

28 Cocking Piece
29 Cocking Piece Pin
30 Cocking Piece Link Washer
31 Mainspring
32 Bolt Head Retaining Pin
33 Firing Pin Assembly
34 Firing Pin Stop Nut Washer
35 Firing Pin Stop Nut
36 Front Sight
37 Rear Sight
38 Front Sight Base
39 Front Sight Screw
40 Front Sight Adjusting Screw
41 Rear Sight Step
42 Rear Sight
43 Front Sight Screw
44 Front Sight Assembly
45 Sear Pin
46 Dummy Screw
47 Recoil Lug
48 Barrel Lock Nut
49 Barrel
50 Receiver
51 Trigger Adjusting Screw Cover
52 Magazine Box
53 Sear Spring
54 Sear Bushing
55 Sear Assembly
56 Buttplate Screws

57 Buttplate
58 Stock
59 Pistol Grip Cap Screw
60 Pistol Grip Cap
61 Trigger Guard Screw
62 Trigger Guard
63 Magazine Follower Assembly
64 Hinge Plate Spring
65 Magazine Spring
66 Hinge Pin
67 Hinged Plate
68 Magazine Latch Retaining Ring
69 Floorplate
70 Floorplate Screw, Rear
71 Magazine Latch Spacer
72 Magazine Latch
73 Magazine Latch Spring
74 Floorplate Screw, Front
75 Magazine Latch Button
76 Stock
77 Escutcheon
78 Floorplate
79 Magazine Assembly
80 Magazine Ejector Spring
81 Magazine Guide
82 Magazine Latch Spring
83 Magazine Latch Pin
84 Magazine Latch

Model 110C and 110CL Bolt-Action Rifle

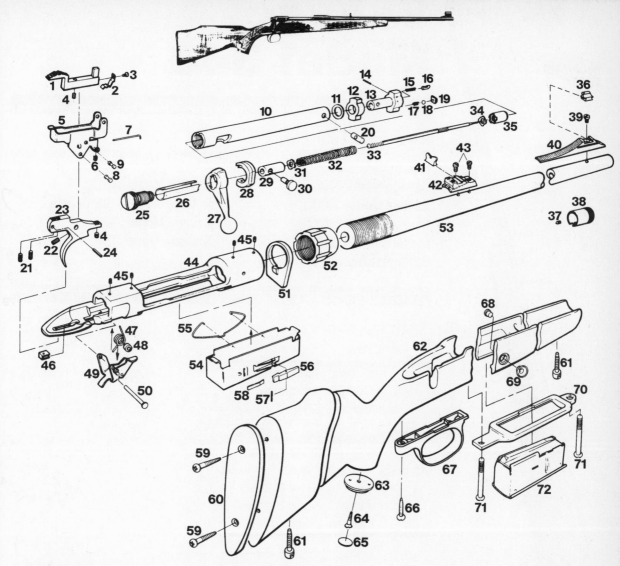

KEY

1	Safety
2	Safety Detent Spring
3	Safety Detent Spring Screw
4	Trigger Pull Adjusting Screw
5	Trigger Bracket
6	Trigger Pull Adjusting Screw
7	Trigger Pull Adjusting Spring
8	Trigger Pin
9	Safety Bearing Pin
10	Bolt Body
11	Front Baffle Friction Washer
12	Front Baffle
13	Bolt Head Assembly
14	Ejector Retaining Pin
15	Ejector Spring
16	Ejector
17	Extractor Spring
18	Steel Ball
19	Extractor
20	Bolt Head Retaining Pin
21	Trigger Travel Adjusting Screws
22	Trigger Pin Retaining Screw
23	Trigger
24	Trigger Spring Pin
25	Bolt Assembly Screw
26	Cocking Piece Sleeve
27	Bolt Handle
28	Rear Baffle Assembly
29	Cocking Piece
30	Cocking Piece Pin
31	Cocking Piece Link Washer
32	Mainspring
33	Firing Pin Assembly
34	Firing Pin Stop Nut Washer
35	Firing Pin Stop Nut
36	Front Sight
37	Front Sight Pin
38	Front Sight Hood
39	Front Sight Screw
40	Front Sight Ramp
41	Rear Sight Blade
42	Rear Sight Base
43	Rear Sight Screws
44	Receiver
45	Dummy Screws
46	Trigger Adjusting Screw Cover
47	Sear Spring
48	Sear Bushing
49	Sear Assembly
50	Sear Pin
51	Recoil Lug
52	Barrel Lock Nut
53	Barrel
54	Magazine Guide
55	Magazine Ejector Spring
56	Magazine Latch
57	Magazine Latch Pin
58	Magazine Latch Spring
59	Buttplate Screws
60	Buttplate
61	Swivel Studs
62	Stock
63	Pistol Grip Cap
64	Pistol Grip Cap Screw
65	Medallion
66	Trigger Guard Screw
67	Trigger Guard
68	Magazine Latch Button
69	Escutcheon
70	Floorplate
71	Floorplate Screws
72	Magazine Box

Savage Model 340

Similar/Identical Pattern Guns

The same basic assembly/disassembly steps for the Savage Model 340 also apply to the following guns:

Savage Model 340B

Savage Model 340D

Savage Model 340V

Stevens Model 322

Springfield Model 840

Savage Model 340C

Savage Model 340S Deluxe

Savage Model 342

Stevens Model 325

Data:	Savage Model 340
Origin:	United States
Manufacturer:	Savage Arms Company Westfield, Massachusetts
Cartridges:	22 Hornet, 222, 223, 225 Win., 30-30
Magazine capacity:	4 rounds (3 in 30-30)
Overall length:	40 and 42 inches
Barrel length:	22 and 24 inches
Weight:	6½ pounds

The Model 340 was intended to be an in-between gun, a low-priced bolt-action repeater chambered for two varmint cartridges and one medium-game round. In this category it gained wide acceptance since 1950, and was discontinued in 1985. For a short time, a carbine version was made in 30-30 only, with an 18½-inch barrel. The basic Model 340 design has been marketed as the Savage Model 342, the Stevens Model 322 and 325, and the Springfield Model 840, among others. They are essentially the same.

Disassembly:

1. Remove the magazine. Pull the trigger all the way to the rear, beyond its normal let-off position, and hold it there. Open the bolt, and remove it toward the rear.

2. With a small brass hammer, tap the cocking lug out of its detent notch at the rear of the bolt, allowing the striker to go forward to the fired position, as shown.

3. Drift out the cross pin that retains the bolt head.

4. Remove the bolt handle and striker assembly toward the rear. If the assembly is tight, use a plastic hammer to tap it gently off.

5. Grip the front portion of the striker firmly in a vise, and push the bolt handle sleeve toward the front until the cocking piece is exposed. Remove the semi-circular key from the top of the cocking piece, and unscrew the cocking piece from the rear of the striker shaft. **Caution:** *Keep a firm grip on the bolt handle, as the striker spring is compressed.*

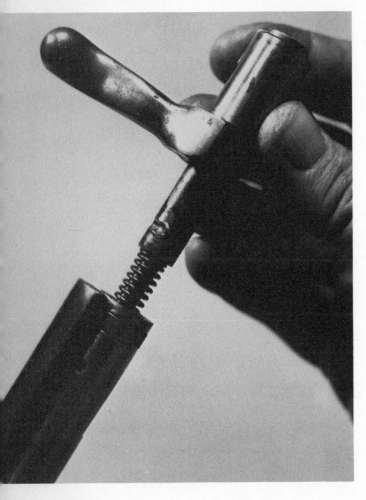

6. Slowly ease off the tension of the striker spring, and remove the striker and spring from the front of the bolt handle unit.

7. Some models of the 340 design have a clip-on extractor unit, and others, such as the one shown, have a hook-in type with a spring and plunger at the rear. To remove this type, restrain the plunger and spring, and pivot the extractor out toward the right and take it off. The clip-on type unit is simply pried out of its recess for removal.

8. The gas shield is retained on top of the bolt by two cross pins, and mounted on twin rings which encircle the bolt. The cross pins are usually staked in place, so if removal is necessary, be sure the shield is well supported while driving out the pins.

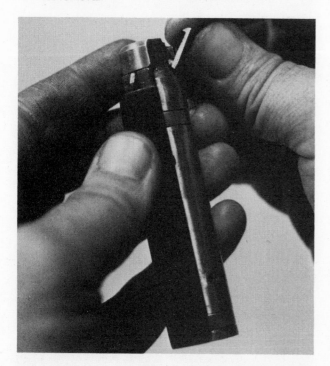

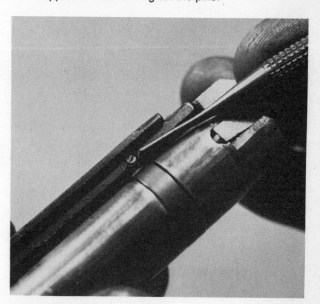

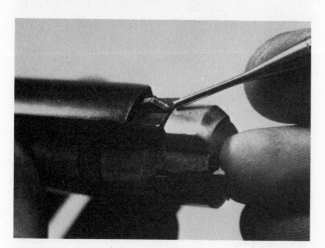

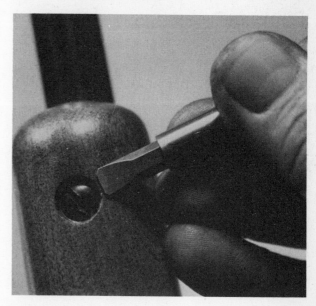

9. When the front gas shield cross pin is drifted out, the gas shield key and its spring will be released along with the shield.

10. Remove the barrel band screw, located on the underside near the front of the stock.

11. Remove the main stock mounting screw, located on the underside in the front tip of the magazine plate. Separate the action from the stock.

12. To remove the barrel band, push the band nut toward the barrel, and disengage its side studs from the holes in the band. The band can then be taken off upward.

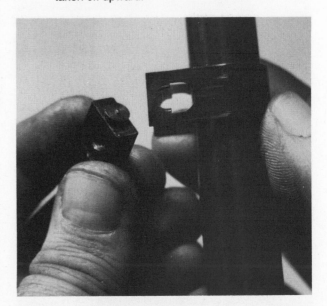

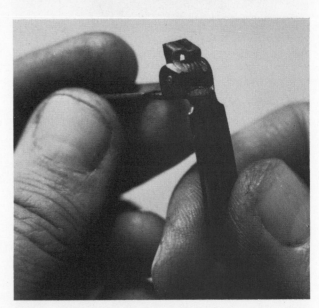

13. The magazine guide is retained on the underside of the receiver by a single screw, and the screw and guide are removed downward.

14. In the 22 Hornet version, the front magazine guide also contains a small cartridge ramp and a torsion spring for the ramp. Drifting out the cross pin will release the ramp and spring for removal, but in normal takedown they are best left in place.

15. The cross pins in the trigger housing that retain the trigger and sear mechanism have large heads on the right side and are semi-riveted on the left. It is not advisable to remove them in normal takedown. If necessary for repair, or if the trigger housing must be removed, the internal parts must be taken out, as the two vertical retaining screws for the housing are obscured by the parts. Drifting out the pin shown will release the trigger and its spring for removal toward the rear and downward.

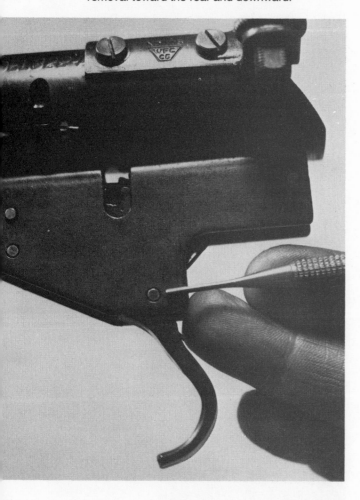

16. Drifting out the cross pin at the upper rear of the trigger housing will release the sear and its spring for removal downward and toward the rear. The spring is under tension, so control it and ease it out.

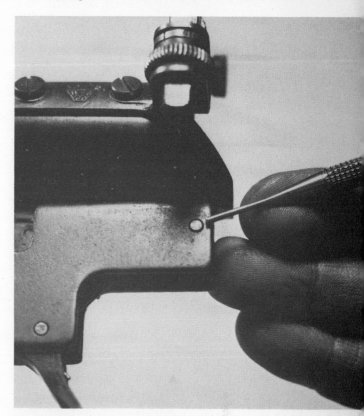

17. Drifting out the lower cross pin at the front of the trigger housing will release the sear lever for removal downward. The upper pin holds the combination sear lever bracket and magazine stop in place, and its removal is not necessary.

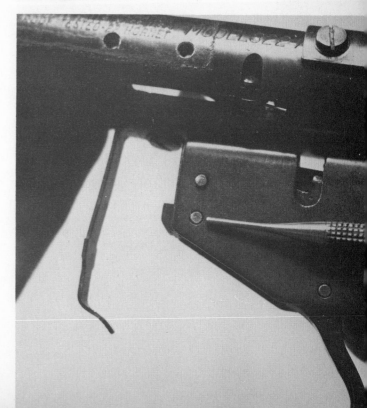

18. Remove the safety-lever screw, and take off the safety toward the right.

19. When the safety-lever is removed, take care not to lose the small safety positioning ball and spring. If they do not come out freely, there is an access hole on the inside of the bolt tunnel in the receiver for insertion of a tool to nudge them out. Removal of the screw on the right side of the housing will allow the main safety-block to be taken off toward the right.

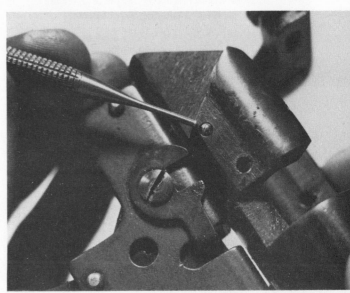

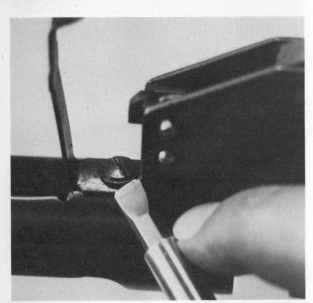

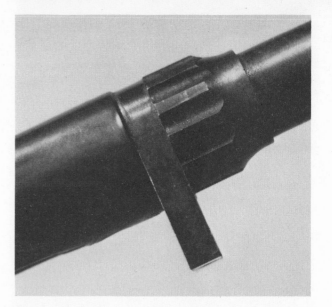

20. After the other parts are removed from the trigger housing, the vertical screws at the front and center will be accessible, and the trigger housing can be removed downward. The magazine catch screw can also be removed, and the catch taken off downward.

21. The barrel is retained in the receiver by a deeply grooved lock nut, requiring a special wrench which is not routinely available. It can be loosened or retightened by using a hammer and non-marring punch in one of the grooves, working in an area normally covered by the stock. Removal of the nut will allow the barrel to be taken out toward the front, and the recoil lug will also be freed for removal. In normal takedown, this system should be left in place.

22. Insert a screwdriver beneath the upper collar of the ejector pivot pin, and pry it out upward and toward the left. The ejector and its spring will be released for removal from their slot in the side of the receiver.

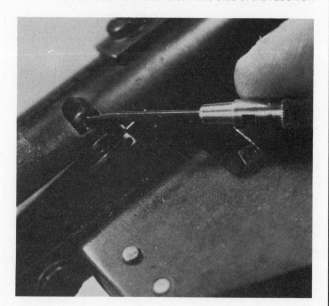

Reassembly Tips:

1. When replacing the cocking piece on the rear of the striker shaft, note that the degree of advancement on the threads controls the protrusion of the firing pin point from the bolt face. Check this by inserting the rear portion of the bolt, with the striker in the fired position, into the front portion of the bolt. If the protrusion is more than the amount shown, turn the cocking piece for adjustment.

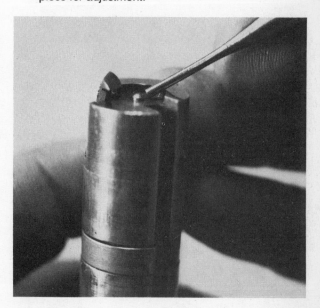

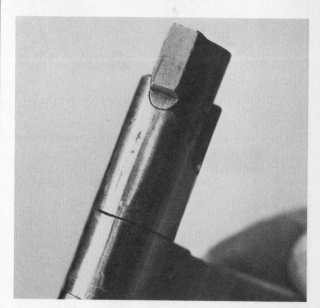

2. Before the reassembled bolt can be put back into the receiver, the gas shield must be aligned with the forward lug of the bolt and the bolt handle base, and the striker must be cocked. When the striker is in the position shown, the bolt can be reinserted.

Model 340, 340B, 340C, 340D and 340V Bolt-Action Rifle

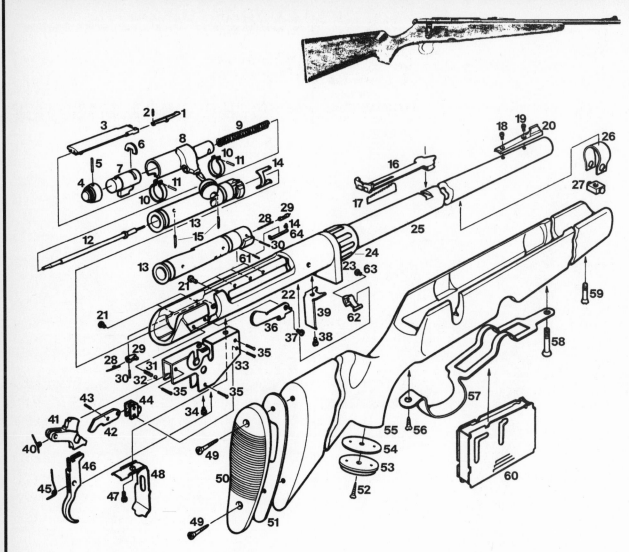

KEY

1	Gas Shield Key
2	Gas Shield Key Spring
3	Gas Shield
4	Cocking Piece Cap
5	Cocking Piece Cap Pin
6	Cocking Piece Key
7	Cocking Piece
8	Bolt Body and Handle
9	Mainspring
10	Gas Shield Clips
11	Gas Shield Clip Pins
12	Firing Pin
13	Bolt Head
14	Extractor
15	Bolt Head Retaining Pins
16	Rear Sight
17	Rear Sight Step
18	Front Sight Screw, Short
19	Front Sight Screw, Long
20	Front Sight
21	Dummy Screws
22	Receiver
23	Barrel Lug
24	Barrel Lock Nut
25	Barrel
26	Barrel Band
27	Barrel Band Nut
28	Ejector Spring
29	Ejector
30	Ejector Pin
31	Safety Spring
32	Safety Plunger Ball
33	Trigger Bracket
34	Trigger Bracket Screw, Short
35	Sear Pins
36	Safety
37	Safety Screw
38	Magazine Retainer Screw
39	Magazine Retainer Spring, Front
40	Sear Spring
41	Sear
42	Sear Lever
43	Sear Cam Pin
44	Magazine Stop
45	Trigger Spring
46	Trigger
47	Trigger Bracket Screw
48	Magazine Retainer Spring, Rear
49	Buttplate Screws
50	Buttplate
51	Buttplate Spacer
52	Pistol Grip Cap Screw
53	Pistol Grip Cap
54	Pistol Grip Cap Spacer
55	Stock
56	Trigger Guard Screw, Rear
57	Trigger Guard
58	Recoil Lug Screw
59	Barrel Band Screw
60	Magazine Assembly
61	Extractor Spring Pin
62	Baffle Block
63	Baffle Block Screw
64	Extractor Spring

Stevens Favorite

Data:	Stevens Favorite
Origin:	United States
Manufacturer:	J. Stevens Arms & Tool Company Chicopee Falls, Massachusetts
Cartridge:	22 Long Rifle
Overall length:	36$\frac{1}{2}$ inches
Barrel length:	22 inches
Weight:	4 pounds

The little Stevens Favorite was certainly well-named. After its introduction in 1889, it became the most popular "boy's rifle" of all time, and lasted through 46 years of production. The gun was simple and reliable, a single shot with a lever-actuated falling block. In 1915 it was redesigned, the most notable internal changes being in the ejector and hammer spring. These differences will be noted in the instructions. The gun covered here is the early model, made prior to 1915.

Disassembly:

1. Back out the barrel retaining screw, located just forward of the lever on the underside of the gun. On guns made after 1915, the head of the screw will be a knurled piece, rather than a ring.

2. Remove the barrel and forend assembly forward.

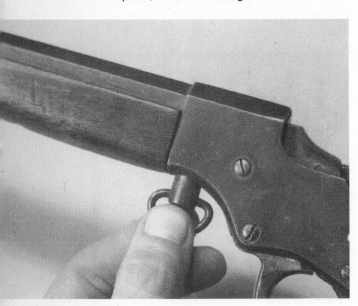

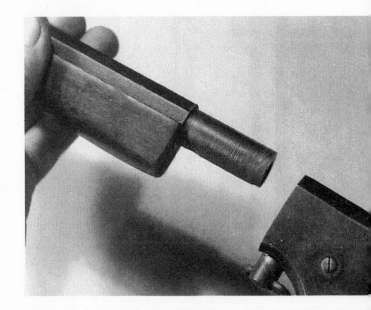

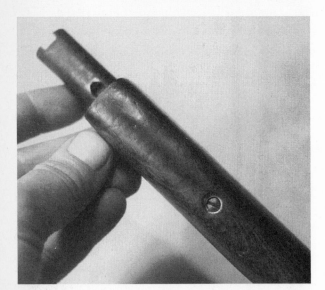

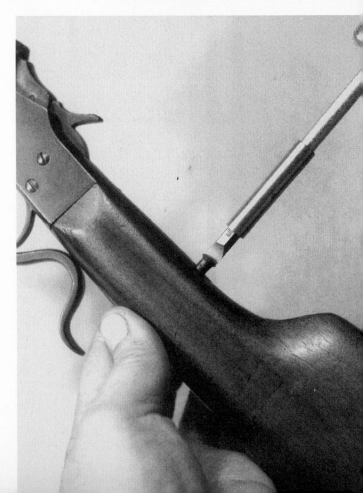

3. The forend is held on the underside of the barrel by a single screw.

4. Remove the screws at the rear tip of the upper and lower receiver tangs to release the stock for removal. Remove the stock toward the rear. If the stock is very tightly fitted, it may be necessary to bump the front of the comb with the heel of the hand or with a soft rubber hammer.

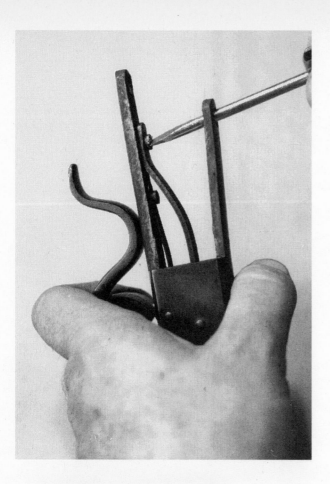

5. The screw that retains the hammer spring can be reached through the stock screw hole in the upper tang. Remove the hammer spring screw and take out the spring toward the rear. On the post-1915 guns, the hammer spring will be a heavy coil with an internal hammer strut and a base sleeve at the rear which bears on a groove in the head of a large screw in the lower tang. On these guns, grip the sleeve firmly with pliers and move it forward, and then upward to clear the base screw. After the hammer spring is removed, in both models, the screw which retains the trigger spring will be accessible. For this screw, use either an offset screwdriver or a screwdriver with the tip cut to an angle.

6. Taking out the hammer and trigger pivot screws will release the hammer for removal upward and the trigger for removal downward.

7. Remove the lever pivot screw, located at the lower edge of the receiver.

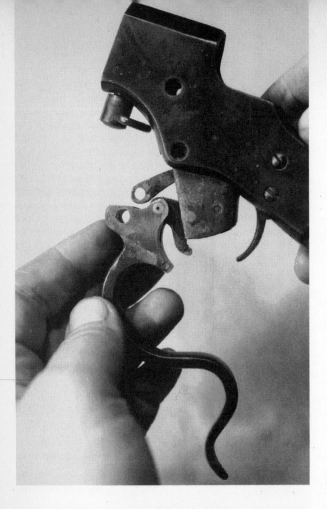

8. Remove the breechblock pivot screw.

9. Remove the lever and breechblock assembly downward. The ejector, which is retained by the lever pivot screw, will also come out at this time.

10. The ejector on the later model guns is different from the one shown. On the post-1915 guns, it has a front lobe which contains a plunger and spring, the plunger bearing on the breechblock pivot. The plunger is staked in place, and removal in routine disassembly is not advisable. Drifting out the upper cross pin in the breechblock will release the firing pin for removal toward the rear. The lower cross pin holds the link to the breechblock, and the pin at the top of the lever retains the lever on the link.

Reassembly Tips:

1. When replacing the lever and breechblock assembly in the receiver, be sure the ejector is in the position shown, with its cartridge rim recess and firing pin groove toward the rear. Also, be sure the link is in the position shown, with its hooked beak downward and pointing toward the rear.

When replacing the lever and breechblock assembly in the receiver, the forward arms of the breechblock should be inserted into the bottom of the receiver first; then the breechblock is tipped into position.

On both models, insert the breechblock pivot screw first; then insert the lever pivot screw, being sure it passes through the lower loop of the ejector. On the later guns, it will be necessary to use a small tool to center the ejector loop while inserting the screw, holding it against the tension of its plunger and spring.

Stevens Favorite Single Shot Rifle

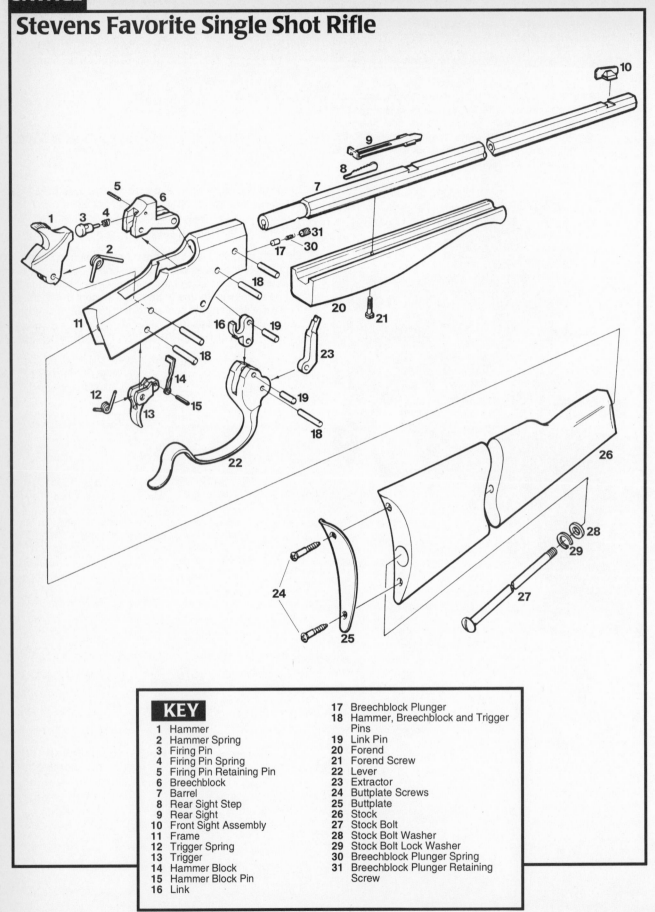

KEY

1 Hammer	17 Breechblock Plunger
2 Hammer Spring	18 Hammer, Breechblock and Trigger Pins
3 Firing Pin	19 Link Pin
4 Firing Pin Spring	20 Forend
5 Firing Pin Retaining Pin	21 Forend Screw
6 Breechblock	22 Lever
7 Barrel	23 Extractor
8 Rear Sight Step	24 Buttplate Screws
9 Rear Sight	25 Buttplate
10 Front Sight Assembly	26 Stock
11 Frame	27 Stock Bolt
12 Trigger Spring	28 Stock Bolt Washer
13 Trigger	29 Stock Bolt Lock Washer
14 Hammer Block	30 Breechblock Plunger Spring
15 Hammer Block Pin	31 Breechblock Plunger Retaining Screw
16 Link	

Swedish Mauser Model 1894

Similar/Identical Pattern Guns

The same basic assembly/disassembly steps for the Swedish Mauser Model 1894 also apply to the following guns:

Brazilian Model 1894 Rifle   **Chilean Model 1895 Rifle**
Mexican Model 1902 Rifle   **Spanish Model 1893 Rifle**
Spanish Model 1893 Short Rifle   **Spanish Model 1895 Carbine**
Spanish Model 1916 Artillery Carbine **Swedish Model 38 Rifle**
Swedish Model 41 Rifle   **Swedish Model 96 Rifle**
Turkish Model 1893 Rifle

Data:	Swedish Mauser Model 1894
Origin:	Sweden
Manufacturers:	Mauser (Germany) & Swedish arsenals
Cartridge:	6.5x55mm
Magazine capacity:	5 rounds
Overall length:	37.6 inches (Carbine)
Barrel length:	17.7 inches (Carbine)
Weight:	7.6 pounds (Carbine)

There are some small differences, but mechanically there is the same basic design in the Spanish Mauser of 1893 and 1895, and the Swedish Model 1894 and Model 1896. Both rifle and carbine versions were made. There is also the Model 38, a shortened conversion of the Model 1896 Swedish rifle. The Model 1894 Swedish carbine was chosen for our takedown sequence because its fore-stock arrangement is slightly more complex than the other guns, which used simple barrel bands.

Disassembly:

1. Open and close the bolt, cocking the striker. Set the safety in its vertical on-safe position. Open the bolt, pull the bolt stop outward, and remove the bolt toward the rear.

2. Unscrew the striker assembly (counter-clockwise, rear view), and remove the assembly toward the rear.

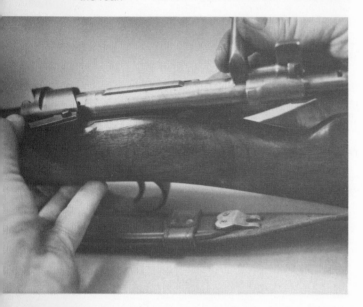

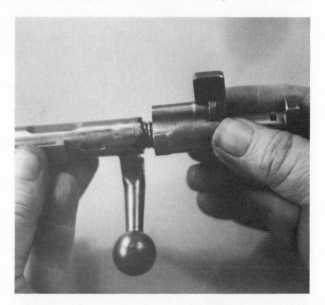

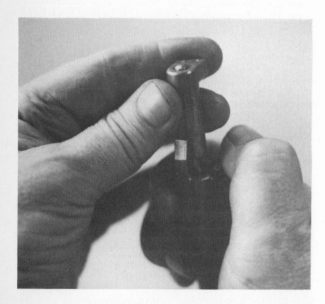

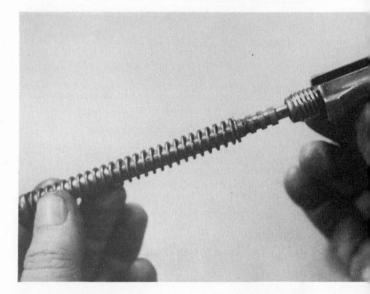

3. Rest the firing pin point on a block of wood, or grip the front shoulder in a padded vise. Using the safety-lever as a handle, push down the headpiece until the sear contact lug on the cocking piece clears. Turn the cocking piece 90 degrees in either direction, and slowly release the spring tension.

4. Remove the cocking piece and the bolt headpiece toward the rear. The spring is easily removed from the shaft of the striker.

5. Turn the safety-lever all the way over to the right, and remove it toward the rear.

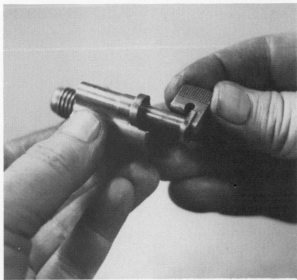

6. Turn the extractor to the bottom of the bolt, and push it off toward the front. The collar that retains the extractor can be removed by spreading it out of its groove, but in normal takedown it is best left in place.

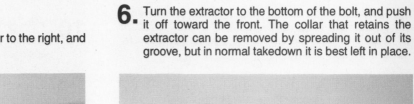

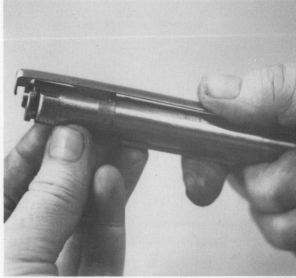

7. Insert a tool in the opening at the rear of the magazine floorplate to depress the latch, and move the floorplate rearward.

8. Remove the magazine floorplate, spring, and follower. These parts are easily separated by sliding the spring out of its recesses in the floorplate and follower.

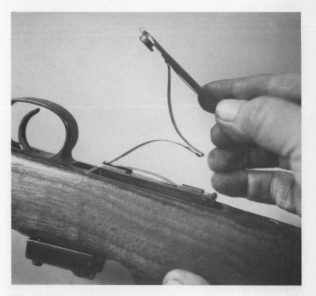

9. Remove the screw from the underplate that extends rearward from the muzzle piece. The screw is located just forward of the bayonet lug, which has been removed from this gun.

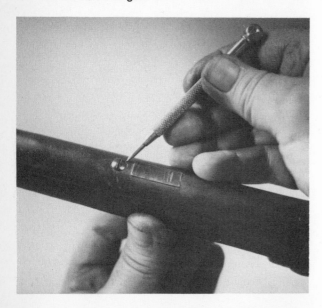

10. Through the access hole on the underside near the muzzle, depress the lock plunger and move the assembly off toward the front.

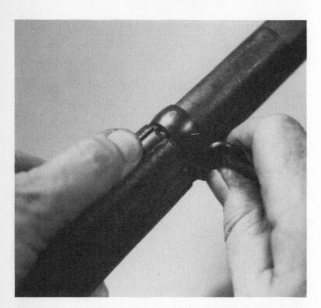

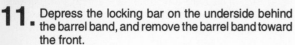

11. Depress the locking bar on the underside behind the barrel band, and remove the barrel band toward the front.

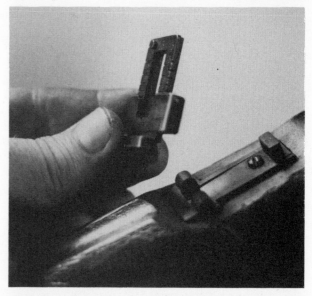

12. Drift out the rear sight cross pin, and remove the rear sight. The rear sight spring is retained by a vertical screw.

13. Lift the upper handguard at the front, and move it forward for removal.

14. Remove the vertical screws on the underside at the front and rear of the trigger guard/magazine housing unit.

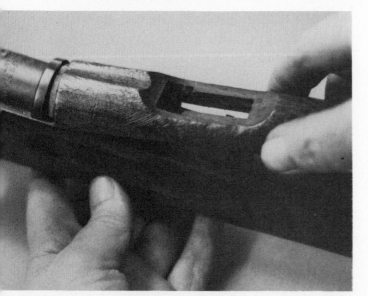

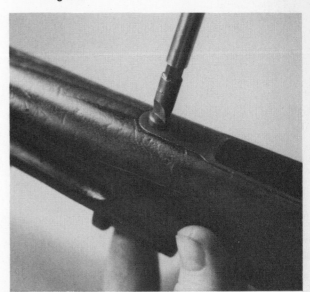

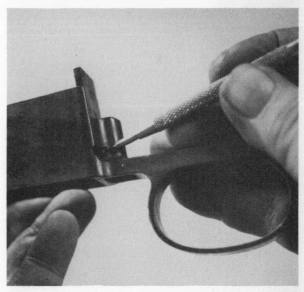

15. Remove the trigger guard/magazine unit downward.

16. The magazine floorplate latch plunger and its spring are retained in the unit by a cross pin.

17. Remove the action from the stock.

18. The bolt stop is pivoted and retained on the left side of the receiver by a vertical screw.

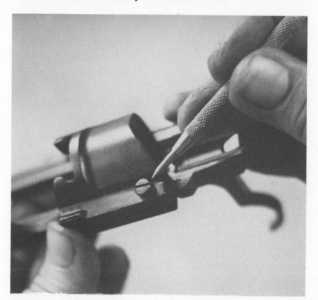

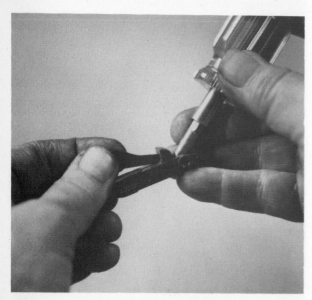

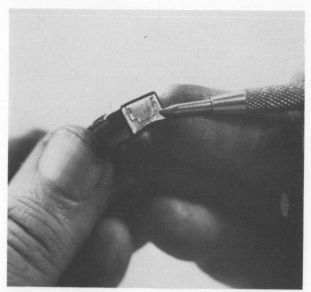

19. The ejector can be removed from the bolt stop by moving it forward and lifting it out.

20. If it is necessary to remove the combination bolt stop and ejector spring, you must grip the bolt stop in a padded vise and drive the spring forward for removal. In normal takedown, the spring is best left in place.

21. Push out the cross pin that retains the trigger and sear assembly, and remove the assembly, and the spring, downward.

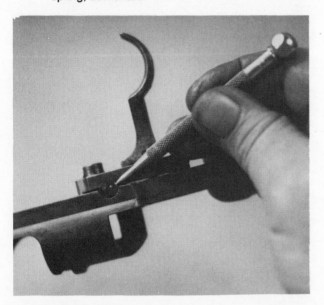

22. The trigger can be separated from the sear by drifting out the cross pin. The spring is easily lifted out of its recess.

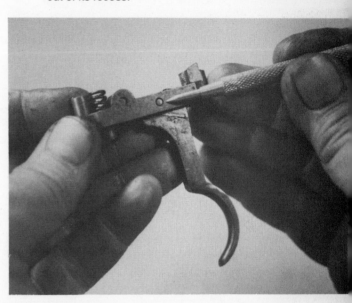

Reassembly Tips:

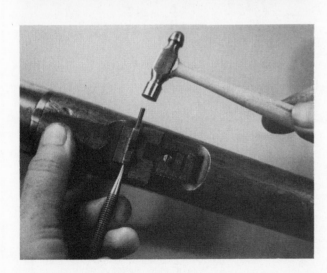

1. Use a drift punch to position the rear sight for reinstallation of the cross pin.

2. When replacing the muzzle unit, it will be necessary to insert a tool to depress the latch plunger as it is moved back into place. Be sure the stepped lip at the rear of the unit goes inside the barrel band.

Model 94 and 96 Bolt-Action Rifle

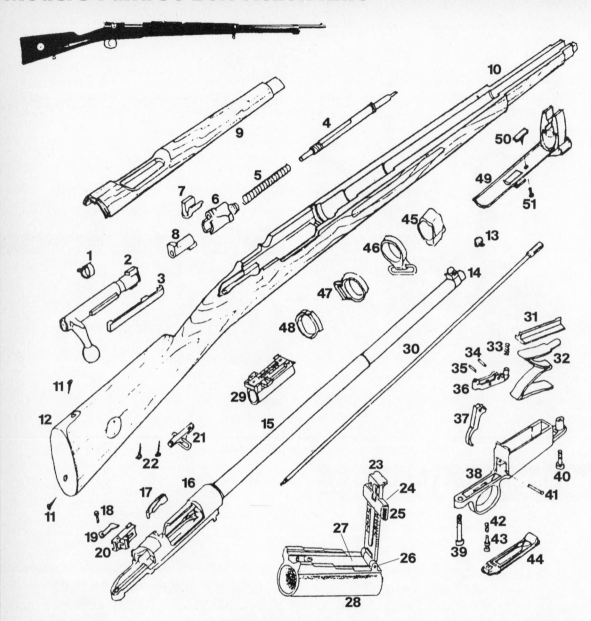

KEY

1 Extractor Collar
2 Bolt Body
3 Extractor
4 Firing Pin
5 Firing Pin Spring
6 Bolt Sleeve
7 Safety
8 Cocking Piece
9 Handguard
10 Stock
11 Buttplate Screws
12 Buttplate
13 Front Sight
14 Front Sight Band
15 Barrel
16 Receiver
17 Ejector Spring and Cover
18 Ejector Screw

19 Ejector
20 Ejector and Bolt Release Housing
21 Rear Sling Swivel
22 Rear Swivel Screws
23 Rear Sight Ladder
24 Rear Sight Slide
25 Rear Sight Slide Catch
26 Rear Sight Ladder Pivot
27 Rear Sight Ladder Spring
28 Rear Sight Base
29 Rear Sight Assembly
30 Cleaning Rod (Mod. 96)
31 Magazine Follower
32 Magazine Follower Spring
33 Sear Spring
34 Sear Pin
35 Trigger Pin
36 Sear
37 Trigger
38 Trigger Guard

39 Rear Guard Screw
40 Front Guard Screw
41 Floor Plate Catch Pin
42 Floor Plate Catch Spring
43 Floor Plate Catch
44 Floor Plate
45 Front Barrel Band (Mod. 96)
46 Rear Barrel Band (Mod. 96)
47 Front Barrel Band (Mod. 94)
48 Rear Barrel Band (Mod. 94)
49 Nose Cap (Mod. 94)
50 Nose Cap Nut (Mod. 94)
51 Nose Cap Screw (Mod. 94)

Parts Not Shown
Barrel Band Spring
Bayonet Stud Spacer (Mod. 96)
Bayonet Stud Spacer Pin (Mod. 96)
Cleaning Rod Stud (Mod. 96)
Rear Guard Screw Bushing

U.S. 30 M-1 Carbine

Similar/Identical Pattern Guns

The same basic assembly/disassembly steps for the U.S. 30 M-1 Carbine also apply to the following guns:

Iver Johnson M-1 Carbine
Universal M-1 Carbine

Plainfield M-1 Carbine
U.S. 30 M1A1

Data:	U.S. 30 M-1 Carbine
Origin:	United States
Manufacturers:	Winchester, IBM, General Motors, and several other contractors
Cartridge:	30 Carbine
Magazine capacity:	15 or 30 rounds
Overall length:	35.6 inches
Barrel length:	18 inches
Weight:	5½ pounds

Designed by an engineering group at Winchester, the Carbine was adopted as a U.S. military arm in 1941. Several sub-models were developed later, such as the M1A1 with folding stock, and the M2 selective fire version. With the exception of the parts that pertain to their special features, the instructions for the standard M1, given here, can be applied to the others. Early and late Carbines will have some small differences, such as the change from a flat-topped bolt to a round one, different rear sight, etc., but none of the changes affect the takedown to any great degree. This can also be said of the post-war commercial versions.

Disassembly:

1. Remove the magazine, and cycle the action to cock the internal hammer. Loosen the cross screw in the lower flanges of the barrel band. It should be noted that if a screwdriver is not available, the rim of a cartridge case can be used to turn the specially-shaped screw head.

2. Depress the barrel band latch, located on the right side, and slide the band and bayonet mount unit toward the front. Move the upper handguard wood forward, and lift it off. Tip the action upward at the front, unhooking its rear lug, and lift it out of the stock.

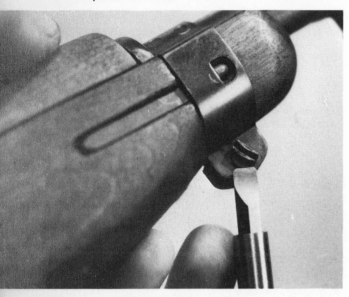

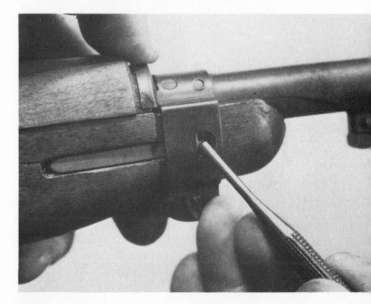

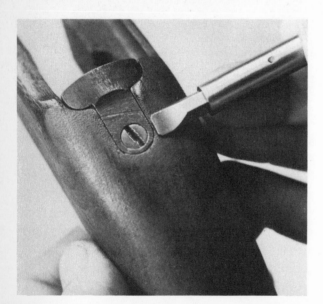

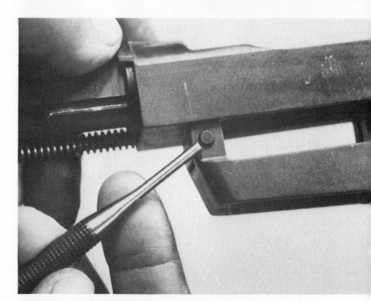

3. The barrel band latch can be removed by drifting its cross post toward the right, using the small access hole on the left side of the stock. Backing out the vertical screw in the tail of the recoil plate will allow removal of the plate upward.

4. Push out the cross pin at the front of the trigger housing, move the housing forward, out of its slots at the rear, and remove it downward.

5. Restrain the hammer, pull the trigger, and ease the hammer down to the fired position. Insert a drift punch through the hole in the front of the hammer spring rod, move the rod toward the rear, and lift its head out of its seat in the back of the hammer. **Caution:** *The spring is under heavy tension, so control it as the rod and spring are eased out upward, and toward the left for removal.*

6. Take out the hammer pivot pin, and remove the hammer upward.

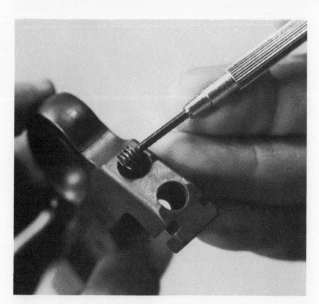

7. Insert a small tool at the rear of the trigger housing, and pull the trigger spring toward the rear until it stops, about as far as shown.

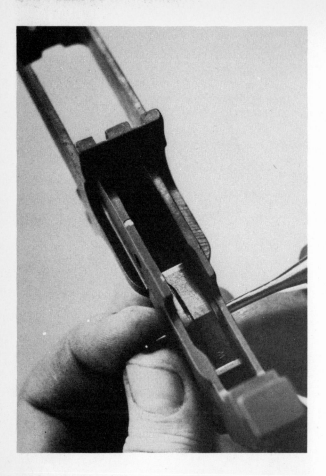

8. Restrain the sear, inside the trigger housing, and push out the trigger pin toward either side.

9. Remove the sear, sear spring, and trigger upward.

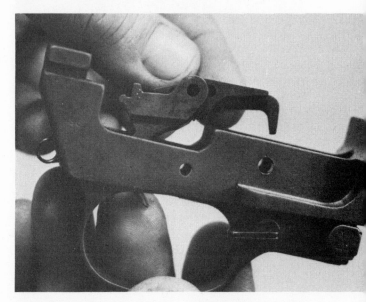

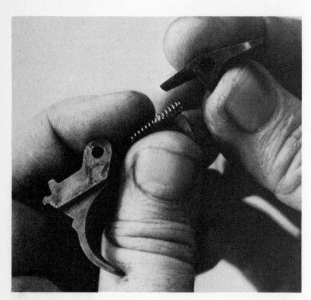

10. The sear and its spring are easily detached from the top of the trigger. After the trigger is removed, the trigger spring can be moved forward out of its well at the rear of the housing and taken out.

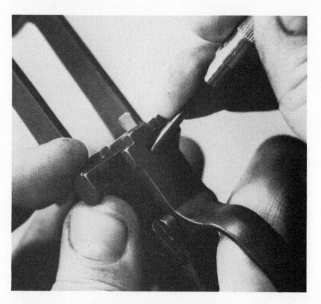

11. Insert a small screwdriver into the hole on the underside of the trigger housing, below the magazine catch, and push the catch retaining plunger toward the rear, holding it there while moving the catch out toward the right, along with its spring and plunger.

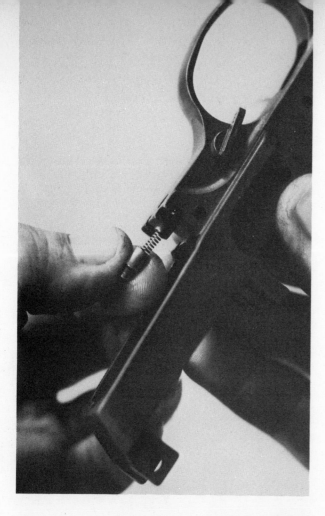

12. Remove the magazine catch retaining plunger toward the front, slowly releasing the tension of its spring. Remove the spring, and the rear plunger which positions the safety. The two plungers are identical, and need not be kept separated.

13. Remove the safety-catch toward the right.

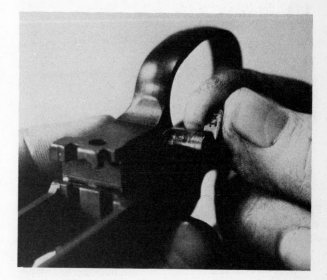

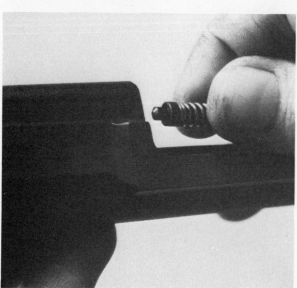

14. Grip the action slide spring and its guide rod firmly, just behind its front tip, and move it just far enough toward the rear to disengage its front stud from the recess on the back of the action slide. Tip the rod and spring away from the slide, and slowly ease the tension, removing them toward the front.

15. Move the action slide toward the rear until its inner projection on the left side is aligned with the exit cut in the barrel groove. Turn the slide toward the left and downward, disengaging the inner projection from the groove. At the same time, the rear lug of the cocking handle will be aligned with its exit cut in the receiver track, and the action slide can be removed.

16. Move the bolt to the position shown, and lift its right lug upward and toward the right. Rotate the bolt, and remove it upward and forward.

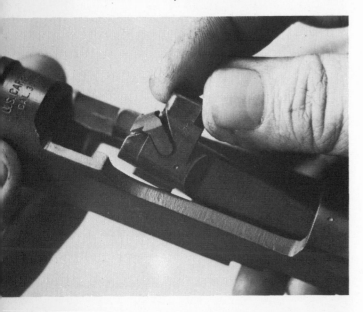

17. Disassembly of the bolt is much easier if the special military tool is used. The knurled knob of the screw is turned to back it out, the bolt is laid in the tool, and the knob tightened, pushing the disassembly nose on the rotary piece against the extractor plunger. At the same time, the ejector is depressed by a post in the front of the tool. With these two parts held in place, the extractor is easily lifted out, the screw backed off, and the other parts removed. In the photo, the tool is shown with the screw tightened, ready for removal of the extractor. It is possible, without the tool, to use a small screwdriver to depress the extractor plunger. If this method is used, be sure to restrain the ejector, as it will be released when the extractor shaft clears its retaining cut.

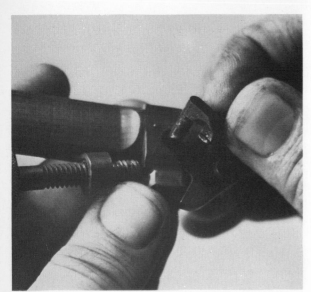

18. A hole is provided in the underside of the tool for pushing out the extractor, and it is removed upward.

19. After the extractor is removed, the screw on the tool is backed off, and the ejector and its spring are removed toward the front. The extractor plunger and its spring can be taken out of their hole at the base of the lug, and the firing pin can be removed from the rear of the bolt.

20. To remove the gas piston, it is best to use the standard military wrench designed for this. The retaining nut is simply unscrewed, and the piston is taken out toward the rear. It is possible to remove the nut without the wrench, with pliers, for example, but the nut is sure to be damaged.

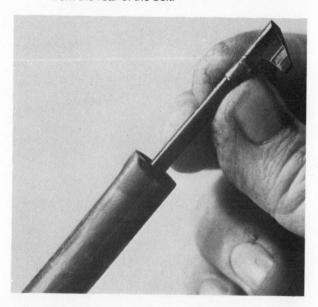

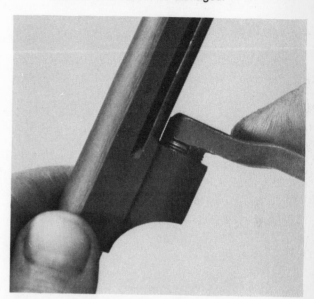

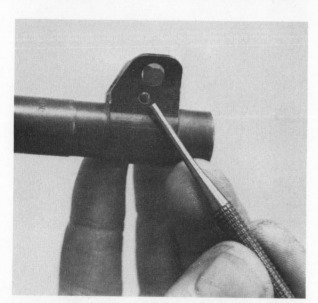

21. The front sight can be removed by drifting out its cross pin, and using a non-marring punch to nudge it off toward the front. When the sight is taken off, be sure the small key inside it is not lost. The barrel band unit can be taken off after the sight is removed.

Reassembly Tips:

1. When replacing the ejector in the bolt, be sure the ejector is oriented as shown for proper engagement with the extractor post.

2. When replacing the tiny extractor plunger, be sure the notch on the plunger is oriented downward, as this surface locks the extractor in place.

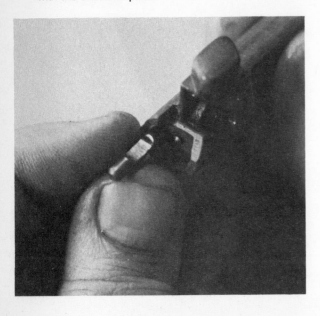

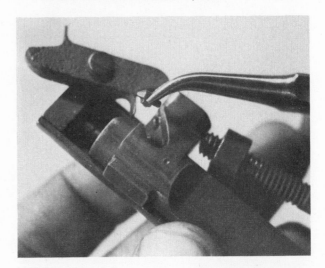

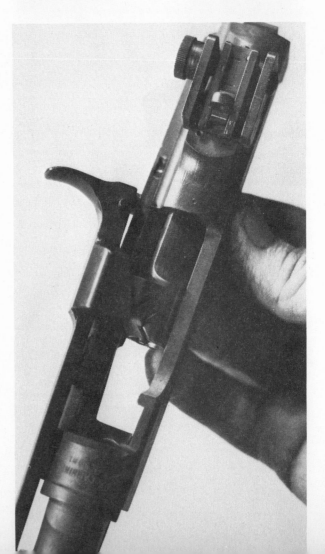

3. When properly assembled, the extractor and its plunger will be engaged as shown.

4. During replacement of the action slide, position the bolt as shown, then bring the slide onto the bolt lug and move it into place in its track.

Insert the trigger spring from the front, and push it back to the temporary rear position, just as in disassembly. After the trigger/sear system is installed, move the spring back toward the front, lifting its forward end to drop into the groove at the upper rear of the trigger.

M-1 Autoloading Carbine

KEY

1	Buttplate Screw
2	Buttplate
3	Stock
4	Slide Lock
5	Slide
6	Slide Lock Spring
7	Recoil Plate Screw
8	Recoil Plate
9	Receiver
10	Recoil Spring
11	Extractor
12	Firing Pin
13	Bolt
14	Bolt Complete
15	Extractor Spring
16	Extractor Spring Plunger
17	Ejector Spring
18	Ejector
19	Rear Sight
20	Gas Piston Nut
21	Gas Piston
22	Hand Guard
23	Barrel
24	Recoil Spring Guide
25	Band Spring
26	Barrel Band with Swivel and Screw
27	Front Sight
28	Front Sight Key
29	Front Sight Pin
30	Trigger Guard Pin
31	Sear
32	Hammer
33	Hammer Spring Plunger
34	Trigger Housing
35	Trigger Housing Complete
36	Safety Spring
37	Safety Spring Plungers
38	Magazine Catch Spring
39	Magazine Catch Plunger
40	Magazine Catch
41	Trigger Pin
42	Safety
43	Hammer Pin
44	Stock Escutcheon
45	Trigger
46	Sear Spring
47	Hammer Spring
48	Trigger Spring

U.S. Model 1903 Springfield

Similar/Identical Pattern Guns
The same basic assembly/disassembly steps for the U.S. Model 1903 Springfield also apply to the following gun:
U.S. Model 1903A3 Springfield

Data:	U.S. 1903 Springfield
Origin:	United States
Manufacturer:	Springfield Arsenal and Rock Island Armory
Cartridge:	30-06 Springfield
Magazine capacity:	5 rounds
Overall length:	43.2 inches
Barrel length:	24 inches
Weight:	8.6 pounds

Adopted by the U.S. as military standard in 1903, this rifle replaced the Krag-Jorgensen and was used until the adoption of the M-1 Garand in 1936. Although officially replaced, the Springfield saw quite a bit of use during World War II. In 1942, the Remington Arms Company did a slight redesign of the gun, mostly to make it easier to manufacture, and this rifle was designated the Model 1903A3. The main differences were in the use of stamped-steel parts to replace several of the machined parts of the original gun, such as the magazine floorplate, and the rear sight was moved to the rear of the receiver. Mechanically, they are essentially the same.

Disassembly:

1. Cycle the bolt to cock the striker, and set the safety-lever in the vertical position. Set the magazine cut-off lever, located at the left rear of the receiver, at its mid-position, angled slightly upward from the horizontal. Remove the bolt toward the rear.

2. Depress the bolt sleeve lock (arrow), located on the left side, and unscrew the sleeve and striker assembly counter-clockwise (rear view). Remove the sleeve and striker assembly toward the rear, taking care not to trip the safety-lever.

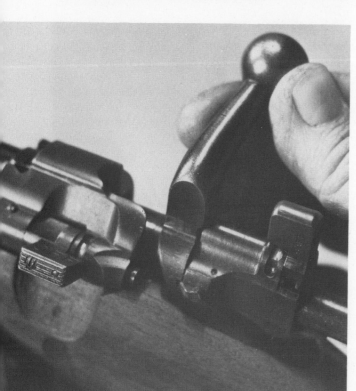

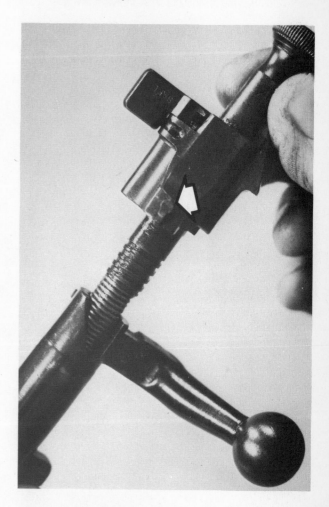

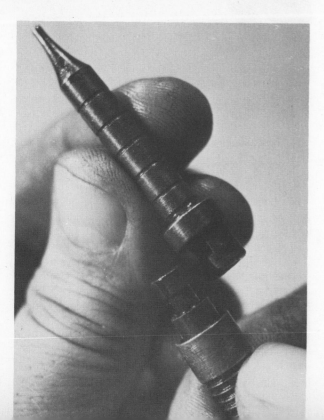

3. Holding firmly to the sleeve and striker knob, turn the safety back to the off-safe position and allow the striker to move forward in the sleeve. Grip the serrated area on the retaining sleeve, just to the rear of the firing pin, and pull the sleeve toward the rear until it clears the back of the firing pin. Remove the firing pin toward the side. **Caution:** *Rest the striker knob on a firm surface during this operation, and keep a firm grip on the firing pin retaining sleeve, as the striker spring is quite strong.*

4. Slowly release the spring tension, and remove the retaining sleeve and the spring toward the front.

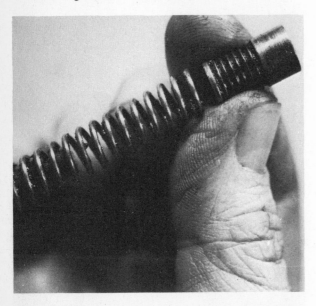

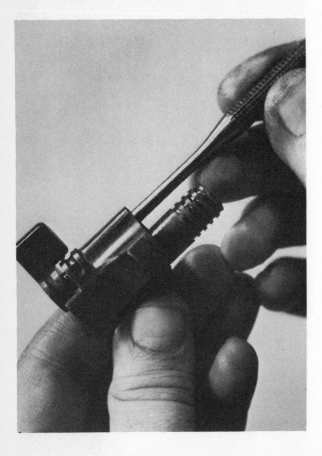

5. Slide the bolt sleeve off the striker rod toward the front.

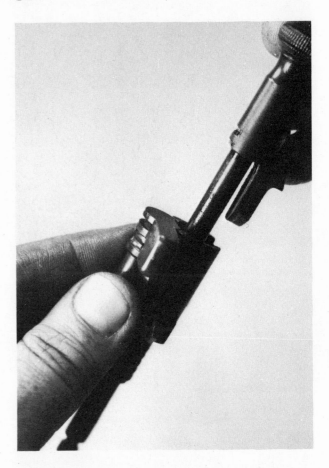

6. Turn the safety-lever back to its mid-position and rest the lower rear edge of the bolt sleeve on a firm surface. Use a drift punch against the front tip of the safety shaft to drive it out toward the rear. Note that the safety plunger and spring will be released as the safety clears the rear of the bolt sleeve, so ease them out and take care that they are not lost.

7. Turn the extractor clockwise (rear view) until its front underlug is out of the groove at the front of the bolt, and is aligned with the ungrooved area on the bolt. Push the extractor forward and off its T-mount on the bolt ring.

8. Insert a drift punch in the hole on the underside, just forward of the trigger guard, and depress the magazine floorplate latch. Move the floorplate toward the rear. Remove the floorplate and the attached spring and follower downward. The spring is easily detached from the floorplate and follower.

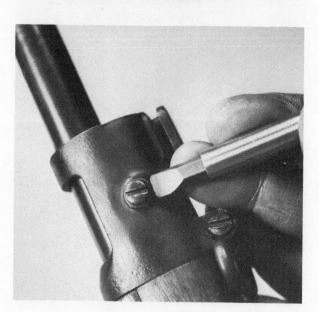

9. Remove the cross screw in the front barrel band, and slide the barrel band forward.

10. Depress the lock spring on the right side, in front of the rear barrel band (after the band screw and sling loop are removed), and slide the band off toward the front. Move the upper handguard wood forward, and take it off.

11. Remove the large vertical screws on the underside at the front and rear of the magazine/trigger guard unit. Remove the action from the stock, and take off the trigger guard unit downward.

12. The ejector is retained on the left side of the receiver by a vertical pin with a slotted screw-type head at its lower end. If the pin is unusually tight, using a screwdriver to turn it will help to loosen it, but for removal it is driven out downward. The ejector is taken out toward the inside of the receiver.

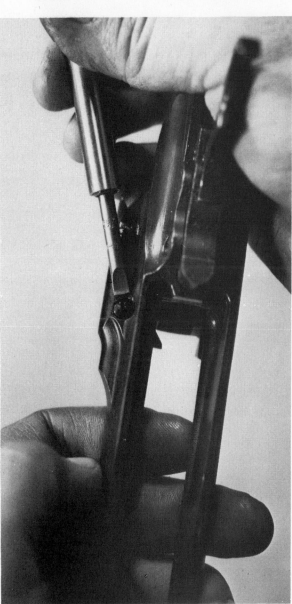

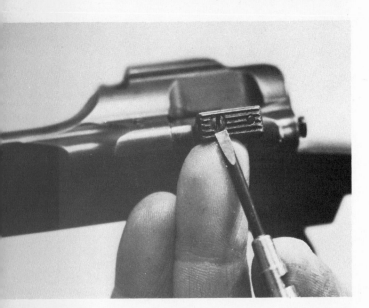

13. Remove the small screw in the serrated end of the bolt stop/magazine cut-off lever.

14. The bolt stop pivot has a cannelure at its rear tip, allowing it to be pulled out with a fingernail or a screwdriver blade. When removing the pivot pin, keep slight inward pressure on the bolt stop, to relieve spring pressure on the pin.

15. Remove the bolt stop/magazine cutoff toward the left, taking care not to lose the positioning plunger and its spring.

16. Push out the sear pivot pin toward the left. As soon as its large head clears its recess in the underside of the receiver, exert slight pressure on the front of the sear to compress the spring and assist withdrawal of the pin.

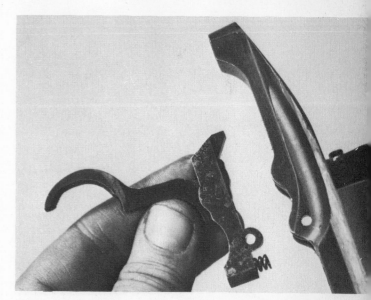

17. Remove the trigger, sear, and sear spring assembly downward. Drifting out the trigger cross pin will allow separation of the trigger from the sear.

18. To take the front barrel band completely off, the front sight must be drifted out of its dovetail to allow the band to pass. The front sight blade is retained in the dovetailed base by a cross pin.

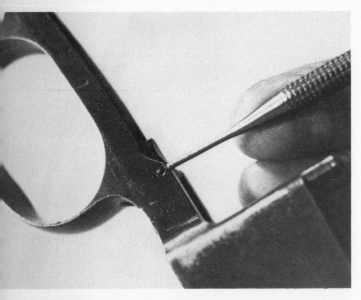

19. Drifting out the cross pin in the trigger guard unit will allow removal of the magazine floorplate latch and its spring upward. The spring is quite strong, so control it and ease it out.

Reassembly Tips:

1. When replacing the safety-lever in the bolt sleeve, insert a small screwdriver to depress the positioning plunger and spring, and note that the lever should be in its midway (vertical) position for installation.

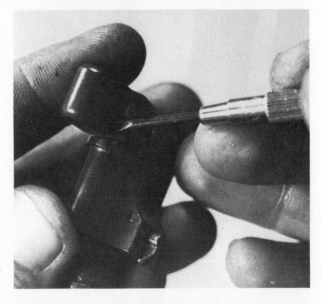

Before the bolt is replaced in the receiver, the striker must be in the cocked position, with the bolt handle raised. Since the Springfield has a cocking knob, this is easily done.

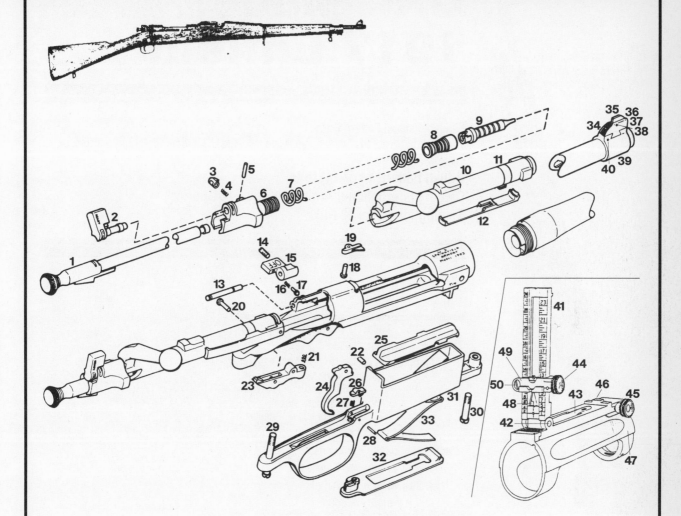

KEY

1 Firing Pin Rod
2 Safety Lock Assembly
3 Bolt Sleeve Lock
4 Bolt Sleeve Lock Spring
5 Bolt Sleeve Lock Pin
6 Bolt Sleeve
7 Mainspring
8 Striker Sleeve
9 Striker
10 Bolt Complete
11 Extractor Collar
12 Extractor
13 Cutoff Spindle
14 Cutoff Screw
15 Cutoff
16 Cutoff Plunger Spring
17 Cutoff Plunger
18 Ejector Pin

19 Ejector
20 Sear Pin
21 Sear Spring
22 Trigger Pin
23 Sear
24 Trigger
25 Follower
26 Floorplate Catch
27 Floorplate Catch Spring
28 Floorplate Catch Pin
29 Rear Guard Screw
30 Front Guard Screw
31 Trigger Guard
32 Floorplate
33 Magazine Spring
34 Front Sight Base
35 Front Sight Blade
36 Front Sight Base Screw
37 Front Sight Base Spline
38 Front Sight Blade Pin

39 Front Sight Band
40 Front Sight Base Pin
41 Rear Sight Leaf
42 Leaf Hinge Pin
43 Rear Sight Leaf Spring
44 Rear Sight Binding Knob, Elevation Slide
45 Rear Sight Windage Knob Assembly
46 Rear Sight Leaf Base
47 Rear Sight Base Collar
48 Rear Sight Drift
49 Rear Sight Slide
50 Rear Sight Slide Cap Screw

Parts Not Shown
Buttplate
Buttplate Trapdoor

U.S. Model 1917 Enfield

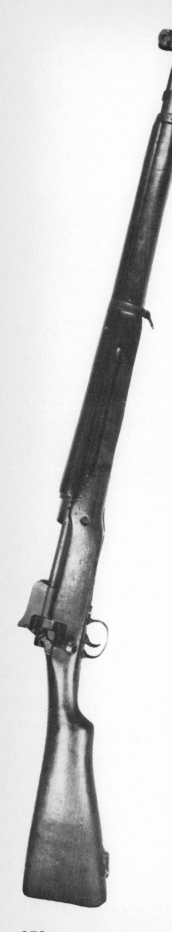

Similar/Identical Pattern Guns

The same basic assembly/disassembly steps for the U.S. Model 1917 Enfield also apply to the following guns:

British Pattern 14 (P-14) Rifle
Century International Arms Centurion 14 Sporter
Remington Model 30 Rifle

Data:	U.S. Model 1917 Enfield
Origin:	United States
Manufacturers:	Remington Arms Company, at Ilion, New York, and Eddystone, Pennsylvania, and Winchester in New Haven, Connecticut
Cartridge:	30-06
Magazine capacity:	5 rounds
Overall length:	46.3 inches
Barrel length:	26 inches
Weight:	9 pounds

This rifle was originally developed by the British between 1910 and 1913, and was chambered for an experimental 276-caliber rimless round. When issued as a substitute standard gun for the British forces, the chambering was for the regular 303 British round, and the rifle was called the Pattern 14 (P-14) Enfield. When the U.S. entered World War I, the supply of 1903 Springfield rifles on hand was small, and a number of P-14 Enfields, left over from British contracts, were converted to 30-06, and designated as the U.S. Model 1917 or P-17 Enfield. More than two million U.S.-spec 1917 Enfields were eventually produced. Sporterized 1917s, like the Century Centurion, are mechanically alike, and these instructions generally apply.

Disassembly:

1. Open the bolt, and pull the bolt stop outward, holding it out while removing the bolt toward the rear.

2. For bolt disassembly, do not remove the bolt from the receiver. Lift the bolt handle about half way, and push forward on it, opening a gap between the rear of the bolt sleeve and the front of the cocking piece. Insert a thin piece of steel (a penny works fine, too) into the gap, trapping the cocking piece at the rear. In some guns, pushing the half-lifted handle forward will not open an adequate gap. In this case, open the bolt and move it toward the rear, turn the safety back to the on-safe position, then push the bolt forward until the gap opens and the steel plate can be inserted.

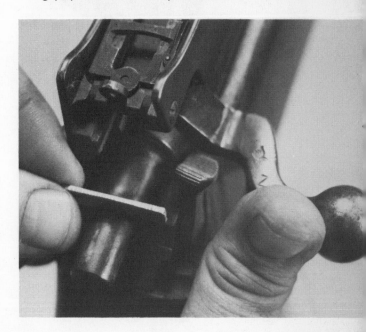

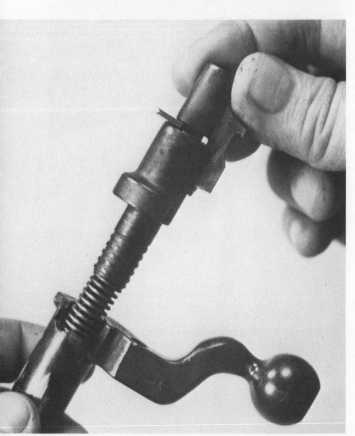

3. Taking care not to dislodge the steel plate, remove the bolt from the receiver as described in step #1, and unscrew the bolt sleeve and striker assembly from the rear of the bolt.

4. With the front of the striker gripped firmly in a padded vise, push the bolt sleeve toward the front, and remove the steel plate inserted earlier. Push the sleeve forward until the rear edge clears the front of the cocking lug, and rotate the cocking piece one-quarter turn in either direction. Remove the cocking piece from the rear of the striker shaft. **Caution:** *Keep the bolt sleeve under control, as the powerful striker spring is compressed.*

5. Release the spring tension slowly, and remove the bolt sleeve and striker spring toward the rear.

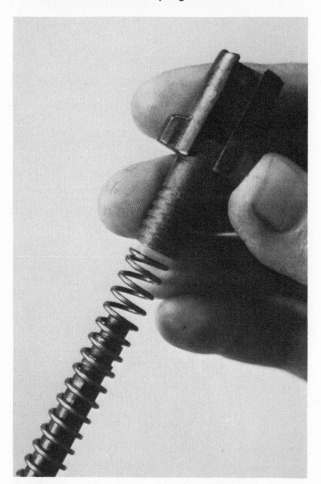

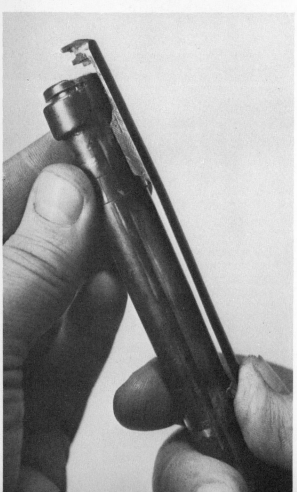

6. Turn the extractor clockwise (rear view) until it is aligned with the gas port, and its front underlug is out of the groove at the front, and push it off its mount toward the front.

7. Insert a drift punch in the hole at the rear of the magazine floorplate, and depress the floorplate latch. Slide the plate slightly toward the rear, and remove it downward, along with the magazine spring and follower. The spring is easily detached from the floorplate and follower by sliding it out of its mounting slots.

8. Remove the cross screw in the front barrel band, slide it toward the front, and take off the front upper handguard wood.

9. Drift out the cross pin in front of the rear barrel band, and move the band forward off the stock. It may be necessary to also loosen the sling loop cross screw at the bottom of the band. The rear upper handguard can now be moved forward, and taken off upward.

10. Remove the screw on the underside, in the front tab of the trigger and magazine housing. Remove the screw on the underside at the rear of the trigger guard, and separate the action from the stock. The magazine box can be removed from the stock, and the guard and magazine housing can be taken off downward.

11. Drifting out the cross pin in the guard will allow removal of the magazine floorplate latch and its spring upward.

12. Drifting out the cross pin in the front sight will allow removal of the front sight assembly toward the front. This unit is usually tight, and may have to be nudged off with a hammer and nylon drift. Take care not to lose the front sight key, which will be released as the sight is removed. The front band, rear band, and the rear upper handguard ring can now be taken off toward the front.

13. Remove the vertical screw that retains the bolt stop, at the left rear of the receiver, and take off the bolt stop and ejector assembly toward the left. The spring rest plug can also be taken out toward the left.

14. Tip the rear tail of the bolt stop spring inward, to lift its front hooks from inside the stop, and remove the spring and ejector toward the rear.

15. Remove the small cross screw at the right rear of the receiver, and take off the safety-lever retainer toward the rear.

16. With the safety-lever in the on-safe position (toward the rear), insert a small-diameter drift punch to depress the safety plunger and spring, and remove the safety toward the right. Restrain the plunger and spring, and ease them out. As the safety is moved toward the right, the drift must be removed to allow the cross piece to pass, then is reinserted to restrain the plunger and spring.

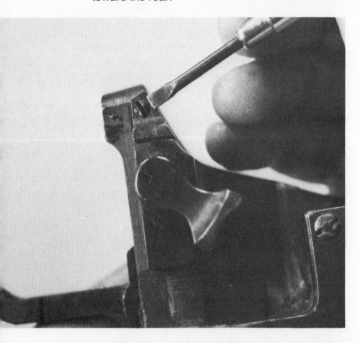

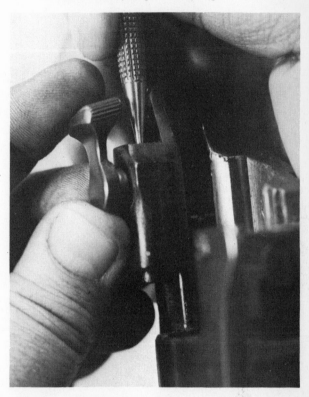

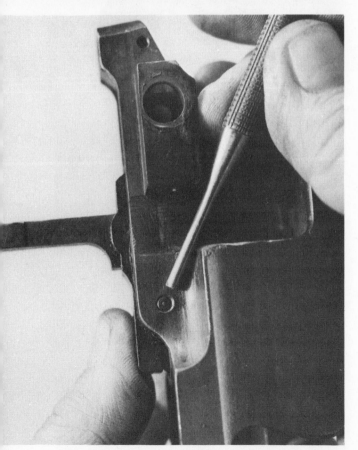

17. Drift out the sear cross pin toward the left. Exert upward pressure on the front of the sear, and the cross pin can be pushed out more easily.

18. Remove the sear, trigger, and sear spring downward. Drifting out the trigger cross pin will allow separation of the trigger from the sear.

Reassembly Tips:

1. When replacing the safety-lever, insert a slim tool from the rear to depress the safety plunger and spring while the safety is inserted.

2. When replacing the extractor, after it is started back onto its flanges on the mounting ring, depress the tail of the extractor while lifting the beak at the front, to clear its underlug over the front edge of the bolt. Lift it only enough to clear.

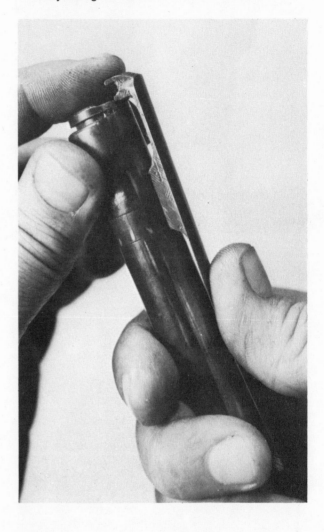

U.S. Model 1917 Bolt-Action Rifle

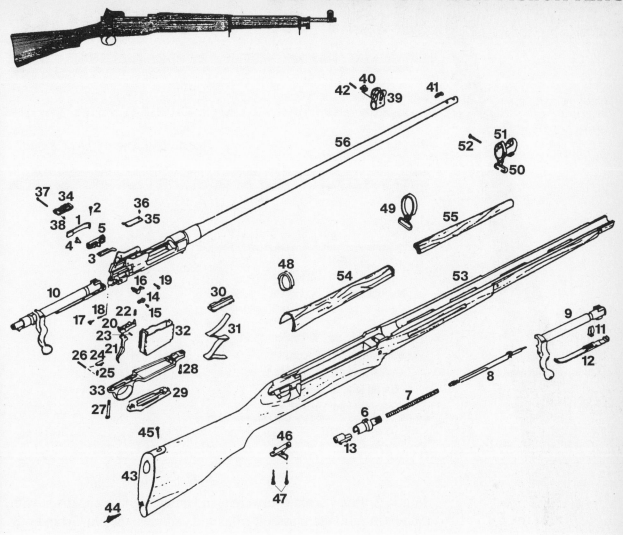

KEY

1	Bolt Stop Spring
2	Bolt Stop Screw
3	Ejector
4	Bolt Stop Spring Rest
5	Bolt Stop
6	Bolt Sleeve
7	Mainspring
8	Firing Pin
9	Bolt, Stripped
10	Bolt, Complete
11	Extractor Collar
12	Extractor
13	Cocking Piece
14	Safety Lock Holder
15	Safety Lock Holder Screw
16	Safety
17	Safety Lock Plunger
18	Safety Lock Plunger Spring
19	Sear Pin
20	Sear
21	Trigger
22	Sear Spring

23	Trigger Pin
24	Floorplate Catch
25	Floorplate Catch Spring
26	Floorplate Catch Pin
27	Rear Guard Screw
28	Front Guard Screw
29	Floorplate
30	Follower
31	Magazine Spring
32	Magazine Box
33	Trigger Guard
34	Rear Sight
35	Rear Sight Base Spring
36	Rear Sight Base Screw
37	Rear Sight Axis Screw
38	Rear Sight Axis Nut
39	Front Sight Carrier
40	Front Sight Blade
41	Front Sight Spline
42	Front Sight Pin
43	Buttplate
44	Buttplate Screw, Large
45	Buttplate Screw, Small
46	Rear Swivel Assembly

47	Rear Swivel Base Screws
48	Handguard Ring
49	Lower Band Assembly
50	Stacking Swivel
51	Upper Band
52	Upper Band Screw
53	Stock
54	Handguard, Lower
55	Handguard, Upper
56	Barrel

Parts Not Shown
Follower Depressor
Front Guard Screw Bushing
Lower Band
Lower Band Screw
Plate Spring
Rear Guard Screw Bushing
Rear Sight Slide
Rear Sight Slide Spring
Rear Swivel Base
Sling Swivel
Stacking Swivel Screw

U.S. M-1 Garand

Similar/Identical Pattern Guns
The same basic assembly/disassembly steps for the U.S. M-1 Garand also apply to the following guns:

Beretta BM-59   **Springfield Armory M-1 Garand**

Data:	U.S. M-1 Garand
Origin:	United States
Manufacturers:	Springfield Armory, Winchester, and other contractors
Cartridge:	30-06 Springfield
Magazine capacity:	8 rounds
Overall length:	43.6 inches
Barrel length:	24 inches
Weight:	9½ pounds

Although it may seem overweight and unwieldy in comparison with today's ultra-modern assault rifles and carbines, the old Garand was the finest military rifle of its day. It was adopted as U.S. military standard in 1936, and served us well through World War II, the Korean conflict, and into the Viet Nam war. The trigger group mechanism is a particularly fine piece of engineering, and in slightly modified form lives on today in the Ruger Mini-14. The weakest point is the magazine system, where a complicated assortment of levers and arms somehow succeed in feeding the cartridges with excellent reliability.

Disassembly:

1. With the internal hammer cocked, the bolt closed, and the safety in the on-safe position, insert a rod or drift punch through the transverse hole at the rear of the trigger guard, and pull it toward the rear and outward, pivoting the guard downward and toward the front. Some late-production guns don't have a hole in the trigger guard, so simply pull toward the rear with the fingers or a non-marring tool.

2. Remove the trigger group downward. Push the buttstock downward, pivoting the receiver and barrel group upward at the rear, and remove the buttstock assembly.

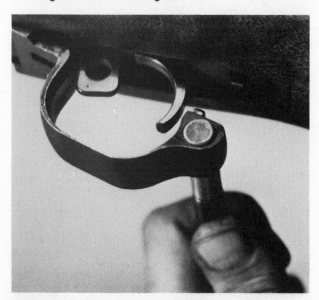

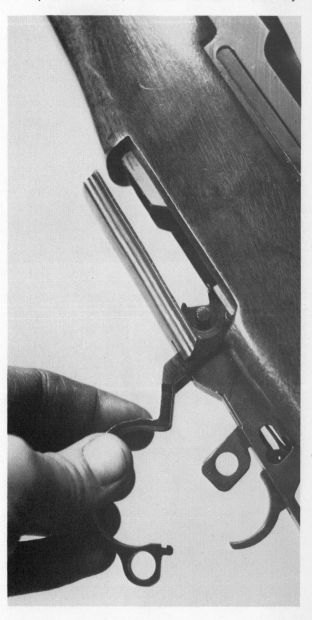

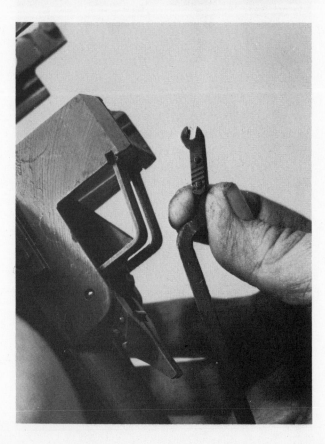

3. Grip the serrated surfaces on the sides of the rear tip of the follower rod, and move it forward, unhooking it from the follower arm. Slowly release the spring tension, and remove the follower rod and spring toward the rear.

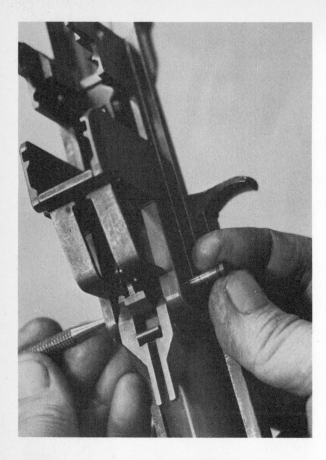

4. Remove the cross pin that pivots the follower arm, pushing it out toward the right.

5. Remove the follower arm, and the operating rod catch, with its attached accelerator, toward the front.

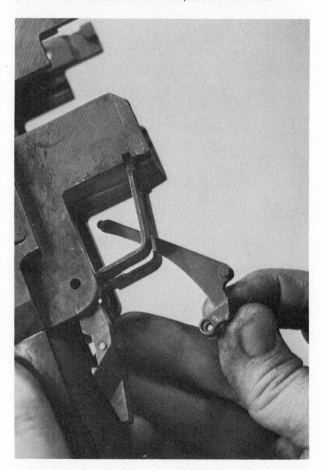

6. The accelerator is mounted in the operating rod catch by a cross pin, and separating these parts is not recommended in normal disassembly.

7. Remove the cartridge guide from the front of the magazine housing.

8. Remove the follower assembly from the bottom of the magazine housing. Disassembly of the magazine follower is definitely not recommended.

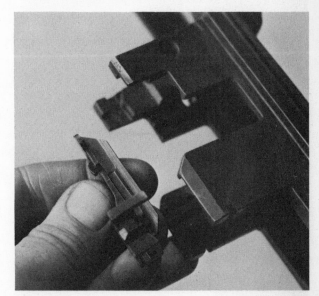

10. Move the bolt back toward the front, until its front is about an inch from the rear of the barrel shroud, then remove it upward and toward the front, lifting it slightly toward the right.

9. Move the operating slide and bolt toward the rear until the lug on the inside of the handle is aligned with the exit cut in the slide track. Push the handle upward, then out toward the left, and turn the slide for removal toward the rear.

11. When disassembling the bolt, a Garand tool is helpful, but not absolutely necessary. It is not difficult to depress the extractor plunger with a small screwdriver while lifting the extractor out of its recess upward. **Caution:** *The ejector will be released as soon as the extractor post clears its retaining cut, and the ejector spring is quite strong, so control it and ease it out.*

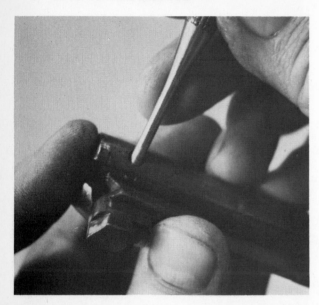

12. Remove the firing pin from the rear of the bolt.

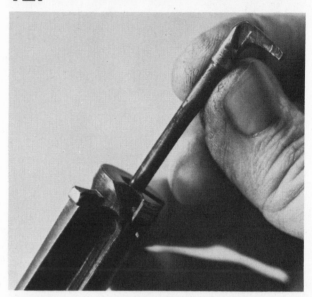

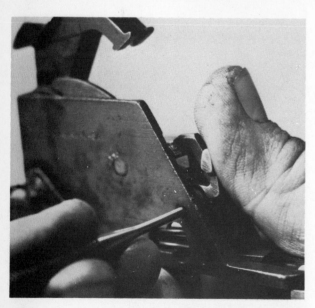

13. Snap the trigger guard back into place, release the safety, restrain the hammer, and pull the trigger. Lower the hammer to the fired position. Exert pressure on the rear of the sear, to slightly compress the hammer spring and relieve tension on the trigger pin, and drift out the trigger pin toward the right. **Caution:** *The hammer spring is quite strong, so keep firm pressure on the back of the sear.*

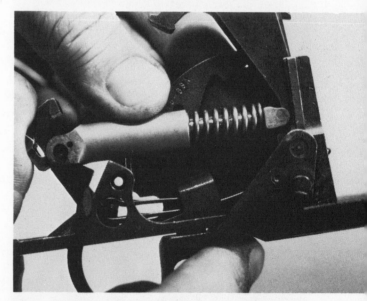

14. Slowly release the spring tension, allowing the trigger/sear assembly and the hammer spring housing to move upward and toward the rear. Control the hammer spring housing with downward pressure, as it will tend to climb out.

15. Remove the hammer spring housing, the spring, and the hammer strut upward and toward the rear. Remove the trigger/sear assembly upward. The sear is cross-pin-mounted on the trigger, but these parts should not be separated in normal disassembly.

16. Push out the hammer pivot pin toward the right.

18. Move the safety to the off-safe position, and tilt its upper arm toward the right, until its pivot post moves out of its hole in the housing, then remove it upward.

17. Move the trigger guard toward the rear. Move the hammer toward the rear, then remove it upward and toward the right.

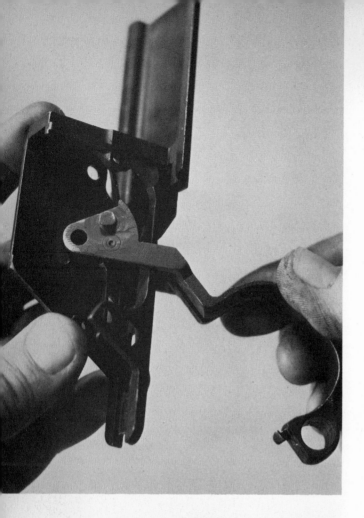

19. Move the trigger guard toward the rear until its right upper arm is aligned with the open space in the housing, and tilt the right arm inward (toward the left), removing the guard downward and toward the right.

20. Use a drift punch to tap the clip ejector spring off its post, working through the access hole in the left wall of the trigger group. The spring can also be simply pried off the post from inside, using a screwdriver blade.

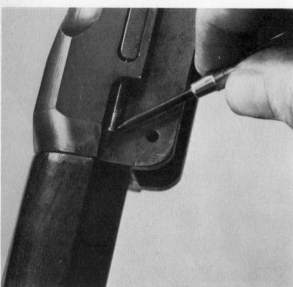

21. Use a drift punch to start the clip latch pin out toward the front, until its larger front tip can be grasped or pushed with a screwdriver blade, and pull the pin toward the front and out. The latch and its spring are then taken off toward the left.

22. Unscrew the gas piston nut, located below the barrel at the muzzle, and remove it.

23. Unscrew the gas cylinder lock, and take it off toward the front.

24. Slide the gas cylinder off toward the front. If it is very tight, tap it with a plastic hammer to free it.

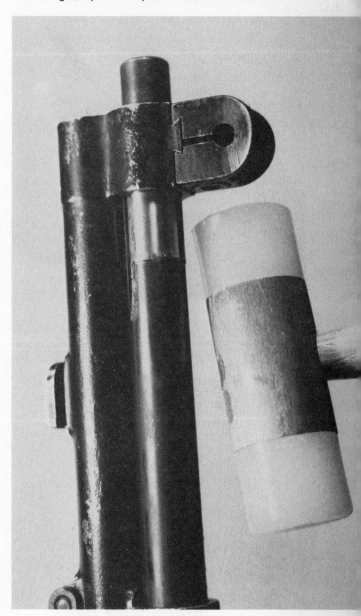

25. Remove the front handguard wood toward the front. Drift out the cross pin in the underside of the rear band, and remove the band toward the front.

26. Snap the rear upper handguard band out of its grooves in the barrel, and remove the handguard.

Reassembly Tips:

1. When replacing the ejector and its spring, be sure the recess on the ejector is properly oriented for engagement with the extractor post. When replacing the extractor, press the front face of the bolt against a hard surface to keep the ejector depressed while inserting the extractor. The extractor has a camming surface beside the plunger, and can just be snapped into place, without depressing the plunger manually.

When replacing the operating slide latch, be sure the hook at its rear engages the top of the inner projection of the clip latch.

When replacing the magazine follower arm, be sure its rear side studs enter the track on the underside of the follower before inserting the cross pin.

When attaching the follower rod hooks to the studs on the follower arm, depress the carrier slightly to allow them to snap into place.

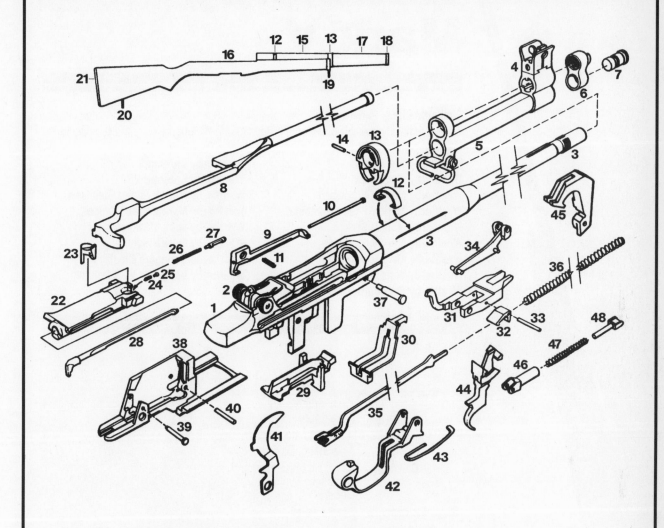

KEY

1 Receiver
2 Rear Sight Assembly
3 Barrel
4 Front Sight
5 Gas Cylinder with Stacking Swivel
6 Gas Cylinder Lock
7 Gas Cylinder Lock Screw
8 Operating Rod
9 Clip Latch
10 Clip Latch Pin
11 Clip Latch Spring
12 Rear Handguard Band
13 Lower Band
14 Lower Band Pin
15 Rear Handguard
16 Stock
17 Front Handguard
18 Front Handguard Ferrule
19 Stock Ferrule and Swivel
20 Buttstock Swivel
21 Buttplate and Screws
22 Bolt
23 Extractor

24 Extractor Spring
25 Extractor Plunger
26 Ejector Spring
27 Ejector
28 Firing Pin
29 Slide and Follower
30 Bullet Guide
31 Operating Rod Catch
32 Accelerator
33 Accelerator Pin
34 Follower Arm
35 Follower Rod
36 Operating Rod Spring
37 Follower Arm Pin
38 Trigger Housing
39 Trigger Pin
40 Hammer Pin
41 Safety
42 Trigger Guard
43 Clip Ejector
44 Trigger
45 Hammer
46 Hammer Spring Housing
47 Hammer Spring
48 Hammer Spring Plunger

Weatherby Mark V

Similar/Identical Pattern Guns
The same basic assembly/disassembly steps for the Weatherby Mark V also apply to the following guns:

Weatherby Alaskan
Weatherby Fibermark
Weatherby Mark V Eurosport
Weatherby Mark V Fluted Synthetic
Weatherby Mark V SLS
Weatherby Mark V Stainless
Weatherby Mark V Ultramark
Weatherby Vanguard Classic II
Weatherby Vanguard Weatherguard

Weatherby Euromark
Weatherby Lazermark
Weatherby Mark V Fluted Stainless
Weatherby Mark V Safari Grade
Weatherby Mark V Sporter
Weatherby Mark V Synthetic
Weatherby Vanguard Classic I
Weatherby Vanguard VGX Deluxe

Data:	Weatherby Mark V
Origin:	United States
Manufacturer:	Weatherby, Inc. Atascadero, California
Cartridges:	A long list of standard and Weatherby Magnum calibers
Magazine capacity:	2 to 5 rounds
Overall length:	43¼ to 46½ inches
Barrel length:	24 or 26 inches
Weight:	6½ to 10½ pounds

From the first Weatherby rifle in 1948 to the present time, the guns of the late Roy Weatherby have established a standard of excellence that is rivalled only by the more expensive custom rifles. The Mark V, first offered in 1955, is still in production. Early actions were made by FN, some Springfield actions were used, and the guns were made in Japan for many years. Recently, production was transferred back to the U.S. In 1970 a lower-priced version of the Mark V, the Vanguard, was introduced, and it shares many of the mechanical features of the Mark V. These instructions will generally apply to the Vanguard rifle as well.

Disassembly:

1. Open the bolt, hold the trigger pulled to the rear, and remove the bolt from the rear of the receiver.

2. Grip the underlug of the cocking piece firmly with smooth-jawed non-marring pliers, and move the cocking piece toward the rear until it can be turned to engage its front step on the inside of the bolt sleeve. This will lock the striker in rear position, as shown.

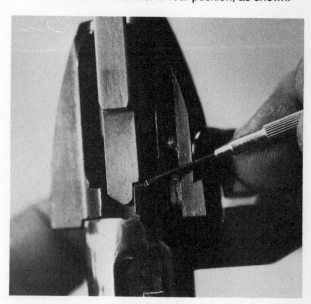

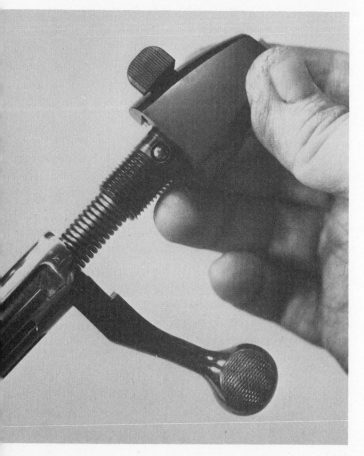

4. Remove the lock ball from its well on top of the bolt sleeve neck, and take care that it isn't lost.

3. Unscrew the bolt from the sleeve and striker assembly and remove it toward the front. Keep the sleeve in the upright position during this operation, as the firing pin lock ball will be freed from its hole at the front of the sleeve as soon as it clears the rear of the bolt.

5. Turn the cocking piece out of its lock step inside the bolt sleeve, and allow it to move forward into its recess on the underside of the sleeve.

6. Note that the base of the firing pin at the front of the striker shaft (not shown) has flat sides. Grip the bolt sleeve firmly, and by hand or with parallel-jaw pliers unscrew the striker shaft from the cocking piece. Keep front-ward pressure on the sleeve, as the striker spring is partially compressed. Ease the spring tension slowly, and remove the striker and spring toward the front.

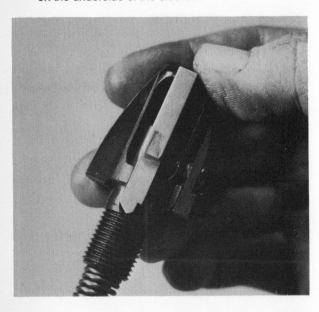

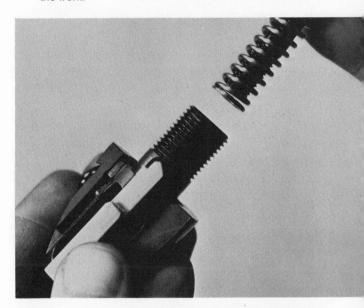

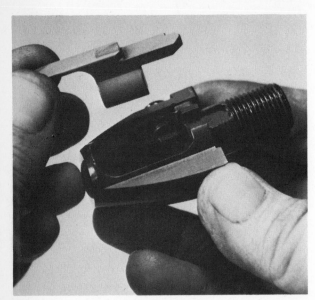

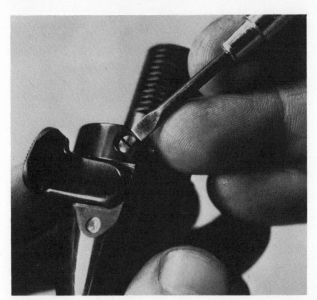

7. Remove the cocking piece from the bolt sleeve.

8. The safety is retained in the bolt sleeve by its positioning lever and spring, and the lever is held by a screw on the right side. Remove the screw, and take out the lever and spring toward the front. The safety is then removed toward the right.

9. The ejector is retained by a cross pin at the front of the bolt. **Caution:** *The ejector spring is under tension. Control the ejector and ease it out toward the front.*

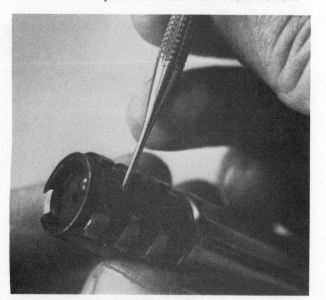

10. The extractor is also retained by a cross pin on the right side at the front of the bolt. Drifting out the pin will free the extractor and its coil spring for removal.

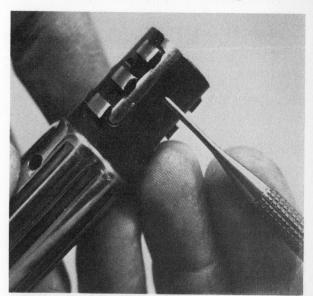

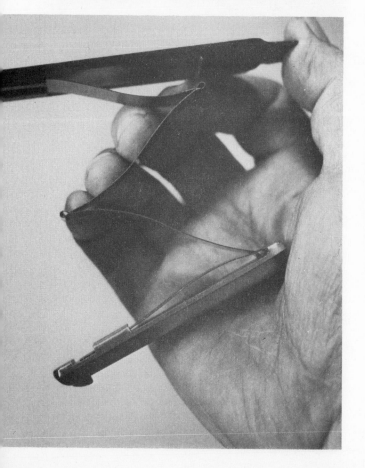

12. Close the floorplate, and remove the large vertical screw at the front of the magazine plate. Remove the large vertical screw at the rear of the trigger guard, and take off the trigger guard assembly downward. Separate the action from the stock.

11. Operate the latch and open the magazine floorplate. Slide the magazine spring out of its slot inside the floorplate. The follower is separated from the spring in the same way.

13. Drifting out the cross pin will allow the magazine floorplate to be removed.

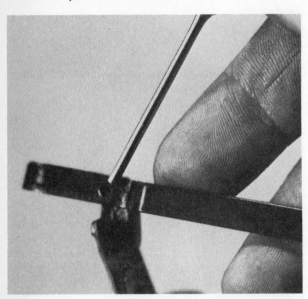

14. Drifting out the roll pin that retains the floorplate latch will allow removal of the latch and its spring downward and toward the front.

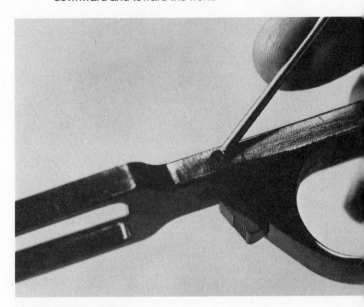

15. When the action is taken out of the stock, the magazine box will be released for removal. Note that there is a spacer plate (in some calibers) at the rear of the box, and take care that it isn't overlooked and lost.

16. On earlier guns, the trigger housing is retained by a post and cross pin. On the late model shown, two Phillips-head screws hold the housing to the underside of the receiver. One screw enters from below, at the front of the housing, and the other enters from above, located in the floor of the bolt track at the rear. Taking out these screws will allow removal of the housing downward, but this will not be necessary in normal disassembly.

17. Early Mark V rifles had a trigger housing with a removable sideplate. Note that on this late gun, the housing is a one-piece casting, and the trigger and sear cross pins are heavily staked in place to discourage disassembly. If necessary, the pins can be removed. The trigger is taken out toward the rear and downward, the sear upward, and the bolt stop upward (after removal of the trigger). Unless something needs repair, it's best to leave these parts in place.

18. The angle of the trigger "shoe" on its lower extension is adjustable by means of a tiny screw on the left side. The shoe can be removed by drifting out its cross pin.

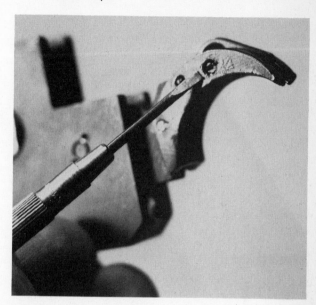

Reassembly Tips:

1. When replacing the magazine box, in those calibers which have a spacer plate at the rear, note that the plate is inserted from below, with its "shelf" turned toward the rear, to seal off the excess space.

2. When replacing the striker, turning its threaded rear back into the cocking piece, note that the striker shaft has recesses on its side which aligns with the lock ball in the neck of the sleeve. Also, note that the depth to which the shaft is turned controls the degree of protrusion of the firing pin point at the bolt face.

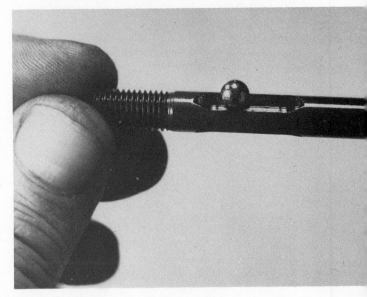

3. When the striker and bolt sleeve system is fully assembled and installed in the bolt, let the striker move forward to the fired position, and check the degree of firing pin point protrusion at the bolt face. If it is more than the one shown, it must be adjusted. Note that the striker must be recocked before the bolt is put back into the receiver.

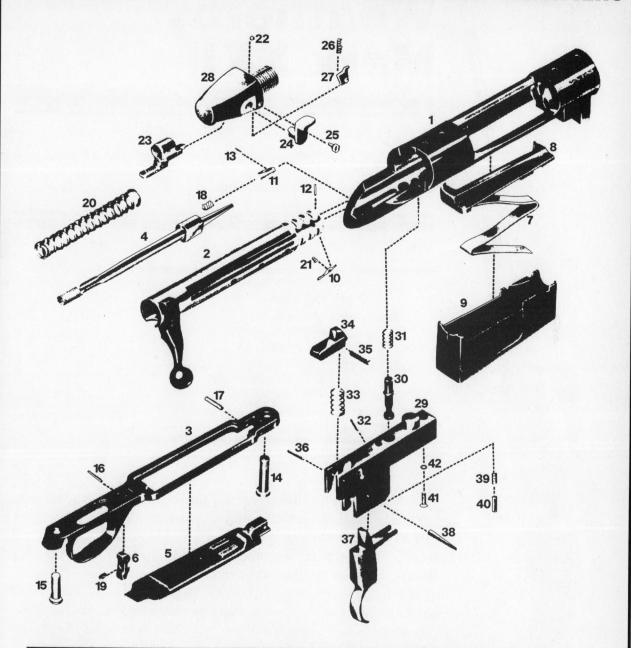

KEY

1 Receiver
2 Bolt Body
3 Trigger Guard
4 Firing Pin
5 Floorplate
6 Floorplate Catch
7 Follower Spring
8 Magazine Follower
9 Magazine Box
10 Extractor
11 Ejector
12 Extractor Pin
13 Ejector Pin
14 Front Trigger Guard Screw
15 Rear Trigger Guard Screw
16 Floorplate Catch Pin

17 Floorplate Pin
18 Ejector Spring
19 Floorplate Catch Spring
20 Firing Pin Spring
21 Extractor Spring
22 Retainer Ball
23 Cocking Piece
24 Safety-Lever
25 Safety Hook Screw
26 Safety Spring
27 Safety Hook
28 Bolt Sleeve
29 Trigger Housing
30 Bolt Stop
31 Bolt Stop Spring
32 Creep Adjustment Screw
33 Sear Spring
34 Sear

35 Sear Lock Pin
36 Sear Pin
37 Trigger
38 Trigger Pin
39 Trigger Spring
40 Pull Weight Adjustment Screw
41 Trigger Housing Attachment Screw, Bottom
42 Star Washer, Bottom Attachment Screw

Parts Not Shown
Barrel
Sear Spring Washer
Stock
Trigger Housing Attachment Screw, Top

Weatherby Mark XXII

Similar/Identical Pattern Guns
The same basic assembly/disassembly steps for the Weatherby Mark XXII also apply to the following gun:
Weatherby Mark XXII Tube Magazine

Data:	Weatherby Mark XXII
Origin:	United States
Manufacturer:	Weatherby, Inc. Atascadero, California
Cartridge:	22 Long Rifle
Magazine capacity:	5 and 10 rounds in box magazines, 15 rounds in tubular magazine model
Overall length:	$42^1/_4$ inches
Barrel length:	24 inches
Weight:	6 pounds

The Mark XXII had the classic Weatherby look and, in addition to its fine fit and finish, it had several unique features. One was a selector lever that allowed the gun to be used as a single shot, with the bolt remaining open after firing until released by the lever. With the lever in its other position, the gun would function as a normal semi-auto. There were two versions of the Mark XXII, the only difference being in the magazine systems—one had a tubular magazine, and the other, shown here, had a detachable box type. Early examples were made in Italy, but the bulk of production came from Japan. The guns will be marked with the old South Gate, California, address. The Mark XXII was made from 1963 to 1989.

Disassembly:

1. Remove the main stock mounting screw, located on the underside, forward of the magazine well. Remove the screw at the rear of the trigger guard on the underside and lift the action straight up out of the stock. It should be noted that it is possible to take off the barrel and receiver unit alone by pushing out the large takedown pin at the rear of the receiver toward the left, and moving the barrel/receiver unit forward and upward, but this will leave the trigger group sub-frame in the stock. After the two screws are taken out, the trigger guard unit can be taken off downward.

2. Push out the cross pin at the rear of the receiver toward the left and remove it.

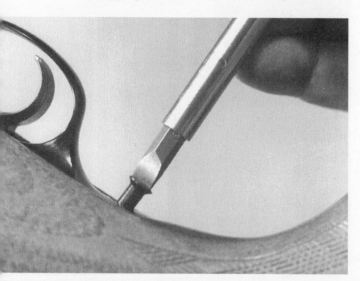

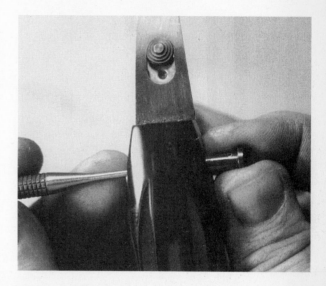

3. Move the trigger group about $1/8$-inch toward the rear and remove it downward.

4. Before any disassembly of the trigger group, hold the hammer against its spring tension, pull the trigger and ease the hammer down to the fired position. The selector lever on the right side of the group is retained by a large C-shaped spring clip. Carefully slide the clip off downward and remove the selector lever toward the right.

5. The pivot and mounting stud for the single shot bolt-catch is retained inside the group by a C-clip. Use a small screwdriver to slide the clip off upward, and take care that it isn't lost. There is an access hole on the left side through which the clip can be reached. The bolt-catch piece is then removed toward the right, along with its pivot-post, unhooking its spring at the front. The torsion spring is held in the group by a roll cross pin.

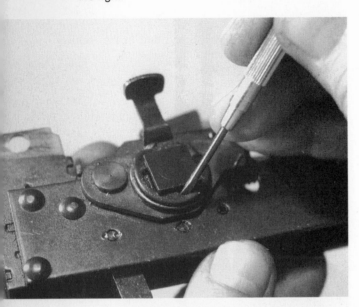

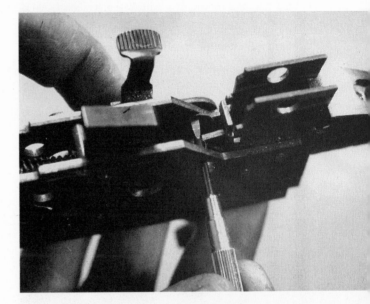

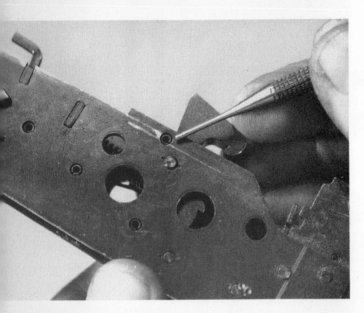

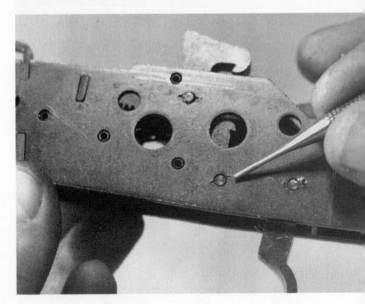

6. Set the hammer on its first step, and drift out the roll cross pin just forward of the hammer at the top edge of the group. Restrain the hammer, pull the trigger to release it and let it go forward beyond its normal down position, relieving the tension of the hammer spring. Drifting out the solid pin just below the roll pin, the hammer pivot, will allow removal of the hammer and its spring and guide upward.

7. The sear is retained by a solid pin near the lower edge of the receiver. Drifting out this pin will allow removal of the sear and its spring downward.

8. The trigger is retained by a cross pin just to the rear of the sear pin. The trigger and its attached sear bar and spring are removed downward. The coil trigger spring will be released as it clears its plate at the rear of the trigger, so restrain it and take care that it isn't lost.

9. Drifting out a small roll pin at the rear of the trigger group will allow removal of the safety bar toward the front. **Caution:** *The safety bar plunger and spring will be released upward as the bar is moved out, so restrain them against loss.* The rear portion of the safety, the button and indicator plate, are not easily removable, as this would require taking off the staked tang plate. This is not advisable in normal takedown.

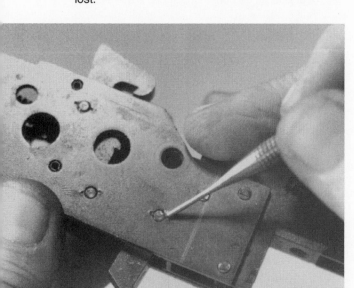

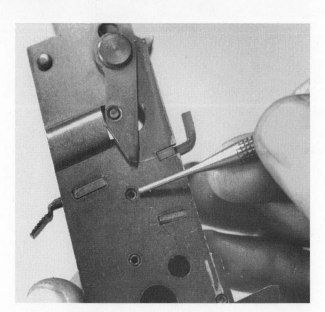

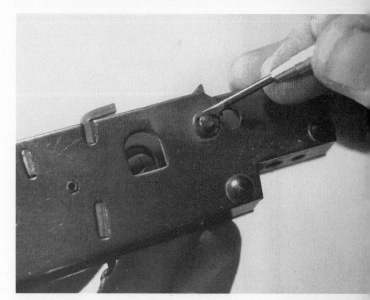

10. The magazine catch and its spring are retained by a roll cross pin. Note the relationship of the spring and the catch before removal, to aid reassembly. The catch and spring are removed downward. The ejector is staked in place between the riveted side-plates of the trigger group and is not removable in normal takedown.

11. The bolt hold open device is retained by a C-clip on the right side of the group, the clip gripping the end of its cross-shaft. Note that there is also a small washer under the C-clip, and take care that it isn't lost. The hold open is removed toward the left.

12. Firmly grasp the bolt handle and pull it straight out toward the right.

13. Invert the gun and move the bolt slowly toward the rear. Lift the front of the bolt enough to clear the receiver, and ease the bolt out forward, slowly relieving the tension of the bolt spring. **Caution:** *Control the compressed spring.* Remove the spring and its guide from the rear of the bolt.

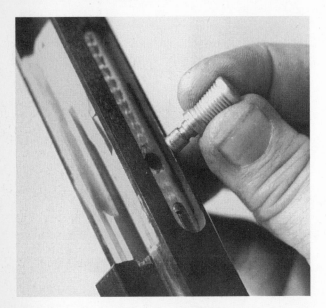

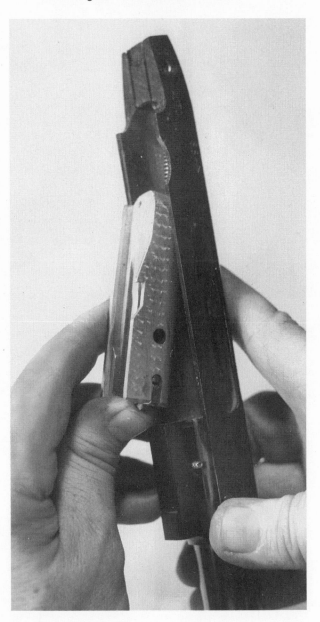

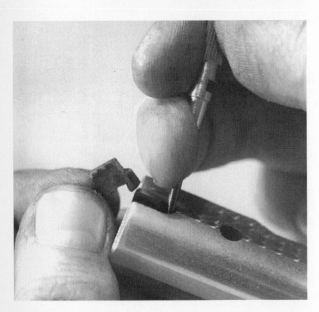

14. Use a small screwdriver to depress the extractor spring plunger, and lift the extractor out of its recess at the right front of the bolt. **Caution:** *Do not allow the screwdriver to slip, as the small plunger and spring will travel quite a distance if suddenly released.*

15. The firing pin is retained by a vertical roll pin located at the left rear of the bolt, and the firing pin and its return spring are removed toward the rear.

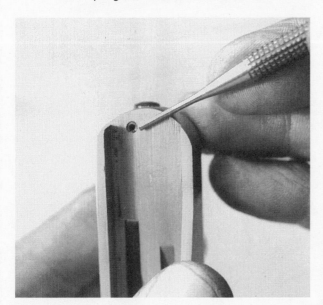

1. When replacing the single shot bolt-catch on the right side of the trigger group, remember to hook the torsion spring under its forward end. The spring may be installed first, and then its end moved out, downward and up to hook it under the part.

When replacing the large takedown cross pin at the rear of the receiver, be sure it is inserted from left to right. Otherwise, the stock will block its removal when the rifle is fully reassembled.

Mark XXII (Tube) Autoloading Rifle (Post-1982)

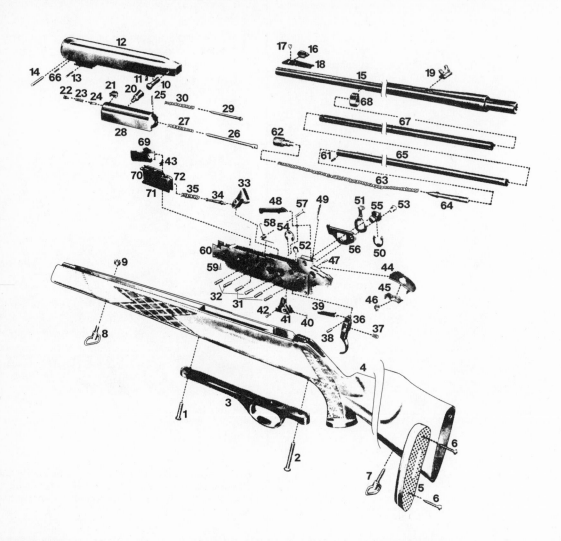

KEY

1	Front Trigger Guard Screw
2	Rear Trigger Guard Screw
3	Trigger Guard
4	Stock
5	Buttpad
6	Buttpad Screws
7	Rear Sling Swivel Assembly
8	Front Sling Swivel Assembly
9	Front Sling Swivel Nut
10	Takedown Pin
11	Takedown Pin Spring
12	Receiver
13	Locating Pin
14	Barrel Pin
15	Barrel
16	Front Sight
17	Front Sight Ramp Screw
18	Front Sight Ramp
19	Rear Sight
20	Operating Handle
21	Extractor
22	Extractor Plunger
23	Extractor Spring
24	Operating Handle Plunger
25	Firing Pin Retaining Pin
26	Firing Pin
27	Firing Pin Spring
28	Bolt
29	Recoil Spring Guide
30	Recoil Spring
31	Hammer, Sear and Trigger Pins
32	Hammer Stop, Sear Stop and Lifter Spring Pins
33	Hammer
34	Hammer Spring Guide
35	Hammer Spring
36	Trigger
37	Trigger Spring
38	Disconnector Pin
39	Disconnector
40	Disconnector Spring
41	Sear
42	Disconnector Spring Pin
43	Lifter Spring
44	Safety Tang Plate
45	Safety Slide
46	Safety Button
47	Safety-Lever Pin
48	Safety-Lever
49	Safety-Lever Spring
50	Selector Stud Retaining Ring
51	Selector Lever
52	Selector Lever Pin Retaining Ring
53	Selector Lever Plate Pin
54	Selector Stud Lock Ring
55	Selector Stud
56	Selector Lever Plate
57	Trigger Assembly Cross Screw
58	Selector Spring
59	Tension Screw
60	Trigger Frame Assembly
61	Magazine Plug Pin
62	Magazine Plug
63	Magazine Spring
64	Magazine Follower
65	Inner Magazine Tube
66	Magazine Tube Pin
67	Outer Magazine Tube
68	Magazine Ring
69	Lifter
70	Cartridge Guide Assembly
71	Left Cartridge Guide
72	Right Cartridge Guide

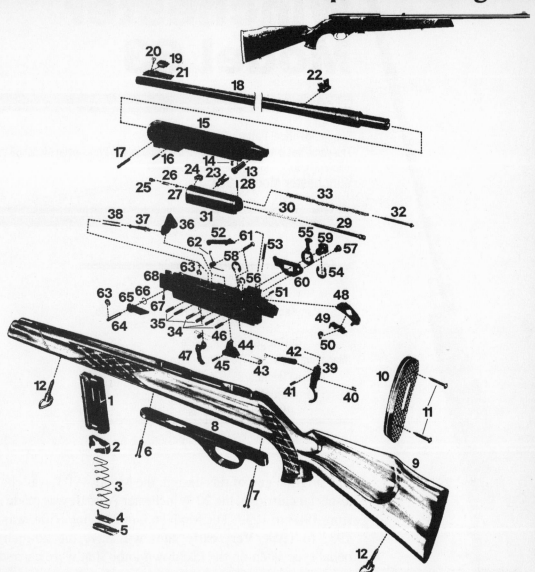

KEY

1	Magazine Box
2	Magazine Follower
3	Magazine Spring
4	Magazine Shoe Retainer
5	Magazine Shoe
6	Trigger Guard Screw, Front
7	Trigger Guard Screw, Rear
8	Trigger Guard
9	Stock
10	Buttpad
11	Buttpad Screws
12	Sling Swivel Assembly
13	Takedown Pin
14	Takedown Pin Spring
15	Receiver
16	Locating Pin
17	Barrel Pin
18	Barrel
19	Front Sight
20	Front Sight Ramp Screw
21	Front Sight Ramp
22	Rear Sight
23	Operating Handle
24	Extractor
25	Extractor Plunger
26	Extractor Spring
27	Operating Handle Plunger
28	Firing Pin Retaining Pin
29	Firing Pin
30	Firing Pin Spring
31	Bolt
32	Recoil Spring Guide
33	Recoil Spring
34	Hammer, Sear and Trigger Pins
35	Hammer Stop, Magazine Release and Sear Stop Pins
36	Hammer
37	Hammer Spring Guide
38	Hammer Spring
39	Trigger
40	Trigger Spring
41	Disconnector Pin
42	Disconnector
43	Disconnector Spring
44	Sear
45	Disconnector Spring Pin
46	Magazine Release Spring
47	Magazine Release
48	Safety Tang Plate
49	Safety Slide
50	Safety Button
51	Safety-Lever Pin
52	Safety-Lever
53	Safety-Lever Spring
54	Selector Stud Retaining Ring
55	Selector Lever
56	Selector Lever Pin Retaining Ring
57	Selector Lever Plate Pin
58	Selector Stud Lock Ring
59	Selector Stud
60	Selector Lever Plate
61	Trigger Assembly Cross Screw
62	Selector Spring
63	Bolt Lock Pin Retaining Ring
64	Bolt Lock Pin
65	Bolt Lock Lever
66	Bolt Lock Spring
67	Tension Screw
68	Trigger Frame Assembly

Winchester Model 63

Data:	Winchester Model 63
Origin:	United States
Manufacturer:	Winchester Repeating Arms Co. New Haven, Connecticut
Cartridge:	22 Long Rifle
Magazine capacity:	10 rounds
Overall length:	$39^1/_2$ inches
Barrel length:	20 and 23 inches
Weight:	$5^1/_2$ pounds

The original gun of this design, the Model 1903, was chambered for a special cartridge, the 22 Winchester Auto. It was made in this form from 1903 to 1932. The Model 63, in 22 Long Rifle, was made from 1933 to 1958. Very early guns will have the 20-inch barrel and pedal-type latch on the takedown knob that were carried over from the 1903 model. Otherwise, mechanically, the two models are practically identical.

Disassembly:

1. Use a coin or a specially shaped screwdriver to loosen the takedown screw at the rear of the receiver. After it is freed, the serrated knob is easily turned by hand. Back it out until it is stopped by its internal pin. **Note:** If you have a Model 1903, or a very early Model 63, the knob will have a pedal-type latch below it which must be depressed to allow turning.

2. Separate the buttstock and trigger group assembly from the receiver, moving the assembly straight toward the rear. Tight fitting may require the use of a rubber mallet for initial separation.

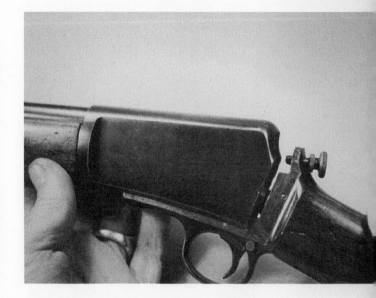

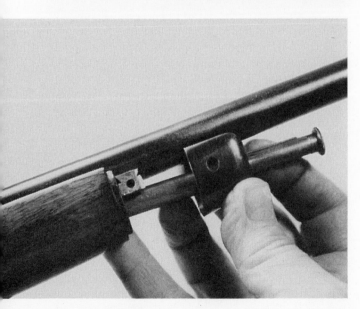

3. Remove the two screws, one on each side, that retain the forend cap. Remove the forend cap and cocking plunger assembly toward the front. The plunger spring is easily removed from inside the plunger. The knob is retained on the plunger by a cross pin.

4. Keep the forend snugged to the rear to avoid damaging it and carefully drift the forend cap base out of its dovetail toward the right. Use a brass or nylon drift to avoid damaging the screw-hole threads. Remove the forend toward the front.

5. Unscrew and remove the recoil spring guide rod. **Caution:** *Restrain the spring as the rod is taken out.*

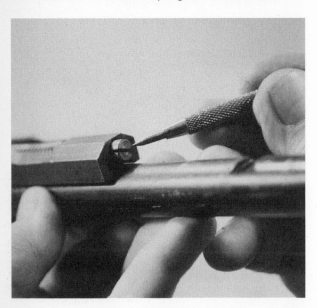

6. One method of controlling the spring during removal of the guide rod is shown here.

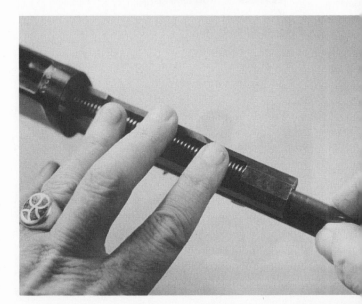

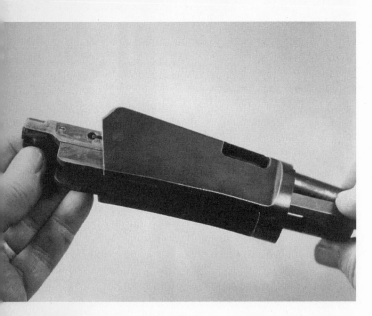

7. Move the bolt assembly rearward and take it out of the receiver.

8. The ejector is retained by a single screw inside the left wall of the receiver, and the screw is accessible through the ejection port. In normal takedown, this is best left in place.

9. Restrain the firing pin and push out the firing pin retaining cross pin.

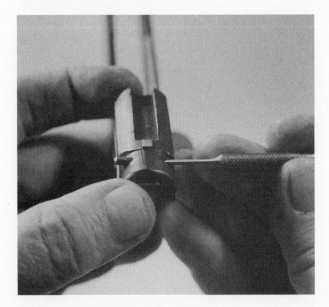

10. Remove the firing pin and its rebound spring toward the rear.

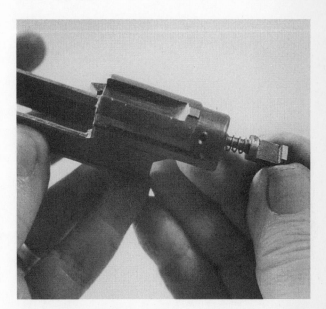

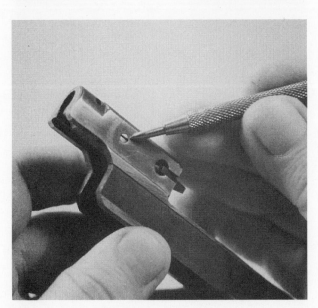

11. Remove the extractor plunger stop screw.

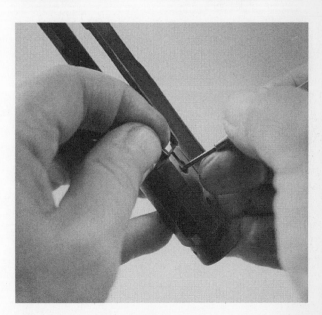

12. Insert a small tool between the extractor and its plunger, and depress the plunger toward the rear. Lift out the extractor. **Caution:** *Control the plunger and its compressed spring.*

13. Remove the inner magazine tube. Take out the two buttplate screws and remove the buttplate.

14. The best way to remove the stock mounting nut is to alter a $5/8$-inch deep socket, cutting away its edge to leave two projections that will engage the slots in the nut. Removal can also be done this way: Use an angled drift punch to break the nut loose.

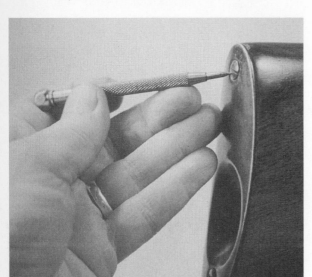

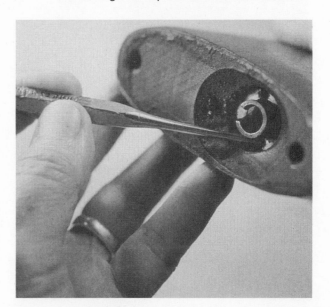

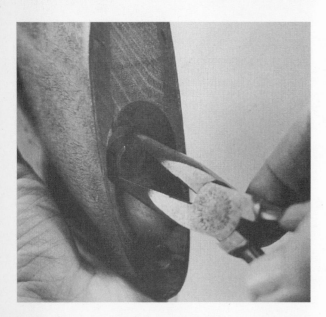

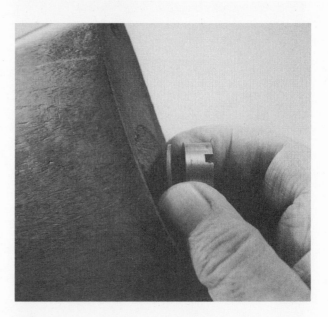

15. Once the nut is freed, an opened sharp-nosed plier can be used to unscrew it.

16. Remove the stock mounting nut and its washer toward the rear.

17. Remove the buttstock toward the rear.

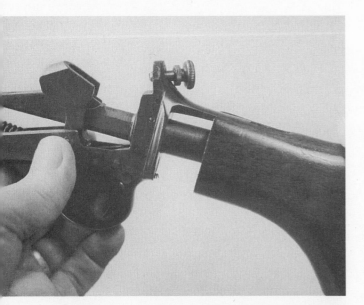

18. Remove the safety detent plunger and spring toward the rear.

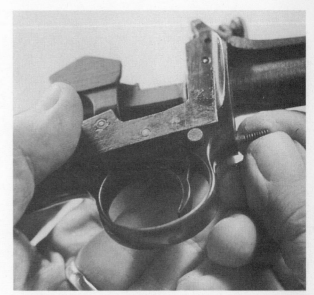

19. Retract the hammer slightly until the cross-hole near the tip of the spring guide is accessible, and insert a small pin to trap the hammer spring. Ease the hammer back forward.

20. Drift out the hammer spring base lock pin.

21. Tip the hammer spring base to the side until its upper portion stops against the frame. This will free it from its recess.

22. Drift out the hammer pivot pin.

23. Remove the hammer and spring assembly toward the front. Pressing the spring base against a slightly opened vise and removing the keeper pin will allow the base and spring to be taken off the guide. **Caution:** *The spring is under tension.* The guide pivot pin can also be removed to take the guide off the hammer.

24. Drift out the trigger cross pin.

25. Take out the sear and its spring from inside the trigger group.

26. Turn the trigger downward into the guard for removal.

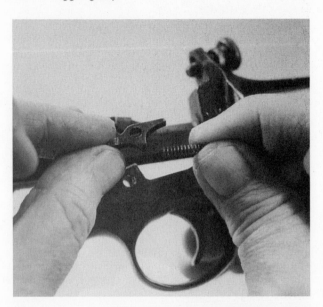

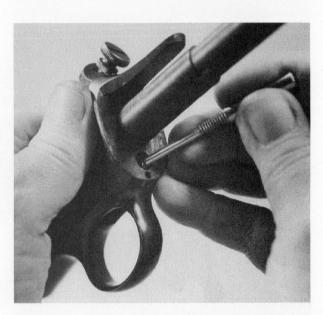

27. Use a tool to push the trigger spring out toward the front, into the receiver, for removal. **Caution:** *Lay a shop cloth over the lower receiver to arrest the spring as it is freed.*

28. Remove the safety button toward either side.

29. If removal of the takedown screw is necessary, determine the smaller end of the cross pin in its tip, and drift that end to push it out. The knob/screw can then be taken off rearward.

30. If you have removed the takedown screw, then drifting out this pin will release the takedown screw lock plunger and its spring for removal upward. **Caution:** *The spring is under tension.*

31. The cartridge stop and its spring can be removed from the magazine housing by pushing out this cross pin. Take care that the small coil spring is not lost.

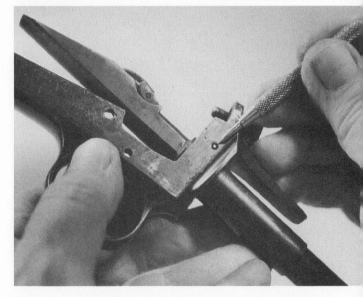

32. In normal takedown, the magazine housing is best left in place. However, if removal is necessary, this cross pin retains it in the lower receiver. After the pin is drifted out, the housing is moved forward out of the lower receiver. In removal of the magazine housing, there is always the possibility of damage.

Reassembly Tips:

1. When reinstalling the safety, remember that the flat recess goes toward the front and also that the shorter of its two ends goes toward the right side, as shown.

2. The trigger spring must be inserted through the trigger guard, and a tool is used to push it back into its tunnel. The proper orientation is shown. You will know it is properly in place when its rear bends are visible at the back of the lower receiver (see step 27).

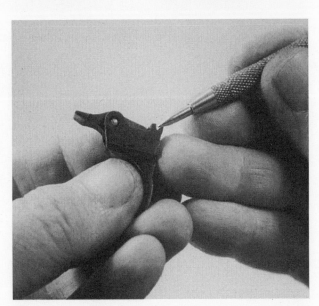

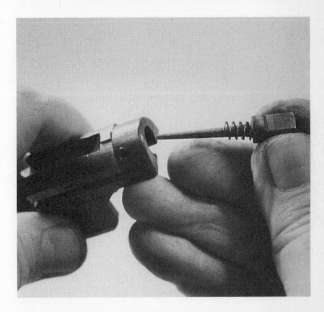

3. When installing the trigger and sear, and the sear spring, it is best to use a short slave pin to pre-assemble them, as shown. The slave pin is pushed out as the trigger pin is inserted. As the assembly is put in place, be sure the recess at the rear of the trigger engages the trigger spring.

4. Be sure the firing pin is installed in the orientation shown, with the long flat on top.

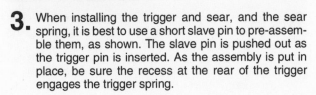

5. In rifles that have seen a lot of use, the firing pin retaining pin may be a loose fit. After it is reinstalled, it is best to stake the pin lightly on each side, as shown.

6. When replacing the recoil spring and its guide, start the spring onto the rod as the rod is pushed toward the rear, moving it in small increments. As the end is neared, use a tool to compress the spring forward while the threads are engaged.

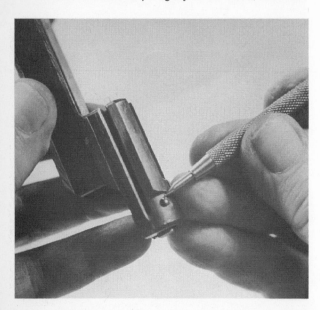

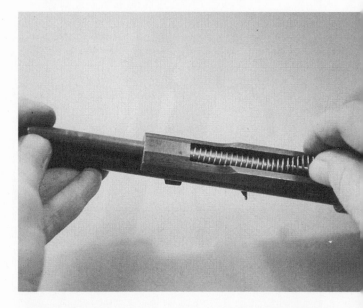

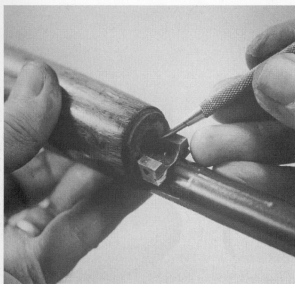
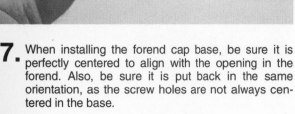

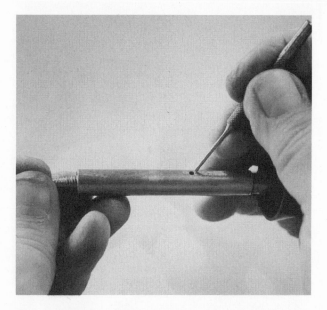

7. When installing the forend cap base, be sure it is perfectly centered to align with the opening in the forend. Also, be sure it is put back in the same orientation, as the screw holes are not always centered in the base.

8. Use a tool to compress the cocking plunger spring, and insert a small tool in the hole provided to trap the spring. When the plunger has engaged the end of the recoil spring guide rod, and just before the forend cap is pushed into place, the tool is removed to release the spring.

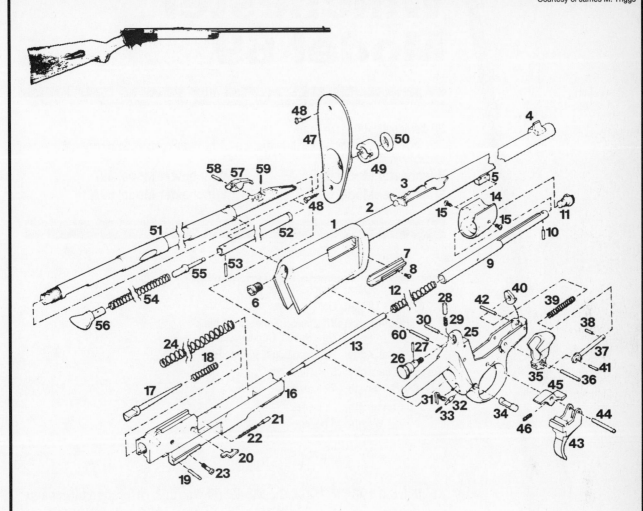

KEY

1	Receiver
2	Barrel
3	Rear Sight
4	Front Sight
5	Forearm Tip Tenon
6	Takedown Screw Bushing
7	Ejector
8	Ejector Screw
9	Operating Sleeve
10	Operating Sleeve Tip Pin
11	Operating Sleeve Tip
12	Operating Sleeve Spring
13	Bolt Guide Rod
14	Forearm Tip
15	Forearm Tip Screws
16	Bolt
17	Firing Pin
18	Firing Pin Spring
19	Firing Pin Stop Pin
20	Extractor
21	Extractor Plunger
22	Extractor Plunger Spring
23	Extractor Plunger Stop Screw
24	Bolt Spring
25	Trigger Housing
26	Takedown Screw
27	Takedown Screw Stop Pin
28	Takedown Screw Lock Plunger
29	Takedown Screw Lock Plunger Spring
30	Takedown Screw Lock Plunger Stop Pin
31	Trigger Spring
32	Trigger Lock Plunger
33	Trigger Lock Plunger Spring
34	Trigger Lock
35	Hammer
36	Hammer Pin
37	Hammer Spring Guide Rod
38	Slave Pin
39	Hammer Spring
40	Hammer Spring Abutment
41	Hammer Spring Guide Rod Pin
42	Hammer Spring Abutment Pin
43	Trigger
44	Trigger Pin
45	Sear
46	Sear Spring
47	Buttplate
48	Buttplate Screws
49	Buttstock Nut
50	Buttstock Nut Washer
51	Magazine Tube, Outer
52	Magazine Tube, Inner
53	Magazine Plug Pin
54	Magazine Spring
55	Magazine Follower
56	Magazine Plug
57	Cartridge Cutoff
58	Cartridge Cutoff Pin
59	Cartridge Cutoff Spring
60	Throat Pin

Parts Not Shown
Forearm
Stock

Winchester Model 69

Similar/Identical Pattern Guns
The same basic assembly/disassembly steps for the Winchester Model 69 also apply to the following guns:
Winchester Model 69T   **Winchester Model 697**
Winchester Model 69M   **Winchester Model 69A**

Data:	Winchester Model 69
Origin:	United States
Manufacturer:	Winchester Repeating Arms New Haven, Connecticut
Cartridge:	22 Short, Long, or Long Rifle
Magazine capacity:	5 or 10 rounds
Overall length:	42 inches
Barrel length:	25 inches
Weight:	5 pounds

Made from 1935 to 1963, the Model 69 was also offered in target and match versions, the only difference in these being the addition of standard sling swivels and two different sights. Since they are mechanically the same, these instructions apply to all guns in the 69 series including the Model 697, except for removal of sights. The basic magazine was a five-shot detachable box type, but a ten-shot version was available as an optional accessory.

Disassembly:

1. Remove the magazine and back out the main stock screw on the underside of the stock, forward of the magazine plate. Remove the action from the stock.

2. To remove the bolt, hold the trigger in the pulled position while opening the bolt and moving it out the rear of the receiver.

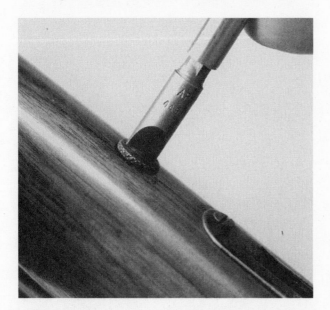

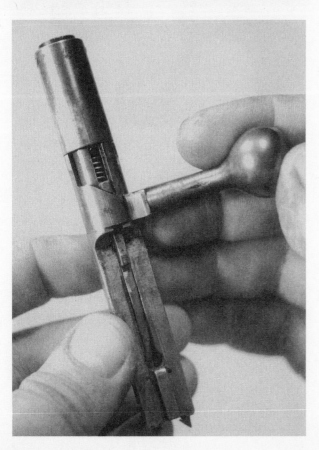

3. Grip the front portion of the bolt in a padded vise and turn the bolt handle to allow the striker to move forward to the fired position, partially easing the tension of its spring. The photo shows the bolt after the handle is turned, with the striker forward.

4. The screw-slotted end piece at the rear of the bolt is *not* a screw. The slot is there to aid reassembly. With the bolt still gripped in a padded vise, exert slight pressure on the end piece to control the tension of the striker spring, and push out the cross pin at the rear of the bolt. **Caution:** *The striker spring is under some tension, even when at rest, so control it and ease out the end piece.*

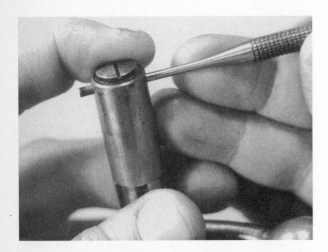

5. Remove the bolt end piece and the striker spring toward the rear.

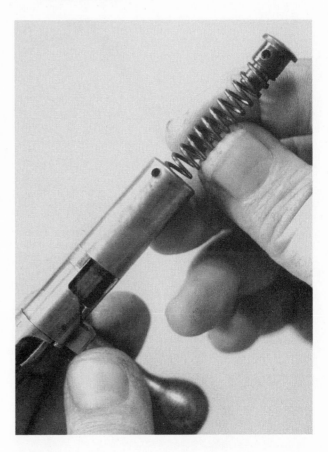

6. Remove the bolt sleeve toward the rear. The sleeve is often tightly fitted, and may require a few nudges with a nylon drift and hammer to start it off.

7. Move the bolt handle sleeve slightly toward the rear until the firing pin (striker) retaining cross pin is exposed and drift out the cross pin.

8. Move the bolt handle sleeve back forward, against its shoulder on the bolt, and turn it until the widest part of its internal opening is aligned with the firing pin on the underside of the bolt. Then, move the firing pin all the way to the rear, tip its rear end downward and remove it from the bolt. The clearances are very close here, so proceed with care.

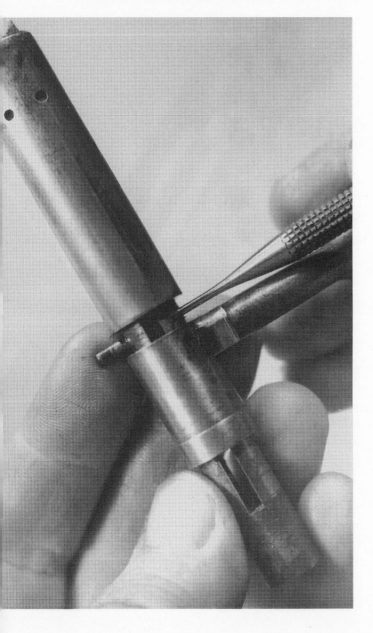

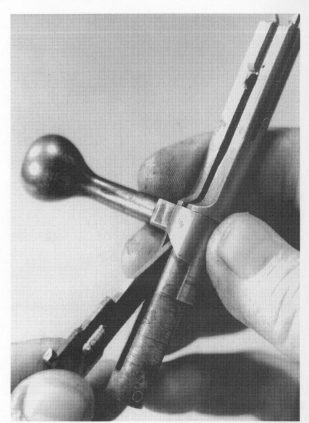

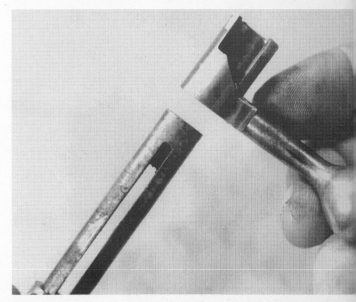

9. Remove the bolt handle sleeve toward the rear.

10. A drift punch of very small diameter is required to remove the vertical pins at the front of the bolt which retain the two extractors. The punch shown was made in the shop for this purpose. The pins must be driven out upward, and the extractors and their small coil springs are taken off from each side.

11. The formed steel that is the magazine catch is secured on the right side of the magazine housing by a single screw.

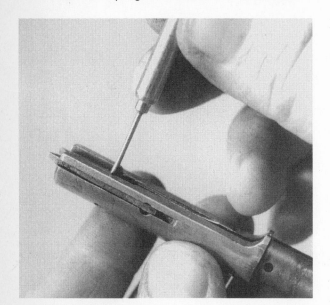

12. Remove the front magazine housing screw.

13. Remove the rear screw from the magazine housing and remove the magazine housing downward.

14. The magazine housing can be taken off without disturbing the trigger spring adjustment screw, but it is best to at least back it off to relieve the spring tension. If this is done, note its depth if the same weight of pull is desired on reassembly.

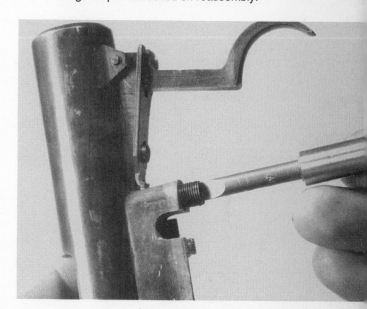

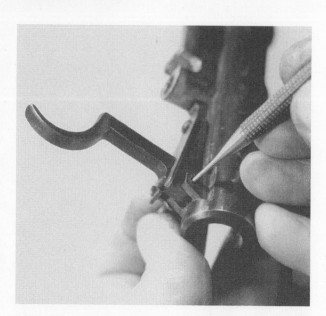

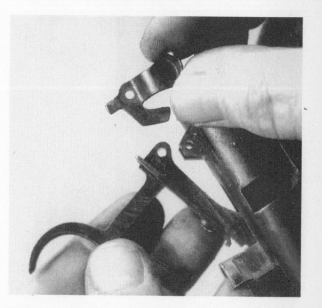

15. Drift out the cross pin that retains the trigger.

16. Remove the trigger and safety-lever downward.

17. Remove the screw on the underside of the front arm of the trigger, and slide the safety plate off toward the front. **Caution:** *Removal of the safety plate will release the safety positioning plunger and spring, so control them as the plate is taken off to prevent loss.*

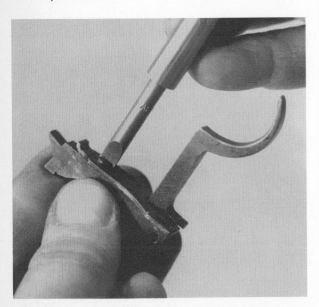

18. The magazine catch release button is retained in the left side of the stock by a circular spring clip which rests in a groove on the button shaft. Push the button in to give access to the clip, move it out of its groove and slide it off the shaft toward the right. The button and its coil spring can then be taken off toward the left.

Reassembly Tips:

1. When replacing the trigger and safety-lever, be sure the upper front arm of the lever goes into its slot in the receiver, and that the lower arm of the lever enters its slot in the safety plate on the trigger. Be sure the holes in the trigger and lever are aligned with the holes in the mount on the receiver before driving in the cross pin.

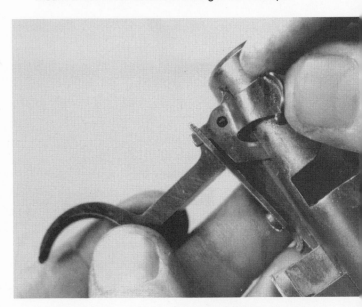

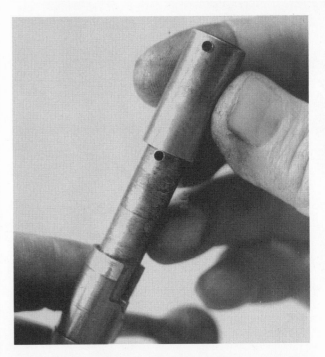

2. When replacing the bolt sleeve, be sure the cross pin holes at the rear are as closely aligned as possible with the holes in the bolt body before tapping the sleeve into place. When the sleeve is fully forward, insert a small drift punch through the holes to complete the alignment.

3. To reinstall the bolt end piece, grip the front portion of the bolt in a padded vise and push the end piece into place, holding it against the tension of the striker spring. Be sure the striker is in the fired position. Use a wide-bladed screwdriver to turn the end piece until the cross pin hole is in alignment with the holes in the bolt sleeve and body, and insert a drift punch to hold the end piece in place while driving in the cross pin.

4. Before the bolt is reinserted in the receiver, the striker must be in cocked position. With the bolt still gripped in the padded vise, turn the bolt handle to cock the striker. The photo shows the striker in the cocked position.

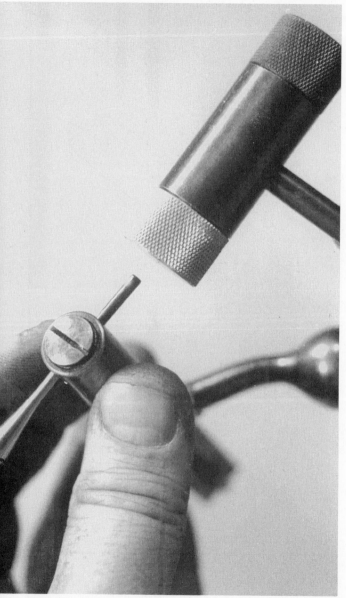

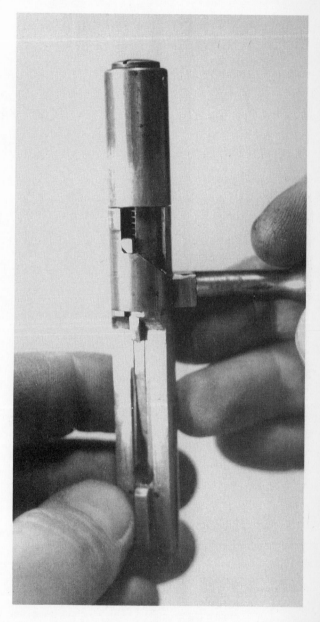

Model 69A Bolt-Action Rifle

Courtesy of James M. Triggs

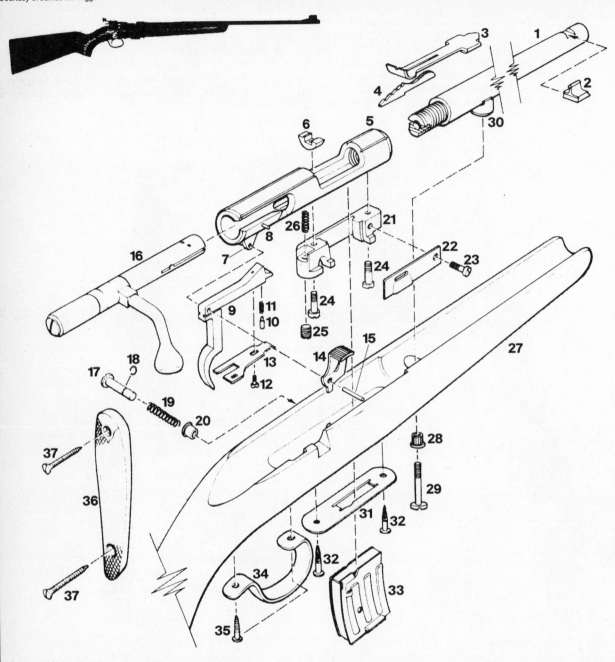

KEY

1 Barrel
2 Front Sight
3 Rear Sight
4 Rear Sight Elevator
5 Receiver
6 Ejector
7 Trigger Base
8 Safety-Lever Stop Pin
9 Trigger
10 Safety Lock Plunger
11 Safety Lock Plunger Spring
12 Safety Lock Screw
13 Safety Lock
14 Safety-Lever
15 Trigger Pin
16 Breechbolt, Complete
17 Magazine Release Plunger
18 Magazine Release Plunger Stop
19 Magazine Release Plunger Spring
20 Magazine Release Plunger Escutcheon
21 Magazine Holder
22 Magazine Catch
23 Magazine Catch Screw
24 Magazine Holder Screws
25 Trigger Spring Adjusting Screw
26 Trigger Spring
27 Buttstock
28 Stock Stud Screw Escutcheon
29 Stock Stud Screw
30 Stock Stud
31 Magazine Plate
32 Magazine Plate Screws
33 Magazine
34 Guard Bow
35 Guard Bow Screws
36 Buttplate
37 Buttplate Screws

Winchester Model 70

Similar/Identical Pattern Guns

The same basic assembly/disassembly steps for the Winchester Model 70 also apply to the following guns:

Winchester Model 70 Featherweight

Winchester Model 70 Lightweight Carbine

Winchester Model 70 Mannlicher

Winchester Model 70 Super Express

Winchester Model 70 Win-Tuff Featherweight, Lightweight

Winchester Model 70A

Winchester Model 670 Carbine

Winchester Ranger

Winchester Model 70 H.B. Varmint

Winchester Model 70 Lightweight Rifle

Winchester Model 70 Sporter

Winchester Model 70 Winlite

Winchester Model 670

Winchester Model 770

Winchester Model 70 Classic Series

Data:	Winchester Model 70
Origin:	United States
Manufacturer:	Winchester Repeating Arms Company New Haven, Connecticut
Cartridges:	From 222 to 458, including several magnum rounds
Magazine capacity:	Varies with cartridges
Overall length:	42½ to 44½ inches
Barrel length:	22 and 24 inches
Weight:	About 7½ pounds

The original Model 70 first appeared in 1936, and was made until 1963. An "economy" version was made between 1964 and 1972, and since that time the original quality was resumed, with some of the innovations of the 1964 version retained. Collectors, and some shooters, treasure the pre-1964 "originals," but in some ways, the later guns, as now currently made, are mechanically superior. A list of the calibers and model variations of the Model 70 would nearly fill an entire page. The gun covered here is a late standard model. On the pre-1964 guns, the bolt detail is quite similar to the standard Mauser pattern. As many readers will be aware, the Model 70 is now made under license by the U.S. Repeating Arms Co.

Disassembly:

1. To remove the bolt, the safety must be in the off-safe position. Open the bolt, and depress the bolt stop, located at the left rear of the receiver. Hold it down, and withdraw the bolt toward the rear. For clarity, the bolt stop is indicated with a drift punch in the photo. It is depressed with a fingertip.

2. Remove the screws on the underside at the front and rear of the trigger guard. Note that on some Model 70 guns the magazine is a through-type, with a hinged cover plate. The one shown in the photos is a closed (blind) type, with a solid stock underside. After the guard screws are removed, the guard can be taken off downward.

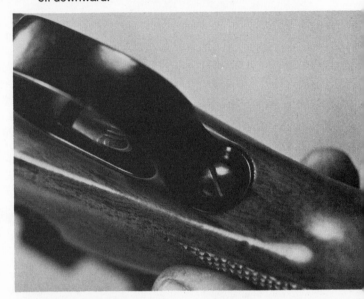

3. Remove the main stock mounting screw, on the underside below the chamber area. If the gun is a through-magazine type, this screw will be in the forward base of the magazine floorplate. When all three screws are removed, the action can be taken out of the stock.

4. If the gun is a blind magazine type, the magazine follower, spring, and internal floorplate can be taken out upward. If the gun has an external floorplate, the floorplate and front hinge plate can be taken off downward. The plate is attached to its base with a cross pin. A cross pin also retains the floorplate catch and its spring in the front of the trigger guard.

5. The magazine box, or housing, is usually a tight press fit on the bottom of the receiver, and can be removed by exerting downward pressure while working it gently from side to side.

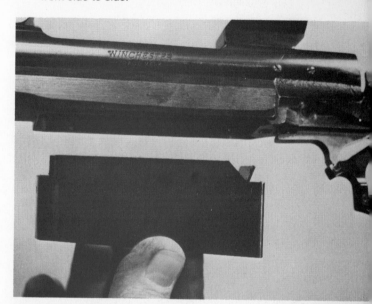

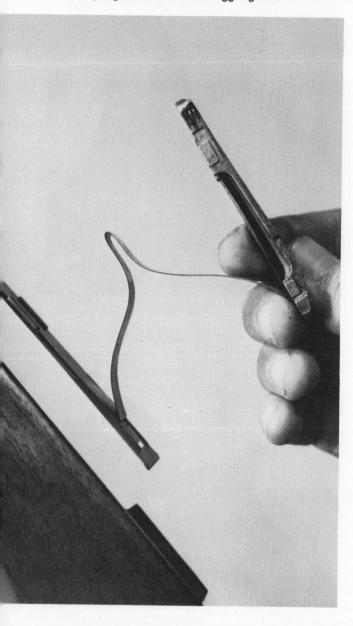

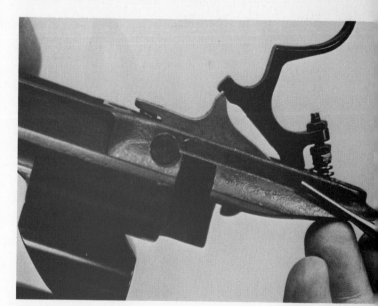

6. A cross pin retains the trigger assembly on the underside of the receiver. Note that the trigger, its spring, and adjustment system can be removed downward without disturbing the adjustment. The cross pin must be drifted out toward the left.

7. Note that the trigger pin has an enlarged head on the left side, and is also the pivot and retainer for the bolt stop and its spring. Before removal, note the relationship of the bolt stop, its spring, and the trigger, to aid reassembly. Restrain the spring as the pin is drifted out, and ease it off.

8. The bolt stop is moved downward and toward the rear for removal.

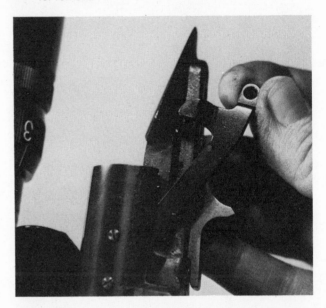

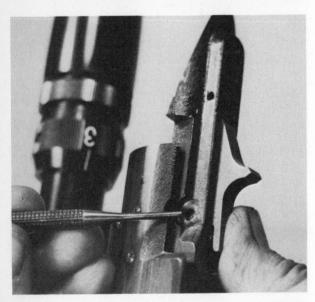

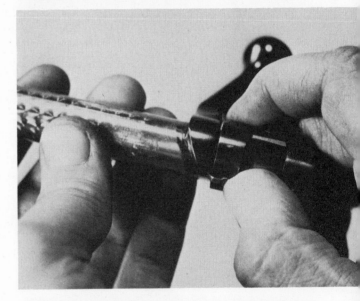

9. The sear is retained on the underside of the receiver by a cross pin which must be drifted out toward the right. Restrain the sear against the tension of its strong spring, and remove the sear and spring downward.

10. Grip the lower lug of the cocking piece firmly in a vise, and move the bolt forward until the safety can be turned back to the safe position. Depress the bolt sleeve lock plunger, located on the left side of the bolt, and unscrew the rear section, the bolt sleeve. During this operation, take care that the safety is not tripped to the fire position.

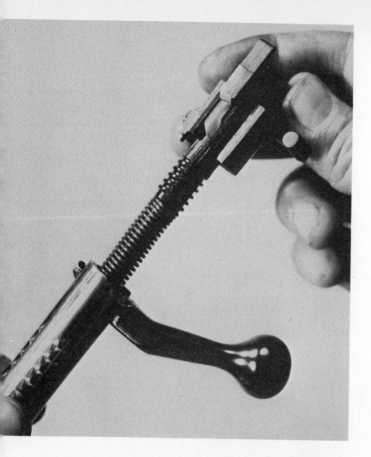

11. When the sleeve and striker assembly has cleared its internal threads, withdraw it toward the rear.

12. Grip the forward portion of the striker firmly in a vise, with the spring retaining C-clip and compression washer just above the vise jaws. Pry the compression washer upward, remove the C-clip, and allow the washer and spring to come down on the vise. With a firm hold on the bolt sleeve, open the vise, and slowly ease the assembly upward, releasing the tension of the spring. Take care not to lose the compression washer. If the gun is an older one, spring removal is done by simply pulling the firing pin sleeve slightly toward the rear, giving it a quarter-turn in either direction, and easing it off toward the front. After the tension is relieved, take off the spring toward the front.

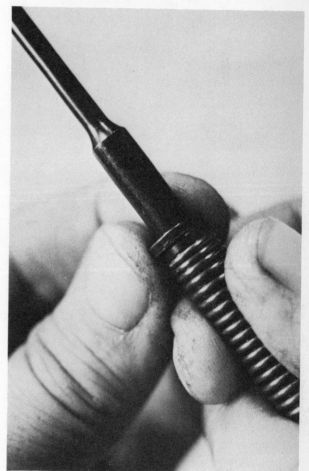

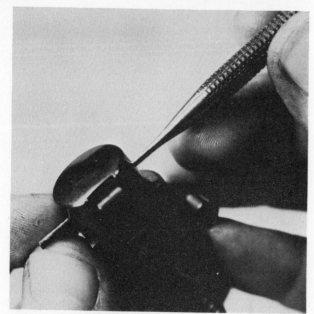

13. Drift out the cross pin in the bolt end piece, at rear of the bolt sleeve.

14. Remove the bolt end piece toward the rear. If it is tight, it can be tapped off by sliding the striker assembly against it.

15. Remove the striker assembly from the rear of the bolt sleeve.

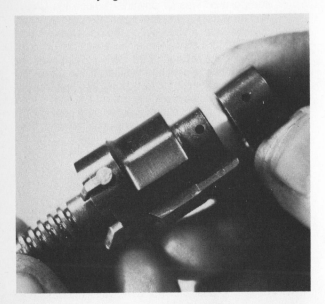

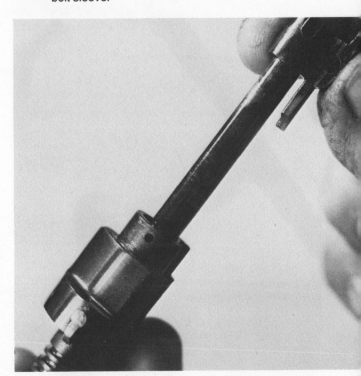

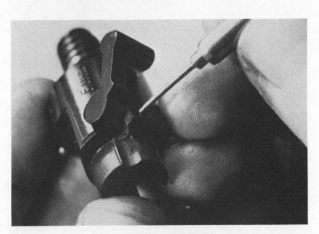

16. To remove the bolt sleeve lock plunger and spring, push out the retaining pin, which runs lengthwise in the sleeve, and take off the plunger and spring toward the side.

17. Use a very small drift punch to push the small pin beside the safety inward, into the interior of the bolt sleeve. The safety-lever should be in the off-safe position.

18. Turn the safety around toward the rear, then move it upward and out of the bolt sleeve. **Caution:** *The safety positioning spring and plunger will be released as the safety clears the sleeve, so restrain them and ease them out.*

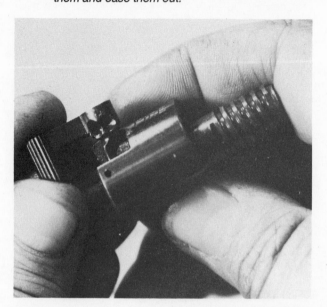

19. To remove the ejector, drift out the angled cross pin at the front of the bolt. **Caution:** *The strong ejector spring will expel the ejector as the drift is removed, so ease the ejector out toward the front, and remove the spring.*

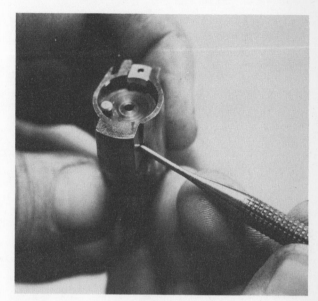

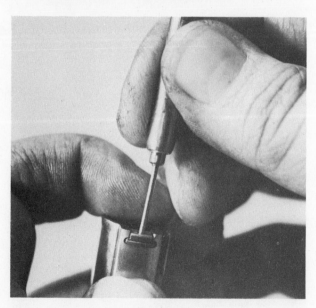

20. To remove the extractor, use a small-diameter drift punch to depress the extractor plunger, accessible through a small hole in the front face of the extractor. While keeping the plunger depressed, move the extractor out of its T-slot in the bolt lug. **Caution:** *Restrain the plunger and spring, and ease them out.* If the gun is an older one, it will have a long external Mauser-style extractor. For removal details on this type, see the Mauser or Springfield sections.

Reassembly Tips:

1. When replacing the striker spring, note that the retaining C-clip has a recess on one side. This side must go toward the front. With the forward part of the striker gripped in a vise (as in disassembly), this means that the recess on the C-clip should be installed downward, toward the vise jaws.

2. Before the bolt sleeve and striker assembly can be installed in the bolt body, the striker must be locked to the rear by placing the safety in the on-safe position. Grip the lower lug of the striker firmly in a vise, push the bolt sleeve toward the front, and set the safety. When the sleeve and striker assembly are back in the bolt body, the safety must be released to the off-safe position before the bolt can be reinserted in the receiver.

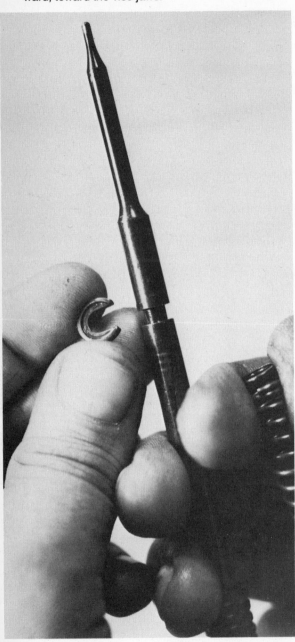

3. If the magazine housing has been removed, insert its rear edge into the recess first, then tap the front gently inward and toward the rear until it is in place.

Model 70 and 70 Featherweight Bolt-Action Rifle

Courtesy of James M. Triggs

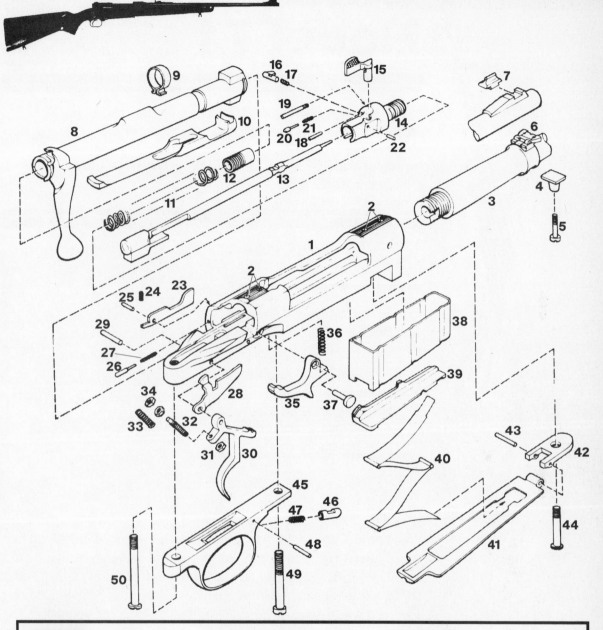

KEY

1 Receiver
2 Receiver Plug Screws
3 Barrel
4 Forearm Stud
5 Forearm Stud Screw
6 Rear Sight Assembly
7 Front Sight
8 Breechbolt
9 Extractor Ring
10 Extractor
11 Firing Pin Spring
12 Firing Pin Sleeve
13 Firing Pin
14 Breechbolt Sleeve
15 Safety Lock
16 Breechbolt Sleeve Lock
17 Breechbolt Sleeve Lock Spring

18 Breechbolt Sleeve Lock Pin
19 Firing Pin Stop Screw
20 Safety Lock Plunger
21 Safety Lock Plunger Spring
22 Safety Lock Stop Pin
23 Ejector
24 Ejector Spring
25 Ejector Pin
26 Bolt Stop Plunger
27 Bolt Stop Plunger Spring
28 Bolt Stop
29 Trigger Pin
30 Trigger
31 Trigger Stop Screw Nut
32 Trigger Stop Screw
33 Trigger Spring
34 Trigger Spring Adjusting Nuts
35 Sear
36 Sear Spring

37 Sear Pin
38 Magazine
39 Magazine Follower
40 Magazine Spring
41 Magazine Cover
42 Magazine Cover Hinge Plate
43 Magazine Cover Hinge Pin
44 Magazine Cover Hinge Plate Screw
45 Guard Bow
46 Magazine Cover Catch
47 Magazine Cover Catch Spring
48 Magazine Cover Catch Pin
49 Front Guard Bow Screw
50 Rear Guard Bow Screw

Parts Not Shown
Buttplate
Buttplate Screws
Buttstock

Winchester Model 71

Similar/Identical Pattern Guns
The same basic assembly/disassembly steps for the Winchester Model 71 also apply to the following guns:

Browning Model 71   **Browning Model 1886**
Winchester Model 1886

Data:	Winchester Model 71
Origin:	United States
Manufacturer:	Winchester Repeating Arms New Haven, Connecticut
Cartridge:	348 Winchester
Magazine capacity:	4 rounds
Overall length:	40 and 42 inches
Barrel length:	20 and 24 inches
Weight:	8 pounds

When production of the venerable Model 1886 ended in 1937, it had already been replaced (a year earlier) in the Winchester line by the excellent Model 71. This gun had all the best features of the Model 1886, and was chambered for a new cartridge, the 348 Winchester. The rifle was discontinued in 1958, but it was very popular in the north country, and many are still in use. Although it externally resembles the other lever-action Winchesters, its internal mechanism is quite different, as the takedown sequence will show. In 1987, Browning Arms Co. exactly reproduced this gun in a limited edition as the Browning Model 71, and the instructions will apply.

Disassembly:

1. Remove the large vertical screw at the rear tip of the upper tang, and take off the buttstock toward the rear. If it is very tight, bump the front of the comb with the heel of the hand to start it.

2. With the hammer in the fired position, drift out the cross pin in the lower tang that retains the hammer spring base. **Caution:** *The powerful hammer spring is under some tension, even when at rest. Control the spring base, and ease it toward the rear.* Take out the base, and the hammer spring, toward the rear.

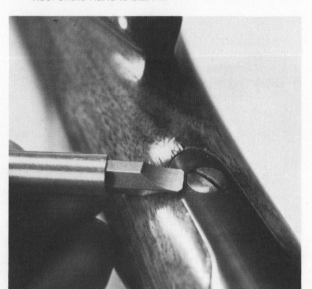

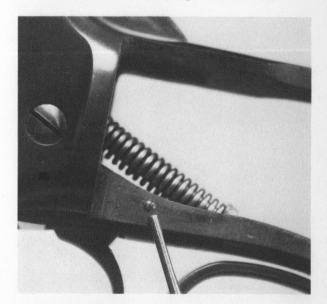

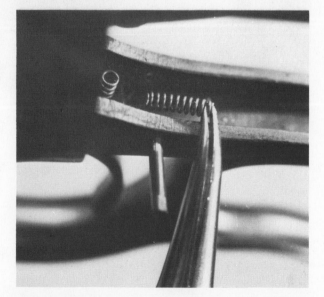

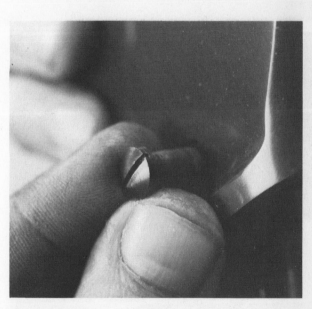

3. When the spring base is removed, the small coil spring that powers the trigger-block safety will be freed for removal from the left side beneath the base. Note that this spring, and the trigger-block safety, are not found on all Model 71 rifles. At this point, the trigger spring can also be removed from the upper rear of the trigger.

4. Remove the hammer screw toward the left.

5. Remove the hammer screw bushing toward the left. If the bushing is tight, there is a small hole inside it to give lodging for a drift point, inserted from the opposite side, to nudge it out.

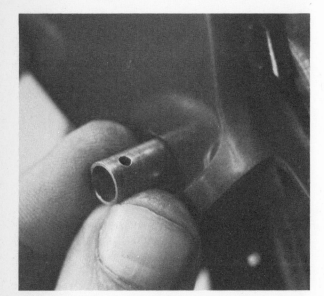

6. Slide the lower tang toward the rear, and remove it. The lever can be partially opened during this operation, for clearance of the trigger.

7. Remove the hammer and the attached hammer strut downward.

8. Drifting out the cross pin in the lower tang will allow removal of the trigger and sear from the tang. If the trigger-block safety is present, taking out the trigger will also free it for removal.

9. Drift out the lever bushing pin toward the right. Note that the left tip of this pin may have the look of a screw slot, but it is actually a split tempered pin which locks the lever pivot bushing.

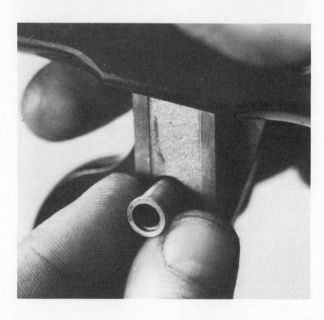

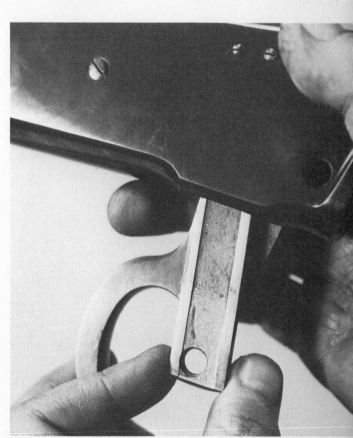

10. Remove the lever pivot bushing toward the left.

11. Remove the left locking block downward. The right locking block is not removed at this time.

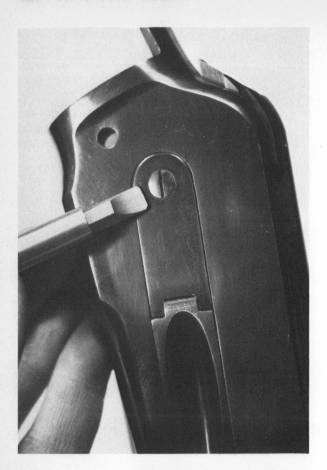

12. Remove the loading gate base screw, on the right side of the receiver, and take off the loading gate assembly toward the right. The gate spring can be removed from its recess on the inside of the base, and drifting out the hinge pin will allow separation of the gate from the base.

13. With the bolt pushed back to the front, and the right locking block pushed partially into place to lock it, align the recess on the front of the locking block with the rear tip of the cartridge guide. Remove the cartridge guide screw, and move the cartridge guide toward the rear to free it from its recess.

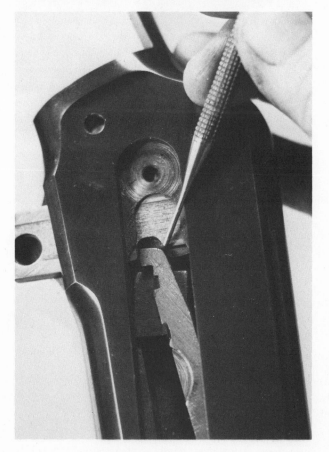

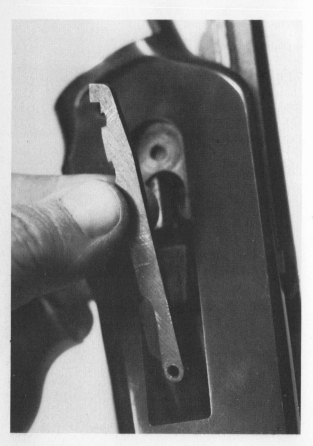

14. Open the bolt, and tip the front end of the cartridge guide inward. Remove the guide from the receiver opening.

15. The right locking block can now be removed downward.

16. Move the bolt all the way to the rear, out of its tracks in the receiver, and tilt the assembly to clear the carrier. Remove the carrier downward. The carrier plunger and spring can be removed by drifting out the pin at the rear of the carrier.

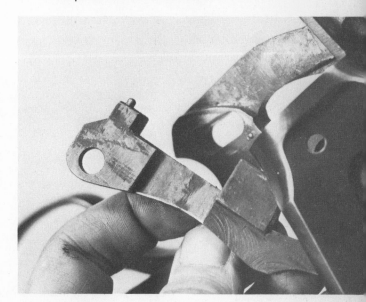

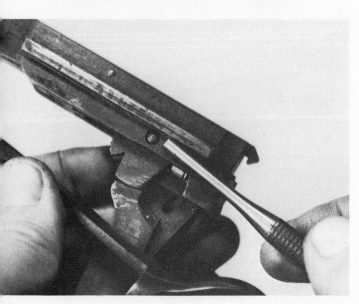

17. Drift out the lever link pin, and separate the lever from the bolt. **Caution:** *This will also release the ejector and its spring and collar, so control them and ease them out.*

18. Remove the lever downward. The lever latch plunger and its spring are retained in the lever by a cross pin. Control the plunger, and ease it out.

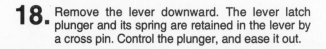

19. When removing the ejector from the front of the bolt, take care not to lose the small collar at the rear of the ejector spring.

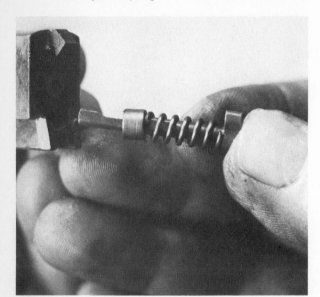

20. Drifting out the cross pin at the lower rear of the bolt will allow removal of the firing pin toward the rear.

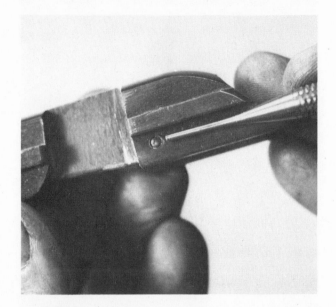

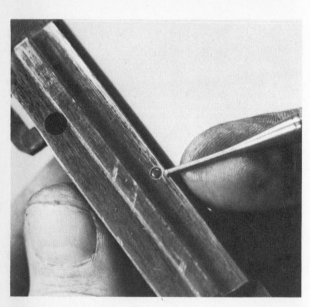

21. Drifting out the cross pin at top center will allow removal of the extractor. Don't lift the extractor upward. Hook a tool under its beak at the front, and lever it out forward.

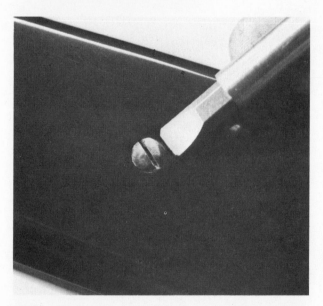

22. Remove the large screw on the left side of the receiver, and take out the cartridge stop from inside the receiver.

23. Remove the screw on the underside, near the front end of the magazine tube, and take out the end piece toward the front. **Caution:** *The magazine spring is partially compressed, so control it and ease it out.* Remove the spring and follower toward the front.

24. Remove the screws on each side of the forend tip, and slide the tip off toward the front.

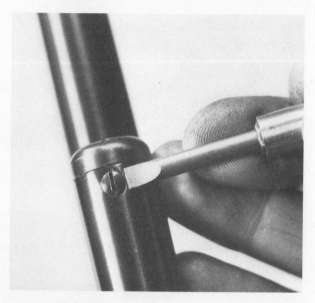

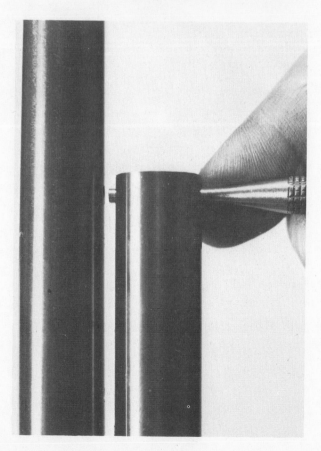

25. Insert a drift punch through the screw holes in the end of the magazine tube, and unscrew the tube counter-clockwise (front view). Remove the tube toward the front. Drift the forend tip tenon out of its dovetail toward the right, and move the forend forward and off.

Reassembly Tips:

1. Before replacing the hammer bushing and screw, insert a tapered drift punch to align the hammer, carrier, and lower tang loops.

2. Replacement of the hammer spring system will be easier if a slave pin is used, as shown, to restrain the spring during installation. If the trigger-block safety is present, install the hammer spring system, then insert the safety spring through the opening in the base, compressing it to snap it into place.

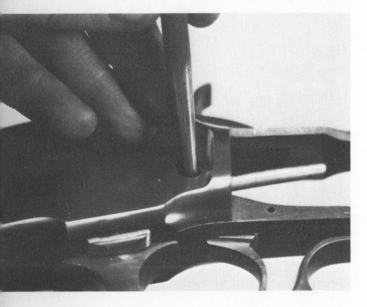

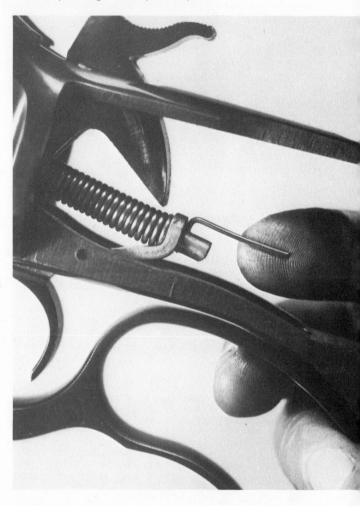

Model 71 Lever-Action Rifle

Courtesy of James M. Triggs

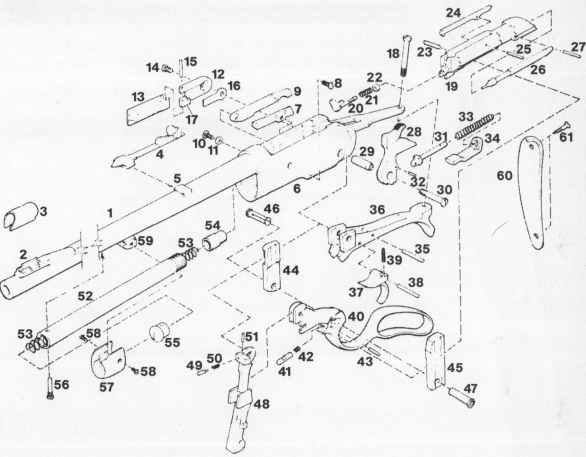

KEY

1 Barrel
2 Front Sight
3 Front Sight Cover
4 Rear Sight
5 Rear Sight Blank
6 Receiver
7 Cartridge Stop
8 Cartridge Stop Screw
9 Cartridge Guide
10 Cartridge Guide Screw
11 Cartridge Guide Screw Bushing
12 Spring Cover Base
13 Spring Cover Leaf
14 Spring Cover Base Screw
15 Spring Cover Leaf Pin
16 Spring Cover Spring
17 Spring Cover Stop Pin
18 Upper Tang Screw
19 Breechbolt
20 Ejector
21 Ejector Spring

22 Ejector Collar
23 Finger Lever Connecting Pin
24 Extractor
25 Extractor Pin
26 Firing Pin
27 Firing Pin Stop Pin
28 Hammer
29 Hammer Screw Bushing
30 Hammer Screw
31 Hammer Spring Guide Rod
32 Hammer Spring Guide Rod Pin
33 Hammer Spring
34 Hammer Spring Abutment
35 Hammer Spring Abutment Pin
36 Lower Tang
37 Trigger
38 Trigger Pin
39 Trigger Spring
40 Finger Lever
41 Friction Stud
42 Friction Stud Spring
43 Friction Stud Stop Pin
44 Locking Bolt, Right

45 Locking Bolt, Left
46 Finger Lever Bushing Pin
47 Finger Lever Bushing
48 Carrier
49 Carrier Plunger
50 Carrier Plunger Spring
51 Carrier Plunger Pin
52 Magazine Tube
53 Magazine Spring
54 Magazine Follower
55 Magazine Plug
56 Magazine Plug Screw
57 Forearm Tip
58 Forearm Tip Screws
59 Forearm Tip Tenon
60 Buttplate
61 Buttplate Screws

Parts Not Shown
Forearm
Stock

Winchester Model 190

Similar/Identical Pattern Guns

The same basic assembly/disassembly steps for the Winchester Model 190 also apply to the following guns:

Winchester Model 290   **Winchester Model 290 Deluxe**

Data:	Winchester Model 190
Origin:	United States
Manufacturer:	Winchester Repeating Arms Company New Haven, Connecticut
Cartridge:	22 Long Rifle
Magazine capacity:	15 rounds
Overall length:	39 inches
Barrel length:	$20^1/_2$ inches
Weight:	5 pounds

Introduced as the Model 290 in 1964, and in a "deluxe" version, this gun was offered in an economy style in 1974 as the Model 190. In this designation, it was made until 1980. Some very early guns will be found to have a plastic rear sight and a combination front sight and magazine tube hanger of the same material, and some elements of takedown involving those parts will be slightly different. However, the instructions will apply to either model.

Disassembly:

1. Cycle the bolt to cock the hammer and move the safety to the on-safe position. Remove the magazine tube and push out the large plastic cross pin located in the receiver just above the trigger. The pin can be pushed out toward either side.

2. Tip the trigger housing down at the rear and move it slightly toward the rear to disengage its forward stud from its recess inside the receiver. Remove the trigger group downward.

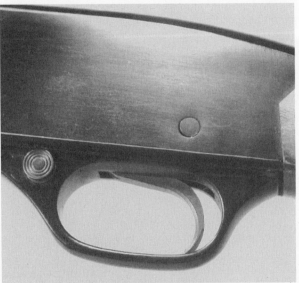

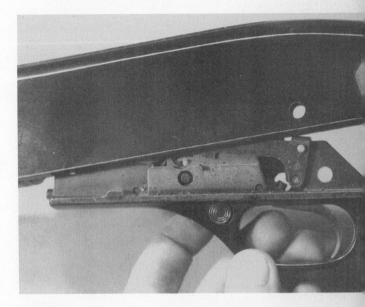

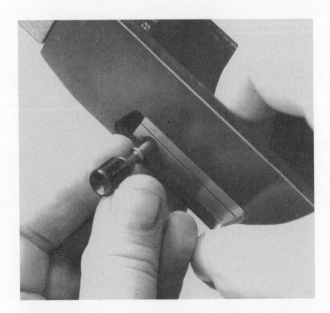

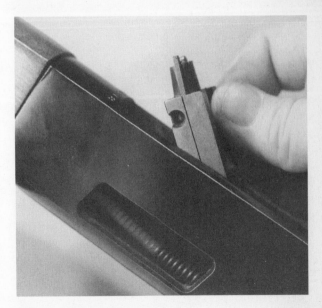

3. With the gun inverted, retract the bolt slightly and use a finger or tool to hold it inside the receiver. Lift the front of the bolt, and remove the bolt handle from its hole in the bolt.

4. Move the bolt toward the rear to clear its forward end from the barrel throat and tip the front of the bolt upward (the gun is still inverted) until it can be removed from the receiver. **Caution:** *The bolt spring is under tension. Ease it out.*

5. Remove the bolt spring and its nylon guide from the receiver.

6. Removal of the buttstock requires a special socket wrench with a very deep end. It is possible to alter an ordinary socket for this, but in normal disassembly it is best to leave the stock in place. If the stock is removed, and the headless mounting bolt taken out, the recoil plate inside the receiver will be released for removal.

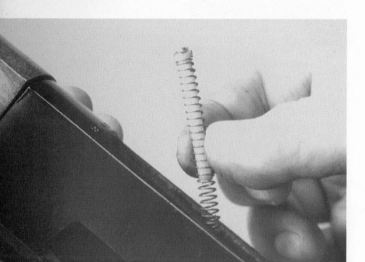

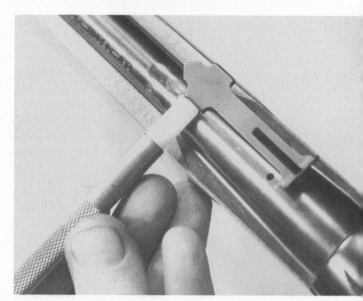

7. Drifting out the small, short cross pin in the magazine tube hanger near the muzzle will release the outer magazine tube for removal toward the front. This will allow the forend to be taken off downward. After removal of the forend, the nylon forend mount is easily slid out of its dovetail toward either side.

8. Flex the rear sight very slightly upward, and take out the sight elevator. Drifting out the rear sight toward the right will release the barrel collar cover for removal upward, giving access to the barrel collar.

9. With the proper wrench (available from Brownells) turn the barrel collar counterclockwise (front view) until it is out of the receiver. Remove the barrel toward the front. **Note:** Because of the permanently attached magazine tube hanger, the barrel collar is not removable from the barrel.

10. If the barrel is very tight in the receiver, grip the barrel in a padded vise and tap the front of the receiver with a wood, leather or nylon hammer, moving the receiver off the rear of the barrel. **Caution:** *Take care not to deform the lower front of the receiver.*

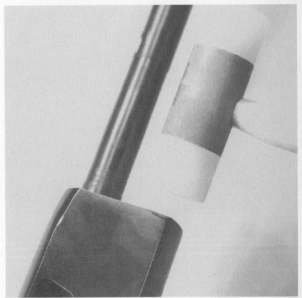

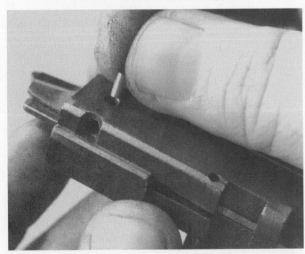

11. Drift out the vertical pin on the left side of the bolt to allow the firing pin to be moved toward the rear, easing the tension of the combination firing pin spring and extractor spring. **Note:** There is a steel ball bearing at each end of the spring. Take care that these are not lost. Remove the extractor pivot pin from its hole in the top front of the bolt. With the spring tension relieved, the pin should come out when the bolt is inverted and tapped with a light hammer. If the pin is tight, it can be nudged out by using a pointed tool in the stake mark on the underside of the bolt. Take care that this very small pin isn't lost.

12. Remove the extractor from the right side of the bolt, taking it out forward and toward the right.

13. Move the firing pin forward to nudge the spring out of its tunnel in the bolt and remove the spring and the two ball bearings from the extractor recess. Again, take care that the ball bearings aren't lost.

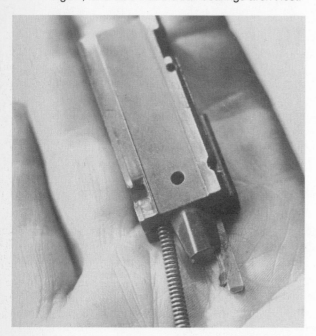

14. Move the firing pin toward the center of the bolt and remove the firing pin toward the rear.

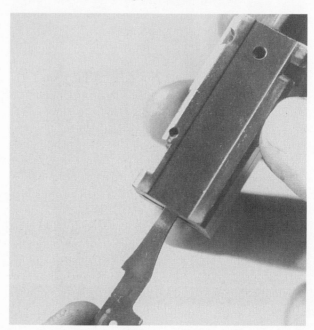

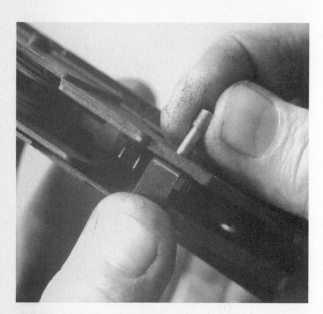

15. Move the safety to the off-safe position, restrain the hammer and pull the trigger, lowering the hammer to the fired position. Restrain the sear/disconnector assembly and remove its pivot pin toward the right.

16. Remove the sear/disconnector assembly upward. The sear and its spring are a permanent assembly inside the disconnector, the pivot pin being riveted in place at the factory. Routine removal is unwise in normal disassembly.

17. Push the hammer pivot out toward either side (left) and remove the hammer assembly upward (right). The hammer spring and its two nylon support pieces are easily removed from the hammer.

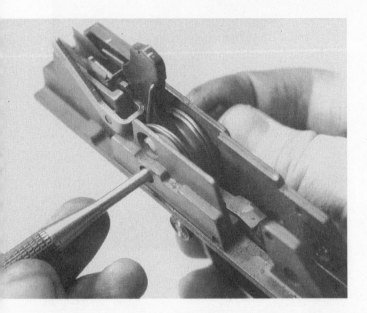

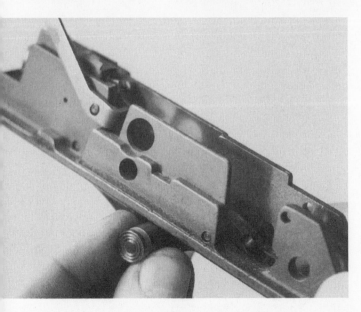

18. The right rear tail of the hammer spring retains the safety, and the safety can now be turned slightly and removed toward the left.

19. Push out the trigger pivot pin and remove the trigger from the top of the trigger housing. The sear contact stud on the trigger is factory-staked at the proper level, and it should not be disturbed.

20. The feed system is retained by three cross pins. The large pin at the rear (upper right in the photo) retains the carrier lever. When drifting it out, restrain the carrier, as its spring is under tension. Moving the carrier out to the rear will release the spring and its plunger, so proceed with caution. The cartridge feed guide is retained by a tiny roll pin near its center and by a larger pin near the lower edge of the housing. When these are removed, the guide can be taken out toward the top.

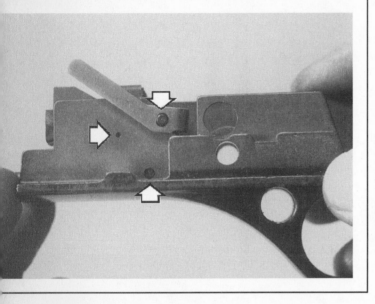

When replacing the safety in the trigger housing, remember that the end with the red ring goes toward the left, and be sure that the positioning recesses on the right side are at the top.

Note that the hammer pivot has one flat side, and be sure both of the nylon hammer spring supports are oriented so that their inside flats will align with the flat on the pin. If not, the support bushings may be damaged as the pin is pushed into place.

When driving in the firing pin stop pin on the left side of the bolt, insert the bolt handle temporarily to prevent the loss of the extractor pivot pin.

When replacing the bolt spring and guide, use a small screwdriver to push in the spring, a few coils at a time, while keeping pressure on the guide toward the rear. When the rear tip of the guide is in the spring hole, restrain the guide and spring with a tool or fingertip while inserting the bolt and bolt handle. Then, move the bolt back, being sure that the head of the guide engages its recess on the rear of the bolt.

When replacing the hammer assembly in the trigger housing, be sure the right lower tail of the hammer spring enters its recess inside the housing, so it will contact the positioning grooves in the safety. Be sure the left tail of the spring lies on its shelf in the housing, or it may bind the trigger.

Reassembly Tips:

1. When replacing the sear/disconnector assembly, be sure the lower end of the sear spring goes toward the rear, down the slope of the trigger.

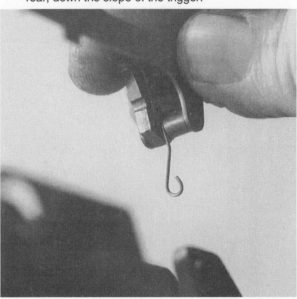

2. When installing the outer magazine tube, be sure it is fully to the rear and the groove in its upper flange is aligned with the cross pin hole in the hanger before inserting the cross pin.

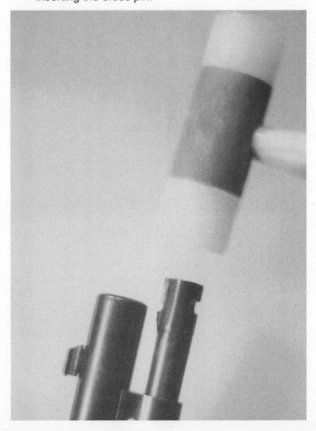

Model 190 Autoloading and Model 150 Lever-Action Rifle

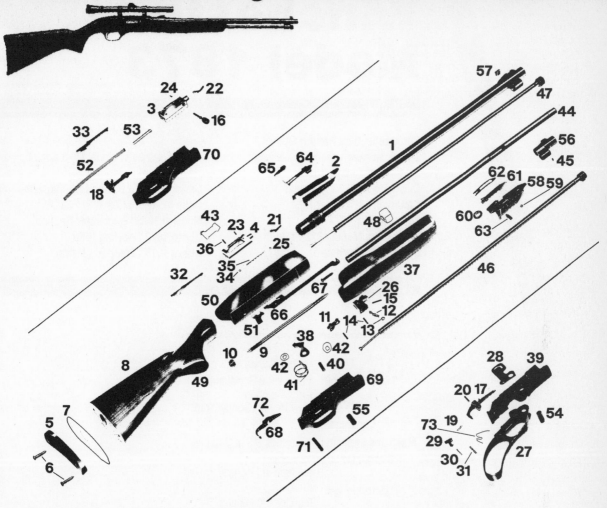

KEY

1	Barrel and Barrel Collar
2	Barrel Collar Cover
3	Breechbolt Complete (Model 190)
4	Breechbolt Complete (Model 150)
5	Buttplate
6	Buttplate Screws
7	Buttplate Spacer
8	Buttstock
9	Buttstock Bolt
10	Buttstock Nut with Washer
11	Carrier
12	Carrier Coil Spring
13	Carrier Coil Spring Plunger
14	Carrier Pins
15	Carrier Stop Pin
16	Cocking Handle
17	Disconnector and Sear Assembly (Model 150)
18	Disconnector and Sear Assembly (Model 190)
19	Disconnector Coil Spring
20	Disconnector Pin
21	Extractor (Model 150)
22	Extractor (Model 190)
23	Extractor Pin (Model 150)
24	Extractor Pin (Model 190)
25	Extractor Plunger
26	Feed Guide
27	Finger Lever
28	Finger Lever Arm
29	Finger Lever Latch
30	Finger Lever Latch Pin
31	Finger Lever Pin
32	Firing Pin (Model 150)
33	Firing Pin (Model 190)
34	Firing Pin Plunger
35	Firing Pin Spring
36	Firing Pin Stop Pin
37	Forearm
38	Hammer
39	Hammer Housing
40	Hammer Pin
41	Hammer Spring
42	Hammer Spring Supports
43	Locking Plate
44	Magazine Tube, Outside
45	Magazine Tube Retaining Pin, Outside
46	Magazine Tube, Inside Assembly (Rifle)
47	Magazine Tube, Inside Assembly
48	Magazine Tube Bracket
49	Pistol Grip Cap Assembly
50	Receiver
51	Recoil Plate
52	Return Spring
53	Return Spring Guide
54	Safety (Model 150)
55	Safety (Model 190)
56	Sight, Front (Plastic)
57	Sight, Front (Metal)
58	Sight Base, Rear
59	Sight Base Screw, Rear
60	Sight Elevator, Rear
61	Sight Leaf, Rear
62	Sight Spring, Rear
63	Sight Windage Screw, Rear
64	Rear Sight
65	Rear Sight Elevator
66	Slide Arm
67	Slide Arm Screw
68	Trigger Assembly
69	Trigger Guard
70	Trigger Guard (Model 190)
71	Trigger Guard Pin, Rear
72	Trigger Pin
73	Trigger Spring

Winchester Model 1873

Similar/Identical Pattern Guns

The same basic assembly/disassembly steps for the Winchester Model 1873 also apply to the following guns:

Cimarron 1873 30" Express	Cimarron 1873 Button Half-Magazine
Cimarron 1873 Short Rifle	Dixie Model 1873
E.M.F. Model 1873	Mitchell 1873 Winchester Replica
Navy Arms Model 1873-Style Rifle	Uberti 1873 Sporting Rifle
Uberti 1873 Carbine	Uberti 1873 "Trapper's Model"

Data:	Winchester Model 1873
Origin:	United States
Manufacturer:	Winchester Repeating Arms Company New Haven, Connecticut
Cartridges:	32-20, 38-40, 44-40
Magazine capacity:	15 rounds (12 in Carbine)
Overall length:	43 inches (carbine, 39 inches)
Barrel length:	24 inches (carbine, 20 inches)
Weight:	8¼ pounds (carbine, 7¾ pounds)

Originally made from 1873 to 1923 by Winchester, the Model 1873 has been reproduced in Italy by Aldo Uberti, and has been offered by several importers. The gun shown here is the version marketed by Dixie Gun Works. There are some small mechanical differences between the modern Italian guns and the original Winchesters, and these will be noted in the instructions.

Disassembly:

1. Remove the large vertical screw at the rear tip of the upper tang. Remove the screw on the underside, at the rear tip of the lower tang.

2. Remove the buttstock toward the rear. If it is tight, bump the front of the comb with a rubber mallet.

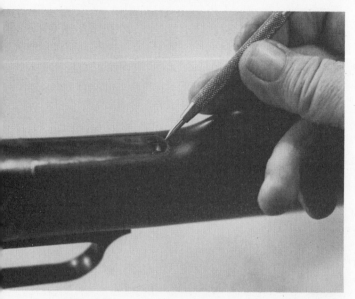

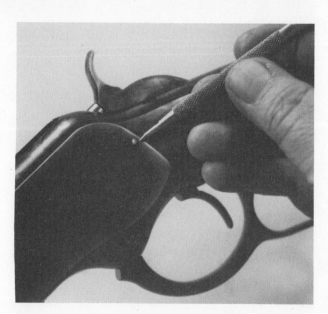

3. Remove the cross screw that retains the sideplates.

4. Tip the sideplates outward at the rear, and remove them. If they are tight, tap the side of the receiver (not the sideplate) with a nylon hammer.

5. The loading gate, which is its own spring, is attached to the inside of the right sideplate with a screw.

6. Remove the left and right link assemblies. Removal of the center pins in the links is not advisable, except for repair.

7. Remove the link pin from the upper arm of the lever. Note that in an original Winchester, this pin is not routinely removed.

8. Remove the two screws on the underside, forward of the lever, and take out the lever detent spring on the left, and the carrier spring on the right.

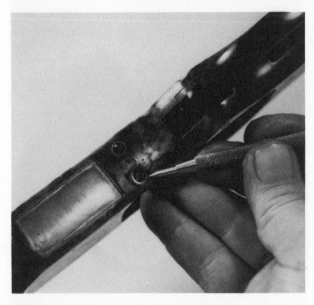

9. Remove the lever cross screw.

10. Remove the lever downward. In an original gun, the lever is not removed at this point.

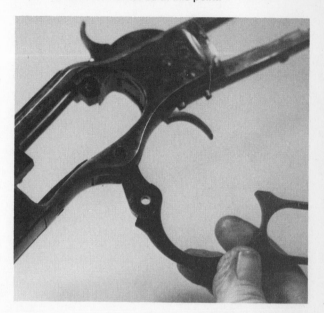

11. With the bolt moved fully to the rear, the carrier lever may be lifted from its recess in the receiver by pushing up on the carrier.

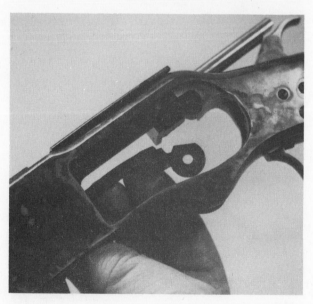

12. With the carrier up, move the lever to the rear. Tip the lever out to the position shown, toward the right, and remove it rearward. Note: This is not possible with an original gun.

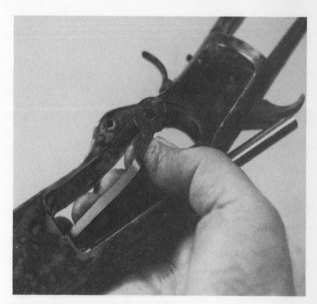

13. Remove the carrier from the receiver. Again, this is a later step with an original gun.

14. Drift out the forward link cross pin in the bolt. If the gun is an original Winchester, this will release the firing pin retractor to be taken out downward, and by depressing the hammer, the combined bolt rod and firing pin can be taken out rearward.

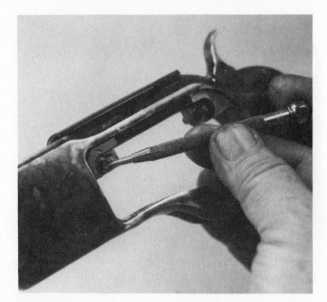

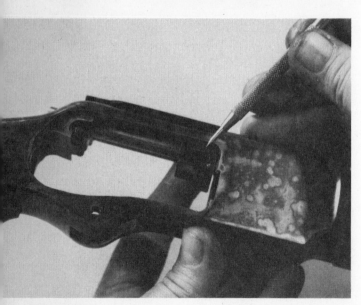

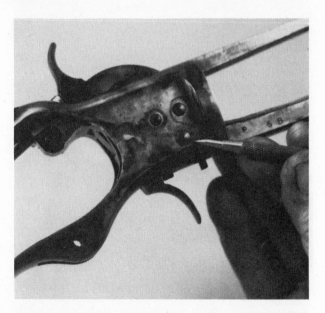

15. In the reproduction gun, there is a rebound spring rather than a retractor. The separate bolt rod, and the firing pin and its spring, are retained at the rear of the bolt by this small cross pin. After removal of the pin, the rod will not clear the hammer for removal, but it can be moved to the rear for access to the firing pin and its spring, for repair purposes.

16. Depress the safety catch, pull the trigger, and set the hammer in its safety notch. Remove the screws at lower rear on each side of the receiver.

17. Remove the lower tang assembly downward. If the gun is an original Winchester, the finger lever, carrier lever and carrier can now be removed.

18. The bolt rod can now be taken out rearward.

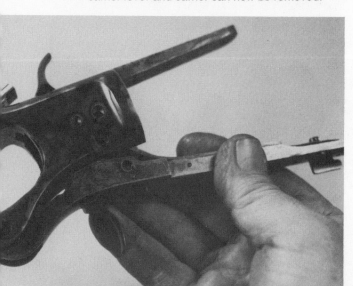

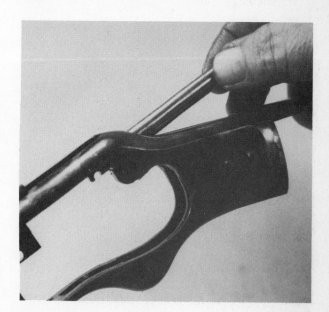

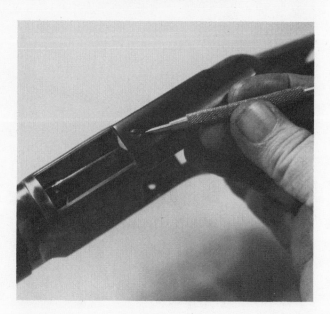

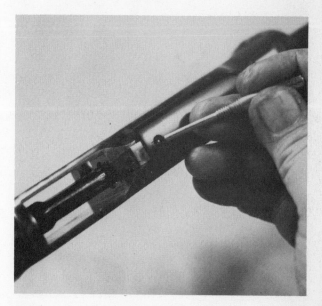

19. Remove the dust cover screw.

20. Move the dust cover to the point shown, and depress the cover tension ball and spring.

21. Move the dust cover off rearward. **Caution:** *Control the ball and spring as they are cleared by the edge of the cover.* Use a magnetized tool to remove the ball and spring.

22. Remove the dust cover base from the top of the receiver.

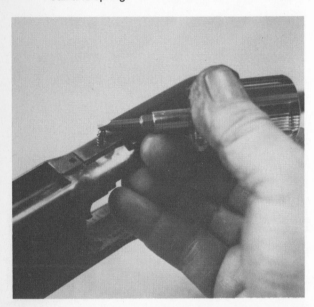

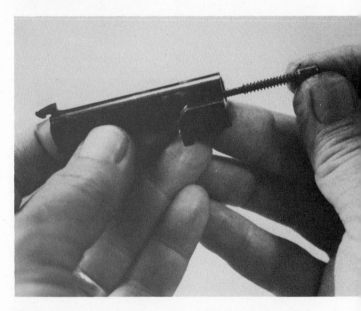

23. Move the bolt rearward, tip it downward, and remove it toward the side.

24. Remove the firing pin and its return spring from the bolt.

25. The extractor is retained by a cross pin, and the ends of the pin are contoured to the curvature of the top of the bolt. Removal should be only for repair purposes. The extractor is its own spring.

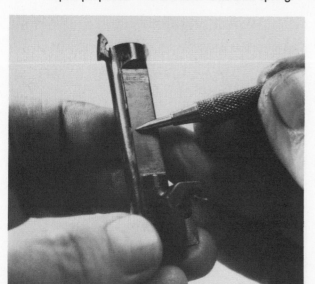

26. Depress the safety catch to free the trigger, **and** release the hammer from its safety step to go all the way over forward. Depress the front of the hammer spring, and unhook the hammer stirrup from the spring.

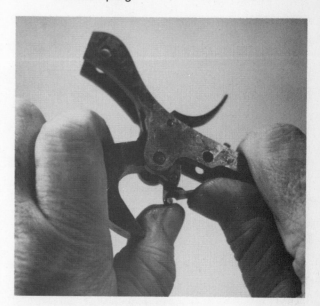

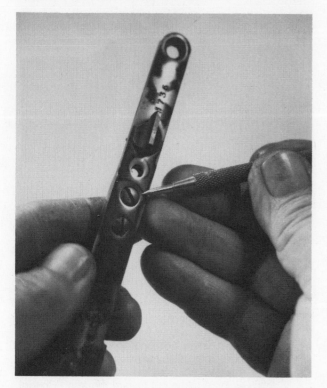

27. Back out the smaller screw, forward of the one indicated, to release any tension on the spring. Remove the spring screw, indicated, and take off the spring.

28. Drift out the cross pin, and remove the hammer.

29. The lever safety catch is pivoted and retained by a cross pin at the rear. The superposed lever safety and trigger springs are retained by a vertical screw. If this system is to be taken apart, remove the screw and springs first.

30. Drifting out the trigger cross pin will free the trigger and sear assembly, including the sear spring, for removal. In an original gun, the trigger and sear are a single part.

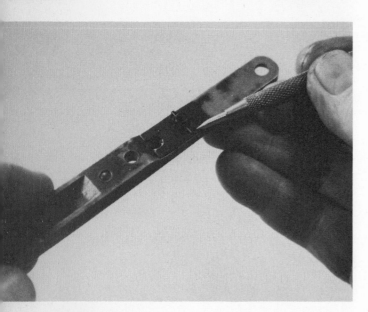

31. The lever latch and its spring are retained by a cross pin at the rear of the tang unit.

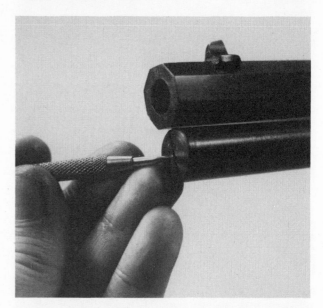

32. On the original Winchester, the magazine end plug is retained by a vertical screw on the underside at the muzzle. On this version, the plug has a screw slot, and it is threaded directly into the magazine tube. Removal will allow the magazine spring and follower to be taken out toward the front. Control the spring.

33. The forend cap is retained by a screw on each side. Full removal of the cap and forend, however, requires removal of the magazine tube.

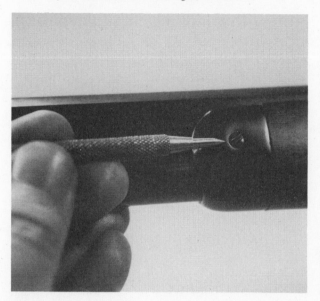

34. The magazine tube is retained by a cross pin in the tube loop. After the pin is drifted out, the tube is taken out toward the front. This will free the forend and its cap for removal. The tube loop and the forend cap base can then be driven out of their dovetail mounts on the barrel.

Reassembly tips:

1. When replacing the carrier, be sure the side with the large cut at the rear is on the right side.

2. When replacing the carrier spring and the lever detent spring, be sure each is on the correct side, and that the in-turned tips bear properly on the lever and the carrier lever. If the springs are not positioned correctly, the sideplates cannot be installed.

Model 1873 Lever-Action Rifle

Courtesy of James M. Triggs

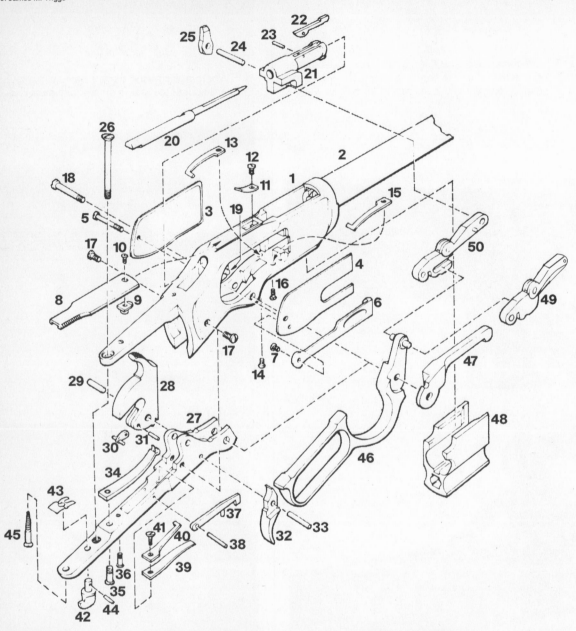

KEY

1	Receiver
2	Barrel
3	Sideplate, Left
4	Sideplate, Right
5	Sideplate Screw
6	Spring Cover
7	Spring Cover Screw
8	Mortise Cover
9	Mortise Cover Stop
10	Mortise Cover Stop Screw
11	Mortise Cover Spring
12	Mortise Cover Spring Screw
13	Finger Lever Spring
14	Finger Lever Spring Screw
15	Carrier Lever Spring
16	Carrier Lever Spring Screw
17	Slide Tang Screws
18	Finger Lever Screw
19	Rear Link Pin
20	Firing Pin
21	Breechblock
22	Extractor
23	Extractor Pin
24	Front Link Pin
25	Firing Pin Retractor
26	Upper Tang Screw
27	Lower Tang
28	Hammer
29	Hammer Pivot Pin
30	Stirrup
31	Stirrup Pin
32	Trigger
33	Trigger Pivot Pin
34	Mainspring
35	Mainspring Screw
36	Mainspring Tension Screw
37	Safety Catch
38	Safety Catch Pin
39	Trigger Spring
40	Safety Catch Spring
41	Trigger and Safety Catch Spring Screw
42	Lever Latch
43	Lever Latch Spring
44	Lever Latch Pin
45	Lower Tang Screw
46	Finger Lever
47	Carrier Lever
48	Carrier Block
49	Link Assembly, Right
50	Link Assembly, Left

Winchester Model 1892

Similar/Identical Pattern Guns
The same basic assembly/disassembly steps for the Winchester Model 1892 also apply to the following guns:

Browning B92	**Rossi M92 SRC**
Rossi M92 SRS	**Spanish "El Tigre" Carbine**
Winchester Model 53	**Winchester Model 65**

Data:	Winchester Model 1892
Origin:	United States
Manufacturer:	Winchester Repeating Arms Company New Haven, Connecticut
Cartridges:	25-20, 32-20, 38-40, and 44-40
Magazine capacity:	14 rounds (rifle), 12 rounds (carbine)
Overall length:	41¾ inches (rifle)
Barrel length:	24 inches (rifle), 20 inches (carbine)
Weight:	6¾ pounds (rifle)

Another of John M. Browning's masterpieces for Winchester, the Model 1892 was made in rifle form until 1932, and in carbine style until 1941. Slim, elegant, and totally reliable, the Model 92 was popular for many reasons, one of which was its chambering for the same cartridges as the Colt revolver in its three larger calibers. In today's market, collectors and shooters vie for the few remaining guns in circulation. I know of several of these guns that are still in regular use as small to medium-size game rifles. The Model 53 and Model 65 Winchesters are mechanically identical. Browning made an exact copy and called it the B92; Rossi of Brazil has two versions (imported currently by Interarms); and the old Spanish "El Tigre" is based on the Model 1892. These instructions generally apply to all versions.

Disassembly:

1. Remove the vertical stock mounting screw, located at the rear of the upper tang, and take off the stock toward the rear. If it's tight, bump the front of the comb with the heel of the hand to start it.

2. Partially open the lever to give access to the hammer spring screw and strain screw, at the rear of the lower tang. Loosening the strain screw will make removal of the spring screw easier, but this is not absolutely necessary. After removal of the spring screw, disengage the spring hooks from the hammer stirrup, and take out the hammer spring toward the rear.

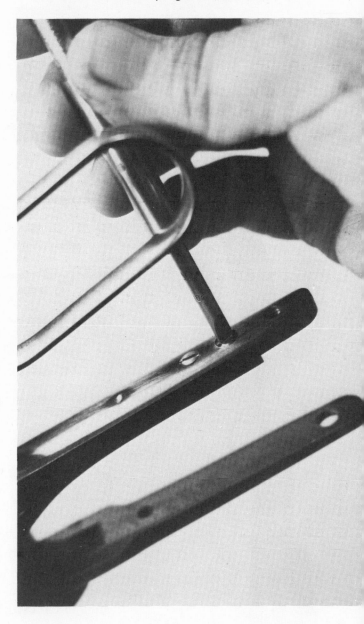

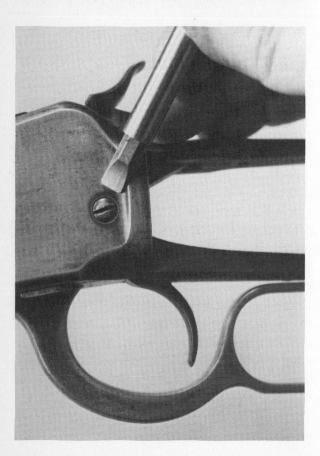

3. Remove the cross screw on the left side at the rear of the receiver that retains the hammer and the lower tang/trigger housing unit. Pulling the trigger to relieve its spring tension on the hammer will make removal of the screw easier.

5. The lower tang/trigger housing unit may now be slid out toward the rear. If the unit is very tight, insert a bronze or aluminum rod through the spring screw hole, which has no threads (not the stock screw hole), and tap the rod to start the unit out. Drifting out the cross pin in the lower tang unit will allow removal of the trigger downward.

4. Hold the trigger to the rear, and remove the hammer upward and toward the rear.

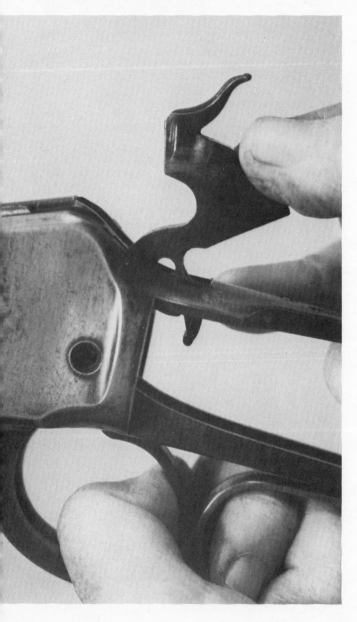

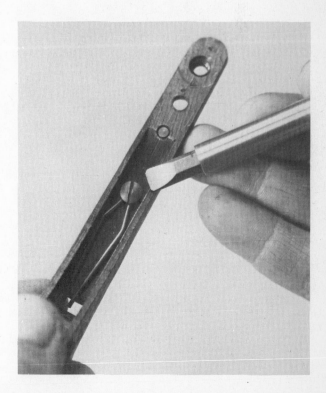

6. The trigger spring is retained by a vertical screw inside the lower tang, and the spring is removed upward. The one shown has a round wire spring, but early guns will have a blade type.

7. With the lever opened, remove the lock screw in the left locking block, the screw nearest its lower edge.

8. The part above the screw, although slotted, is not a screw. It is the cross pin that links the locking blocks to the lever. Push out the cross pin toward the left. Then remove the right and left locking blocks downward.

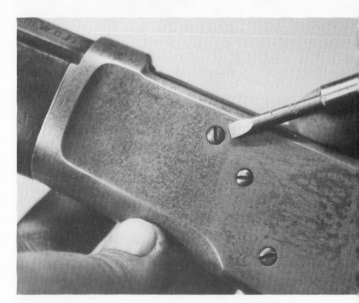

9. Remove the lever pin cover screw, located on the left side of the receiver at the upper front.

10. Move the breechblock (bolt) to the fully closed position, and insert one of the locking blocks from below to hold it in place. Insert a drift punch into the access hole on the right side of the receiver, and push out the lever/bolt connecting pin toward the left. Remove the lever downward and toward the rear.

11. Drifting out the cross pin in the base of the lever will allow removal of the lever latch plunger and its spring toward the rear. **Caution:** *This is a strong little spring, and it is under tension, so control it and ease it out.*

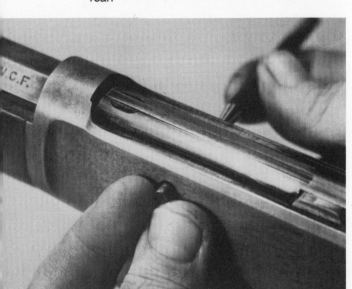

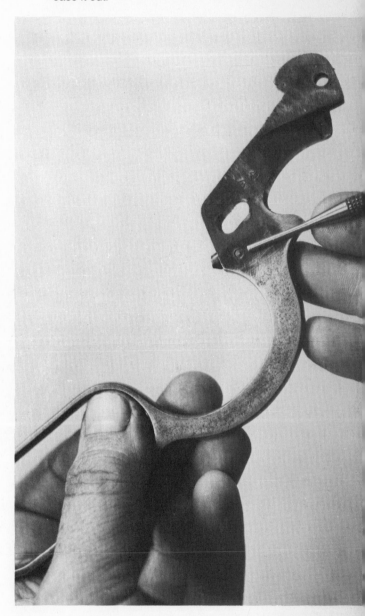

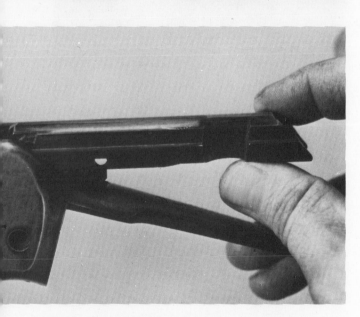

12. Remove the temporarily inserted locking block, and take out the breechblock toward the rear.

13. Removal of the lever pin will also have freed the ejector and its collar and spring, and these can now be taken out of the breechblock toward the front.

14. Drifting out the smaller cross pin near the top of the bolt will allow removal of the extractor.

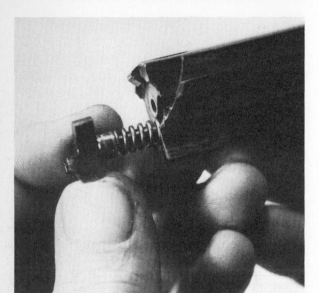

15. After the pin is drifted out, do not lift the extractor upward, as this may break its tempered tail. Hook a small screwdriver under the forward beak of the extractor, and lever it straight out toward the front.

16. Drift out the larger of the two cross pins in the bolt, the firing pin retaining pin, and take out the firing pin toward the rear.

17. Remove the carrier screws, one on each side of the receiver.

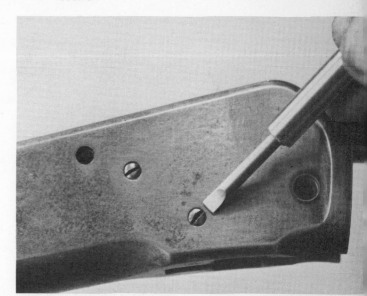

18. After the screws are removed, move the carrier toward the rear, and take it out downward. Note that the carrier plunger may jump into one of the screw holes during removal, and a drift punch will then have to be inserted to depress the plunger and free it.

19. The carrier plunger and its spring are retained in the carrier by a vertical pin. The spring is under tension, so restrain the plunger during removal.

20. Removal of the cartridge guide screws, one on each side, will release the guides to be taken out of the inside of the receiver. The left guide has the cartridge stop mounted on a vertical pin at its forward end, and the cartridge stop spring is in a recess in the back of the guide. The spring is freed by removal of the guide mounting screw, so take care that it isn't lost during removal of the guide.

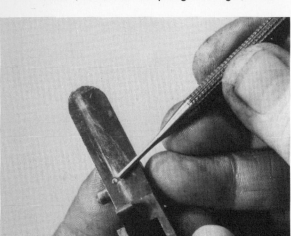

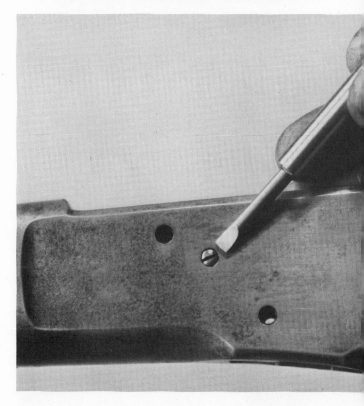

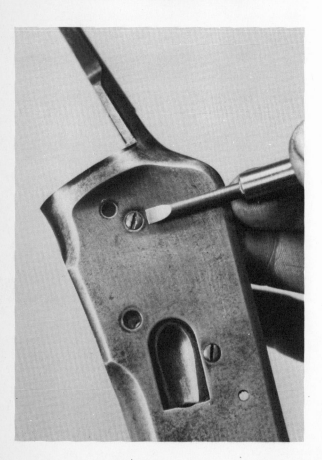

21. The loading gate is its own spring, and is retained by a screw on the right side, near the rear of the receiver. After removal of the screw, the gate is easily taken out.

22. Removal of the screw on the underside of the magazine tube near the muzzle will allow the end plug, magazine spring, and magazine follower to be taken out toward the front. **Note:** Some magazine springs have more tension than others. To be safe, restrain the end plug and ease it out.

23. Remove the screws on each side of the forend cap, and move the cap forward along the magazine tube.

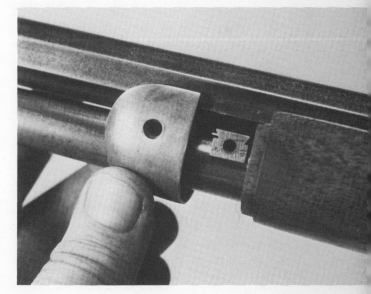

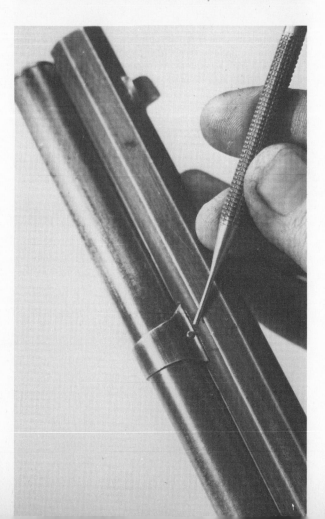

24. Drift out the small cross pin in the magazine tube hanger loop, and remove the magazine tube toward the front. The forend is now moved forward, then downward and off.

Reassembly Tips:

1. When replacing the carrier in the receiver, it will be necessary to insert a small screwdriver to depress the carrier plunger to clear the inner frame wall at the rear.

2. When replacing the ejector in the front of the bolt, note that the collar goes at the rear of the spring, to contact the spring base hook below the bolt. Keep the receiver slanted upward during insertion of the bolt, to prevent the ejector assembly from dropping out.

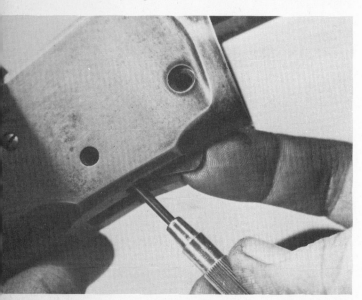

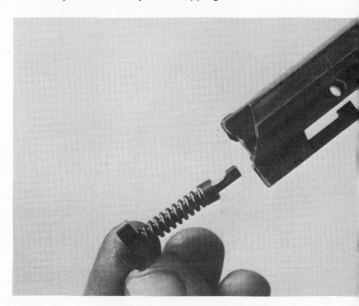

When replacing the lever and its bolt connector pin, once again insert a locking block from below, to hold the bolt in full forward position during replacement of the pin. Also, note that the pin is beveled on one end, and this end should be inserted.

When replacing the left cartridge guide, be sure the cartridge stop spring is properly in place in its recess, with its forward tip hooked beneath the rear tab of the cartridge stop, and the concave side of the spring toward the inner wall of the receiver.

3. When replacing the locking blocks in the receiver, remember that the one with the lock screw goes on the left side.

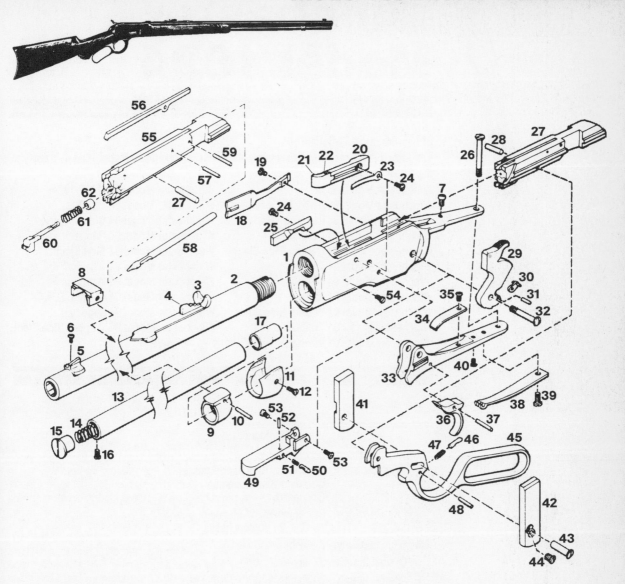

KEY

1 Receiver
2 Barrel
3 Rear Sight Assembly
4 Rear Sight Elevator
5 Front Sight
6 Front Sight Screw
7 Tang Sight Screw
8 Forend Tip Tenon
9 Magazine Ring
10 Magazine Ring Pin
11 Forend Tip
12 Forend Tip Screw
13 Magazine Tube
14 Magazine Spring
15 Magazine End Cap
16 Magazine End Cap Screw
17 Magazine Follower
18 Spring Cover
19 Spring Cover Screw
20 Cartridge Guide, Left

21 Cartridge Stop
22 Cartridge Stop Joint Pin
23 Cartridge Stop Spring
24 Cartridge Guide Screws
25 Cartridge Guide, Right
26 Upper Tang Screw
27 Breechbolt
28 Lever and Breechbolt Pin
29 Hammer
30 Hammer Stirrup
31 Hammer Stirrup Pin
32 Hammer Screw
33 Lower Tang
34 Trigger Spring
35 Trigger Spring Screw
36 Trigger
37 Trigger Pin
38 Mainspring
39 Mainspring Screw
40 Mainspring Strain Screw
41 Locking Bolt, Right
42 Locking Bolt, Left

43 Locking Bolt Pin
44 Locking Bolt Pin Screw
45 Finger Lever
46 Friction Plunger
47 Friction Plunger Spring
48 Friction Stud Stop Pin
49 Carrier Assembly
50 Carrier Stop
51 Carrier Stop Spring
52 Carrier Stop Pin
53 Carrier Screws
54 Lever and Breechblock Pin Hole
   Plug Screw
55 Breechbolt Assembly
56 Extractor
57 Extractor Pin
58 Firing Pin
59 Firing Pin Stop Pin
60 Ejector
61 Ejector Spring
62 Ejector Collar

Winchester Model 1894

Similar/Identical Pattern Guns

The same basic assembly/disassembly steps for the Winchester Model 1894 also apply to the following guns:

Winchester Model 55	Winchester Model 64 (1972-1974)
Winchester Model 94 Antique Carbine	Winchester Model 94 Big Bore
Winchester Model 94 Big Bore Side Eject	Winchester Model 94 Classic Series
Winchester Model 94 Deluxe	Winchester Model 94 Ranger
Winchester Model 94 Ranger Side Eject	Winchester Model 94 Side Eject
Winchester Model 94 Trapper	Winchester Model 94 Win-Tuff
Winchester Model 94 Wrangler	Winchester Model 94 Wrangler II
Winchester Model 94 XTR	Winchester Model 94 44 Mag. S.R.C.
Winchester Model 94 Walnut Side Eject	Winchester Model 94 Legacy
Winchester Model 94 Trails End	Winchester Model 94 Trapper Side Eject
Winchester Model 94 Wrangler Side Eject	

Data:	Winchester Model 1894
Origin:	United States
Manufacturer:	Winchester Repeating Arms Company New Haven, Connecticut
Cartridge:	357 Magnum, 44 Magnum, 45 Colt, 30-30 Winchester
Magazine capacity:	6 rounds
Overall length:	37 inches
Barrel length:	20 inches
Weight:	6½ pounds

To say that this gun needs no introduction would be an understatement. However, since some younger readers might not have been with us long enough to have learned its history, let's briefly pass along the information that it was designed by John M. Browning, and has been produced continuously by Winchester since 1894. It was originally chambered for two blackpowder loads, but for most of its production life the calibers have been the 30-30 and 32 Winchester Special, the latter discontinued in the late 1970s. There have been several slight internal design changes along the way, but the instructions will generally apply to all 94s. As most readers will be aware, the gun is now made by U.S. Repeating Arms Co.

Disassembly:

1. Use a screwdriver with a wide, thin blade to remove the lever pin cover screw, located on the left side of the receiver at the upper front.

2. Use a drift punch to push out the lever pin toward the left. This is accessible through a small hole on the right side of the receiver, just above the front of the loading gate.

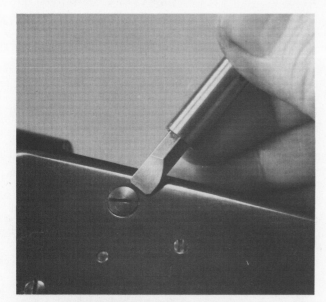

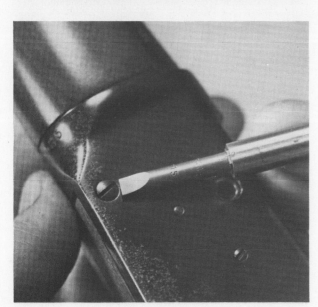

3. Remove the cross screw that pivots the link plate at the lower left front of the receiver.

4. Move the lever downward, along with the attached link, then move them forward, disengaging the rear of the link from the locking block. The lever and link assembly are then removed downward.

5. Drifting out the large cross pin in the link plate will release the lever for removal. Drifting out the small cross pin at the rear of the link plate will release the plate latch plunger and its spring toward the rear. The spring is under tension, so restrain the plunger and ease it out.

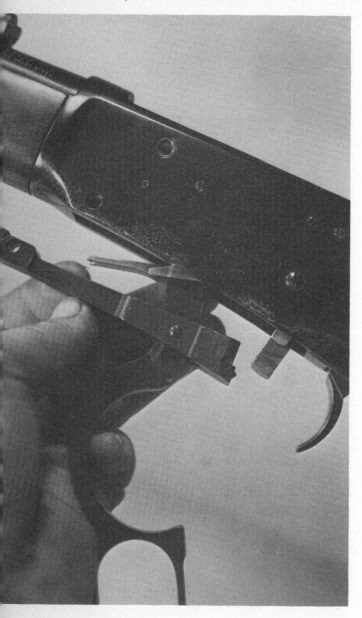

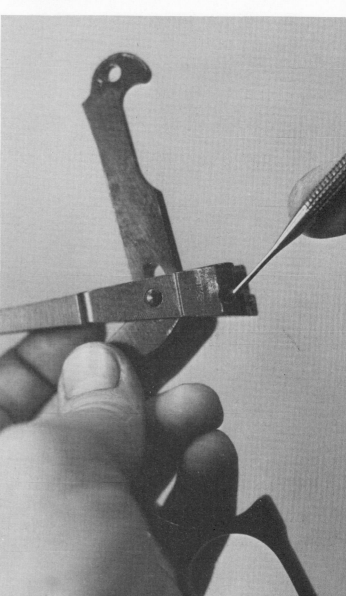

6. Remove the carrier pivot screw toward the left. Note that on early guns, there are two separate screws, one on each side of the receiver.

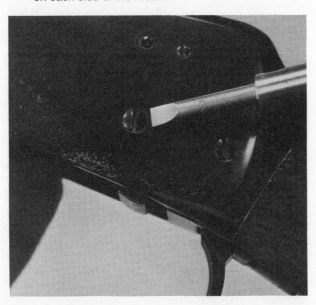

7. Remove the carrier downward.

8. It should be noted that removal of the lever will have released the firing pin (in late guns), and if it needs to be taken out for repair, this can be done without further disassembly. In early guns, a firing pin retaining pin at the lower rear of the bolt must also be removed. Also, the extractor can be taken out by moving the bolt to the rear and drifting out its cross pin or cross pins (later guns have two).

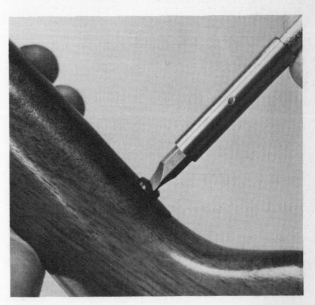

9. Remove the vertical screw at the rear of the upper tang, and take off the stock toward the rear. If the stock is tightly fitted, bump the front of the comb with the heel of the hand to start it.

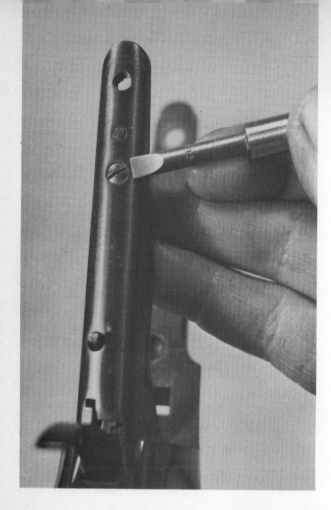

10. With the hammer lowered to the fired position, remove the hammer spring screw, located on the inside of the lower tang at the rear. This will be made easier by first backing out or removing the hammer spring strain screw, as shown.

11. Removal of the hammer spring screw will require an offset screwdriver, or one with an angled tip, as shown. After the screw is removed, the spring and its angled base are taken out toward the rear.

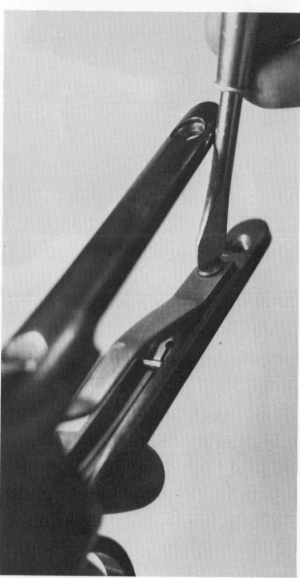

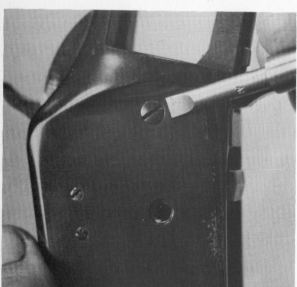

12. Remove the cross screw that retains both the hammer and the lower tang/trigger housing. Remove the hammer upward and toward the rear.

13. Remove the lower tang/trigger housing unit toward the rear. If this assembly is tight, use a drift punch of nylon or some other non-marring material to nudge it out.

14. The locking block can now be removed downward. Drifting out the roll cross pin near the top of the locking block will allow removal of the short firing pin striker.

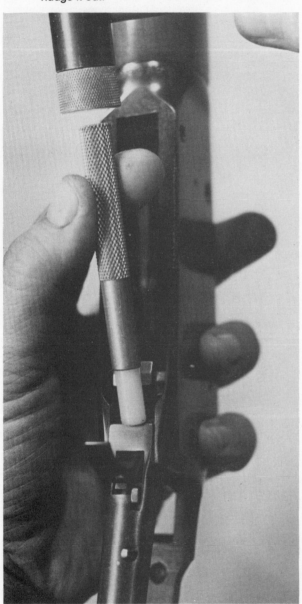

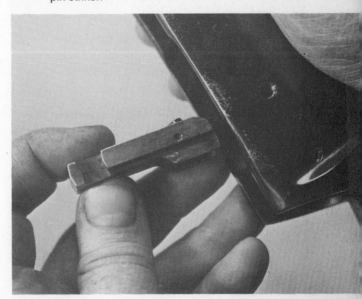

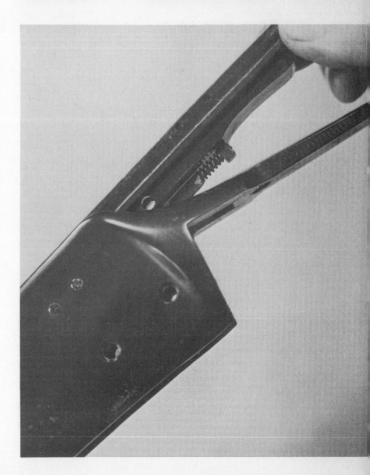

15. The breechblock (bolt) can now be moved straight out of the receiver toward the rear.

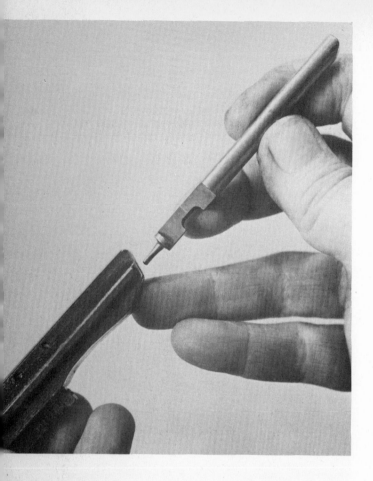

16. If it has not been previously removed, the firing pin can now be taken out of the bolt toward the rear. In early guns, a small retaining cross pin at the lower rear of the bolt must be driven out to release the firing pin.

17. The extractor is retained in the top of the bolt by a single solid cross pin (early guns), or by two roll cross pins (late guns). After these are drifted out, the extractor is removed upward.

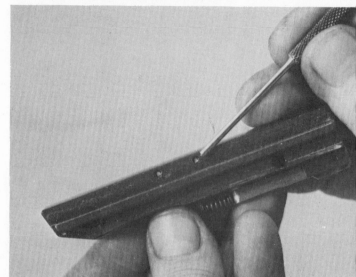

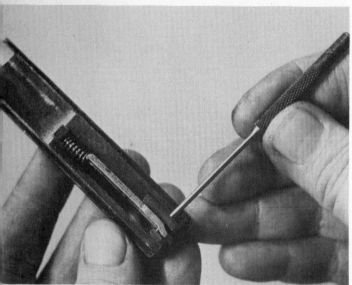

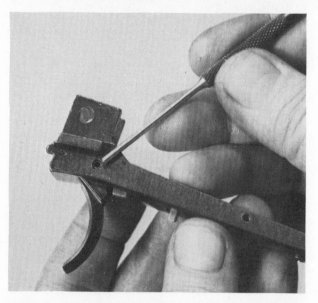

18. The ejector and its spring are retained on the underside of the bolt by a single cross pin at the lower front. Use a roll pin drift to remove the pin, and take out the ejector and its spring toward the front.

19. The trigger and sear are retained in the trigger housing by a roll cross pin that is the pivot for both parts. After the pin is drifted out, the trigger is removed downward, the sear toward the front.

20. A cross pin at the center of the lower tang unit retains both the trigger stop and the combination spring that powers the stop and the sear. Drift out the pin toward the left, so the spring will be released first.

21. Remove the screw on the right side of the receiver directly to the rear of the loading gate, and take out the loading gate from inside the receiver.

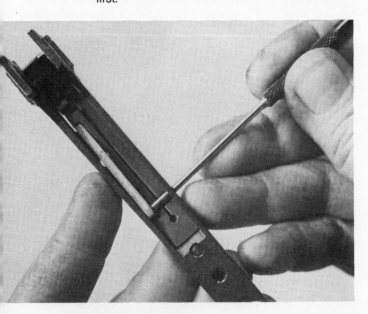

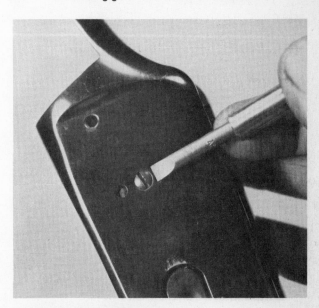

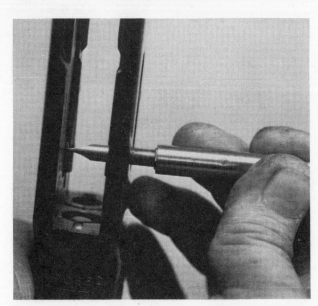

22. With the loading gate removed, the screw that retains the carrier spring will be accessible through the front portion of the loading port. Remove the screw, and take out the spring from inside the receiver.

23. There are two small screws, one on each side of the receiver, the one on the right being just above the loading port. These retain the right and left cartridge guides inside the receiver. In normal take-down, these are best left in place, as any slight misalignment during reassembly can cause problems, one of which is possible stripping of the screws.

24. Removal of the vertical screw at the forward end of the magazine tube will allow the magazine plug, magazine spring, and follower to be taken out toward the front. **Caution:** *The magazine spring is under some tension, so control it and ease it out.*

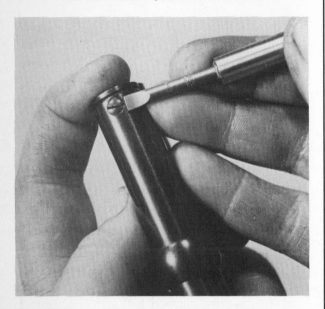

25. Remove the cross screw from the front barrel band. Remove the cross screw from the rear barrel band, and slide the barrel band forward, off the front of the forend wood. The magazine tube can now be moved out toward the front, and the forend can he moved slightly forward and taken off downward.

Reassembly Tips:

1. When replacing the locking block in the receiver, note that the upper wings of the block must be toward the rear.

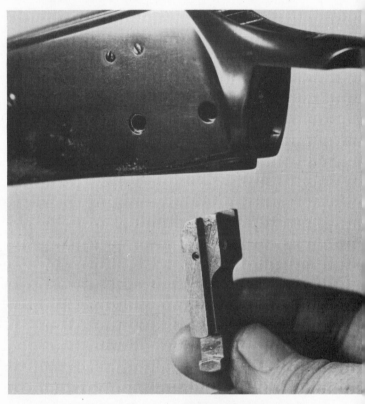

When replacing the firing pin in the breechblock, note that it must be oriented for insertion of the lever, with its front recess on the left side—see step number 16.

When replacing the loading gate, hold it in position inside the receiver with a fingertip, centering the hole for insertion of the screw. To align the screw for proper start, allow the front tip of the gate to protrude from the loading port. As soon as the screw is started, though, be sure to depress the front of the gate inside the port before tightening the screw.

New Model 94 Lever-Action Carbine

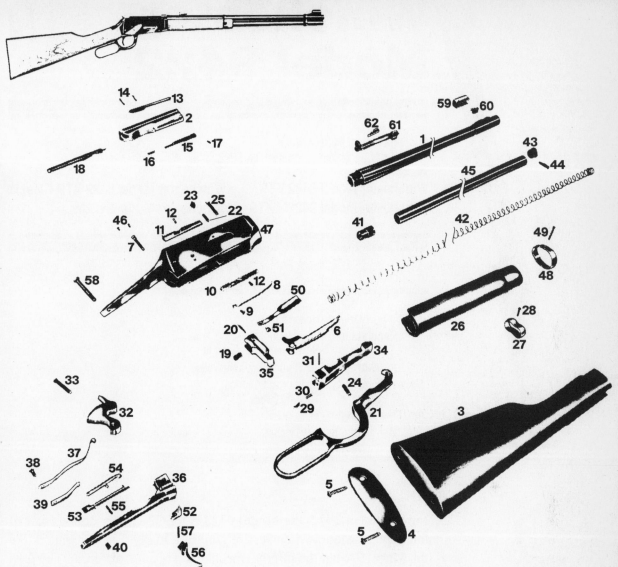

KEY

1 Barrel	**21** Finger Lever
2 Breechbolt	**22** Finger Lever Pin
3 Buttstock	**23** Finger Lever Pin Stop Screw
4 Buttplate	**24** Finger Lever Link Pin
5 Buttplate Screws	**25** Finger Lever Link Screw
6 Carrier	**26** Forend
7 Carrier Screw	**27** Front Band
8 Carrier Spring	**28** Front Band Screw
9 Carrier Spring Screw	**29** Friction Stud
10 Cartridge Guide, Right	**30** Friction Stud Spring
11 Cartridge Guide, Left	**31** Friction Stud Stop Pin
12 Cartridge Guide Screws	**32** Hammer
13 Extractor	**33** Hammer Link Screw
14 Extractor Pins	**34** Link
15 Ejector	**35** Locking Bolt
16 Ejector Spring	**36** Lower Tang
17 Ejector Stop Pin	**37** Mainspring
18 Firing Pin	**38** Mainspring Screw
19 Firing Pin Striker	**39** Mainspring Base
20 Firing Pin Striker Pin	**40** Mainspring Strain Screw
	41 Magazine Follower
	42 Magazine Spring

43 Magazine Plug
44 Magazine Plug Screw
45 Magazine Tube
46 Sight Plug Screws
47 Receiver
48 Rear Band
49 Rear Band Screw
50 Spring Cover
51 Spring Cover Screw
52 Sear
53 Trigger Stop Spring
54 Trigger Stop
55 Trigger Stop Pin
56 Trigger
57 Trigger Pin
58 Upper Tang Screw
59 Front Sight Cover
60 Front Sight
61 Rear Sight
62 Rear Sight Elevator

Winchester Model 9422

Similar/Identical Pattern Guns

The same basic assembly/disassembly steps for the Winchester Model 9422 also apply to the following guns:

Winchester Model 9422 XTR   **Winchester Model 9422 XTR Classic**

Winchester Model 9422M XTR   **Winchester Model 9422M**

Data:	Winchester Model 9422
Origin:	United States
Manufacturer:	Winchester Repeating Arms Co. New Haven, Connecticut
Cartridge:	22 Short, Long, Long Rifle
Magazine capacity:	21 Shorts, 17 Longs, 15 Long Rifles
Overall length:	37$^{1}/_{8}$ inches
Barrel length:	20$^{1}/_{2}$ inches
Weight:	6$^{1}/_{2}$ pounds

Introduced in 1972, the Model 9422 is the 22-caliber counterpart of the popular Model 94 centerfire gun. Externally it is very much like the Model 94, but the internal mechanism is quite different. The feed system is similar to the one used in the Model 61, making malfunctions extremely unlikely. The Model 9422 is fairly simple for a lever action, and with the exception of the cartridge stop and its spring, takedown and reassembly are relatively easy.

Disassembly:

1. Remove the magazine tube and take out the large coin-slotted cross screw at the rear of the receiver. A nickel fits the slot best. Separate the two sections of the gun, moving the rear portion down and toward the rear.

2. Remove the bolt assembly from the receiver toward the rear.

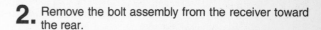

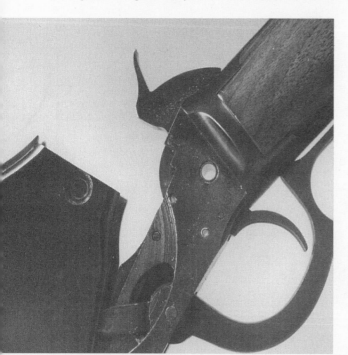

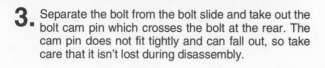

3. Separate the bolt from the bolt slide and take out the bolt cam pin which crosses the bolt at the rear. The cam pin does not fit tightly and can fall out, so take care that it isn't lost during disassembly.

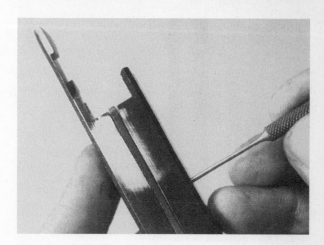

4. Use a roll pin punch to drift out the cross pin in the bolt slide and remove the firing pin striker upward.

5. The firing pin is retained in the bolt by a roll pin across the upper rear, and the firing pin and its return spring are removed toward the rear.

6. A vertical pin on the left side of the bolt retains three parts—the left extractor, the ejector, and the carrier pawl retainer. The extractor and pawl retainer are removed toward the left, and the ejector is moved out toward the rear. Take care that the small coil springs with the ejector and inside the carrier pawl are not lost.

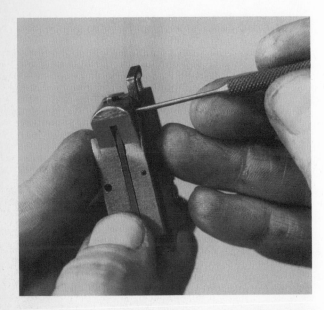

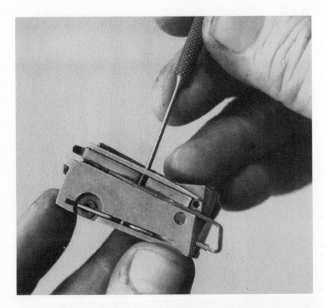

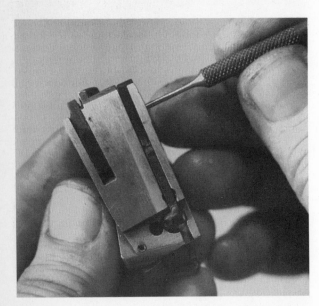

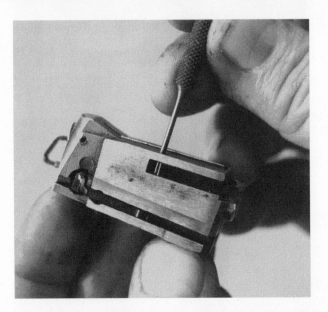

7. The right extractor is retained by a vertical roll pin on the right side of the bolt. The pin is accessible through a hole in the bottom right of the bolt, and is driven out upward. The extractor and its coil spring are taken off toward the right.

8. The lower extractor, part of the feed system, is retained by a vertical roll pin, accessible through a hole in the top of the bolt on the right side, and the pin is driven out downward. The lower extractor and its spring are then removed toward the right. Keep the spring with the lower extractor, and don't get it confused with the upper one, as they are not interchangeable.

9. Remove the buttplate, and use a B-Square stock bolt tool, or a long screwdriver, to take out the stock retaining bolt. When the bolt is out, take off the buttstock toward the rear.

10. Before removing the carrier and cartridge stop, carefully note the position and relationship of the combination spring which powers these parts, to aid in reassembly. Push out the cross pin which pivots and retains the cartridge stop, carrier, and the spring. All are removed upward, but the cartridge stop must be moved slightly forward before being lifted out. **Caution:** *The spring is under some tension, so keep the parts under control when pushing out the cross pin.*

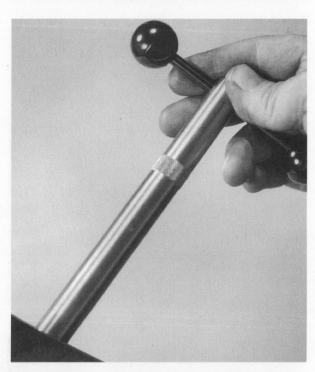

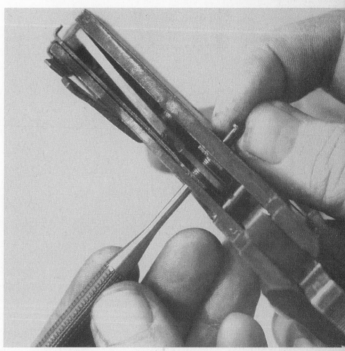

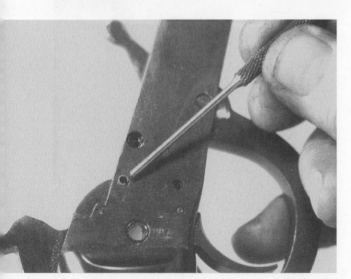

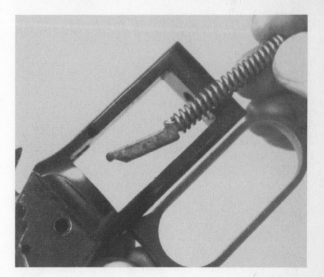

11. Use a roll pin punch to drift out the hammer stop pin, located just forward of the hammer. Set the hammer on its safety step while the stop pin is drifted out.

12. Restrain the hammer against its spring tension, pull the trigger to release it, and ease the hammer forward, past its normal down position. This will relieve the tension of the hammer spring, and the spring and its guide strut can then be removed from the rear, toward either side.

13. The hollow hammer pivot is now easily pushed out toward either side, and the hammer is removed upward. If the hammer pivot is tight, use a non-marring tool as large as its diameter, and take care not to deform its end edges.

14. With an Allen wrench of the proper size, take out the screw that retains the lever tension spring and its plate, and remove the plate and spring upward.

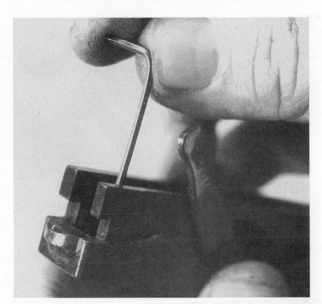

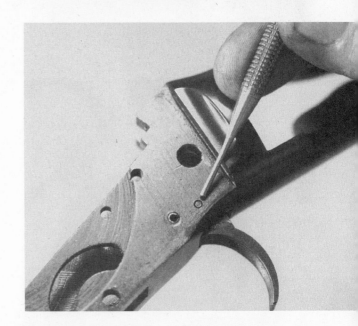

15. Push out the lever pivot pin toward the left, and remove the lever downward. Tip the upper lever arm toward the left as it is lifted out of its semi-circular opening and remove it.

16. Drifting out the solid cross pin above the trigger will release the trigger downward. The trigger spring is retained by a roll pin, just forward of the trigger pin.

17. Remove the cross screw in the rear barrel band, and slide the band off toward the front. If the band is very tight, it will be necessary to nudge it with a nylon drift and hammer. Nudge it equally, on alternate sides, to avoid binding.

18. Remove the cross screw from the front barrel band, and slide the outer magazine tube out toward the front. Remove the forend forward and downward.

19. The barrel is retained in the receiver by a cross pin that is riveted on the right side. The pin must be driven out toward the left. The barrel can then be gripped in a padded vise and the receiver driven off with a wood or nylon mallet. In normal disassembly, however, the barrel is best left in place.

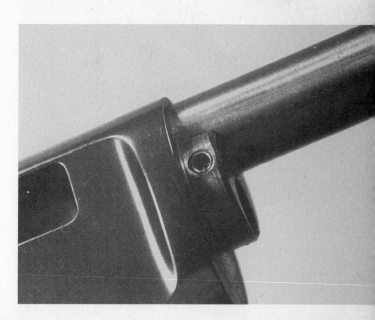

Reassembly Tips:

1. When replacing the outer magazine tube, be sure it is installed to its proper depth, and that the shallow groove in its top is aligned with the cross screw hole in the front barrel band.

2. To install the carrier, cartridge stop, and combination spring without great difficulty will require the use of a slave pin, a short length of rod stock to hold the parts together while they are positioned for insertion of the cross pin. The photo shows the proper arrangement of the parts and the spring, with the slave pin in place. The longer left arm of the spring goes below the hammer stop pin.

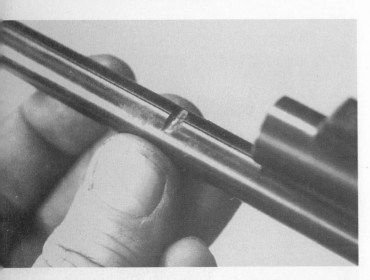

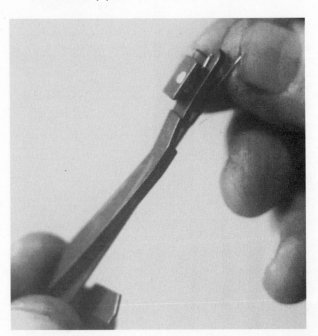

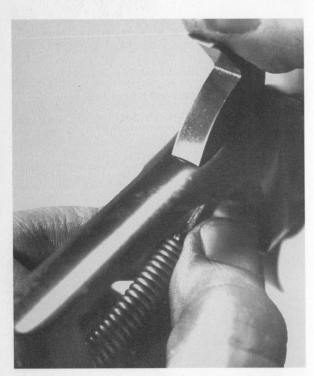

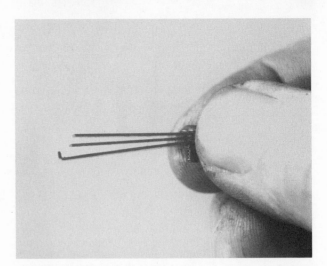

3. When replacing the hammer strut and spring, guide the spring at the rear to position the rear tip of the strut in alignment with its hole in the rear vertical bar of the trigger group. Be sure the front tip of the strut enters its recess on the rear of the hammer as the hammer is drawn back to the safety step.

4. When replacing the lever tension system in the front of the trigger group, note that the single or double spring leaves go on top, and the L-shaped plate on the bottom, with the short arm of the "L" upward.

5. When replacing the lever, note that the upper arm of the lever must be in position in the trigger group before the lever is moved into place.

6. When replacing the bolt assembly in the receiver, the bolt and bolt slide should be engaged as shown, with the bolt in the unlocked position, as the assembly is moved into the rear of the receiver.

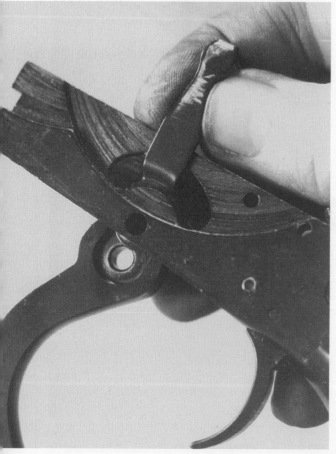

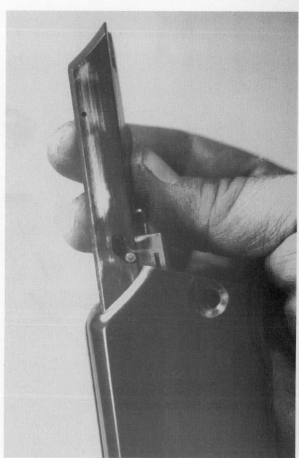

Model 9422 Lever-Action Carbine

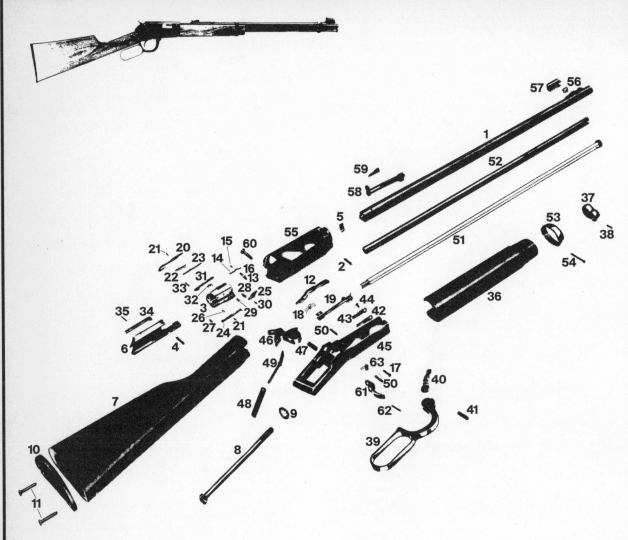

KEY

1	Barrel	22	Ejector Spring
2	Barrel Retaining Pin	23	Extractor, Left
3	Breechbolt	24	Extractor, Right
4	Bolt Cam Pin	25	Extractor, Upper Right
5	Bolt Guide with Pad	26	Extractor Spring, Right
6	Bolt Slide	27	Extractor Helper Spring, Right
7	Buttstock	28	Extractor Spring, Upper Right
8	Buttstock Bolt	29	Extractor Helper Spring, Upper Right
9	Buttstock Bolt Washer	30	Extractor Pin, Upper Right
10	Buttplate	31	Firing Pin
11	Buttplate Screws	32	Firing Pin Spring
12	Carrier	33	Firing Pin Retainer Pin
13	Carrier Pawl	34	Firing Pin Striker
14	Carrier Pawl Retainer	35	Firing Pin Striker Retaining Pin
15	Carrier Pawl Retainer Pin	36	Forend
16	Carrier Pawl Spring	37	Front Band
17	Carrier Pin	38	Front Band Screw
18	Carrier Spring	39	Finger Lever
19	Cartridge Cutoff	40	Finger Lever Arm
20	Ejector	41	Finger Lever Pin
21	Ejector and Extractor Pins	42	Finger Lever Spring
		43	Finger Lever Spring Plate
44	Finger Lever Spring Screw		
45	Frame		
46	Hammer		
47	Hammer Pivot Bushing		
48	Hammer Spring		
49	Hammer Spring Guide Rod		
50	Hammer Stop and Trigger Spring Pins		
51	Magazine Tube Assembly, Inside		
52	Magazine Tube, Outside		
53	Rear Band		
54	Rear Band Screw		
55	Receiver		
56	Front Sight		
57	Front Sight Cover		
58	Rear Sight		
59	Rear Sight Elevator		
60	Takedown Screw		
61	Trigger		
62	Trigger Pin		
63	Trigger Spring		